GREAT LIVES
FROM
HISTORY

GREAT LIVES FROM HISTORY

American Women
Series

Volume 3
Gor-Lup

Edited by

FRANK N. MAGILL

SALEM PRESS

Pasadena, California   Englewood Cliffs, New Jersey

∞ The paper used in these volumes conforms to the
American National Standard for Permanence of Paper for
Printed Library Materials, Z39.48-1984.

Library of Congress Cataloging-in-Publication Data
Great lives from history. American women series /
edited by Frank N. Magill.
    p.   cm.
Includes bibliographical references and index.
    1. Women—United States—Biography. 2. Women—
Canada—Biography. 3. Women—United States—His-
tory. 4. Women—Canada—History. I. Magill, Frank
Northen, 1907-   . II. Title: American women series.
HQ1412.G74   1995
305.4′0973—dc20
ISBN 0-89356-892-9 (set)   94-38308
ISBN 0-89356-895-3 (volume 3)   CIP

PRINTED IN THE UNITED STATES OF AMERICA

LIST OF BIOGRAPHIES IN VOLUME THREE

LIST OF BIOGRAPHIES IN VOLUME THREE

GREAT LIVES
FROM
HISTORY

RUTH GORDON

Born: October 30, 1896; Quincy, Massachusetts
Died: August 28, 1985; Edgartown, Massachusetts
Areas of Achievement: Theater and drama, film, and literature
Contribution: A world-renowned actress, Ruth Gordon was also a playwright, film writer, and novelist. Her acting career included stage, film, and television.

Early Life

Ruth Gordon was born Ruth Jones, the daughter of Clinton Jones, a seaman who became a factory foreman, and Annie Tapley Ziegler Jones, a housewife. Ruth had an unremarkable but happy childhood. The family was just poor enough to rejoice in such special treats as Clinton's bringing home a bucket of oysters. Although the Joneses never lacked the necessities, they had little excess income for luxuries.

Ruth was bright and resourceful. Before she was of school age, she was convinced that she could accomplish anything she wished to as long as she worked hard enough at it. She urged people never to be helpless and projected sufficient self-assurance to stand as a model for others. Ruth Gordon admitted in the last year of her life that she had never faced facts or listened to sage advice, but somehow she usually attained her goals.

The turning point came for Gordon in 1912, when, at the age of fifteen, she saw a performance of the play *The Pink Lady* (pr. 1912) starring Hazel Dawn. Dawn's performance convinced Gordon that what she wanted most in life was to act. Her father, who had his heart set on her becoming a teacher of physical education, was dubious about the new direction his daughter's life was taking.

When she pinned fifty dollars into her corset and set out for the American Academy of Dramatic Arts in New York City at age seventeen, however, Clinton gave her his blessing as well as his old spyglass, telling her that if she needed to borrow money, she could use it as collateral, something she never did even though she sometimes had to pawn other possessions during those early days.

Gordon's theatrical beginnings were singularly unpromising. So bad was her performance in the annual review during her junior year at the Academy that the school's president told her she would never be an actress and insisted that she withdraw from the institution. Gordon was undaunted. She played some small parts in silent films, after which she played a taxi dancer in Vernon and Irene Castle's initial film, earning a little more than a dollar a day for her performance.

Late in 1915, Gordon played Nibs to Maude Adams' Peter Pan in a Broadway production of *Peter Pan* (wr. 1904). This performance got her a starring role in Booth Tarkington's *Seventeen* (pr. 1916), but her first major theatrical debut ended disastrously. The critics detested her acting. Through this role she met Gregory Kelly, an actor whom she married the following year. Gordon credits Kelly with teaching her how to act.

Life's Work

Shortly after their marriage, Ruth Gordon and her husband formed a repertory company in Indianapolis, Indiana. When the company failed financially, the two took to the road, playing stock for short runs in small towns. When they had saved enough money to rescue their theater, they quit the stock company and returned to their theater in Indianapolis.

Before Kelly succumbed to a heart attack in 1927, Gordon acted regularly in their repertory theater, honing her skills under his patient tutelage. Her seven years in Indianapolis helped her to emerge as the actress she eventually became. During this apprenticeship, she acted in such productions as *Tweedles* (pr. 1923), *Mrs. Partridge Presents* (pr. 1924), *The Fall of Eve* (pr. 1924), *The Phantom Ship* (pr. 1942), *Holding Helen* (pr. 1925), and *Collision* (pr. 1926).

After Kelly's death, Gordon returned to the East Coast, giving her first performance there at the New Rochelle Women's Club in Maxwell Anderson's *Saturday's Children* (pr. 1928), which later moved to Broadway. Following *Saturday's Children*, she had roles in *Serena Blandish* (pr. 1929), *Hotel Universe* (pr. 1930), and *The Church Mouse* (1931). She was establishing her reputation as an able, highly professional actress.

A hiatus occurred, however, between Gordon's role in *The Church Mouse* and her role in John Wexley's *They Shall Not Die* (1934), because she had, through a liaison with producer Jed Harris, become pregnant. Harris, who was already married and a father, could not marry Gordon. Because of the need to keep word of her pregnancy from his wife and family, Harris sent Gordon to Europe when her pregnancy became apparent. Her only child, Jones Harris, was born in Paris.

By 1935, Gordon was receiving acclaim for her sensitive portrayal of Mattie Silver in the stage adaptation of Edith Wharton's *Ethan Frome*. Following this performance, she was cast in the role of Mrs. Pinchwife in a New York revival of William Wycherley's *The Country Wife* (wr. 1673), which moved to London for the 1936-1937 theatrical season. Gordon, the first American actress to perform at the Old Vic, won praise for her role in *The Country Wife*. Alexander Wollcott's review said that Gordon had turned in the most richly comic performance he could recall.

While in England, Gordon saw a great deal of Robert and Madeline Sherwood at Great Enton, their house in Surrey. When Sherwood's *Abe Lincoln in Illinois* (pr. 1938) became a success on Broadway, it was decided to make the play into a film to be released in 1939. Gordon made her motion picture debut as Mary Todd Lincoln. Meanwhile, she had triumphed as Nora Helmer in Henrik Ibsen's *A Doll's House* (wr. 1879), which was produced on Broadway in 1938.

After making *Abe Lincoln in Illinois*, Gordon stayed on in Hollywood to play Mrs. Ehrlich in *Dr. Ehrlich's Magic Bullet* (1940), and she later played roles in films such as *Two-Faced Woman* (1941), *Action in the North Atlantic* (1943), and *Edge of Darkness* (1943). During the 1942-1943 Broadway season, however, she was back in New York, newly married to Garson Kanin, twenty years her junior, and playing Natasha in a revival of Anton Chekhov's *The Three Sisters* (wr. 1900).

From 1943 to 1945, Gordon played the lead in the first of several plays she wrote,

Over Twenty-One (pr. 1943). The play's success encouraged Gordon, who went on to write *Years Ago* (1947) during the same year in which she and Kanin collaborated on the film script *A Double Life* (1947) for Universal Studios.

Gordon produced three more dramatic scripts, *The Leading Lady* (pr. 1948)—an adaptation of a Philippe Heriat play—in which she played a leading role on Broadway; *A Very Rich Woman* (1965); and *Ho, Ho, Ho* (1976). She and Kanin also produced a film script, *The Actress* (1953), adapted for Metro-Goldwyn-Mayer from her play *Years Ago*. The couple's other film scripts include *Adam's Rib* (1949) for Metro-Goldwyn-Mayer; *The Marrying Kind* (1952) for Columbia Pictures; and *Pat and Mike* (1952) for Metro-Goldwyn-Mayer. Both *Adam's Rib* and *Pat and Mike* were written specifically as acting vehicles for Katharine Hepburn and Spencer Tracy.

The following Kanin-Gordon collaborations won nominations for the awards that follow their titles parenthetically: *The Actress* (Academy Award and Writers Guild Award); *Pat and Mike* (Academy Award and Writers Guild Award); *The Marrying Kind* (Writers Guild Award); and *Adam's Rib* (Academy Award and Writers Guild Award), which won the Box Office Ribbon Award.

In 1954, Gordon played Dolly in Thornton Wilder's *The Matchmaker*, later transformed into the musical *Hello, Dolly*, in New York, London, and Berlin. When she had first read the play, then titled *The Merchant of Yonkers* (wr. 1938), which Wilder had written especially for her, she had rejected the part.

Twenty-three years after *Edge of Darkness*, Gordon returned to the screen, playing a sinister older woman in *Inside Daisy Clover* (1965). Her performance proved so successful that it won her a Golden Globe Award and a nomination for an Academy Award. Her next role was as the satanic neighbor in *Rosemary's Baby* (1968), for which Gordon won the Academy Award as best supporting actress.

Gordon's film career escalated from that point as she played sinister or eccentric older women in *Whatever Happened to Aunt Alice?* (1969), *Where's Poppa?* (1970), *Harold and Maude* (1971), *Every Which Way But Loose* (1978), and *Any Which Way You Can* (1980). *Harold and Maude*, the story of an elderly woman who is romantically involved with an eighteen-year-old man, although not originally a commercial success, eventually attracted a cult following.

During this period, Gordon's career as a television actress advanced. She acted in five made-for-television films, *Look What's Happened to Rosemary's Baby* (1976; later retitled *Rosemary's Baby II*), *The Great Houdini* (1976); *Perfect Gentlemen* (1978); *Don't Go to Sleep* (1982); and *The Secret World of the Very Young* (1985), for which she received an Emmy Award nomination. She also made guest appearances on the television shows *Kojak, Rhoda, The Bob Newhart Show, The Love Boat, The Flip Wilson Show*, and *Taxi*, in which her appearance won for Gordon an Emmy Award for the best guest appearance on a television series.

Gordon's first novel, *Shady Lady*, was published in 1981. It tells the story of a stage-struck girl who goes first to Chicago and then to New York as a Ziegfeld Girl.

Gordon succumbed to a stroke in her home on Martha's Vineyard in her eighty-ninth year. She had performed almost to the end of her life. In 1984, her hometown of

Quincy, Massachusetts, dedicated its Ruth Gordon Center for the Performing Arts to her. She was also inducted into the Theatre Hall of Fame.

Summary

Ruth Gordon was, from childhood, self-confident, convinced that people who want something can, by their own initiative, attain it. Her life exemplifies the validity of this belief. In her teens, she was discouraged from becoming an actress both by teachers of acting and by critics. Shortly after she was thirty, she lost her first husband, and soon after that she became a single parent.

During this period, Gordon continued acting, perfecting her art, ever ready to learn. By the mid-1930's, she enjoyed considerable success and soon embarked on what was to be a fruitful career in films. Many people mocked her marriage to Garson Kanin in 1941 because he was twenty years younger than she. Gordon made neither apologies nor explanations for this marriage, but helped to turn it into a productive collaboration that yielded five excellent film scripts.

At seventy, Gordon revived her film career and, during the next fourteen years, had important roles in fourteen films, winning an Oscar for one. Her career as a television actress began when she was eighty and continued until the year of her death at eighty-eight. At eighty-five, she published her first novel.

Gordon stands today as an example of an indomitable spirit. While others complained of lack of opportunity, she was busy creating opportunities for herself.

Bibliography

Brockett, Oscar G., and Robert R. Findlay. *Century of Innovation: A History of European and American Theatre and Drama Since 1870*. Englewood Cliffs, N.J.: Prentice-Hall, 1973. The authors discuss Gordon briefly. They make the interesting point that, like many players of her day—notably Alfred Lunt, Lynne Fontanne, the Barrymores, Tallulah Bankhead, Laurette Taylor, and Jane Cowl—Gordon subscribed to no specific school of acting.

Gordon, Ruth. *My Side: The Autobiography of Ruth Gordon*. New York: Harper & Row, 1976. Of the three autobiographies, this work seems to be the most complete. Although it is not a systematic telling of Gordon's life, it is reasonably accurate.

——————. *Myself Among Others*. New York: Atheneum, 1971. In this first of her three autobiographical works, Gordon details the events of her early life. She then chronicles in a nonchronological way her life as an actress and playwright. Each of her autobiographies is somewhat guarded.

——————. *Ruth Gordon: An Open Book*. Garden City, N.Y.: Doubleday, 1980. This highly readable book is interspersed with aphorisms from well-known historical figures. It does not go into significant detail about many of the salient elements of Gordon's life, such as the birth of her son or her marriage to Garson Kanin.

Houghton, Norris. *Entrances and Exits: A Life In and Out of the Theatre*. New York: Limelight Editions, 1991. Houghton mentions Gordon's early contributions to repertory theater in Indianapolis. He also describes her slow start in the rehearsals of John Wexley's *They Shall Not Die* in 1934 and discusses how she suddenly came into her own in the later rehearsals.

McGilligan, Pat. "Garson Kanin: Self-Expression." In *Backstory 2: Interviews with Screenwriters of the 1940s and 1950s.* Berkeley: University of California Press, 1991. This interview with Gordon's husband, Garson Kanin, provides perceptive insights into their collaboration as scriptwriters. Includes a chronology of their theater and film writing credits, alone and together.

Oppenheimer, George, ed. *The Passionate Playgoer: A Personal Scrapbook.* New York: Viking Press, 1958. This book contains numerous passing references to Gordon. It also reproduces in full her *New York Times* piece "Those Years After Years Ago."

R. Baird Shuman

KATHARINE GRAHAM

Born: June 16, 1917; New York, New York

Areas of Achievement: Publishing and journalism
Contribution: The only woman to serve as publisher of a major American newspaper during the twentieth century, Graham built *The Washington Post* into a national institution and helped bring down an American president.

Early Life

Katharine Meyer was born on June 16, 1917, into financial power, social privilege, and public life. The fourth child of Eugene Meyer and Agnes Ernst Meyer, Katharine had almost limitless options when she graduated from the University of Chicago in 1938 after spending her first two years of college at Vassar. By numerous accounts, her father was one of the more remarkable Americans of his time—a man who consciously chose to marry a white Anglo-Saxon Protestant (WASP) so his children would not have to fight the anti-Semitism that stung him at an early age; a man who had amassed a fortune of more than $50 million in careers in merchandising and in investment by 1917, when he liquidated his holdings to embark on government service; and a man who had successfully pursued more than a half-dozen different careers by 1933, when at fifty-seven years old, and almost as a hobby, he purchased at a bankruptcy sale a discredited newspaper, *The Washington Post.*

As her father pursued the task of bringing the *Post* to a level of journalistic respectability, Katharine—alone among the Meyer children—chose journalism as a career, working initially as a reporter on the *San Francisco News* for a year before joining *The Washington Post* in 1939. According to Carol Felsenthal's biography of Katharine Graham, her father had mailed her daily issues of the *Post* throughout her stay at the University of Chicago, where she had gone to pursue her interest in journalism after two unchallenging years at Vassar College. The year on the West Coast served as something of a first and last apprenticeship before joining the *Post.*

Although Katharine's entry in *Who's Who in America* indicates that she served on the editorial staff of *The Washington Post* from 1939 to 1945, and although she did throw herself wholeheartedly into that job upon her arrival there, Felsenthal maintains that her interest in a career in journalism ended the moment she met her future husband, Philip L. Graham, one of Washington's most eligible bachelors and a man endowed with a commanding presence who could also be engagingly charming. They married on June 5, 1940, within six months of their first meeting. Katharine Meyer had found a mainline WASP to marry. More important, in Philip Graham, a former editor of *The Harvard Law Review*, she had also found a man to whom her father would turn to manage the *Post.*

Life's Work

Her marriage lasted for nearly a quarter of a century, but few of those years appear to have been easy ones for Katharine Graham. Her husband was allegedly capable of thinking of her and his father-in-law in terms of vile ethnic slurs even as he loved the one and respected the success of the other. Over time, he became a philanderer, separated from his wife only to return to her later, took over the *Post* and expanded its operations by opening overseas bureaus in 1957, and threw himself increasingly into national politics as an undisguised booster of Lyndon Johnson in the latter's struggle with John Kennedy for the Democratic Party's 1960 presidential nomination. Bouts of depression and self-doubt increasingly injected themselves into his otherwise often manic lifestyle to the point that he was finally willing to seek institutionalized treatment.

For her part, Katharine Graham concentrated on retiring from her involvement in the paper and into private life, and on rearing their four children, a daughter, Elizabeth, and sons Donald, William, and Stephen. Then, on August 3, 1963, Philip Graham checked out of the Chestnut Lodge treatment center to spend a day with his wife, played tennis with Katharine in the morning, and killed himself while she took an early afternoon nap. Katharine Meyer Graham in that moment became the head of *The Washington Post*.

As the newspaper's publisher, president (1963-1973, 1977), chairman of the board (1973-1993), and chief executive officer (1973-1991), Katharine Graham ran the *Post* for most of the next thirty years. During those decades, she continued and improved upon the efforts of first her father and then her husband to build the *Post* into a great journalistic institution and, eventually, into a profitable *Fortune 500* company. The task required considerable physical and emotional effort. As Kenneth Berents, a respected newspaper analyst, observed in *The New York Times* article (of September 10, 1993) covering Graham's formal retirement as the *Post*'s chairman of the board, Graham often spoke of herself as "an oddity [in a world dominated by men], and looked upon as such." Breaking down gender bias took time and diligence; however, as that time passed, she gained confidence in both her ability to manage the newspaper and in the men she chose to run it. By the time she began cutting back on her involvement in the operations of the *Post* and turned the publisher and chief executive responsibilities over to her son Donald (in 1979 and 1991, respectively), *The Washington Post* had become not only a world-class newspaper but also the centerpiece in a respected media conglomerate including the *International Herald Tribune* (on which Graham served as cochairman), *Newsweek* magazine, and cable and broadcast television properties. Not surprisingly, during those years—in Berents' words—Graham herself came to be viewed as "one of the industry's great ladies." Indeed, she had become the only woman to head a major American newspaper.

Summary

Just as Katharine Graham broke new ground as a woman heading a media empire, so her newspaper constantly broke new ground in covering the news under her steadying influence, care in selecting the *Post*'s management team, and willingness to support her subordinates even when under tremendous pressure to do otherwise.

To write of these developments is to relive the America covered by the *Post* during Katharine Graham's directorship. The years following Graham's succession to the newspaper's leadership were turbulent ones for the United States, with Washington serving as the center stage in a changing America. Only months after her husband committed suicide, President John F. Kennedy was assassinated in Dallas. Then came the Lyndon Johnson-Barry Goldwater campaign of 1964 and the buildup of American military forces in Vietnam the following year. Civil rights marches declined, antiwar protests commenced, and the cities began to explode. The Tet offensive in Vietnam in early 1968 persuaded President Johnson not to seek reelection; Robert Kennedy was killed in June campaigning for the Democratic Party's nomination to succeed him. In between, Martin Luther King, Jr., was also assassinated, and the Washington riots that followed his assassination provided *The Washington Post* with a fast-breaking story quite literally on its doorsteps, complete with photo opportunities of machine-gun emplacements on the steps of the Capitol. Its coverage of the event was perhaps the key moment in the *Post*'s emergence among the elite national newspapers in the United States.

The *Post* remained in that company with its openly critical coverage of the Johnson and Nixon administrations' conduct of the Vietnam war and its publication in June of 1971 of "The Pentagon Papers." In fact, and much to the annoyance of Ben Bradlee, Graham's hand-picked editor of *The Washington Post*, *The New York Times* broke the story two days before the *Post* obtained its own copy of the documents chronicling America's often governmentally choreographed entry into the Vietnam war. By the time the case reached the Supreme Court to test the government's ability to squelch the publication of the documents on the grounds of national security considerations, *The Washington Post* had become an equal party to the action.

Graham's greatest impact on the newspaper and public affairs, however, was still to come—in the *Post*'s investigative coverage of a minor break-in conducted in the early morning hours of June 17, 1972, at the headquarters of the Democratic National Committee. *The Washington Post* would stay with that story long after other news organizations and newspapers had abandoned it. Requests to drop the story would come from such important personages as Secretary of State Henry Kissinger. Veiled and not-so-veiled threats of action against the *Post* and its media empire came from the offices of President Nixon's special counsel, Charles Colson, and from former Attorney General John Mitchell. Still, with the same determination she would else-where show in facing down strikers at her newspaper, Graham never wavered in her support of her staff. In the end, the trail led from Watergate to the White House, the affair cemented *The Washington Post*'s growing reputation for journalistic respect-ability and independence, and the *Post*'s coverage of the Watergate affair made celebrities out of Katharine Graham as well as Ben Bradlee and the reporter team of Bob Woodward and Carl Bernstein. It was President Richard Nixon who would have to resign from office in disgrace, not the publisher of the *Post*.

Bibliography

Bernstein, Carl, and Bob Woodward. *All the President's Men*. New York: Simon & Schuster, 1974. No study of Katharine Graham and the *Post* would be complete without this rendition of the Watergate affair. The crucial decisions at the newspaper were not made by Mrs. Graham so much as by the executives she trusted and by whom she stood throughout their pursuit of the story.

Davis, Deborah. *Katharine the Great: Katharine Graham and Her "Washington Post" Empire*. 3d ed. New York: Sheridan Square Press, 1991. The third edition of a work that originally appeared in 1979, this book has been updated to cover Graham's years in the quasi-retirement that followed her 1979 decision to turn her publisher's duties over to her son Donald.

Felsenthal, Carol. *Power, Privilege, and the "Post": The Katharine Graham Story*. New York: G. P. Putnam's Sons, 1993. Something of an unauthorized biography on Katharine Graham. Reputedly published without interviews with Graham (who was working on her memoirs), it was published shortly before her official retirement from *The Washington Post*.

Gilbert, Ben W., and the staff of *The Washington Post*. *Ten Blocks from the White House: Anatomy of the Washington Riots of 1968*. New York: F. A. Praeger, 1968. The 1968 riots provided the *Post* with a major story several years before the flaps over the Pentagon Papers and the Watergate affair. This work provides a good account of how Graham's newspaper covered that story.

Sussman, Barry. *The Great Coverup: Nixon and the Scandal of Watergate*. New York: New American Library, 1974. A well-crafted, readable outsider's account of the Watergate scandal and the role of the *Post* and its management in the downfall of the Nixon administration.

Ungar, Sanford J. *The Papers and the Papers: An Account of the Legal and Political Battle over the Pentagon Papers*. New York: Columbia University Press, 1989. An outstanding analysis of the struggle over the Pentagon Papers, this reprint of the 1972 book released by E. P. Dutton captures some of the drama behind the decision of both *The New York Times* and *The Washington Post* to publish the secret documents concerning the Vietnam War. The focus is on *The New York Times* as a party in the court case arising from the publication of the Pentagon Papers.

The Washington Post Staff. *The Fall of a President*. New York: Delacorte Press, 1974. An excellent collection of the *Post*'s coverage of the Watergate affair, from its early, limited reporting on the Watergate break-in to the House of Representatives' consideration of Articles of Impeachment against President Richard Nixon.

Joseph R. Rudolph, Jr.

MARTHA GRAHAM

Born: May 11, 1894; Allegheny, Pennsylvania
Died: April 1, 1991; New York, New York
Area of Achievement: Dance
Contribution: Graham is generally accepted as the greatest single figure in American modern dance.

Early Life

Although her name is virtually synonymous with modern dance, Martha Graham did not have a single dance lesson until she was twenty-two years old. Her father, George Graham, was a doctor who specialized in nervous disorders and, consequently, was intrigued by physical movement. He warned his daughters never to be dishonest because he would know they were lying by the tension in their bodies. Although he would not allow Martha to study ballet because of the social taboos of the era and on the pretext that it would interfere with her schoolwork, Martha credits her father with being her first dance teacher, for he taught her the importance of the body's language and of honesty.

George Graham was the son of an Irish immigrant, while Martha's mother, Jane Beers Graham, could trace her heritage back to Miles Standish and the *Mayflower*. Martha's upbringing consisted of a strict Puritan code of ethics, and she and her two younger sisters were required to attend church and daily prayers. As an outlet for their mischievousness, however, the sisters were permitted to play "dress up" and to create their own plays. Because she was a physically plain child, this early role playing gave Martha a means of escape as well as a means of channeling her explosive temper. As an adult, she would create her own brand of glamour, but the temper and the subsequent tantrums would only become more pronounced.

The young Martha was a voracious reader who appeared to be mesmerized by the drama of life and called to reveal its mysteries. One of these mysteries was the impact of ritual, and when the Grahams hired a nanny, Lizzie Pendergast, who took the girls with her to Catholic mass, Martha was fascinated by the ceremony and the music.

When Martha Graham was in her teens, her sister Mary was diagnosed with asthma, and, in an effort to seek a better climate, Jane Graham moved with the girls to Santa Barbara, California. Martha immediately acclimated to her new environment and was drawn to the pageantry of the Asian population in the area. This pageantry, coupled with the recollected Catholic mass, would eventually become the root of her creations.

Although she was still not allowed to study dance formally, Martha was active in other areas; in high school, she edited the literary magazine, acted in the school play, and played basketball. Many of these interests decreased in importance, however, when in 1911, Martha saw her first ballet, a performance by Ruth St. Denis at the Mason Opera House in Los Angeles. Martha memorized some of the moves, tried them at home, and sealed her fate. Even though her parents would not give their blessings to this chosen profession, Martha took her first step toward her career by giving up sports in order not to injure her legs.

In 1913, Martha enrolled in an arts-oriented junior college, the Cumnock School. With her father's reluctant assent, she studied acting, play writing, and dance. During her years at the Cumnock, two events took place which affected the course of her future. In 1914, George Graham died, leaving enough investments for his daughters to finish their educations, and, in 1915, Martha's idol, Ruth St. Denis, and her husband Ted Shawn opened a dance school in Los Angeles.

Immediately after being graduated from the Cumnock School, Martha auditioned for and was accepted to the Denishawn School. Denishawn was the most innovative training available, because St. Denis believed in teaching holistic dance, not merely ballet. Although Martha adored St. Denis, the feeling was not reciprocated, and she was sent to study with Ted Shawn. While working with Shawn, she performed the lead in *Serenata Morisca*, memorizing the steps after seeing them demonstrated only four times, and it became her trademark piece, transforming her from a student into a professional.

By 1918, she had become Shawn's principal teacher, and a dance he created especially for her marked her entry into modest fame. The dance was *Xochital*, about an assault on an Aztec maiden. Putting her emotional being into the performance, Graham was a terrifying figure of wildness and fury in defending her virtue, and often her partners were bleeding as they came off stage. She performed the number from coast to coast for two years, until it was scheduled for a European tour and St. Denis appropriated the role for herself.

Because of their artistic and temperamental differences, Martha Graham and Ted Shawn came to despise each other, and Martha looked for a way out. In spite of the animosity, she studied and worked as a teacher and principal dancer with Denishawn for almost eight years until an offer to return to New York in 1923 permitted her to strike out on her own.

Life's Work

The liberating offer was from the Greenwich Village Follies, a vaudeville revue. At long last, Martha Graham was encouraged to create her own dances within the exotic parameters of glamour required by the Follies management. Although the position garnered her a certain amount of fame and financial comfort, she knew it was not her life's work. She felt destined to be an "artist," which in her view translated as "worker"; in 1925, she left Broadway to teach and, more important, to learn in the newly created dance department of the Eastman School of Music in Rochester.

Founded by George Eastman, the inventor of the Kodak camera and a patron of the arts, the school became the launching pad for the creative genius of Martha Graham. Since she was given autonomy, she threw out the old, standardized modes of teaching dance and began to experiment with and through her students.

Using several of her most gifted disciples as a company, the true Martha Graham emerged in 1927 with *Revolt*, which related man's injustice to man, followed closely by *Heretic* and *Vision of the Apocalypse*. Discarding the traditional flow of ballet, her dancers used spastic jerks, trembling, and falls to the floor to illustrate their themes. The press and the public were shocked. This was not entertainment, they believed; this was disturbing, which was exactly the response Graham had hoped to elicit.

In 1929, beginning with her former Eastman students, Martha initiated her own company, the Martha Graham School of Contemporary Dance. From that point, she was unfailingly experimental and uncompromising, and she was frequently the source of bewilderment and angry resistance. People were rarely indifferent to her, and she was surrounded by debate throughout her career. Whether it was adoration or disgust, it was impossible to view one of her performances without experiencing a definite emotional reaction. Known for her tyranny and her temper, she nevertheless instilled hero worship in her students, who followed her in a cult-like procession. They knew that although she demanded perfection and absolute obedience, she could also be genuinely kind, caring, and surprisingly sentimental.

Thematically, Martha Graham delved into every dark corner of the human mind through physical expression. She was fascinated by rituals, psychological conflicts, and mythology, a subject she considered the ancestor of psychotherapy. Throughout her career, she composed more than one hundred dances and choreographed more than one hundred eighty works, each of which was extremely complex in terms of symbolic meaning and literary allusion.

Although condemned by some for her use of the body and her frank acknowledgment of human sexuality, Graham proclaimed she was tracing the genealogy of the soul of humanity, that she wanted to "chart the graph of the heart." Holding her work-worn hands skyward and performing in bare feet, she moved to themes that dealt with archetypes and rituals so old that humankind could not understand them because it had forgotten them. Her fame led to world tours, and she traveled extensively in both Europe and Asia. She became an honorary ambassador for the United States and was courted by both the Nazi party in 1936 and the communists in the 1950's. She rejected both groups.

Although she excelled as a choreographer, Graham insisted that she was primarily a performer. Thus, when she was forced to retire from the stage in 1969 at the age of seventy-five, the media and her company expected her to wither away. After a cycle of hospitalization and convalescence, Martha recovered, thanks, in part, to the encouragement of a young photographer, Ron Protas, who adored her. Through his care, she regained her will to live, and in her eighties, Martha Graham staged a comeback, including tours of the United States and the Far East and a full return to teaching.

In 1991, after completing a fifty-five-day tour of the Far East with her troupe, Martha Graham contracted pneumonia. Two months later, on April 1, she died of cardiac arrest. She was ninety-six years old.

Summary

Frequently ranked with Pablo Picasso, Igor Stravinsky, and James Joyce for developing a form of expression that broke the traditional mold, Martha Graham is generally accepted as the greatest single figure in American modern dance and the symbol of it in the popular mind. She invented a new and codified language of dance and began a whole fashion with respect to stage design and costuming, symbolic props, and mobile scenery. During her long career, she won virtually every honor an artist can receive, including the Presidential Medal of Freedom and the French Legion of Honor. She performed for heads of state and was granted honorary degrees from Harvard and Yale, among other universities.

Despite the acclaim, it was her ground-breaking style, her refusal to compromise, and her depiction of the American woman on the threshold of a new life for which Martha Graham will be remembered. Seeking the key to woman's present dilemma, Graham laid bare the mythos surrounding the feminine role and in the process created such memorable pieces as *Primitive Mysteries*, for which she was awarded a Guggenheim Fellowship, *Appalachian Spring*, which won a Pulitzer Prize for Aaron Copland's score, and *Letter to the World*, which depicted the inner and outer life of poet Emily Dickinson and was considered by some to be Graham's masterwork. She was also the first choreographer consistently to employ African American and Asian dancers and to incorporate the spoken word into her dances.

Because it deals with myth, ritual, and the unconscious, the substance of her work is intangible and cannot be analyzed; it involves a total sensory impression that can only be experienced. Martha Graham shall remain, in the words of her biographer, Agnes de Mille, the "most startling inventor and the greatest performer who trod the native stage."

Bibliography
Anderson, Jack. *Dance*. New York: Newsweek Books, 1974. This work is a brief overview of the entire range of ballet history. It includes biographical information on dancers, including Graham, and a selected bibliography.
Balanchine, George. *Balanchine's New Complete Stories of the Great Ballets*. Edited by Francis Mason. Garden City, N.Y.: Doubleday, 1968. Written by one of the great masters in dance, this work includes plot summaries of ballets, including those devised by Martha Graham. A chronology of significant events in ballet history, an annotated list of recordings, and a selected bibliography are included.
de Mille, Agnes. *Dance to the Piper*. Boston: Little, Brown, 1952. Although this book is de Mille's autobiography, much information on Graham is included. The two were contemporaries and friends, and de Mille eventually became Martha Graham's biographer.
——————— . *The Life and Work of Martha Graham*. New York: Random House, 1991. This biography of Graham was written by one of the greatest figures in twentieth century dance, an artist who is ideally qualified to discuss Graham and her work.
Lloyd, Margaret. *The Borzoi Book of Modern Dance*. New York: Alfred A. Knopf, 1949. Biographical information on Martha Graham and a discussion of her work are included in this volume. Additionally, the book contains information on the conversion of classical ballet into legitimate theater.

Terry, Walter. *Frontiers of Dance: The Life of Martha Graham.* New York: Thomas Y. Crowell, 1975. Written by a former student of Graham's, this book depicts the life and work of Martha Graham from the early years through the initial stages of her comeback.

Joyce Duncan

ANGELINA GRIMKÉ and SARAH GRIMKÉ

Angelina Grimké

Born: February 28, 1805; Charleston, South Carolina
Died: October 26, 1879; Hyde Park, Massachusetts

Sarah Grimké

Born: November 26, 1792; Charleston, South Carolina
Died: December 23, 1873; Hyde Park, Massachusetts

Areas of Achievement: Social reform and women's rights
Contribution: Because their gender hindered their activity in the abolitionist movement, the Grimké sisters realized the necessity for women's rights and worked to establish them.

Early Life

Sarah Moore Grimké was the sixth child born to John and Mary Grimké, well-to-do South Carolinians. The Grimkés spent November to March on their rice plantation, which was operated by a large number of slaves, including field hands as well as house and personal slaves. When Eli Whitney's gin made growing cotton more profitable, Judge Grimké turned to cotton production.

In April, to avoid the unhealthy summer months, the family went to Charleston, where they joined the social scene as upper-class planters and respected Episcopalians. Beyond the plantation, John Grimké sat on the South Carolina bench, for a time as chief justice. He also served in the South Carolina House of Representatives. Active in the coming of the Revolutionary War, John joined a handful of South Carolinians in protesting the Boston Port Bill of 1774, which resulted from the Boston Tea Party. Once war began, he fought as a captain in the Continental Army.

When Sarah was thirteen, Mary Grimké gave birth to her fourteenth child, Angelina. Devoted to her new sister, Sarah became the infant's godmother and helped with her rearing to the extent that Angelina called her older sister "mother."

Sarah, influenced by both her father and her older brother Thomas (born September 26, 1786), wanted to study law. Thomas, who studied at Yale, earned a distinguished position as an attorney, politician, and reformer. Active in both the temperance and peace movements, and a founding member of the South Carolina branch of the American Colonization Society, he undoubtedly influenced his younger sisters in their reform endeavors. Sarah's gender, however, hampered her goal of following in his, and their father's, footsteps.

Both Sarah and Angelina grew up in an aristocratic, conservative environment dominated by slavery and the authoritarian Episcopal Church. Both sisters knew firsthand the abuses of slavery; indeed, Angelina fainted at school after witnessing the results of a beating administered to a young male slave.

Sarah showed a certain degree of emancipation in her mid-twenties when she accompanied her father to Philadelphia, where he sought medical attention. Unfortunately, the prescription of rest proved unsuccessful, and Sarah was with him at his death. She stayed on, living for two months with a Quaker family. The simplicity of their lifestyle, plus the absence of slaves, had a profound effect on her, as did her reading of a book by the antislavery Quaker John Woolman. His spirituality and abolitionist leanings moved Sarah. She returned to Charleston, but after a few years she rebelled against the family's lifestyle by moving to Philadelphia in the early 1820's. In a conscious break with her past, she joined the Society of Friends. Angelina also rebelled, converting to Presbyterianism while still in Charleston. Still dissatisfied, she went to Philadelphia in 1829 and joined the Society of Friends.

Life's Work

The joining of Angelina and Sarah Grimké in Philadelphia set them on a path toward social reform. Although Angelina seemed to be the dominant figure, they both devoted their lives first to the antislavery crusade and then to women's rights when they found that their gender hampered their pursuit of their reformist goals.

While the Society of Friends had been active in the antislavery crusade since the American Revolution, most historians date the beginning of abolitionism to 1831, when William Lloyd Garrison began publishing *The Liberator*. In 1834, he printed a letter written by Angelina opposing slavery. The next year, she attended lectures by Andrew Gordon and George Thompson, both of whom advocated the immediate end of slavery. These lectures prompted the sisters' enthusiastic entry into the antislavery crusade. They joined the free produce movement, refusing to buy or consume any products grown by slave labor. Angelina also joined the Philadelphia Female Anti-Slavery Society, her name appearing as a committeewoman in May, 1835. Others who influenced them were merchants Arthur Tappan and Lewis Tappan and seminary student Theodore Weld. The sisters' outspoken opposition to slavery forced them out of the Society of Friends, because of the Society's seemingly ambiguous stance on immediate abolition. First Sarah and then Angelina withdrew.

Together, the sisters moved to New York to be closer to the center of the abolition crusade. There, bringing a fresh perspective to antislavery based on their southern upbringing, they joined the Anti-Slavery Society. Angelina wrote *An Appeal to the Christian Women of the South*, a pamphlet that appeared in 1836. In it, she wrote that slavery abrogated the teachings of Jesus, human law as given by God to Adam, and the Declaration of Independence. Although the pamphlet received favorable reviews from abolition supporters, southern postmasters burned it, and Angelina was threatened with arrest if she returned to Charleston. Because of this work's popularity, the sisters began speaking to small groups of women. They urged the women, who could not vote and therefore did not make law, to influence their husbands, fathers, and brothers. They further encouraged any women who owned slaves to free them and pay them wages for their labor.

Both sisters continued to write. Sarah produced *Address to Free Colored Americans*, while Angelina wrote *Appeal to the Women of the Nominally Free States* (1837). It became increasingly obvious to these women that gender equality was intimately associated with antislavery and that it was impossible to work for one without the other. This caused a split in the antislavery ranks: Those who supported the activities of the Grimké sisters fought with their more traditional male counterparts, who believed that a woman's place was in the home. Angelina and Sarah refused simply to report the positions of others; they worked to shape antislavery policy, thus furthering the movement as well as introducing women's rights.

In part to heal the growing rift, the Anti-Slavery Society sponsored a New England speaking tour for Angelina and Sarah. There the sisters began speaking to public audiences of women and then groups of men and women. This activity brought criticism from a variety of places, including ministerial associations, which spurred the sisters' interest in women's rights to protect their work in the abolitionist movement. The highlight of their tour came when Sarah was scheduled to address the Massachusetts Legislature on the subject of abolition. Illness prevented her appearance, and Angelina appeared in her stead. In all, the women spent six months in New England. They delivered some eighty speeches in sixty-seven communities, speaking to a combined audience of at least 40,000. In their wake, they left several local chapters of the Anti-Slavery Society.

Upon returning to New York, Angelina began a correspondence with fellow abolitionist Theodore Weld, which blossomed into romance. Despite his pledge not to marry until slavery ended, Angelina and Theodore were married in Philadelphia on May 14, 1838, in a ceremony fitting two reformers. They wrote their own wedding vows, contravening the established custom of male superiority. Sarah gave the couple her blessing, although she appeared to be playing the role of martyr throughout (when she first arrived in Philadelphia, Israel Morris, a Quaker, courted Sarah, but she rejected his proposal of marriage).

The couple, joined by Sarah, bought a small farm in New Jersey, near New York City. Despite a variety of illnesses, Angelina gave birth to three children, and Sarah helped to rear them. Their apparent closeness and affection for each other notwithstanding, Sarah and Angelina did not always get along, and at one point Sarah struck out on her own. She returned to the Weld household soon, however, probably because of the children.

Theodore, a major abolitionist in his own right, had injured his voice during one of his many speaking tours and had retired from speaking to farm. He did, however, continue to work for the Anti-Slavery Society. Angelina and Sarah also gave up public speaking in favor of farming and editing Weld's works; they assisted him with *Slavery as It Is* (1839).

In keeping with their simple lifestyle, they adopted the dietary plan of Sylvester Graham. They also continued to boycott any products produced by slave labor (sugar, for example). They always lived simply and never accumulated any wealth; at the same time, their home was always open to other reformers.

For a time, while in New Jersey, the Welds joined other reform movements. They were briefly associated with the Millerites, a millennial group. Later, they joined the Raritan Bay Union, a New Jersey Utopian association for which Weld ran a school and the sisters taught. They also operated a boarding school, with Weld as principal, Angelina teaching history, and Sarah teaching French. Still later, they had a school in Hyde Park, Massachusetts, where Sarah wrote an unpublished biography of Joan of Arc.

Angelina and Sarah were prolific writers. Their major works on women's rights are, for Angelina, *Appeal to the Women of the Nominally Free States* (1837), and for Sarah, *Letters on the Equality of the Sexes and the Condition of Woman* (1838). Both these works appeared a full decade before the Seneca Falls Convention, which is generally regarded as the advent of the women's rights movement in the United States. Although neither sister attended, both continued to be active in women's rights. For example, they wore, briefly, the outfit associated with the women's movement and made famous by Amelia Bloomer. Several major figures in the women's rights movement, including Elizabeth Cady Stanton, Lucy Stone, and Susan B. Anthony, acknowledged their debt to the Grimké sisters.

During the Civil War, Theodore Weld returned to the lecture circuit, despite fears for his voice, while Angelina and Sarah worked with the Woman's Central Committee. In 1865, Angelina's favorite theme, to fulfill the Declaration of Independence through an end to slavery, was achieved.

Late in life, the sisters learned that their brother Henry had three male children by a slave woman. Accepting these young men as their nephews, they supported their educational endeavors and were pleased with their success.

Later in life, the Welds and Sarah moved to Massachusetts, where all three taught in Hyde Park. Sarah died in 1873, and Angelina, incapacitated by a series of strokes, died six years later in 1879.

Summary

Angelina and Sarah Grimké lived to see slavery abolished in the United States with the passage of the Thirteenth Amendment, but they died long before the women's rights movement achieved success with the passage of the Nineteenth Amendment. They did, however, see the progress made by the women's rights activists they inspired. Women of exceptional dedication and courage, the Grimké sisters turned their frustration over being limited in the antislavery crusade to good advantage when they began speaking and writing about women's rights. Neither Angelina nor Sarah compromised; instead, they broke with their family and their community in favor of their position. When their gender stood in the way of further achievements, they worked to change the attitudes of the dominant male culture. The sisters refused to play secondary roles in the antislavery movement because of their gender; through the written and spoken word, Angelina and Sarah Grimké helped define the abolitionist movement, and through that effort pointed the way to the women's rights movement.

Bibliography

Barnes, Gilbert H. *The Antislavery Impulse: 1830-1844.* Gloucester, Mass.: Peter Smith, 1957. Although dated, this classic provides a solid foundation for a study of the abolitionist crusade. Includes several references to Angelina and Sarah as well as to Theodore Weld.

Birney, Catherine. *The Grimké Sisters: Sarah and Angelina Grimké, the First American Women Advocates of Abolition and Women's Rights.* Westport, Conn.: Greenwood Press, 1969. A reprint of the 1885 edition of an important work on the Grimkés.

Hersh, Blanche Glassman. *The Slavery of Sex: Feminist-Abolitionists in America.* Urbana: University of Illinois Press, 1978. An insightful examination of the interconnections between the antislavery movement and women's rights.

Lerner, Gerda. *The Grimké Sisters from South Carolina.* Boston: Houghton Mifflin, 1967. Standard biography of the sisters and their role in both abolition and women's rights.

Lumpkin, Katharine. *The Emancipation of Angelina Grimké.* Chapel Hill: University of North Carolina Press, 1974. Focuses on psychological and religious factors in the lives of the Grimkés and Theodore Weld.

Perry, Lewis, and Michael Fellman, eds. *Antislavery Reconsidered: New Perspectives on the Abolitionists.* Baton Rouge: Louisiana State University Press, 1979. Two essays consider the connection between the antislavery movement and women's rights.

Duncan R. Jamieson

CATHY GUISEWITE

Born: September 5, 1950; Dayton, Ohio

Areas of Achievement: Journalism and art

Contribution: After building a successful career in advertising, Cathy Guisewite created *Cathy*, an immensely popular comic strip that illustrates the life of a young, single, working woman in contemporary society. In a national poll by newspaper editors for *World Almanac and Book of Facts*, Guisewite has twice been selected as one of "America's Twenty-Five Most Influential Women."

Early Life

Cathy Lee Guisewite was born September 5, 1950, the middle daughter of William Lee and Anne Duly Guisewite, and grew up in the small town of Midland, Michigan. William Lee Guisewite owned an advertising agency, and his wife had worked in advertising before her marriage. Anne Guisewite later taught graduate school, but she regarded rearing her children as a rewarding career. A full-time mother, she encouraged her daughters to create their own greeting cards and to illustrate miniature books for gifts.

Cathy attended the University of Michigan, where she majored in English. Continuing the family tradition of illustrated gifts, she created "A College Girl's Mother's Guide to Survival" for a Mother's Day gift. Anne Guisewite sent the guide to American Greetings Corporation, but despite enthusiasm there, it was never published.

After receiving her B.A. degree in 1972, Cathy worked for advertising agencies, where she wrote radio commercials and magazine ads for such products as automobile brakes and shock absorbers. In 1974, she joined the prestigious W. B. Doner & Co. in its Southfield, Michigan, headquarters. She specialized in retail accounts and became the firm's first female vice president in 1976, heading a group of writers and artists. It was a key experience; Cathy was one of the most popular employees the firm ever had, and she found Doner a nourishing environment where she could develop her creative gifts and sense of humor.

Cathy's professional success was not, however, matched by social success. On long evenings at home she wrote a diary, eventually supplementing the text with stick figures. When she saw herself in the diary, she was able to perceive the humor in her social mishaps. Instead of letters, she sent diary entries to her parents to assure them she was coping. Her mother, sensing the possibilities for a comic strip, sent Cathy a list of syndicates to query. Within an hour of reading eighteen samples she sent, the executives of Universal Press Syndicate unanimously agreed to offer Cathy a contract. Despite the rudimentary quality of her drawing, they believed that her work mirrored the lives of contemporary, single, working women.

Although Cathy did not feel secure enough to leave her job at W. B. Doner & Co. until nine months later, the first *Cathy* appeared on November 22, 1976, in about sixty newspapers. After choosing the title for the strip at the urging of Universal, she admitted that the comic strip Cathy is very similar to her creator.

Life's Work

Cathy Guisewite developed her artistic skills by studying books on how to draw cartoons, by following suggestions from the syndicate, and by studying the work of other cartoonists. She has cited the strips *Beetle Bailey* and *Peanuts* as particularly strong influences, the latter for creating facial expressions with very few lines. As Guisewite's talent has developed over the years, Cathy's appearance has changed. Originally defined by weak, shaky lines, she is now drawn in firm, expressive ones. Her wardrobe has grown from pants and a long-sleeved shirt with a heart in the middle to a wide assortment of outfits. Cathy's character has also developed as Guisewite has changed, becoming more assertive in her attitudes and relationships.

The basic themes of the comic strip are consumerism, food, career, mother, and romantic relationships. Each strip is an arena for Cathy's insecurities, which sometimes lead to turmoil and sometimes to insight. Different facets of Cathy's personality are brought out by different characters. One of the central relationships in the strip is between Cathy and "Mom," who is based at least partly on Guisewite's own mother. Cathy's Mom is totally supportive and nurturing, sometimes to the point of being maddening. She refers to Cathy as "my baby," and often treats her as if she were still a child. Constant scheming to encourage her daughter to marry and have a child is treated with good-humored tolerance by Cathy yet contributes to Cathy's chronic insecurity. In 1987, a list of housekeeping, health, and travel tips titled *Motherly Advice from Cathy's Mom, with Illustrations by My Beautiful and Talented Daughter* was published by Andrews, McMeel and Parker. Guisewite often receives fan mail from mothers who send the strips to their daughters to make a point.

Cathy's friendship with Andrea, her best friend and an ardent feminist, is another important relationship in the strip. Andrea has married and has two young children but also works full time. She is a character who strives for perfection and is a perfect means for Guisewite to illustrate the perils and pitfalls of being a contemporary working mother. Andrea also functions as a kind of alter ego for Cathy; she often gives advice based on feminist ideology about how to do things better.

Cathy's boyfriend, Irving, is ostensibly a modern, enlightened man, but he wants her to do his laundry, pick up beer, play golf with him, and watch football. Cathy's feelings toward him are ambiguous and range from total infatuation to intense irritation. She spends much time trying to elicit commitments and compliments from Irving, yet she hates herself for it. No matter how annoying he is, Irving represents the core of the male-female conflict in the strip and provides some satisfaction in Cathy's life. The relationship represents a real schism between Cathy's intellectual and emotional self.

A successful innovation introduced in the 1980's was the adoption of a puppy, Electra. The dog, who seems to be able to communicate with her owner, soon became a sounding board for Cathy's struggles with relationships, mother, and weight problems. Often, Cathy's pet has more insight into people or problems than Cathy has. Meanwhile, Electra has developed her own humorous character as she has struggled to work out her canine difficulties.

Guisewite's own experiences are often the basis for episodes in the strip. She has even left an argument with a boyfriend to jot down details for later use. Yet Guisewite avoids risqué subjects; she likes to keep things vague and let the readers interpret the specifics as they like. Politics proved to be off-limits for *Cathy* during the last two weeks of the 1988 presidential election campaign. Cathy's friend Andrea urged women to vote and recommended Democratic candidate Michael Dukakis because of his support of various women's issues. The editors of about twenty papers pulled the strip or moved it to the Op-Ed page.

Guisewite's first television special, *Cathy*, took four years to plan and appeared on CBS in May, 1987, with her own father supplying the voice for the character "Dad." *Cathy's Last Resort*, a second television special, appeared in November, 1988. On May 8, 1993, NBC aired *Mother's Day Sunday Funnies*, a show that featured Guisewite's cartoon characters played by real people, including Patti Johns as Cathy. Each year, the daily *Cathy* comic strips are gathered into a collection published by the United Press Syndicate company Andrews and McMeel, while Ballantine Books irregularly publishes collections of selected cartoons. *Glamour* runs a monthly *Cathy* strip on its "Viewpoint" page. With the assistance of a part-time secretary and a graphics designer, Guisewite spends afternoons designing and writing copy for an assortment of *Cathy* products aimed at adult women. These include greeting cards, beach towels, T-shirts, mugs, sleepwear, posters, and stationery, among other things.

When she left Michigan in late 1980, Guisewite traveled up and down the West Coast before settling in Santa Barbara, California, which reminded her of the peaceful town of her childhood. It proved too quiet for her, however, and in 1984 she relocated to Los Angeles, where she moved into a spacious, modern, home-studio in the Hollywood Hills. Guisewite admits she is a workaholic and believes that total dedication to her work precludes romantic attachments. The only activity she actively pursues beyond her work is walking her dog. She likes being single and avoids any relationships that might threaten her professional commitment. When she started *Cathy*, writing the strip took all of Guisewite's working hours, but after years of practice she creates the daily strip in about two hours and a Sunday comic in about five. For feedback and advice, she turns to her younger sister Mickey, who works in advertising and is unfailingly candid with her opinions. In 1993, Bantam published *Dancing Through Life on a Pair of Broken Heels: Extremely Short Stories for the Totally Stressed*, written by Mickey Guisewite and illustrated by Cathy Guisewite. The book explores the fears, foibles, and embarrassments suffered by many apparently successful women.

Guisewite maintains public contact through speaking engagements and promotions, and she uses these occasions to interview people and find out their reactions to *Cathy*. In 1982, Guisewite won the Outstanding Communicator of the Year Award from the organization Los Angeles Advertising Women and was included in a San

Mateo, California, museum exhibit as one of the "ten influential twentieth-century cartoon artists." Guisewite was nominated for the National Cartoonist Society's Reuben Award, which honors the "Outstanding Cartoonist of the Year" in 1990, 1991, and 1992. She finally received the Reuben statuette in May, 1993, at a time when *Cathy* appeared in more than one thousand newspapers. At the awards ceremony, Charles Schulz, the creator of *Peanuts* whose work Guisewite had studied to improve her own drawing, tore open the Reuben envelope, smiled broadly, and announced her the winner.

Summary

From time to time, *Cathy* has been criticized by ardent feminists, who are irritated by such Cathy statements as "Deep down, I think I really *like* to be pushed around." In the early years of the strip, Cathy lost more battles than she won, but she has gradually become more assertive. Cathy Guisewite considers herself a feminist and imagines Cathy to be caught between two social ideals that she would like to reconcile: traditionalism and feminism.

The strip appeals most strongly to women in the eighteen to thirty-four age group, who find Cathy struggling with the problems similar to their own, and who suffer from the same weaknesses. Guisewite also mirrors current trends that influence everyone, such as popular television shows and new medical "miracles." Cathy incarnates Everywoman as she shops for consumer electronics, worries about her car repairs, succumbs to the pitch of a real-estate broker, agonizes over taxes, and sums up an important relationship: "You aren't the person I was pretending you were!!" *Cathy* reflects the lives of contemporary women with humor and insight, and Guisewite's popularity in a field that has been primarily a male bastion has broadened opportunities for women in cartoon journalism.

Bibliography

Astor, David. "Guisewite Works Overtime on Cathy." *Editor & Publisher*, June 25, 1983, 37-38. This interview chronicles the phenomenal popularity of the *Cathy* strip. Guisewite discusses why the strip is a success, her working habits, and her fan mail.

Guisewite, Cathy. *The Worse Things Get, the Better We Eat*. New York: Ballantine, 1989. A collected sample of some of the best of the cartoon strip, focusing on the acquisition of Cathy's puppy Electra. Electra brings out the obsessions and insecurities of Cathy, Irving, and Mom.

Millner, Cork. *Santa Barbara Celebrities*. Santa Barbara, Calif.: Santa Barbara Press, 1986. An informal talk with Cathy Guisewite is included in this collection of interviews. Guisewite answers questions about herself and about the genesis of *Cathy* and the characters who appear in it.

Robbins, Trina. *A Century of Women Cartoonists*. Northampton, Mass.: Kitchen Sink Press, 1993. This large-format book presents an overview of the contributions of women comic strip artists since the beginning of the medium. Written with a feminist slant, it describes the struggles that women cartoonists have undergone to achieve recognition.

Serchia, Paul. "'Cathy' Mentions Kasdan Films." *Editor & Publisher* 125 (April 25, 1992): 29-30. Serchia discusses the ethical problems involved in mentioning commercial products, including films, in cartoon strips. Comic strip Cathy's ecstatic reaction to *Grand Canyon* may have something to do with Guisewite's relationship with the film's director.

Sheila Golburgh Johnson

SARAH JOSEPHA HALE

Born: October 24, 1788; Newport, New Hampshire
Died: April 30, 1879; Philadelphia, Pennsylvania
Areas of Achievement: Literature and journalism
Contribution: The author of poetry, novels, plays, and cookbooks, as well as an important history of women, Hale is best known as the editor of *Godey's Lady's Book*, the most popular magazine in the United States before the Civil War. As editor of this women's magazine, Hale encouraged and supported women writers, and she advocated improved opportunities for women's education and work.

Early Life

Born October 24, 1788, on a farm outside Newport, New Hampshire, Sarah Josepha Buell was one of four children of Gordon and Martha Whittlesey Buell. Though opportunities for formal schooling for girls were limited at the time, Buell received a good education at home, and she credited her mother with inspiring her love of literature. Despite limited access to books, Buell read widely during her youth. By the time she was fifteen, for example, she had read all of William Shakespeare's works. Other favorites included the Bible, John Bunyan's *Pilgrim's Progress* (1678, 1684), and Ann Radcliffe's *The Mysteries of Udolpho* (1794). Buell also benefited from tutoring by her brother Horatio, who attended Dartmouth College. During Horatio's summer vacations at home, the two studied Latin, Greek, philosophy, English grammar, rhetoric, geography, and literature. Hale drew on her strong education when, at age eighteen, she opened a private school for children. She continued to teach until 1813, when she married David Hale, a lawyer in Newport.

During her marriage, Sarah Josepha Buell Hale continued her education. As she later recalled, she and her husband spent two hours each evening reading current literature and studying topics ranging from composition and French to science. During this period, Hale also worked on her own writing, publishing a few poems in local magazines.

Hale's life changed considerably when, in 1822, shortly before the birth of their fifth child, Hale's husband died suddenly. Concerned with providing for her family, Hale turned first to the millinery business, but she soon focused on becoming an author. Her first volume of poetry, *The Oblivion of Genius and Other Original Poems*, appeared in 1823. After winning several literary prizes and becoming a regular contributor to magazines and gift annuals, Hale published her first novel, *Northwood: A Tale of New England*, in 1827. Though highlighting New England character traits, as the subtitle suggests, the novel focused on the contrasts between the North and South, including issues of race relations and slavery.

Life's Work

Soon after the publication of *Northwood*, Sarah Josepha Hale, at the age of thirty-nine, launched what to a great extent would become her life's work as a magazine editor. When a new periodical, the *Ladies' Magazine*, first appeared in January of 1828, Hale edited it from her home in Newport, but within a few months she moved to Boston, where the magazine was published. Though the *Ladies' Magazine* was not the first periodical intended for American women or edited by an American woman, it did differ considerably from earlier efforts, which often focused on fashion. Hale's *Ladies' Magazine* included fashion plates during part of its nine-year existence, but it was much more intellectual than previous women's magazines had been. Sketches of famous women were common features, and Hale's editorial columns often addressed issues of social reform, such as property rights for married women and the importance of women's education.

Publishing both poetry and fiction, the magazine also had a significant literary component, and Hale's support of American authors is particularly noteworthy. Whereas other magazine editors relied on anonymous material and reprinted British literature (generally without permission), Hale's magazine featured American authors, and she repeatedly encouraged her readers to recognize authorship as a legitimate profession. Therefore, she favored original submissions rather than re-prints, encouraged attribution of authors, and supported the idea that authors should be paid for their work.

Throughout her editorship of the *Ladies' Magazine*, Hale continued her efforts as an author. Her own writings appeared frequently in the magazine, and some of them were published separately in book form. Her *Sketches of American Character* (1829) and *Traits of American Life* (1835) first appeared in the *Ladies' Magazine*. During this time, Hale also published two poetry collections, including *Poems for Our Children* (1830), which contained the poem "Mary's Lamb" (now famous as "Mary Had a Little Lamb").

Hale's career took an important turn in 1837, when after nine years of managing the *Ladies' Magazine*, Hale accepted a new position as editor of Louis Godey's *Lady's Book*, which Godey had founded in 1830 in Philadelphia. For the first several years, Hale edited the magazine from her home in Boston, but in 1841 she moved to Philadelphia. Even before the move, however, Hale carefully reformed the magazine, which initially lacked the intellectual and literary focus Hale had developed in the *Ladies' Magazine*. With Hale as editor, however, the *Lady's Book* (now often referred to by its later name, *Godey's Lady's Book*) became an important literary magazine for women. Though the magazine continued to publish the so-called "embellishments" for which Louis Godey had become famous (engravings, fashion plates, and so forth), Hale continued her earlier positions supporting American writers and improved opportunities for women's work and education. This combination of Godey's "embellishments" and Hale's literary and educational essays proved popular. By 1860, the magazine boasted 150,000 subscribers, making it the most popular U.S. magazine of its day.

With such a large audience, Hale was able to exert considerable influence on a number of social issues. Some of these, such as her efforts to preserve the Bunker Hill Monument and Mount Vernon, demonstrate her strong patriotic impulses. Many more of Hale's editorial campaigns were related to her belief in the power of what she and many of her contemporaries called "woman's sphere." Believing that women were innately more moral than men, Hale voiced strong support of women's charitable organizations, such as the Seaman's Aid Society, which tried to improve the lives of Boston's seamen and their families by founding schools, a library, a boarding house, and a clothing shop. Though Hale believed that the domestic space was part of women's sphere, she did not wish to confine women within the home. Quite the contrary, Hale encouraged women to extend their influence as widely as possible. Thus, for example, Hale voiced strong support for the founding of Vassar College (the first U.S. college for women), campaigned for women's medical colleges, and repeatedly called for women to take professional positions as teachers and with the post office. Hale also took a particular interest in issues of women's health, arguing, for example, for women's physical education and denouncing tight corsets as unhealthy (a charge that was later fully substantiated). Though the *Lady's Book* sometimes prided itself on avoiding political topics, many of Hale's editorial campaigns had significant political implications. Her long-standing efforts to establish Thanksgiving as a national holiday, for example, were based on her belief during the antebellum period that if a nation shared a meal together once a year, it would be less likely to engage in civil war. Though Hale's ultimate goal of preventing civil war was, of course, unsuccessful, she did manage to convince President Lincoln to declare Thanksgiving a national holiday.

Throughout her editorship of the *Lady's Book*, Hale continued to publish her own work. In addition to contributing material to the *Lady's Book*, she published a number of poetry volumes and several short novels, and following the success of Harriet Beecher Stowe's *Uncle Tom's Cabin* in 1852, she issued a revised edition of *Northwood*. Hale also wrote a number of very popular cookbooks. Hale's efforts as a writer were well regarded by her peers, and she was featured in many of the gift annuals and literary anthologies published before the Civil War. One of Hale's most ambitious projects as a writer was her 1853 *Woman's Record: Or, Sketches of All Distinguished Women from "The Beginning" till A.D. 1850*. This nine-hundred-page work presents biographical essays on more than two hundred women, with brief mentions of more than two thousand others.

After five decades as a magazine editor, Hale published her last column with the *Lady's Book* in December, 1877. She died on April 30, 1879, at the age of ninety and was buried in Philadelphia.

Summary

Though she was not the first woman magazine editor, Sarah Josepha Hale enjoyed a longer and more influential career than had any American woman before her. During her fifty-year editorial career, Hale made significant contributions to American literature and to women's issues. She published or reviewed the work of such writers as Edgar Allan Poe, James Fenimore Cooper, and Herman Melville. As editor of a popular women's magazine, Hale was able to support women writers, many of whom, such as Harriet Beecher Stowe and Lydia Sigourney, published their work in her magazines.

Through her editorial columns, Hale was also able to support other issues related to women. Although she did not advocate women's voting rights, she was a strong spokeswoman for property rights for married women, improved women's education, and increased opportunities for women's wage-earning work. Ultimately, one of Hale's most lasting contributions may have been in encouraging other women to pursue careers in publishing and periodicals. By proving that a women's literary magazine could be the nation's most popular periodical and by demonstrating that a woman could manage such a magazine, Hale undoubtedly helped to pave the way for later women editors, authors, and journalists.

Bibliography
Entrikin, Isabelle Webb. *Sarah Josepha Hale and "Godey's Lady's Book."* Lancaster, Pa.: Lancaster Press, 1946. A published dissertation, this work provides a good overview of Hale's editorial career and includes a bibliography of Hale's published works.
Finley, Ruth E. *The Lady of Godey's: Sarah Josepha Hale.* Philadelphia: J. B. Lippincott, 1931. The first full-length biography of Hale, this work provides a good overview of Hale's life, including her work as an author and editor and her support of issues such as national union and women's education.
Hoffman, Nicole Tonkovich. *"Legacy* Profile: Sarah Josepha Hale." *Legacy: A Journal of Nineteenth-Century American Women Writers* 7, no. 2 (Fall, 1990): 47-55. This short sketch of Hale's life and career includes a selected bibliography as well as an excerpt from one of Hale's editorials.
Mott, Frank Luther. *A History of American Magazines, 1741-1850.* Vol. 1. New York: D. Appleton, 1930. Though subsequent studies show less bias against sentimental literature than evident here, this pivotal work includes a detailed sketch of *Godey's Lady's Book* and valuable information about the periodical industry.
Okker, Patricia. *Our Sister Editors: Sarah J. Hale and the Tradition of Nineteenth-Century American Women Editors.* Athens: University of Georgia Press, 1995. In addition to identifying more than six hundred women who edited periodicals in the nineteenth century, this work provides an in-depth analysis of Hale's editorial career, focusing specifically on her literary significance.
Rogers, Sherbrooke. *Sarah Josepha Hale: A New England Pioneer, 1788-1879.* Grantham, N.H.: Tompson & Rutter, 1985. Though it presents little new information, this biography is particularly suited to older adolescents.

Patricia Okker

ALICE HAMILTON

Born: February 27, 1869; New York, New York
Died: September 22, 1970; Hadlyme, Connecticut
Areas of Achievement: Medicine and social reform
Contribution: A physician turned social reformer, Alice Hamilton became one of the
world's leading experts on industrial poisons and pioneered the development of the
new field of industrial medicine in the United States.

Early Life

Alice Hamilton was born on February 27, 1869, in New York City, the second of
the five children—four girls and one son—of Montgomery Hamilton and Gertrude
Pond Hamilton. She grew up in Fort Wayne, Indiana, on the estate of her wealthy and
socially prominent grandmother Hamilton. Her father proved ill-suited for the business world and ended up a heavy drinker, but her mother encouraged her and her
sisters to aspire to personal independence and professional achievement. Her older
sister, Edith Hamilton, would become a distinguished classicist. Alice had a lively and
vivacious personality. From childhood, she displayed a restlessly curious mind and a
keen sense of humor. At the same time, the strongly Presbyterian atmosphere in which
she was reared inculcated an abiding concern with the welfare of others and a lifelong
impulse toward social reform.

First educated at home, she attended Miss Porter's School in Farmington, Connecticut, from 1886 to 1888. Turning to medicine as a way of earning a living while
simultaneously doing good, she made up her deficiencies in science at the Fort Wayne
College of Medicine and entered the medical department of the University of Michigan in March, 1892. She received her M.D. the following year and interned at the
Northwestern Hospital for Women and Children in Minneapolis and the New England
Hospital for Women and Children in Boston in 1893 and 1894. Because her personal
interests lay more in research than in the care of patients, she pursued advanced study
in pathology and bacteriology at the University of Michigan, the universities of
Leipzig and Munich in Germany, and The Johns Hopkins University Medical School.

Life's Work

In 1897, Alice Hamilton was appointed professor of pathology at the Woman's
Medical School of Northwestern University in Chicago. Upon moving to Chicago,
she became a resident of Jane Addams' Hull House settlement. She found herself,
however, caught in a continuing emotional tug of war between the demands of
day-to-day social settlement work and her scientific ambitions. When the Woman's
Medical School closed in 1902, she accepted a position as a bacteriologist at the new
Memorial Institute for Infectious Diseases and undertook further study at the Pasteur
Institute in Paris. Her reading, apparently in 1907, of the pathbreaking exposure of the
dangers of occupational diseases by the British investigator Oliver Thomas in his
book *Dangerous Trades* (1902) led her to pursue what would become her life's

work—the investigation and elimination of industrial poisons.

She was appointed a member of the Illinois Commission on Occupational Diseases in 1908. She supervised the state's 1910 survey of industrial poisoning, with its first-ever combination of modern laboratory techniques and field work. The study focused on lead—the most widely used industrial poison—and her documentation of the extent of lead poisoning led to the adoption of the pioneering Illinois law requiring safety measures and medical examinations to protect at-risk workers. Early in 1911, Hamilton accepted an appointment as a special investigator for a federal agency that later became the Bureau of Labor Statistics of the Department of Labor. In that capacity, she was instrumental in bringing to public attention the problem of industrial poisoning, first in lead-using industries and later in munitions and steel plants. As she explained in a 1929 article, European programs of medical insurance for workers provided a handy source of data about the extent of occupational diseases in those countries. In the United States, however, the investigator "must pick up what information he can . . . here and there from doctors, hospitals, priests, apothecaries, and by following clues through city tenements and workers' cottages."

In 1919, Hamilton became Harvard University's first woman faculty member when she accepted an appointment as assistant professor of industrial medicine in the School of Medicine (after 1925, in the School of Public Health). She insisted on a half-time appointment to leave herself enough time to continue with field work, but the major focus of her activities shifted from scientific investigation to fund-raising and publicity. She was a moving force behind the publication of the *Journal of Industrial Hygiene and Toxicology*, which began in 1919. Her *Industrial Poisons of the United States* (1925), the first American textbook on the subject, established her reputation as one of the world's top experts in the field. That reputation was reinforced by her *Industrial Toxicology* (1934). She was instrumental in the calling of national conferences to draw attention to new poisons: the first on tetraethyl lead in 1925, the second on radium in 1928. She served two terms (1924-1930) as a member of the Health Committee of the League of Nations.

Turning more and more to political activism, she became a forceful advocate of woman suffrage, birth control, a national child labor law, and state health insurance. Her favored remedy was to extend the coverage of workmen's compensation laws to include occupational diseases. If industry were required "to bear the cost of all its own wastage in human material," firms would be forced to adopt safety precautions against work-produced diseases.

During World War I, she was active in women's rights and pacifist activities, attending the first (1915) and second (1919) International Congress of Women. In the 1920's, she opposed the proposed Equal Rights Amendment because of its threatened elimination of protective legislation for women. She spoke out against the execution of Nicola Sacco and Bartolomeo Vanzetti, the anarchists who had been found guilty of murder after what many thought was an unfair trial. She was invited to the Soviet Union in 1924 to investigate the state of industrial hygiene. Although she deplored the suppression of free speech, she was more positive than negative in her appraisal. She was a member of President Herbert Hoover's Research Committee on Social Trends (1930-1932), whose survey of American life was a landmark in social science research.

Never promoted above the level of assistant professor, Hamilton was forced to retire from Harvard because of age in 1935. Although she turned down the position of head resident of Hull House, she accepted the invitation from Secretary of Labor Frances Perkins to become a consultant to the Labor Department's newly established Division of Labor Standards. The result was her last field survey—an investigation of the viscose rayon industry (1937-1938). A visit to Germany in 1933 left her with an abiding revulsion toward Adolf Hitler and the Nazi regime. In 1940, she abandoned her former pacifism to support U.S. resistance to Hitler.

Hamilton served as president of the National Consumer's League (1944-1949); wrote her autobiography, *Exploring the Dangerous Trades: The Autobiography of Alice Hamilton, M.D.* (1943); and in cooperation with Harriet L. Hardy published a revised edition of her *Industrial Toxicology* (1949). During her last years, she took the typical liberal positions of the time: She reversed her former opposition to the Equal Rights Amendment in 1952; she complained about the obsessive anticommunism of U.S. foreign policy and the accompanying threat to civil liberties at home; and she called in 1963 for an end to American military involvement in Vietnam. She died of a stroke at Hadlyme, Connecticut, where she had lived with her sister Margaret since retiring from Harvard, on September 22, 1970.

Summary

At the time that Alice Hamilton began her work in industrial toxicology, a number of British and European investigators had begun to demonstrate the link between work and disease. Even in the United States, the pathbreaking work of such insurance company statisticians as Frederick L. Hoffman of the Prudential Life Insurance Company and Louis Dublin of Metropolitan Life was showing the impact of workplace conditions upon workers' health. Yet doctors and public health officials in the United States largely ignored those findings and paid little attention to the problems of the industrial worker and the work site. Industrial hygiene was not a recognized field. Hamilton probably did more than any other person to transform this situation. In so doing, she fulfilled the goal she had set for herself during her twenties: of leaving behind "something really lasting . . . to make the world better."

Almost single-handedly at the start, she drew public attention to the extent to which workers suffered from toxic hazards in the workplace. Her reputation for scientific accuracy, her skills as a negotiator, and her tact and personal charm made her highly successful in persuading manufacturers to introduce safety measures voluntarily. Even more important was her contribution—through fact-finding, publicity, and lobbying—to the passage of more effective factory inspection laws, stricter safety regulations, and expanded workers' compensation laws covering occupational diseases. Her most important long-term legacies were the adoptions of the federal Mine Safety and Health Act in 1969 and the Occupational Safety and Health Act in 1970.

Bibliography

Grant, Madeleine P. *Alice Hamilton: Pioneer Doctor in Industrial Medicine.* London: Abelard-Schuman, 1967. A biography aimed at young people. Although the treatment is admittedly fictionalized, Grant drew upon interviews with Hamilton, her sister, and her friends. The contemporary photographs are an attractive plus.

Hamilton, Alice. *Exploring the Dangerous Trades: The Autobiography of Alice Hamilton, M.D.* Boston: Little, Brown, 1943. Hamilton recounts her career with self-effacing modesty. An intensely private person, she shied away from exposing her inner self. Even her account of her public activities suffers from a blandness that plays down the conflicts and controversies in which she was involved.

_____ . "Nineteen Years in the Poisonous Trades." *Harpers Magazine* 159 (October, 1929): 580-591. A handy brief survey of Hamilton's investigations into the extent of industrial poisoning.

Rosner, David, and Gerald Markowitz, eds. *Dying for Work: Workers' Safety and Health in Twentieth-Century America.* Bloomington: Indiana University Press, 1987. An important collection of articles that illuminate the context in which Hamilton made her contribution. The two most directly concerned with Hamilton are Rosner and Markowitz's "'A Gift of God'? The Public Health Controversy over Leaded Gasoline During the 1920s" and Ruth Heifetz's "Women, Lead, and Reproductive Hazards: Defining a New Risk."

Sicherman, Barbara. "Alice Hamilton." In *Notable American Women: The Modern Period*, edited by Barbara Sicherman et al. Cambridge, Mass.: The Belknap Press of Harvard University Press, 1980. A brief but perceptive biographical sketch by the leading student of Hamilton's career with accompanying bibliographical information about available sources.

_____ . *Alice Hamilton: A Life in Letters.* Cambridge, Mass.: Harvard University Press, 1984. Reprints 131 of Hamilton's letters, selected with a twofold goal: first, to illustrate her "character, modes of thinking, or way of life"; second, to "reflect the range of her personal, professional, and political interests." Sicherman admits that the letters are more revealing about Hamilton as a person than about her work in industrial medicine, but the accompanying text is excellent on the "nature and significance of her contribution to industrial toxicology."

John Braeman

GORDON HAMILTON

Born: December 26, 1892; Tenafly, New Jersey
Died: March 10, 1967; British Columbia, Canada
Areas of Achievement: Education and sociology
Contribution: Hamilton was a leader in changing emphases in the training of social workers through her teaching, writings, and practice of the profession. She advocated a better world through social work practice that was informed by the social sciences and psychology as well as scientific approaches to casework.

Early Life

Gordon Hamilton was born Amy Gordon Hamilton in 1892. As a female leader in social work education from the 1930's through the 1950's, she did not use her first name professionally. Many of the professional positions she later held were usually offered to men during that time. Especially as a professor and author, Hamilton found it advantageous to attempt to avoid gender discrimination that could be directed against her as a social work leader.

Hamilton was the youngest of four children born to her parents. Her father, George Hamilton, had immigrated from Scotland to Canada in the 1870's; her mother, Bertha Torrance Hamilton, brought him to New Jersey after their marriage. Amy Gordon Hamilton's childhood there was difficult, especially because she was a victim of respiratory illnesses that continued throughout her life. Like many young women of her era, she was educated at home and was discouraged by her family from entering college; her mother disapproved of the sciences, and Hamilton was poorly prepared in those academic areas. When she was able to convince them of her need to have external tutoring in geography, Hamilton began to achieve some educational and social independence. By 1911, she had entered Bryn Mawr College, making a decisive break with her family's traditions and interests. In college, she majored in both Greek and English. Her career goal then was to become a writer and journalist.

Gordon Hamilton's interest in social work developed after her graduation in 1914 from Bryn Mawr College. She spent one year in London but, because of World War I, returned to the United States. Between 1917 and 1920, she worked for the Red Cross Home Service in Colorado. She had moved to Colorado hoping that its climate would improve her health. It was during this time that she was encouraged to seek a position as a social caseworker. She accepted employment with the Charity Organization Society of New York City, a job that marked the beginning of her career in social work.

Life's Work

Gordon Hamilton was comprehensive in her professional interests and developed broad practical experiences in social work as well as academic credentials for teaching and writing. She met Mary Richmond, a social work leader, in Colorado, and Richmond became a major influence on Hamilton's career. Richmond's recommendations allowed Gordon Hamilton to pursue her social work career, and eventually

Hamilton became interested in conducting research in the field. In 1922, after she had moved to New York, Hamilton investigated mental retardation and also participated in studies of social work agencies.

In 1923, Hamilton joined the faculty of the New York School of Social Work, her first teaching position. Her work as a professor there and her mastery of both the practical and theoretical aspects of her subject were so appreciated by students and faculty alike that she remained at the New York School as professor for thirty-four years. Despite her busy teaching load, she did not abandon her social work involvements in the field: From 1925 to 1932, she also served as a social service director and research adviser at Presbyterian Hospital in New York. This practical research was explained in her first book, *Medical Social Terminology* (1927). The volume discussed the correlation in the languages of medicine and social work; it was an early indicator of much of Hamilton's later work, which attempted to link social work with many adjacent academic areas.

Although Hamilton's major influence on social work was through her continued writings, she maintained an activist approach throughout her teaching and writing careers. In 1935 and 1936, she directed social services for the Temporary Emergency Relief Administration; between 1947 and 1950, she served as a research consultant at the Jewish Board of Guardians in New York; from 1944 through 1952, she often volunteered her services as a seminar leader or consultant for many international service organizations, including the United Nations Relief and Rehabilitation Administration and Church World Service. She did not perceive her academic interests as removed from the larger society and limited to classroom expressions; instead, she interpreted social work as well as her own involvements with it as intimately related to actual events that were occurring during her life, and she constructed many of her social work theories from experiences she had had when relating to individual people and social groups. Gordon Hamilton claimed that the social worker should not be limited by academic or practical barriers while attempting to create a better world in which people could live harmoniously. This positive goal and her optimistic assessment of human beings was debated by cautious analysts, but it fit her idea that the social worker ultimately is a social reformer who uses whatever methods and ideas are necessary to aid this process.

All of Hamilton's writings were accomplished after she accepted the teaching position at the New York School of Social Work in 1923. Her early book, *Social Case Recording*, published in 1936, emphasized the integral relation between diagnostic thinking and interpretation in recording social work data. Her main point was that there is no separation between theory and practice as the social worker collects data about people in need. A case record of a client must be intellectually sound, with an awareness of academic principles as well as showing awareness of the individual client's needs. Acute thinking by the social worker will help give him or her a more adequate base from which to diagnose and interpret his or her client's needs. *Social Case Recording* particularly emphasized the need for social workers to be intellectually well-grounded; Hamilton sought to refute the prevailing opinion that the profession consisted merely of unthoughtful or poorly trained "do gooders" and insisted instead that the profession was the expression of a legitimate academically oriented practitioner.

One of the most influential of Hamilton's writings was *Theory and Practice of Social Casework* published in 1940 again during her long teaching career at the New York School of Social Work. As with all of her major books, it was published by Columbia University Press and, as with several of her books, it was translated into other languages. In this volume, the author emphasized the philosophy that can support a service profession such as social work. She was explicit in borrowing from psychology and adopted a Freudian frame of reference as she discussed theories of personality and the psychodynamics of human behavior. This mix of social work theory and psychological theory was innovative at the time and showed Hamilton's continuing attempt to interpret social work as scientifically oriented as well as to correlate it with adjacent disciplines. She presented two major ideas as part of her argument: first, that the person's social environment must always be considered when diagnosing his or her social needs; and second, that social work as a profession must include both scientific knowledge and social values if it is to be successfully practiced. With these ideas, she challenged assumptions that a social worker need not be broadly informed in social theory, particularly concerning personality theory. She also challenged assumptions that being "scientific" excluded a commitment to ethics and values. With her eclectic academic approach, Gordon Hamilton believed strongly that the discipline of social work should be comprehensive enough to incorporate both other sciences and personal and social ethics. She claimed that a client cannot be adequately served if the professional social worker is either scientifically incompetent or disregards the values that impact on his or her social environment.

Theory and Practice of Social Casework became a standard text for social workers in the two decades following its publication. Not only did it correlate academic disciplines and emphasize ethics, it also was one of the clearest statements of the objectives of social work. Hamilton explicitly wrote about social work having two particular objectives: ensuring the economic well-being of the individual and encouraging the individual to establish satisfying social relations. Each of these objectives, according to Hamilton, reinforces the other: A person develops good relations most easily when he or she experiences economic stability, while this same individual can develop economic well-being most adequately if his or her social relationships are satisfying. For Hamilton, social work as a profession has special methods to help attain these objectives for individuals. The methods are expressed in subfields of social work such as social welfare planning, social group work, and social casework. Hamilton continued her ongoing emphases on the importance of intellectual development among social workers, as she wrote that these subfields must be continually informed by serious social research.

Theory and Practice of Social Casework was so widely read that it was reissued in 1951; the author, however, called this second edition a "radical revision." Between 1940 and 1951, Hamilton had been even more influenced by advances in both the social sciences and in psychiatry, especially by social scientific theories about the environment and psychiatry's discussions of ego psychology and of psychoanalytic procedures. As a result of changes in her thinking, she used this revision to insist that social workers needed to understand personality dynamics more adequately by being further informed by psychology and psychiatry, and that social workers should reemphasize the use of environmental or social therapy in their practices. She also strongly and repeatedly acknowledged how culture relates to social casework practices and how a full understanding of culture relies on social scientific discoveries. The revision is characteristic of all of Gordon Hamilton's writings and of her approach to social work as a profession: She evidences an openness to any thinking from any academic area or from any human experience that can support the profession's objectives.

In 1946 and 1947, Columbia University Press published two other influential works by Hamilton: *Principles of Social Case Recording* and *Psychotherapy in Child Guidance: A Study Based on the Practice of the Jewish Board of Guardians*. These were her last major writings before she resigned from the New York School of Social Work in 1957. In the first book, Hamilton emphasized how casework records result from more than technical adequacy; they must evidence the purpose of casework practice itself, namely, reform of the individual client. In the second book, she addressed the dispute over whether social workers should attempt direct treatment of people with emotional difficulties and personality problems or whether they should limit their treatment to resulting social problems. Hamilton gathered her data in a social agency where social workers did psychotherapy. She attempted to clarify the psychological roles of social workers by supporting these roles when the caseworker's competency is assured. While her book did not resolve the dispute, it was an explicit affirmation of an expanded social worker responsibility and an evidence of how adjacent academic fields could function together through the practice of social work.

Gordon Hamilton left teaching in 1957 largely because of continuing poor health, but she maintained her influence on the field by becoming the first editor-in-chief of *Social Work*, the professional journal of the National Association of Social Workers. Her editorials were controversial and innovative, and they elicited responses from academicians in many academic areas. Hamilton was too eclectic in her sources and thought to be easily labeled as a representative of a single school of thought. She was, however, decisively influenced in her early years as social worker and teacher by one person, Mary Richmond. Richmond's early book, *Social Diagnosis* (1917), was the major text about casework until Hamilton's *Theory and Practice of Social Casework* in 1940. Hamilton's teaching and writing expanded far beyond Richmond's, because she was able to borrow from and correlate her own findings with social and psychological thinking as it developed in the 1930's through the 1950's. She extended concepts about social casework and was far more interdisciplinary than her mentor, Mary Richmond, could have envisaged. When Hamilton died in 1967, she was recognized as a consummate teacher, author, and practitioner in the field of social work.

Summary

Gordon Hamilton has left a legacy of writing that has had a profound impact on social work education since her death. Nevertheless, her clarification of the purpose of social work, her emphasis on the scientific approach to casework, and her innovative alliances with other academic fields while practicing social work are not often explicitly attributed as advances introduced by Hamilton. She was honored by universities and social service organizations in several countries before she died, but her name did not register much recognition, even within the field of social work, after the 1960's. Her impact on the theory and practice of social work continues despite her lack of name recognition. Her contributions find their legacy in the students she taught, the readers for whom she wrote, and the service organizations for which she worked; through these efforts, many of her innovative ideas have become accepted in the field of social work.

In 1958, Hamilton was awarded the Florina Lasker Award for superior achievement as a practitioner, scholar, author, thinker, and leader in the profession of social work. Although there is little that has been written about her, she is one example of the many women who have made significant contributions to American academic life and whose ideas have had a practical effect in her profession.

Bibliography

Blanck, R. *Practice Theory Then and Now*. New York: Institute for the Study of Psychotherapy, Smith College Studies in Social Work, 1977. A review of antecedents of modern practice theory that explains both the intellectual heritage of social work and how social work ideas have been put in practice. Gordon Hamilton's *Theory and Practice of Social Casework* (1940) is one of the three major sources for this study, and its ideas are thoroughly considered as an example of social caseworkers' attempts to develop an authentic body of knowledge from which to practice.

Encyclopedia of Social Work. New York: National Association of Social Workers, 1977. The decennial edition of this encyclopedia contains a brief entry on Hamilton. Places her accomplishments within the context of her profession.

Hartman, Ann. "Gordon Hamilton." In *Notable American Women: The Modern Period*, edited by Barbara Sicherman et al. Cambridge, Mass.: The Belknap Press of Harvard University Press, 1980. One of the few biographical sketches of Hamilton, this profile provides useful insights into her intellectual development and her commitment to improving the field of social work.

Kempshall, Anna. "Gordon Hamilton: Some Intimate Glimpses." *New York School of Social Work Newsletter*, June, 1957, pp. 11-12. This article is one of the few published materials about Hamilton's life and career. It attempts to assess her experiences as a teacher and a woman in the environment of her time. Sympathetically portrays her as one of the New York School of Social Work's most complex yet charming faculty members, a role model who served as a mentor to hundreds of interested students.

Shoshani, Batya Shneider. *Gordon Hamilton: An Investigation of Core Ideas*. Ann Arbor, Mich.: UMI, 1985. This dissertation, written by Shoshani in fulfillment of her D.S.W. degree in 1984, constitutes the first full-scale biography of Hamilton. Particularly useful for its discussion of her social work theories and her relationships, both personal and professional, with other women in the field of social casework.

Walton, Ronald G. *Women in Social Work*. London: Routledge and Kegan Paul, 1975. A general history of women's contributions to the profession of social work. The author does not assess Hamilton's ideas directly, but does consider the ideas of Mary Richmond, her early mentor. The sections on Richmond give the reader a sense of those theories that were attractive to Hamilton and formed the foundation of her own later work.

William T. Osborne

LORRAINE HANSBERRY

Born: May 19, 1930; Chicago, Illinois
Died: January 12, 1965; New York, New York
Area of Achievement: Literature
Contributions: A writer and an activist, Lorraine Hansberry was the first African American woman to win the New York Drama Critics' Circle award.

Early Life

Lorraine Vivian Hansberry was born on May 19, 1930, into a middle-class family on the south side of Chicago, Illinois. The youngest of four siblings, she was seven years younger than Mamie, her older sister. The oldest were two boys, Carl, Jr., and Perry.

Lorraine's father, Carl Augustus Hansberry, the son of two teachers, was a former U.S. deputy marshal who worked as a banking accountant and later founded his own bank. His real success, however, came in the real estate business, where he earned the name "Kitchenette Landlord" for buying properties and converting them into kitchenettes. Lorraine's mother, Nannie Hansberry, the daughter of a bishop, who had attended Tennessee State University, became a teacher and later a ward committeeman of the Republican Party.

Hansberry was born in the Depression era, but lived in affluence as a result of her father's wealth. Nevertheless, her middle-class background did not insulate her from the racism and segregation of the time. Living in a ghetto community, she attended Betsy Ross Grammar School, a crowded public school. Fortunately, her enlightened father had a library of classic books, encyclopedias, and the works of black writers. In addition, Carl Hansberry was an avowed nationalist and a member of the National Association for the Advancement of Colored People (NAACP) and the Urban League. Prominent black figures such as W. E. B. Du Bois, Langston Hughes, Paul Robeson, Duke Ellington, and Jesse Owens were regular visitors to the Hansberry home. Lorraine met them all.

By age ten, Lorraine had read most of the books in her father's library and had developed a consciousness that was unusual for children of her age group. Her uncle, William Leo Hansberry, a professor of African history at Howard University and a renowned Africanist for whom a college was named at the University of Nigeria in Nsukka, had a lasting influence on her. From him, she learned of the greatness of Africa and its ancient civilizations, such as old Ghana, Mali, and Songhai. She also heard about colonialism in Africa and its impact on the people. She drew a parallel between the exploited Africans and the subjugated African Americans. These early influences were clearly reflected later in Hansberry's works.

Hansberry also witnessed history. At age eight, she watched her defiant father buy a house in a white neighborhood and challenge the restrictive covenants that promoted segregation by taking his case to court. When the lower court ordered him to vacate the residence, he appealed to the U.S. Supreme Court and won, in the *Hansberry v.*

Lee decision of 1940. His victory did not, however, grant him immunity from bigotry and hostility. As he was contesting his case in the court, a mob attacked his family, hurling stones and bricks at them. Carl Hansberry, who also campaigned for a Republican seat in Congress in 1940 but lost, became disillusioned by racism and with the American justice system. He bought a house in Polanco, Mexico, to settle there permanently with his family, but died shortly afterward, at the age of fifty-one.

The segregational experience left an indelible mark in young Hansberry's mind which was manifested in her future works, particularly in her award-winning play *A Raisin in the Sun* (pr. 1959). When Hansberry was graduated from Englewood High School in 1948, she attended the University of Wisconsin. It is not known why she chose a white college, considering her orientation and her family's choice of black schools. Her sister Mamie attended Howard University. It seems likely that Hansberry had a global vision and did not deem attending a white school a betrayal or an abdication of her black causes.

Hansberry spent three years at the University of Wisconsin. Her freshman courses included physical geography, drawing, and fine arts. Her concern about racism and the general plight of black people found expression in her drawings and sketches. A drawing of herself on the help wanted page of a newspaper followed by the drawing of a man being lynched served as an indication of a war that she would later wage in newspapers, public speeches, and literature.

When Hansberry saw a production of Sean O'Casey's *Juno and the Paycock*, she was captivated by the story and performance. She identified with the plight of Irish men as portrayed in the play. Going to the theater became one of her favorite activities.

While testing the artistic waters by drawing and going to the theater, she experimented with politics, becoming a supporter of Henry Wallace and campaigning for him. Although she attended a white school, Hansberry's interest in black experience continued; while taking her regular courses, she continued to immerse herself in black history, literature, and culture. Unsustained by the school's curriculum, she bid goodbye to her friends and left for New York in 1950.

Life's Work

Lorraine Hansberry continued her education at the New School for Social Research and settled on a career in journalism. After writing briefly for the Young Progressives of America, she went to work for *Freedom*, a monthly magazine published by Paul Robeson. With contributors such as W. E. B. Du Bois, Charles White, and Alice Childress writing on black and Pan-African issues, *Freedom* was a natural choice for Hansberry. Her interests in arts, African history, and politics found outlets in the magazine, and concern for women's rights was also articulated. Distinguishing herself as a versatile writer of "consciousness," she soon rose from the position of staff writer to become associate director of *Freedom*. In five years, she contributed more than twenty-two articles, and several reviews of books and plays.

Among her articles were "Child Labor Is Society's Crime Against Youth," "Negroes Cast in Same Old Roles in T.V. Shows," and "Gold Coast's Rulers Go: Ghana

Moves to Freedom." While writing, she participated in different protest movements, picketed, spoke on street corners, and demonstrated against segregation by helping evicted African Americans move their furniture back to their apartments. When the U.S. government denied Paul Robeson a passport to attend the intercontinental Peace Congress in Montevideo, Uruguay, Hansberry risked reprisal from the government and took a treacherous flight to Uruguay to represent Robeson. The experience broadened her interest in people of color and in world issues.

While still working for *Freedom*, Hansberry developed an interest in creative writing. She wrote stories, poetry, and plays. One of her sketches was performed during a commemoration of *Freedom*'s first anniversary.

While on an assignment in 1951, Hansberry met Robert Nemiroff, a white Jewish graduate student and a communist, at a picket line protesting the exclusion of African American students from the New York University basketball team. After less than two years of courtship, they married in 1953, to the chagrin of black nationalists, who felt betrayed by Hansberry's interracial marriage. Although he was a Jewish American, Nemiroff shared the same social consciousness as Hansberry, and both loved arts and creativity. Marriage to Nemiroff was in no way a contradiction to Hansberry, who had a broad concept of life and a vision for humanity.

After the marriage, the young couple struggled for a couple of years. Hansberry, who had resigned her position with *Freedom* in 1953 to concentrate on her writing, wrote drafts of three plays while working temporarily as a typist, hostess, store clerk, camp program director, and teacher. Their fortune changed when Nemiroff wrote a successful hit song, "Cindy, Oh Cindy," in 1956. Hansberry became a full-time writer. It was at that time that she completed *A Raisin in the Sun*, a play that was to bring her fame. It received its title from Langston Hughes's poem "Harlem," which posed the question, "What happens to a dream deferred? . . . Does it dry up like a raisin in the sun? . . . Or does it explode?"

Hansberry provided the answer. Set in a ghetto in Chicago, *A Raisin in the Sun* centers on a black widower, Lena, who at age sixty harbors her grown son, Walter Lee, Jr., his wife, Ruth Younger, their son, Travis, and her youngest daughter Beneatha in a cramped kitchenette. They live in abject poverty but have dreams and aspirations for a better life. When a long-awaited life insurance check of $10,000 for the death of Lena's husband, Walter, Sr., arrives, the family sees it as a means of escape. Walter wants to buy a liquor store; Beneatha wants to use her share for medical tuition; Lena wants a house and surprises everyone when she reveals that she has made a down payment on one in all-white Clybourne Park. Walter, Jr., does not approve, but when a representative of the white neighborhood tries to dissuade the family from moving into their new house by suggesting monetary compensation, Walter joins his mother and family in rejecting the offer. They move to the bigger home triumphantly, their dream fulfilled.

A Raisin in the Sun is not only about dreams; it is about culture, black identity, and black pride. It is also about feminine strength, as exemplified by Lena, a strong matriarch who keeps her family together, offering love and care without compromising discipline. Since the play affirms the human spirit, it has a universal appeal and offers hope to all struggling people.

One of the first people to read Hansberry's *A Raisin in the Sun*, Phil Rose, Nemiroff's friend and music associate, optioned it for Broadway production. Unfortunately, Broadway producers were not eager for a realistic and positive black play, but Ross was not discouraged. With the help of a coproducer, David S. Cogan, money was raised from different sources, and a production directed by Lloyd Richards toured New Haven and Philadelphia, receiving astounding reviews. The play moved to Chicago, and an agreement was reached to produce it on Broadway.

On March 11, 1959, *A Raisin in the Sun* opened at Broadway's Barrymore Theater and received rave reviews from such influential critics as Brooks Atkinson of *The New York Times* and Walter Kerr of the *New York Herald Tribune*. Superb casting and fine acting by the original cast, Sidney Poitier, Diana Sands, Ruby Dee, and Claudia McNeil, helped to make the play a success. In April, the play won the New York Drama Critics' Circle Award for Best Play of the Year, making Hansberry the first black playwright and the fifth woman to win the prestigious award. At age twenty-nine, she was also the youngest person to achieve that honor.

An instant celebrity, Hansberry was courted by producers from Hollywood. In 1960, she was commissioned to write the opening segment for a television series on the Civil War. When she finished her segment on slavery, *The Drinking Gourd*, it was considered controversial and was not produced. In 1959, Columbia Pictures bought the film rights to produce *A Raisin in the Sun* for the screen. After the film script underwent several rewrites, the film opened in 1961.

Hansberry worked on several scripts following the success of *A Raisin in the Sun*. She started research on *The Sign in Sidney Brustein's Window* in 1959 and completed the play in 1961. *The Sign in Sidney Brustein's Window*'s protagonist is a Jewish intellectual, and the play is based on the people Hansberry knew while living in Greenwich Village. Hansberry used the play as an appeal for intellectuals to pay attention to social and international issues. In 1962, Hansberry completed *What Use Are Flowers?*, a play on the Holocaust and its devastating effects, and embarked on another project, *Les Blancs*. She continued to write articles for newspapers and to make public appearances and talk about causes in which she believed. She talked about black oppression in America and about peace and justice. She wrote essays and articles on black history, art, and culture, and on racism, women, and homophobia. One of her major articles serves as her manifesto today. The article "The Negro Writer and His Roots," was delivered to a black writers' conference on March 1, 1959. Hansberry used it to call on black intellectuals to become involved in world affairs.

Another unpublished article, "Simone de Beauvoir and the Second Sex," expressed concern regarding the status of women and homophobia. As Hansberry worked feverishly in 1963 to complete multiple projects, she became ill. She was to die a slow and painful death from cancer of the pancreas. In the same year, she and Nemiroff obtained a divorce. The divorce was unknown to most of their friends, since the two maintained an intimate and professional relationship. The last two years of

Hansberry's life were to be spent in and out of the hospital. She continued to write, to make public appearances, and to revise *Les Blancs* and *What Use Are Flowers?* She also attended meetings and rehearsals for the production of her play *The Sign in Sidney Brustein's Window*.

When *The Sign in Sidney Brustein's Window* opened at the Longacre Theater on October 15, 1964, it was not as well received as *A Raisin in the Sun* had been. Critics who were baffled by Hansberry's choice of a Jewish subject and the intellectual complexity of the play responded unfavorably. In spite of mixed reviews and relatively low attendance, Hansberry's friends and contemporaries rallied around the producers, ensuring that the play was moved to Henry Miller's theater when Longacre was about to close its doors. Both the play and its playwright were struggling to survive.

On January 12, 1965, Hansberry drew her last breath. *The Sign in Sidney Brustein's Window* was closed for the night in Hansberry's honor as thousands mourned her death.

Summary

Lorraine Hansberry lived for not quite thirty-five years, but she accomplished a full lifetime's work. As Martin Luther King, Jr., predicted in his letter of eulogy to her, her life and work have remained "an inspiration to generations yet unborn."

Her former husband and literary executor edited, produced, and published most of her uncompleted scripts. Among them are *To Be Young, Gifted, and Black*, an autobiographical text, and *Les Blancs: The Collected Last Plays of Lorraine Hansberry*. The latter volume includes *Les Blancs*, *The Drinking Gourd*, and *What Use Are Flowers? To Be Young, Gifted, and Black* was adapted for the stage, and it became the longest-running drama of the time when it was produced Off-Broadway in 1968 and 1969. A film based on the play was released in 1972.

Other uncompleted scripts were "Mary Wollstonecraft"; an adaptation and a film version of *Masters of the Dew*, by the Haitian author Jacques Roulmain; a musical adaptation of the novel *Laughing Boy*, by Oliver La Farge; an adaptation of *The Marrow of Tradition*, by Charles Chestnut; *Achanron*, a play about an Egyptian pharaoh; and *Toussaint*, which was published in 1968 in an anthology of plays by black women edited by Margaret B. Wilkerson.

Nemiroff also polished and promoted Hansberry's existing works. *A Raisin in the Sun* was adapted as a musical and was produced on Broadway in 1972. In 1987, a television production of which Hansberry would have been proud was released by the Public Broadcasting System. The script included original segments that had been omitted in earlier productions. Committed to a better world, Hansberry represented different causes and advocated social and political changes in the United States and throughout the world. She also pressed for the rights of women, whom she described in an interview with Studs Terkel as "the most oppressed group of any oppressed group." She saw a link between racism, homophobia, and the oppression of women, and she envisioned a world in which men and women could unite in a fight for human rights. Hansberry should be remembered as a writer of remarkable talent and as a dedicated humanitarian.

Bibliography
Carter, Steven R. *Hansberry's Drama: Commitment Amid Complexity*. Urbana: University of Illinois Press, 1991. Carter begins his analysis of Hansberry's works with an overview of her commitment in life as expressed in her actions and her nonliterary as well as literary writings.
Cheney, Anne. *Lorraine Hansberry*. Boston: Twayne, 1984. This book is an intimate biography of Hansberry and an analysis of her plays. One chapter is devoted to black nationalists, such as W. E. B. Du Bois, who had a significant influence on the playwright.
Hansberry, Lorraine. *Les Blancs: The Collected Last Plays of Lorraine Hansberry*. Edited by Robert Nemiroff. New York: Random House, 1972. Published posthumously, this collection of Hansberry's plays *Les Blancs*, *The Drinking Gourd*, and *What Use Are Flowers?* contains a critical introduction by Robert Nemiroff and an introduction by Margaret B. Wilkerson.
_____ . *The Movement: Documentary of a Struggle for Equality*. New York: Simon & Schuster, 1965. This photo-essay examines the history of the Civil Rights movement.
_____ . *A Raisin in the Sun*. New York: Random House, 1959. This work, Hansberry's first play, describes an African American family whose dream of escaping poverty and living a better life is fulfilled when the female protagonist makes a down payment on a house in an all-white neighborhood.
_____ . *The Sign in Sidney Brustein's Window*. New York: Random House, 1965. Hansberry's second play, which deals with a Jewish intellectual and his circle of friends, examines the role of intellectuals in politics.
_____ . *To Be Young, Gifted, and Black: Lorraine Hansberry in Her Own Words*. Adapted by Robert Nemiroff. New York: New American Library, 1970. This book contains materials from Hansberry's speeches, essays, journals, memoirs, interviews, letters, and various unpublished works. Includes a foreword by Robert Nemiroff and an introduction by James Baldwin.
Whitlow, Roger. *Black American Literature*. Rev. ed. Chicago: Nelson-Hall, 1976. In the section devoted to Lorraine Hansberry, Whitlow gives a brief biographical account of Hansberry and analyzes *A Raisin in the Sun*.

Nkeonye Nwankwo

PAMELA DIGBY CHURCHILL HARRIMAN

Born: March 20, 1920; Farnborough, England

Area of Achievement: Government and politics
Contribution: A leading fund raiser for the Democratic Party in the 1980's, Harriman
became U.S. Ambassador to France in 1993.

Early Life

Born March 20, 1920, Pamela Digby was the oldest of four children of Edward
Kenelm, eleventh Baron Digby, and grew up on the family's 1,500-acre estate and
dairy farm, Minterne, in Dorset, England. Her father commanded a battalion of the
Coldstream Guards, served in the House of Lords, and was governor of Dorset.
Renowned for his gardening, he was president of the Royal Agricultural Society and
nicknamed "Carnation" Digby. Her mother, Constance Pamela Alice Bruce Digby of
the Barons Aberdare, was an active woman who encouraged her children to follow
suit. Pamela became an expert equestrian, winning many prizes. She attended Down-
ham, a prestigious boarding school, and was presented to King George VI at Buck-
ingham Palace in May, 1938. Among the three hundred other debutantes was John F.
Kennedy's sister Kathleen, with whose family Pamela began a lifelong friendship.

After her presentation, Pamela traveled abroad, studying in France and Germany.
Rumblings of World War II ended her stay on the Continent, and she returned to
England to work as a translator-secretary in the Foreign Office in London. On a blind
date she met journalist Randolph Churchill, the only son of Winston Churchill, and
they became engaged within weeks. After their marriage in 1939, Randolph went back
to war while Pamela moved into 10 Downing Street when her father-in-law became
prime minister in 1940. In October of 1940, Pamela's son Winston was born at
Chequers, the Churchill country estate.

Pamela wrote years later of the daily intensity of life with her father-in-law during
World War II. She was a constant companion, sharing his fears, desperation, and
courage throughout the critical attacks of the Luftwaffe in the Battle of Britain, and
his hospitality and wit when he entertained world leaders at Chequers. The prime
minister was fond of bezique, a six-pack card game, and she frequently played with
him. Intensely loyal to him, she lamented his loss of office in July, 1945.

Meanwhile Pamela's relationship with her husband deteriorated. He looked to her
to pay the gambling debts he incurred playing with fellow officers. Randolph Churchill's boss in civilian life, the publisher Lord Beaverbrook, wrote Pamela a check to
cover the debts and secretly provided shelter for his young godson Winston at his
country home. Having secured the services of a nanny to care for her baby at the
Beaverbrook estate, Pamela moved into the Dorchester Hotel in 1941 and started
working as a secretary at the ministry of supply. Pamela and Randolph Churchill's
marriage was essentially over after two years, and they were divorced in 1947 after a
three-year separation.

Pamela began to make a life of her own and to display an independence of spirit that would bring her friends, lovers, adventures, and notoriety. During 1941, Lord Beaverbrook concerned himself with eliciting further aid from the United States in hopes of securing its entry into the war. Beaverbrook enlisted Pamela's help in entertaining his American guests, and she soon met W. Averell Harriman, Franklin Roosevelt's special envoy to Britain. Her affair with Harriman during the war allegedly provided intelligence information to the British. After he left for Moscow to serve as U.S. Ambassador to Russia, she spent time with the war correspondent Edward R. Murrow. When peace returned to Europe, Pamela worked as a journalist for the Beaverbrook Press from 1946 to 1949, writing articles for Beaverbrooks' *Evening Standard* from New York, Jamaica, and the south of France.

Pamela's search for adventure and independence took her to Paris in 1949. After enrolling young Winston in a Swiss school, she immersed herself in the world of art, culture, and theater. Through her social connections, she could move in high political circles, and she excelled in bringing people from diverse backgrounds together. Intellectuals and celebrities such as Jean Cocteau, André Malraux, and Christian Dior attended salons held at her house on Sunday nights. During this period, she had a number of well-publicized romances, including a five-year affair with Fiat heir Gianni Agnelli that ended in 1952. Following this came a liaison with Elie de Rothschild, head of his family's vineyard at Chateau Lafite. She also was romantically linked to Prince Aly Khan, Frank Sinatra, and others.

Pamela began to spend more time in America. During a visit to New York in 1958, she was introduced by friends to Leland Hayward, producer of the musicals *State of the Union* (1945), *Mister Roberts* (1948), *South Pacific* (1949), *Call Me Madam* (1950), *Gypsy* (1959), and *The Sound of Music* (1959). He also produced the plays *Anne of the Thousand Days* (1948), and *The Trial of the Catonsville Nine* (1971). He divorced his wife and was married to Pamela in 1960. Through Hayward, Pamela was introduced to Hollywood and Broadway film and theater circles. Pamela faced the hostility of stepchildren from Hayward's two former marriages, and stepdaughter Brooke wrote a best-seller, *Haywire* (1977), in which Pamela was depicted as a wicked stepmother. Leland Hayward died on Pamela's birthday, March 20, 1971.

Life's Work

Pamela Churchill Hayward's network of friends, which she assiduously cultivated all her life, rallied to comfort her. In July of 1971, newspaper publisher Katharine Graham invited Pamela to a party in Washington, D.C., where she rekindled her friendship with W. Averell Harriman, who was then a widower. They were married in September of 1971; he was seventy-nine and she was fifty-one years old. She presented him with a unique wedding present—her citizenship papers.

Averell Harriman, heir to the Union Pacific Railroad fortune, had advised every Democratic president since Franklin Roosevelt. Harriman had served as governor of New York from 1954 to 1958, was once a presidential hopeful, and was appointed as U.S. ambassador-at-large under President John F. Kennedy. After their marriage,

Pamela and Averell spent most of their time at their Georgetown home in Washington, D.C. They helped Robert Strauss gain the chairmanship of the Democratic National Committee in 1972, and, in return, Strauss had Pamela take his seat on the board of Braniff Airlines. Her expertise at entertaining turned to organizing fund-raising parties for the Democrats. The Harrimans supported Jimmy Carter's SALT II and Panama Canal Treaties. Named Democratic Woman of the Year in 1980, Pamela worked with Averell to rescue the Democratic Party after the Republican sweep of the White House and Senate and inroads into the House in that year.

Pamela's knowledge of politics and her skill at bringing people together came to fruition, and as her husband grew frailer, she became more active. During the Reagan years of the 1980's, Averell and Pamela organized Democrats for the '80's, a political action committee that raised money for federal, state, and local Democratic candidates. Nicknamed PAMPAC, this committee raised $14 millon in ten years. Pamela and Averell also helped to stake out the Democratic agenda, hosting nearly a hundred "issue evenings" at their house. Policy analysts and members of Congress shared ideas while Pamela facilitated and adjudicated. Presidential hopefuls such as Jay Rockefeller (whom Pamela favored), Al Gore, and Bill Clinton were included as speakers.

Pamela also kept up her interest in foreign policy. Averell included her in his trips to the Soviet Union and China. After his death in July of 1986, Pamela continued to travel to the Soviet Union every two years, and maintained her memberships on the boards of the Friends of the Kennan Institute for Advanced Russian Studies and the Council on Foreign Relations.

Averell Harriman left Pamela the means ($75 million) to do whatever she wanted in life, and rumors circulated that she wanted an ambassadorship. She doggedly worked to assure a Democratic presidency to achieve this goal. In 1990, she disbanded PAMPAC and became chair of the Quarterly Policy Issues Forum of the Democratic Governors Association. She then served as national cochair of the Clinton-Gore Campaign. She lent her house in Middleburg, Virginia, to the Democratic National Committee for a crucial hashing out of positions in 1991. In May of 1993, President Bill Clinton recognized her efforts by appointing Pamela to serve as the U.S. Ambassador to France.

Summary

Pamela Digby Churchill Hayward Harriman grew up in an age when women attached themselves to men and lived through them. She was an attractive young woman with blue eyes and fiery red hair who was presented to society as a debutante and given a finishing school education in Europe. World War II interrupted any hopes of a higher education and served as the background to Pamela's failed marriage and several affairs. She came into her own after her marriage to Averell Harriman, a multimillionaire and ardent Democrat.

Pamela received a political education through her family—seven of them were in Parliament when she was growing up—and marriage to Winston Churchill's only son.

She capitalized on her family and social connections to make friends on the continent, where her independent spirit and search of adventure took her. She was good-looking, charming, intelligent, and a good listener. All the above traits, in addition to her courage, tough-mindedness, and breeding, made her bold enough to hold a salon in Paris.

These skills and talents were further developed when she helped Harriman revive and revamp the Democratic Party. The press called her the "Queen of the Democrats" or "Life of the Party." Her political sagacity proved correct when she recognized Bill Clinton as a comer and appointed him head of the board of PAMPAC after he lost reelection as governor of Arkansas in 1981. Speaker of the House Tom Foley credited her with the Democratic win in 1992.

Slowly she began to reach out on her own and become a force in her own right. She authored an article for *American Heritage* (1983), and gave the Samuel D. Berger Memorial Lecture at the Institute for the Study of Diplomacy at Georgetown University (1988). Harriman was an honorary member of the Executive Committee of the Brookings Institute, Vice Chairman of the Atlantic Council, a trustee of Rockefeller University, and a member of the Trustees Council of the National Art Gallery. Also, she served on the boards of the Winston Churchill Foundation of the United States, the Franklin and Eleanor Roosevelt Institute, and various philanthropic foundations.

Her career demonstrates the power of the American feminist movement, which has enabled women to carve out their own identity. Although Pamela was never a part of the movement, without it she could not have aspired to be an ambassador and head an embassy with an 1,100-member staff. She has a new appreciation of women's issues and is proud of her granddaughter Marina Churchill, a barrister in London.

As ambassador to France she can use her skills of entertaining and bringing diverse peoples together. She speaks French and knows French culture and personages. With her own van Gogh, Cezanne, and Sargent paintings as backdrop, Harriman has already convened French and American politicians to discuss their commonalities and differences.

Bibliography
Duffy, Martha. "And Now, an Embassy of Her Own." *Time* 142 (July 5, 1993): 52-54. Article on Harriman by a seasoned reporter that summarizes her past and present linkages with famous men as well as reviewing her new status as ambassador. Contains a photograph of her in front of her van Gogh painting *Roses* (1890).
Fairlee, Henry. "Shamela." *The New Republic* 199 (August 22, 1988): 21-23. Critical article profiling Averell and Pamela Harriman. The author has a cynical attitude toward Washington's preoccupation with and worship of money, glamour, and image-making. Fairlee doubts Harriman's intellectual abilities and repeats the gossip of her affairs and strained relations with stepchildren.
Gross, Michael. "Queen Mother of the Clinton Court." *New York* 26 (January 18, 1993): 24-34. A biographical sketch searching for explanations of her behavior in her forebears.

Harriman, Pamela C. "Churchill's Dream." *American Heritage* 34 (October/ November, 1983): 84-87. In this intimate portrait of her father-in-law, Pamela reveals his self-doubts after being voted out of office in 1945. She prefers to remember his confidence and courage during World War II.

Ogden, Christopher. *Life of the Party: The Biography of Pamela Digby Churchill Hayward Harriman*. Boston: Little, Brown, 1994. Based on research and interviews accumulated during Ogden's brief attempt at ghostwriting Harriman's official autobiography, this profile is full of telling details of Harriman's social ascent. Unfortunately, it provides little in the way of analysis to account for the complexity of her character or the decisions that shaped her life.

Walton, William. "Profiles: Governor and Mrs. W. Averell Harriman." *Architectural Digest* 41 (June, 1984): 106-113. Interviews the Harrimans about their lives and includes photographs of them, with influential people, and of their houses in New York, Virginia, Washington, D.C., and Barbados. (A fifth house in Sun Valley, Idaho, is barely mentioned.) Although something of a puff piece, the article does provide insight into how Pamela acquired her tastes in decorating and her passion for beautiful gardens.

Virginia W. Leonard

JULIE HARRIS

Born: December 2, 1925; Grosse Pointe, Michigan

Areas of Achievement: Theater and drama and film

Contribution: The outstanding actress of her generation, Harris has performed on stage as well as in films and television. She not only has won awards for her work in all three media but also has encouraged new playwrights to develop roles for women.

Early Life

Julia Ann Harris, who later adopted the first name Julie for the stage, was born on December 2, 1925, in Grosse Pointe, a well-to-do suburb of Detroit, Michigan. Her father, William Pickett Harris, was an investment broker whose hobby had been the study of mammals and who, before entering business, had made trips to Africa to pursue his interests; he brought back as souvenirs African artifacts, which aroused his daughter's interest enough to commission a play, many years later, about the continent. When he was an undergraduate at Yale University, he became attracted to the drama and took part in student productions there, an activity that his daughter claimed would also involve her in the theater. Her mother, Elaine Smith, had trained as a nurse in New York City and was also a theater enthusiast; whenever possible, she took her young daughter and her sons to the playhouse.

Later, Harris attended Grosse Pointe Day School. She did not enjoy her stay there, however, and she persuaded her mother to let her study with a drama coach, Charlotte Perry, who headed the Perry-Mansfield Theatre Workshop in Denver, Colorado. By then, Harris had become determined to make acting her career, a choice that did not please her parents, who understood the odds against success in that profession. Harris' work with Charlotte Perry was so outstanding, however, that her parents agreed to send her to the Yale Drama School in New Haven, Connecticut, in 1944. The school had been founded by a distinguished Shakespearean scholar, George Pierce Baker, who taught at Harvard and was lured to Yale by the promise of having a theater built there where he could teach playwriting. (Among those who passed through his classes was the young Eugene O'Neill.) When Baker first headed the Yale school—the first of its kind in the United States—in the 1920's, he added teachers of acting, directing, lighting, and scene and costume design, making his school so famous that English playwrights such as Henry Arthur Jones dedicated their plays to him in gratitude for his work. It was the perfect place for the young Harris to complete her training.

In spring of 1945, a director visiting the school saw Harris in a class production and was so impressed by her that he offered her a part on Broadway in New York City. Harris accepted and opened in the comedy *It's a Gift* at the Playhouse Theatre in March, 1945. It was a small role in a play that closed after a few performances, but the authors, Curt Goetz and Dorian Olvos, had made it possible for Harris' work to be seen professionally. She returned to Yale to finish out her year and then decided to brave New York again. While there, she studied at the Actors Studio, headed by Lee Strasberg, who also trained performers such as Paul Newman and Marlon Brando, both of whom became stars in American films. Harris took a walk-on part in Shakespeare's *Henry IV, Part 2* and in Sophocles' *Oedipus Rex* when English actor Laurence Olivier brought his company to New York in 1946; she also had a walk-on part in English actor Michael Redgrave's production of Shakespeare's *Macbeth* in 1948. She had her first opportunity to play a more important role in Richard Nash's *The Young and the Fair* at the Fulton Theatre toward the end of November, 1948. The play concerned a theft at a girl's school which the new head of the school is trying to trace. Harris distinguished herself in the part of Nancy, a neurotic teenager accused of the crime. It was probably her interpretation in this drama that led to her engagement in the play that first brought her national acclaim, Carson McCullers' *The Member of the Wedding*, which opened at the Empire Theatre in 1950.

Life's Work

Taking the role of Frankie, a twelve-year-old, though by now the actress was twenty-five, Julie Harris offered a touching portrait of an adolescent who feels that she does not belong. Her only friend is the cook-housekeeper, who was unforgettably played by Ethel Waters, one of America's finest African American singer-actresses. When Frankie's brother announces that he is going to be married and introduces his bride before they go away on their honeymoon, Frankie decides to go with them, because she wants to be a part of something. She discovers that she has no place in such a journey. Understanding at last what it means to grow up and accepting the fact that people are always alone, Frankie bravely comes to terms with a world that she does not understand. So moving was her performance that Harris received that year's Donaldson Award, given to the best supporting actress on Broadway. One year later, she was to repeat her role in the film version of the play, her movie debut.

In November of 1951, John van Druten, a British-born. American-based playwright, adapted novelist Christopher Isherwood's *Berlin Diaries*, the author's fictionalized memories of his youth in Germany in the 1920's. Called *I Am a Camera*, the play opened in the Empire Theatre and gave Harris the opportunity of her career: She took the role of Sally Bowles, the amoral, feckless, delightful heroine of the story. What amazed both the critics and the audience was the range that Harris displayed: The roles of Frankie and Sally could not have been more disparate. As a result of this performance, her name went up in lights over the play's title, indicating that Harris had now officially become a star. She also received her first Tony, Broadway's highest award, for the best performance in a starring role.

In 1955, Harris opened at the Longacre Theatre, starring in the title role of French playwright Jean Anouilh's *Mademoiselle Colombe*. She played the part of an actress whose love affairs stir her husband to jealousy. This play marked the second time Harris had been directed by Harold Clurman, with whom she had first worked in *The Member of the Wedding*. Clurman, an outstanding drama critic and director as well as one of the founders of the Group Theatre in the 1930's, was to lavish high praise on

Harris for her dedication and her versatility. Though Harris radiated considerable charm with her red hair, blue eyes, grace of movement, and presence, she was short and slight of stature and did not possess a strong voice. Knowing how important the voice was, she worked hard to improve her projection; in those days, actors did not have microphones to amplify their voices, and they would not even have dreamed of resorting to artificial means. It took time and effort for Harris to achieve the effect she wanted vocally, but she finally did.

Harris opened in another Anouilh play, *The Lark*, in 1955 at the Longacre, playing the role of Joan of Arc. She headed the cast that included Boris Karloff, long known to motion pictures fans for his horror films but this time playing with great effectiveness the part of a priest who tries to help Joan. All the critics remarked on Harris' newfound vocal power and praised her for growing with each part she played, again undertaking something totally different from what she had done before. For this role she received a second Tony.

In the same year, Harris returned to Hollywood to repeat the role of Sally Bowles for the camera. She then acted in the film *East of Eden*, directed by Elia Kazan, who had won eminence for his stage and screen work with America's foremost playwright, Tennessee Williams. Harris played opposite James Dean, a young film actor whose promising career was cut short when he died in a car crash. He has since become a cult figure to succeeding generations of actors and fans. Although Dean had a reputation for being difficult to work with, director Kazan and all those associated with the film attributed the relative calm on the set to Harris' tact and patience, acknowledging that only she seemed capable of keeping Dean in good humor. Over the years, that particular trait of hers has been as much admired as her talent.

Deciding that she would like to revive a classic play, Harris chose the role of Margery Pinchwife in a Restoration comedy by William Wycherley, *The Country Wife* (1675). Since American actors have never been particularly receptive to such stylized pieces, the production was not successful. Still, Harris seemed determined to enlarge her horizons, and she appeared in two Shakespeare plays in Stratford, Ontario, in 1960: She took the role of Juliet in *Romeo and Juliet* and that of Blanche in *King John*. Like a number of other performers, she believes that the American theater, though it produces fine playwrights, does not give actors enough opportunities to work in revivals of great plays, which is one reason that English actors are often more effective in such roles.

In her quest for something different, in 1963 Harris took on the lead in *Marathon, '33*, a play by American actress June Havoc that dealt with the Depression years when dancing couples earned money by engaging in public dance contests. It was not the best who won, but those who could dance longest without leaving the floor. The play provided a horrific view of American history, and when it opened at the ANTA theatre, critics who remembered the degrading practice praised both the play and the production. Again, it was an entirely new kind of role for Harris.

After appearing in several trifling and forgettable comedies, Harris next chose a musical, *Skyscraper*, with a book by Peter Stone and music and lyrics by Sammy Cahn and James van Heusen. It opened at the Lunt-Fontanne Theater in 1965, and much was made of Harris' attempt in this new form, which was respectable, but musicals clearly were not her forte. Far more effective was her next assignment, *Forty Carats*, an adaptation by Jay Allen of a comedy by French playwrights Pierre Brillet and Jean-Pierre Gredy, which opened at the Morosco in 1968. Playing the part of a fortyish woman who, to the horror of her family, marries a man half her age because he is besotted with her charm, Harris proved that she could convince audiences that she was a glamour queen; although ordinarily she might not have been cast in such a role, she was able to sustain the illusion as well as to prove how skillful she was at light comedy, a chance she was seldom given. The role remained one of her favorites because, as she said, it gave her one of her few opportunities to wear fashionable clothes. It also earned for her a third Tony.

In her late forties, Harris was finding it more difficult to appear in plays that suited her. She went back to Hollywood now and again to make films; one of her best opened in 1963, a Gothic tale based on Shirley Jackson's short story "The Haunting." It was at this point that Harris commissioned her first play, *The Last of Mrs. Lincoln*, by James Prideaux, which opened in 1972 at the Fulton. A sympathetic study of Abraham Lincoln's wife, it became the first of her historical roles and won for Harris her fourth Tony. She took the play on tour, believing, as actors of another generation had believed, that audiences outside New York were entitled to see successful Broadway plays with the original stars, an attitude that most younger actors did not share. Following the tour, she appeared on Broadway with Rex Harrison in a new play by English dramatist Terence Rattigan. *In Praise of Love* opened at the Morosco in 1974 and again cast her in one of her heavier roles—that of a dying woman whose marriage is failing. Whatever success it enjoyed it owed to the presence of the two stars.

From that point on, although Harris worked in films and on television (in the 1980's, she had a running part in an evening soap-opera, *Knot's Landing*, for seven years) she believed that the stage, which she preferred to other avenues of acting, could offer her few opportunities unless she created them herself. Her choice was either to take Broadway plays on tour, even if she had not starred in them in New York, because her popularity with outside audiences remained undimmed, or to go on encouraging new playwrights who might design a role for her. She chose the latter approach, and *The Belle of Amherst*, a one-woman show by William Luce, opened at the Longacre in 1976 and proved to be an enormous success. Based on the life of poet Emily Dickinson, it enjoyed a long run both in New York and on tour; for it, Harris won her fifth Tony—more than any actress had ever received. For her work in television, she has won two awards, called Emmys: The first in 1959, was for the role of a nun in a play about Ireland, *The Little Moon of Alban*, by James Costigan; the second, in 1962, was for the title role in *Queen Victoria*, by Laurence Housman. To date, Julie Harris has been the most honored actress in the United States.

Summary

Julie Harris has continued to follow the pattern she laid out for herself. As a result, a play she commissioned, *Under the Ilex*, by a new dramatist, Clyde Tamage, opened in 1983 in St. Louis, Missouri, and toured the country without coming to New York. It was a two-character study of the relationship between the well-known English literary figures Lytton Strachey and Dora Carrington. In 1988, Harris toured in a one-woman show, *Brontë*, by William Luce, based on the life of English novelist Charlotte Brontë; this time, Harris also toured the college and university theaters, knowing that the subject would be of interest to the students. In 1989, another commissioned play, *But Is He Dead?*, by Donald Freed, had its premiere at the Long Wharf Theatre in New Haven, Connecticut. This two-character play dealt with a period in the life of Irish writer James Joyce and his wife Nora; the idea for it was suggested by Harris herself. In 1991, William Luce, the writer who had provided Harris with several of her most recent pieces, offered her *Lucifer's Child*, a solo play dramatizing incidents from the life of Baroness Blixen, a Danish writer better known as Isak Dinesen. Harris brought this play to Broadway, but it was not successful although she was praised for her performance. Increasingly, critics lamented that she was always so much better than the material she was given. In 1993, she chose to appear Off-Broadway in a new play by Timothy Mason, *The Fiery Furnace*, playing the part of a grandmother trying to protect her family.

What has marked Harris as unique in her profession is her fierce determination not to desert the stage despite the shrinking opportunities, to continue to bring plays to the hinterlands as a means of assuring audiences that "live" actors still care about them, to encourage new writers not only because they may provide roles for her but also because the theater needs their scripts in order to survive, and to remind writers that better-paying jobs in film and television should not replace their work for the stage. To this end, Harris annually sponsors and funds a playwriting contest; theater professionals and critics serve as judges. More and more, she has come to favor playing historical roles of strong women who can control their lives. Art, she contends, whether it is a symphony, a painting, or a play, "tells us something about ourselves. It's a way of expressing our humanity."

Bibliography
Botto, Louis. *At This Theatre*. New York: Dodd, Mead, 1984. Contains a brief discussion of Harris' roles in the theaters in which she played. Pictures of her in *The Member of the Wedding*, *Mademoiselle Columbe*, and *The Lark* are included.
Clurman, Harold. *The Collected Works of Harold Clurman*. New York: Applause Books, 1994. Clurman, a drama critic and director, discusses Harris both as a person and as a performer. He characterizes her as "an actress of inspired invention."
Dowd, Maureen. "Julie Harris at Sixty-five: Gossamer and Grit." *The New York Times*, March 31, 1991, p. H1. This interview with Harris on the eve of her appearance in *Lucifer's Child* provides a useful overview of her career. Includes details about her early life and her marriages as well as her philosophy about acting in the theater.
Kazan, Elia. *A Life*. New York: Alfred A. Knopf, 1988. In his discussion of Harris,

Kazan concentrates on his work with her in the film *East of Eden*. She was, he wrote, "an angel on the set," calming everyone with her humor, tenderness, and sensitivity. The book includes a picture of Harris with her costar James Dean.

Kerr, Walter. *Journey to the Center of the Theatre*. New York: Alfred A. Knopf, 1979. In an appraisal of his reviews as drama critic for *The New York Times*, Kerr bestows particular praise on Harris for her performance as Emily Dickinson, admiring the craft that she so "painfully, stubbornly, at last stunningly acquired. She is magic."

Oppenheimer, George, ed. *The Passionate Playgoer*. New York: Viking, 1958. A collection of reviews by various writers. Marya Mannes discusses Harris' performance in *The Lark*, noting that "no Joan was ever more lonely and vulnerable" and commending her "earthy, peasant shrewdness and gamine vitality."

Mildred C. Kuner

HELEN HAYES

Born: October 10, 1900; Washington, D.C.
Died: March 17, 1993; Nyack, New York
Area of Achievement: Theater and drama
Contribution: In more than sixty years on stage and screen, Hayes became the "first lady of the American theater."

Early Life

Born Helen Hayes Brown on October 10, 1900, in Washington, D.C., Helen was the granddaughter of Patrick and Ann Hayes, who emigrated from Ireland to the United States during the potato famine. Her great aunt, Catherine Hayes, was a famous Irish singer (the "Swan of Erin") who entertained large crowds in London as well as "forty-niners" in America. Helen's mother, Catherine "Essie" Hayes, an aspiring but unsuccessful actress, directed her early career. Helen's father, Francis Arnum Brown, was a wholesale meat salesman.

Like many "stage mothers," Catherine Hayes brought her child into the world of drama. Essie took Helen to her first theater experience: Franz Lehar's *The Merry Widow*. Nicknamed "the white mouse" by her family, Helen immediately acquired a strong affection for the theater. Shortly thereafter, she gave her first performance, as Peaseblossom, in *A Midsummer Night's Dream.*

Helen's early education enhanced her theatrical ambition. First at Holy Cross Academy, then later at Sacred Heart Convent, Helen came under the influence of Roman Catholic nuns who encouraged her interests in acting and music. She also attended Minnie Hawke's School of Dance, which sponsored several musicals in which the young girl could sing and dance. Since Helen's singing was better than her dancing, she concentrated on the latter, resulting in her first professional performance in *The Prince Chap.*

At the age of eight, Helen accompanied her mother to a New York audition for Broadway's Lew Fields. Fields, impressed with Helen's singing, signed her for a leading role in Victor Herbert's 1909 presentation *Old Dutch.* This began a series of stage performances in Fields's presentations.

Despite Helen's youthful successes, her childhood was not without its heartaches. Her mother began to drink excessively, and Helen, like many children of alcoholics, believed that somehow it was her fault. Caring for a drunken mother was not easy for the young girl and her father. Eventually, it became too much for Francis Brown. Although the Browns never divorced, they separated for life.

Helen's stage career also produced its share of difficulties. In 1918, following her exceptional performance in *Dear Brutus*, she received her first starring role on Broadway as a flapper in *Bab* (1920). The latter was a growing experience. By her own admission, she suffered from poor posture and an inability to relax on stage. Her shrill voice bothered critics, including one who dismissed her performance as an unsuccessful effort to get by on her cuteness.

Although these criticisms bruised Helen's youthful ego, she resolved to develop sufficient discipline to correct all of her major weaknesses, and she did. Improving her posture and relaxing the tenseness (by curling her toes), Helen entered the world of light comedy, in which she quickly excelled. In 1926, her performance in *What Every Woman Knows* not only restored Helen to the critics' good graces but also made the play one of her signature presentations, and she repeated it in 1938 and 1954.

Helen's subtlety and power in *What Every Woman Knows* so impressed producer Jed Harris that he cast her for the leading role in *Coquette* (1927), in which she played an aristocratic Southern belle who commits suicide after becoming pregnant by a poverty-stricken young man. Although veteran Broadway observers doubted the wisdom of casting a light comedienne in such a dramatic role, the critics raved and the audience gave her sixteen curtain calls.

Coquette established Hayes's Broadway career. The distinguished British writer Noël Coward, who was not known for giving out compliments, summarized Helen's performance as "astonishingly perfect. . . . She ripped our emotions to shreds." At the age of twenty-seven, Hayes was now a full-blown star.

Hayes's personal life also reached fruition during these formative stages. In 1925, while preparing for *Caesar and Cleopatra*, she met a Chicago newspaper reporter and aspiring playwright named Charles MacArthur. It was love at first sight. Over the protests registered by Helen's mother and both of MacArthur's parents, and despite the fact that he was married (although separated) at the time, the mutual attraction was overwhelming. Their marriage followed shortly after his successful collaboration with Ben Hecht in *The Front Page* (1928). With professional and personal foundations established, Hayes embarked on one of the most remarkable careers in American theater.

Life's Work

Following her wedding and the birth of her daughter Mary in February, 1930, Helen Hayes entered the most productive phase of her career. Although *Mr. Gilhooley* (1930) produced little praise, and *Petticoat Influence* (1930) and *The Good Fairy* (1931) fared only slightly better, Hayes entered Hollywood's cinematic world with a flourish, attaining instantaneous national stardom in *The Sin of Madelon Claudet* (1931), which won for her an Academy Award for Best Actress.

Madelon Claudet's amazing success was made even more remarkable by the fact it was not only her first Hollywood film but also her first talking picture. Editing problems (preview audiences booed during private screenings) nearly prevented the film's release. Producer Irving Thalberg saw brilliant potential and saved the film by making only slight alterations. Helen's performance as Madelon, a French mother forced into prostitution through her efforts to save her illegitimate son, left audiences weeping all over America.

Since winning an Oscar established Hayes's cinematic reputation, her film career immediately scaled new heights. First, she played opposite Ronald Coleman in Sinclair Lewis' *Arrowsmith* (1931); next came a costarring appearance with an emerging young actor named Gary Cooper in another American classic, Ernest Hemingway's *A Farewell to Arms* (1932). Her next film, which paired Hayes with the "King of Hollywood," Clark Gable, was *The White Sister* (1933). Still not finished, Hollywood exploited Hayes by featuring her in four more films in less than two years.

When Hayes returned to New York in 1933 to play *Mary of Scotland*, her reputation as a film celebrity preceded her. Helen's box-office appeal was so great that she played to packed houses for several months. Although the actress stood only five feet tall, she somehow managed to capture the six-foot queen's essential spirit and presence.

The techniques that Helen employed in *Mary of Scotland* served as a successful basis for her tour de force performance of *Victoria Regina* in 1935. It was this portrayal of the great English monarch that won for her the medal awarded by the Drama League of New York for the best stage achievement by an actress that year. *Victoria Regina* probably was Hayes's most famous role in her long career.

Audiences and critics alike applauded her contribution to American culture. The play enjoyed a run of 969 performances in front of America's toughest crowds. The acting challenge was formidable, requiring Hayes to age more than fifty years throughout the evening—complete with sagging face and swelling cheeks. Reflecting first youth, then maturity, and finally old age required talent rarely seen even on the New York stage. So successful was her depiction of the aging queen that some members of the audience did not even recognize her.

The play went on the road throughout the United States. For millions of Americans, Hayes was Queen Victoria. In Washington, D.C., Eleanor Roosevelt saw the play three times and "could not stop clapping." Invited to the White House by the first lady, Hayes met President Franklin D. Roosevelt, who inquired, "And how is your majesty?" *Victoria Regina* left an indelible imprint upon the history of acting in America.

Hayes never again matched the heights she achieved in *Victoria Regina*, although memorable stage and screen performances followed during her long career. In 1938, Hayes and MacArthur adopted a seven-month-old son, James MacArthur, who later spent twelve years playing detective Danny "Danno" Williams on the television show *Hawaii Five-O*. In the late 1930's, Hayes and her husband strongly supported America's entry into World War II, which was already raging in Europe. After the Japanese attack on Pearl Harbor on December 7, 1941, Charles MacArthur volunteered his services to the military, while Helen sold war bonds.

Hayes's stage and screen career flattened out during the war years until she succeeded in 1943 with *Harriet*, a historical play based on Harriet Beecher Stowe's classic *Uncle Tom's Cabin* (1852). Hayes's great concern with civil rights for African Americans undoubtedly accounted for the emotional commitment that she made to this work. Critics also praised her work in *Happy Birthday* (1946).

Tragedy struck Hayes in 1949, when polio claimed the life of her nineteen-year-old daughter Mary MacArthur, a budding actress who had just appeared with her mother in *Good Housekeeping*. Hayes later wrote that "nothing is more difficult to accept than the death of a child."

More adversity followed Mary's death. First, Hayes's alcoholic mother, Catherine

Hayes Brown, died shortly after her granddaughter's death. Then, Charles MacArthur, also an alcoholic, began drinking incessantly because he was unable to cope with the loss of his daughter. According to Hayes, her husband "set about killing himself. It took seven years, and it was harrowing to watch." MacArthur died in 1956.

Coping with the loss of three of the people she loved most dearly became Hayes's greatest challenge. After first believing that she had caused her husband's death, Hayes came to understand that only MacArthur could have sought help for himself. When she accepted that fact, she was able to go on with her future. With grim determination, Hayes turned to her son and her profession for solace. She also returned to the Roman Catholic church, which had excommunicated her following her marriage to the divorced MacArthur. Together, her faith, her son, and her profession sustained her throughout her remaining years.

Although Hayes had not undertaken a significant film since *Vanessa, Her Love Story* in 1935, friends urged her to make *Anastasia* (1956) with Ingrid Bergman and Yul Brynner. The result might have pleased other actresses, but for Hayes it represented only an average performance.

Hayes also returned to Broadway with renewed vigor. Four plays in four years followed: *The Skin of Our Teeth* (1955), *The Glass Menagerie* (1956), *Time Remembered* (1957), and *A Touch of the Poet* (1958). Hayes also took to television in her later years. Television viewers enjoyed her performances in *The Snoop Sisters* (1972), *Victory at Entebbe* (1976), *Murder Is Easy* (1982), *A Caribbean Mystery* (1983), and *Murder with Mirrors* (1985).

Hayes appeared in several films near the end of her career, and in 1971 Hollywood gave her a second Academy Award (Best Supporting Actress) for her role in *Airport* (1970). She retired from the stage following her performance in Eugene O'Neill's *Long Day's Journey into Night* (1972). Helen Hayes died of heart failure at the age of ninety-two on March 17, 1993.

Summary

Helen Hayes was one of the great stars within the American theatrical firmament. Although her talents came to her naturally, it was her great determination, durability, and many years of toiling under the lights that made her one of America's consummate troupers. Work, "plain hard steady work," was the most satisfying thing in her life.

No task was too great or small for this diminutive woman who threw herself into all areas of theatrical performance. On Broadway and in Hollywood, on radio and television, her willingness to work hard without complaining complemented the great natural talent she displayed in rising to the top of her profession.

Hayes suffered through her share of disappointments, but when tragedy seemed to block her way, she never gave up hope or faith. Life's setbacks never deterred her from her ultimate goals. Reared by unhappy parents, rejected by the church of her childhood, married to an increasingly alcoholic husband whom she loved, staggered by the tragic death of her only biological child, Hayes more than persevered in the face of sometimes overwhelming adversity—she triumphed.

Her achievements were many, both in and out of the acting profession. Two Academy Awards and the New York Drama League Medal symbolized the contributions of this actress who was honored as the "first lady of the American theater." In August, 1988, President Ronald Reagan presented her with the National Medal of Arts award for artistic excellence. There was more: Hayes was president of the American Theater Wing and the American National Theater and Academy, chairwoman of the March of Dimes, and the winner of the Catholic Interracial Council of New York's award for her civil rights activities.

Although Hayes was more than America's leading theatrical actress, acting remained her greatest achievement. *The New York Times* called her one of the three great women of the American theater. When she died, the lights of Broadway dimmed in honor of the little lady who bestrode the theatrical world like a colossus.

Bibliography

Eames, John Douglas. *The MGM Story*. Rev. ed. New York: Crown, 1979. Since Helen Hayes did a number of films for Metro-Goldwyn-Mayer, this collection of articles and photographs makes a solid contribution toward an understanding of her film career.

Hayes, Helen. *On Reflection*. New York: M. Evans, 1968. Hayes's autobiographical contributions are always valuable primary sources, and this is no exception. Hayes is refreshingly self-analytical and self-critical. Her honest analyses, however anecdotal and impressionistic, usually are very helpful in assessing the strengths and weaknesses of her career and life.

Hayes, Helen, with Lewis Funke. *A Gift of Joy*. New York: M. Evans, 1965. Written nine years after her husband's death, this deeply penetrating memoir is an excellent philosophical, psychological, and spiritual exposition of Hayes's professional and personal life. Includes Hayes's favorite poetry and some speeches and quotations that inspired her.

Hayes, Helen, with Katherine Hatch. *My Life in Three Acts*. San Diego: Harcourt Brace Jovanovich, 1990. Hayes's final work is more revealing than previous efforts, particularly in areas deemed controversial or painful. This autobiography is especially helpful in understanding the pitfalls of being the child of an alcoholic and being married to an alcoholic.

Houghton, Norris. *Advance from Broadway*. New York: Harcourt Brace, 1941. Houghton traveled 19,000 miles to observe America's theatrical patterns. In the process, he discovered the incredible impact that Hayes exerted on the general public in the "sticks."

Robbins, Jhan. *Front Page Marriage*. New York: G. P. Putnam's Sons, 1982. A fine study of the relationship between Hayes and her husband, Charles MacArthur.

J. Christopher Schnell

LE LY HAYSLIP

Born: December 19, 1949; Ky La, Vietnam

Areas of Achievement: Literature and social reform

Contribution: Advocating forgiveness and healing on both sides in the wake of the Vietnam War, Le Ly Hayslip created the East Meets West Foundation to build clinics, schools, and rehabilitation centers in Vietnam with the assistance of American veterans and other donors.

Early Life

Phung Thi Le Ly was born the sixth child of Vietnamese peasants in the village of Ky La (later Xa Hoa Qui) near Danang, where she lived until the age of fifteen. A premature baby who survived against great odds, she was called *con troi nuoi* (she who is nourished by God) by the villagers. From her father, Phung Trong, she learned to revere her family, her ancestors, and Vietnamese tradition. Her mother, Tran Thi Huyen, taught her humility and the strength of virtue. Le Ly attended a village school through the equivalent of the third grade, her formal schooling cut short by the Vietnam War. From the age of twelve, she supported and worked for the Viet Cong against the American and South Vietnamese (ARVN) armies. Her two brothers also served Ho Chi Minh: Bon Nghe as the leader of a North Vietnamese Army reconnaissance team and Sau Ban as a soldier killed in the South by an American mine.

In her autobiography, *When Heaven and Earth Changed Places*, Le Ly describes how the people of her village were forced to labor for government soldiers by day and assist the Viet Cong by night. Such a schizophrenic existence led to Le Ly's imprisonment and torture by the ARVN as well as a traumatic death sentence and rape at the hands of the Viet Cong.

Forced to flee her village, Le Ly first took a job as housekeeper for a family in Danang and then went with her mother to Saigon, where her sister Lan was living. There, Le Ly and her mother found positions as servants to Anh, a wealthy textile factory owner. Giving in to Anh's affection, sixteen-year-old Le Ly became pregnant with her first child, James (Hung), born in 1967. Anh paid for their return trip to Danang, where Le Ly, with her baby and mother, lived with Lan, who worked as a bar girl.

Le Ly's father, Phung Trong, remained in the village to keep watch over ancestral land and shrines, but he became more and more depressed over the war's effects on the village and his family, particularly his daughters. Lan by then was earning money as a prostitute, while Le Ly hawked cigarettes and drugs on the black market. When Le Ly's father committed suicide, the family risked their lives to give him a traditional funeral. In a moment of shame, Le Ly accepted $400 to have sex with a soldier, but did so knowing that the money would support her family for a year. She worked as a nurse's aide at the Nha Thuong Vietnamese Hospital in Danang and later as a cocktail waitress at a Korean-owned nightclub.

Life's Work

Le Ly Hayslip sprang to national prominence with the publication of her first book, *When Heaven and Earth Changed Places* (1989), in which she chronicled her life as a peasant girl during the Vietnam War in and around her village of Ky La near Danang. One of the first publications to give expression to Vietnam experiences in the ten-year-old war, her book stunned Americans of all political persuasions with the truth that many villagers were tortured and oppressed by both sides in the war. A second book, *Child of War, Woman of Peace*, appeared in 1993, chronicling her arrival in the United States as the wife of an American much older than herself, a second marriage, and fulfillment of her long-held dream to create the East Meets West Foundation to fund projects that would assist both her own people and the American veterans who were still suffering from their war experiences.

Le Ly Hayslip's life in the United States began when she married Ed Munro, a sixty-year-old construction worker who sought a young Asian-born wife who would care for him in his old age. Attracted by his promise of education for Jimmy and the opportunity to escape from Vietnam, Le Ly consented. Her second son, Tommy, was born before they left.

Arriving in the United States in 1970, Le Ly adjusted with difficulty to life in San Diego, California, with her in-laws. When Ed's job prospects failed, they returned to Vietnam and Ed took a construction job at An Khe. There, Le Ly fell in love with an American officer, Dan, who was instrumental in helping her and her children to flee An Khe during a major battle in 1972. Shortly afterward, Ed and his family returned to the United States, where he died of pneumonia.

After the death of her first husband, Le Ly hoped to find happiness with Dan. Because Dan was reluctant to divorce his wife, however, Le Ly married Dennis, who made a heroic trip to Vietnam to rescue her sister Lan and her children as South Vietnam was falling to the Communists in 1975. Unfortunately, Dennis manifested an unstable personality, which found an outlet in fundamentalist Christianity and compulsive gun collecting. During this time, Le Ly began to turn more frequently to Buddhism in search of spiritual comfort and enlightenment. Angered by her resistance to Christianity, Dennis kidnapped their son Alan, Le Ly's third child, and threatened her life. Following a court order which banned him from his wife's household, Dennis died accidentally while burning charcoal in a closed van. After his death, Le Ly sought to pacify his angered spirit through Buddhist rituals and find peace of her own. Her thoughts turned to the possibility of returning to her family in Vietnam.

Terrified of the Communists and fearful of right-wing Vietnamese in the United States, yet resisting efforts of the CIA to co-opt her as a spy, Le Ly Hayslip traveled to Vietnam in 1986 to visit her family. She found a desperately poor country where people were still starving and the war was still going on in the hearts and minds of everyone there. Although her brother Bon would not eat the American food she had brought, her mother and sister welcomed her lovingly. Nevertheless, it was Anh, the father of her first son, who encouraged Le Ly not to settle down again in Vietnam, as she contemplated, but to "help people overcome the pain of war—to learn trust where they feel suspicion; to honor the past while letting go of it; to learn all these things so that they, in turn, may teach."

After returning to the United States, Le Ly went to Hawaii to marry Dan, who was by that time divorced from his wife. Once she arrived, she discovered that he intended to become an arms merchant and had little in the way of personal assets. The marriage never took place, since Le Ly refused to be allied with anyone who marketed weapons and was so obviously interested in her money. Through taking community college courses, workshops, and attending spiritual retreats, Le Ly had educated herself and gained considerable business acumen. Her financial knowledge had accrued from her experiences in various settings: an assembly-line position at National Semiconductor, an aborted attempt at starting her own delicatessen, a partnership in an Oriental restaurant, real estate transactions, and experimentation with the stock market. Yet it was in meeting and talking with American veterans who flocked to the restaurant that Le Ly realized how desperately in need of healing they were.

Determined to use her assets to build a clinic in Quang Nam province, Le Ly acquired licences from the U.S. State Department, assembled medical equipment and supplies, and established the East Meets West Foundation in 1987. She was assisted in her efforts by Cliff Parry, a wealthy individual later convicted as a professional swindler. Having been disillusioned once again, Le Ly resolved no longer to center her life on a man, and instead set about making humanity the love of her life. She worked with writer Jay Wurtz to publish *When Heaven and Earth Changed Places* and also traveled to the Soviet Union with Youth Ambassadors of America to learn about communism and the Cold War. Returning to Vietnam, Le Ly talked with Hanoi officials about her project, burned incense at her father's shrine in Ky La, and visited various assistance projects supported by Vietnam Veterans of America.

On her return to the United States, she enlisted the aid of Veterans-Vietnam Restoration Project, endured the wrath of some individuals in the Vietnamese American community, and earnestly began to raise money for the clinic. On a third trip, she won permission to build a clinic at Ky La. A public announcement by Vietnamese officials eased relations between Le Ly's mother and villagers suspicious that she was hiding money from her "American" daughter. On a fourth trip, accompanied by an American news crew, Le Ly took her sons with her, allowing Jimmy to meet his father Anh, for the first time. With the financial help of film director Oliver Stone, who became interested in Le Ly's story and her project, the Mother's Love Clinic was opened near Ky La in 1989. In her speech to the assembled crowd, Le Ly stated that "America made me a citizen and has let me come back with these presents which she gives you freely and without reservations. What she wants more than anything, I think, is to forgive you and be forgiven by you in return."

A second project of the East Meets West Foundation was the creation of a twenty-acre rehabilitation center for the homeless and handicapped at China Beach, the site where 3,500 Marines landed in Vietnam to begin the American buildup in 1965. A full-service medical center and a school are among the center's efforts to break the circle of vengeance that has kept the countries of Vietnam and the United States, as well as individuals, locked in paralyzing hatred. Her vision is one of reconciliation and spiritual connection. In adapting Le Ly Hayslip's first two books for the screen, Oliver Stone's film *Heaven and Earth* (1993) tells her story as the third film in his Vietnam trilogy (the first two films were *Platoon* [1986] and *Born on the Fourth of July* [1989]). Sadly, this film fails to convey the transformative vision by which she has healed her own painful war memories and enabled thousands more to regain spiritual energy through love, mutual understanding, and cooperation.

After settling in San Francisco, Le Ly Hayslip continued to serve as executive director of the East Meets West Foundation, a charitable relief and world peace organization that funds health care and social service projects in Vietnam. She has devoted much of her time to raising money for the foundation through lecture tours, book signings, and newsletters that keep donors apprised of projects completed and needs still to be met. Working together to coordinate the foundation's efforts with those of other grass-roots organizations offering material assistance to Vietnam, Hayslip has also encouranged veterans to help with various privately funded assistance projects in that country. Involved in frequent trips to Vietnam to oversee East Meets West Foundation projects, Hayslip has begun research on a third book dealing with the theme of healing from the war.

Summary

Out of the chaos, hardship, and upheaval of her early life, Le Ly Hayslip developed courage and self-reliance that allowed her to launch her efforts to heal the physical and emotional wounds left by the Vietnam War at a time when such efforts were viewed with great suspicion. Drawing upon her own reserves as a survivor, Hayslip has written two autobiographical memoirs to document the war experience from a Vietnamese perspective. Although her memoirs had a mixed reception among the highly political and polarized Vietnamese community in the United States, Hayslip struck a sympathetic chord among many American veterans of the Vietnam War. In forming the East Meets West Foundation, Hayslip managed to build a bridge between her native country and her adopted country—one that would allow individuals in Vietnam and the United States to understand one another more completely and to effect a more lasting reconciliation than could be provided by diplomatic agreements.

Bibliography
Abramowitz, Rachel. "The Road to 'Heaven.'" *Premiere* 7 (January, 1994): 46-50. A feature story on the making of Oliver Stone's film *Heaven and Earth*, this article includes a personal profile of Le Ly Hayslip and the contributions she made in helping to create an authentic portrait of her life during the Vietnam War.
Hayslip, Le Ly. "A Vietnam Memoir." *People Weekly* 32 (December 18, 1989): 147-150. In this autobiographical profile, which appeared shortly after the publication of *When Heaven and Earth Changed Places*, Hayslip discusses her life and the impact that the Vietnam War continued to have upon her long after the conclusion of the fighting.

Hayslip, Le Ly, and James Hayslip. *Child of Peace, Woman of War*. New York: Doubleday, 1993. This second autiographical volume chronicles Hayslip's difficult life in the United States as the foreign-born wife of an American citizen and provides a detailed account of her efforts to return to Vietnam and establish various rehabilitation projects there.

Hayslip, Le Ly, and Jay Wurtz. *When Heaven and Earth Changed Places*. New York: Doubleday, 1989. One of the few accurate descriptions of life in rural Vietnamese villages during the Vietnam War, this autobiography also interweaves the narrative of Hayslip's astonishing return to her native country in 1986.

Klapwald, Thea. "Two Survivors Turn Hell into 'Heaven and Earth.'" *The New York Times* 143 (December 19, 1993): H22. A dual portrait of Oliver Stone and Le Ly Hayslip and their collaborative efforts on the film *Heaven and Earth*. Includes a discussion of their individual efforts to heal the wounds that remain in the wake of the Vietnam War.

Mydans, Seth. "Vietnam: A Different Kind of Veteran and Her Healing Mission." *The New York Times* 139 (November 28, 1989): A10. A biographical profile of Hayslip written shortly after the publication of her first book. Gives details about her work on behalf of refugees in the United States and in her native country.

Janet M. Powers

RITA HAYWORTH

Born: October 17, 1918; Brooklyn, New York
Died: May 14, 1987; New York, New York
Area of Achievement: Film
Contribution: A dazzling film star, Hayworth was renowned worldwide as one of the
favorite pinup queens of American servicemen during World War II.

Early Life

Rita Hayworth was born Margarita Carmen Cansino in Brooklyn, New York, on October 17, 1918, the first child of Eduardo Cansino, a Spanish-born vaudeville dancer, and Volga Haworth, a showgirl. Although Haworth was herself a dancer with a promising career, her husband preferred to keep together his own successful act, the Dancing Cansinos. In it he and his sister Elisa starred. Volga Cansino gave up all thought of resuming her career when her daughter Margarita was born, to be followed soon by two sons.

Margarita was eight when the family rented a home in New York City and she was finally able to attend school and play with other children. Until then, she had traveled constantly from one theatrical hotel to another while the family was on the road with the Dancing Cansinos. Vaudeville was nearing its end, however, and Cansino moved his family to California in 1927 so that he could try to break into films at the start of the sound era. He never achieved success in films, and in 1931 Cansino revived the Dancing Cansinos. His daughter Margarita, who had been dancing since she was four, became his partner.

Her education again became secondary to the needs of the Dancing Cansinos. Since California law forbade minors from performing in clubs where alcohol was served, the act was booked in offshore gambling ships and in clubs in Tijuana, Mexico, near San Diego. Margarita was exploited in every possible way: She was removed from school and denied any chance of having a normal education and friends her age, was made to perform in nightclubs while she was several years underage, was required to learn how to be sexually alluring onstage, and (according to biographer Barbara Leaming) was forced to have sexual relations with her father.

Two Margarita Cansinos had begun to emerge: a shy, insecure girl who was denied the chance to be a normal teenager, and a sensuous young dancer. After she had been dancing professionally for about two years, Eduardo Cansino decided that his daughter should have a career in films. She failed her first screen test at the age of fifteen, but in 1934 Fox pictures signed her to a contract. She now served two masters, her father and the studio, which required her to slim down through exercise and dieting, to take dancing, acting, and riding lessons, and to change her name to Rita.

Rita Cansino soon began to find out that a young actress received many offers from older men claiming they could do something for her career. She did begin to pay attention to Edward Judson, a thirty-nine-year-old wheeler-dealer who approached her through her father. As usual, Eduardo Cansino was trying to control his daughter's career and hoped to use Judson's interest in her to his advantage. She, in turn, was willing to use Judson to revive her career (her contract had been dropped when Fox was taken over by Twentieth Century) and to liberate herself from Eduardo Cansino's domination. Judson did succeed in getting Rita small roles as a freelance performer in several minor detective and Western films. Early in 1937, Columbia Pictures put her under contract, and Rita, her career once again on track, married Judson.

Life's Work

Judson, who was living mainly on his wife's income, began to pay even more attention to creating a star. Rita Cansino had to walk as he wanted, take voice and diction lessons, and undergo over a two-year period the painful treatment of electrolysis to alter her eyebrows and her hairline. She also took riding and tennis lessons so that she would be able to behave properly when she met the right people. To see that she did meet such people, Judson squired her to clubs where she could meet Hollywood's power brokers, hired a publicist for her, and apparently even suggested that she offer her sexual favors to the right men.

Columbia officials also had a hand in molding their new property, and to help break with the Latin image she had developed in her early days in films, they changed her name from Rita Cansino to Rita Hayworth. The "y" was added to clarify the pronunciation and to anglicize the name. Ambitious herself, the actress also spent countless hours with makeup and wardrobe specialists to improve her appearance, and she dyed her brown hair auburn.

The actress got her first good role in a major film when she was cast as the other woman in the 1939 adventure *Only Angels Have Wings*, which starred Cary Grant and Jean Arthur. Harry Cohn, the Columbia mogul, now replaced Judson as Hayworth's prime image maker. Cohn wanted her brought along slowly, casting her in good parts in several low-budget films and lending her to other studios such as Warner Bros., for whom she appeared in *The Strawberry Blonde* (1941) with James Cagney and Olivia de Havilland. That same year Hayworth also acted in Twentieth Century-Fox's *Blood and Sand*. Although Linda Darnell had the female lead, Hayworth stole the film with a scene in which she seduced leading man Tyrone Power.

The Columbia publicity specialists then went to work in earnest, sending out innumerable photos and thousands of stories on Hayworth. The buildup achieved its goal when *Life* magazine featured Hayworth in a black lace and white satin negligee on the cover of its August 11, 1941, issue. The photo became one of the popular pinups on the walls of servicemen's quarters during World War II. More than five million copies of it were eventually distributed.

Although she had again played a Latin "femme fatale" in *Blood and Sand*, the Rita Hayworth of 1941 could project another image as well—one more likely to appeal to wartime film audiences. The image was that of a beautiful and desirable woman who was undeniably American. It was this Hayworth that Columbia teamed with dancing great Fred Astaire in *You'll Never Get Rich* (1941), the first of two pictures they did together. Both critics and Astaire praised Hayworth's dancing. Hayworth's own favorite film of this period was *Cover Girl*, a 1944 release in which she danced superbly with costar Gene Kelly. In it she wore contemporary clothing as well as lavish costumes that showcased her beauty. As in her other musicals, Hayworth's songs were dubbed.

Hayworth made news on and off the screen. Her marriage was in trouble, partly because Hayworth was questioning Judson's handling of her income and partly because she and Judson both had other romantic involvements. Hayworth wanted a divorce, and when acrimony and negative publicity threatened to erupt, Columbia attorneys stepped in to end matters as quietly as possible.

On the day the divorce became final in September, 1943, Hayworth married actor Orson Welles, then regarded as a prodigy for his *Citizen Kane* (1941). Partly because she became pregnant, Hayworth starred in only one film, the musical *Tonight and Every Night* (1945), between her marriage and the end of the war. She did make numerous visits to training camps and military hospitals and did volunteer work at the Hollywood Canteen, where servicemen could relax while on leave. To the studio's relief, the birth of her daughter, Rebecca Welles, late in 1944 did not detract from her image of sensuality.

In 1946, Hayworth had her greatest screen success: *Gilda*. Although the plot was convoluted, the film was a box-office hit that returned Hayworth's screen image to that of temptress. Despite the dress and language codes that then governed the film industry, Hayworth performed a remarkably sensuous dance and uttered such lines as "If I'd have been a ranch they would have called me the Bar Nothing." Her sexual allure was so compelling that *Life* soon did a feature on her in which Hayworth was acclaimed as the "love goddess."

By this time, Hayworth's second marriage was in trouble. Shy and insecure, the actress did not readily fit into Welles's world, which was filled with intellectuals and politicians. Both began drinking, and Welles was openly involved with other women.

The one project they undertook together was *The Lady from Shanghai*, filmed in 1946 but not released for two years. For it, Welles got Hayworth to cut her hair and bleach it blonde, a vivid contrast with the Hayworth that fans had come to know. The film failed at the box office, but critics would later consider it a minor classic. Before the film was even released, Hayworth left Welles, taking their daughter with her.

Soon Hayworth was involved in another affair, became pregnant, and had an abortion. She took pains to keep news of it out of the media. Her next romance was with Prince Aly Khan, heir to one of the largest fortunes in the world. Their affair attracted enormous publicity, much of it negative, since Aly Khan was still legally married and since Hayworth globetrotted with Aly Khan, keeping Rebecca with her. When his divorce became final in 1949, Hayworth and Aly Khan were married. Hayworth and Aly Khan had one daughter, Princess Yasmin Khan, but fatherhood did not keep Aly Khan from becoming involved with other women. The couple divorced in 1951.

Hayworth was still under contract to Columbia, and in 1952 the studio teamed her with Glenn Ford, her leading man from *Gilda*, in *Affair in Trinidad*. Her first film in four years, it was a hit at the box office. The following year Hayworth starred in *Miss Sadie Thompson*, a role that emphasized her sensuality but required her to portray the character of Sadie as aging and somewhat weary.

Her personal problems continued. Hayworth had numerous affairs and was married twice more, to singer Dick Haymes and to producer James Hill. The marriage to Haymes was especially troubled and also cost Hayworth much of her money, which she squandered on Haymes's unwise film projects and in paying for assorted legal problems.

By the time she played Sadie Thompson, Hayworth had also begun to have the problem that many actresses face: how to cope with aging when their film success had been built on glamour and beauty. Perhaps hoping to put the love goddess image behind her, she apparently handled the transition with grace, becoming more selective of her roles. In 1957, she appeared as a well-to-do older woman in *Pal Joey*, a musical in which Frank Sinatra leaves her for Columbia's youthful new sex object Kim Novak. Hayworth then appeared in *Separate Tables* (1958) and *They Came to Cordura* (1959). In the latter film, a twentieth century Western costarring Gary Cooper, Hayworth did not even wear makeup. A worn, weary look was called for. *Variety* called her performance in that film the best of her career.

Hayworth performed infrequently during the 1960's and had no screen successes. She began to make television appearances and twice was to have been in Broadway shows: *Step on a Crack* in 1962 and, a few years later, *Applause*. The transition to the unfamiliar routines of stage acting, however, caused her great anxiety. Rehearsals became such an ordeal for her that she could not perform in either show.

At the time, no one understood why such an experienced actress had such problems, but even in films—her last film was in 1972—she began to have trouble with her lines. Later evidence indicated that she might have already begun to suffer from Alzheimer's disease, an affliction that can cause sharp mood swings and difficulty in remembering. Consumption of alcohol (which she apparently gave up about ten years before her death) can aggravate these problems. Eventually, the disease robbed her of control over her body functions and of her ability to think. Medical experts had little understanding of the disease until the 1970's and did not diagnose Hayworth's disorder until 1980. During her last years, she was placed under the guardianship of her daughter Yasmin, who used the media attention paid to her mother's plight to raise money for research into the causes and treatment of Alzheimer's disease.

Summary

Rita Hayworth once seemed to have everything—beauty, glamour, and financial success. The height of Hayworth's fame came during and immediately after World War II. Even though she starred in only half a dozen major films prior to *Gilda*, her screen magnetism, her good performances (primarily in musicals), the studio's media blitz, and the needs of servicemen to escape the stress of war through pinups and other reminders of home combined to establish the Hayworth legend.

Perhaps more than any of her film contemporaries—even Lana Turner and Betty

Grable, who vied with her in popularity as World War II pinup queens—Hayworth transcended reality to become an icon of popular culture, the "love goddess," an image largely created before the war and fixed by her performance in the otherwise undistinguished film *Gilda*. Her public, however, was unaware that years of work by Hayworth and by professional publicists had preceded the creation of the love goddess figure. As she aged, publicists would no longer labor to create a new image appropriate to a woman in her forties. She would have to make the difficult transition unaided, for by the 1950's the publicity mill was at work trying to create new love goddesses— Kim Novak, Jayne Mansfield, and Marilyn Monroe.

Many of Hayworth's anxieties and problems undoubtedly derived from her childhood experiences and from the early onset of Alzheimer's disease. Hayworth's career also exacted its costs, however, which provides a clear example of the difficulties that can arise from the needs of the American people to have larger-than-life heroes and heroines—in Hayworth's case, the love goddess—and the need of the rare performer who is elevated to this status to have privacy and a life apart from the image.

Bibliography
Brady, Frank. *Citizen Welles: A Biography of Orson Welles*. New York: Charles Scribner's Sons, 1989. A detailed account of the legendary Welles, Hayworth's second husband and one of the many men who manipulated her career.
Hill, James. *Rita Hayworth: A Memoir*. New York: Simon & Schuster, 1983. Hill, an acclaimed motion picture producer, married Hayworth in 1958. In writing this memoir of their years together, Hill tries to provide insight into the woman he knew while correcting the public image of the star.
Kobal, John. *Rita Hayworth: The Time, the Place, and the Woman*. New York: W. W. Norton, 1977. Interviews with Hayworth and many of her coworkers give this book special value. One wonders, however, whether the author, who emphasizes her inner strength, was overprotective of Hayworth.
Leaming, Barbara. *If This Was Happiness: A Biography of Rita Hayworth*. New York: Viking, 1989. The fullest account of Hayworth, this is the first study to say that she was the victim of incest as a child. Also includes many interviews.
Morella, Joe, and Edward Z. Epstein. *Rita: The Life of Rita Hayworth*. New York: Delacorte Press, 1983. This brief volume offers nothing new but has many illustrations and a filmography.
Parish, James Robert, and Don E. Stanke. *The Glamour Girls*. New Rochelle, N.Y.: Arlington House, 1975. Hayworth is only one of nine actresses profiled in this book, but the lengthy account of her is valuable for its efforts to assess her career in the context of the studio system. Includes a filmography.
Ringgold, Gene. *The Films of Rita Hayworth: The Legend and Career of a Love Goddess*. Secaucus, N.J.: Citadel Press, 1974. Provides a brief synopsis of each of Hayworth's films, a description of her role in each film, a selection from the reviews, and an abundance of illustrations, many rarely seen.
Stanke, Don E. "Rita Hayworth." *Films in Review* 23 (November, 1972): 527-545. In

this valuable overview of Hayworth's career, Stanke shows clearly how a Hollywood legend was created.

Thomas, Bob. *King Cohn: The Life and Times of Harry Cohn.* London: Barrie & Rockliff, 1967. A useful biography of the Columbia Pictures magnate who controlled Hayworth's career during its peak. An index makes it easy to find the material bearing directly on Hayworth.

Vincent, William. "Rita Hayworth at Columbia, 1941-1945: The Fabrication of a Star." In *Columbia Pictures: Portrait of a Studio,* edited by Bernard F. Dick. Lexington: University Press of Kentucky, 1992. A fascinating attempt to show how Hayworth's managers and Columbia Pictures combined to create a sultry star from a young, insecure woman.

Lloyd J. Graybar

H. D.
Hilda Doolittle

Born: September 10, 1886; Bethlehem, Pennsylvania
Died: September 27, 1961; Zurich, Switzerland
Area of Achievement: Literature
Contribution: The works of H. D., the first great modernist poet, formed the true core of Ezra Pound's Imagist movement and exercised an extraordinary influence on modern poetics. She explored images taken from classical mythology from a profoundly feminine and personal perspective in spare, taut poems.

Early Life
Hilda Doolittle—better known by the nickname "H. D.," given her by Ezra Pound—was born September 10, 1886, in Bethlehem, Pennsylvania, into a world of mystical pietism. Her father was a noted astronomer, her mother was artistic and musical, and the family as a whole was deeply involved in the social and religious life of Bethlehem, stronghold of the Moravian Brotherhood. The profound and eccentric Christianity of Moravianism was to remain an interest of H. D.'s throughout her life. In 1895, the Doolittle family moved to Philadelphia, leaving the close-knit world of the Brotherhood for the more cosmopolitan academic sphere: H. D.'s father became Flower Professor of Astronomy and founder of the Flower Observatory at the University of Pennsylvania.

In 1901, H. D. met Ezra Pound, who was then a student at the university. She was fifteen and he was barely a year older, but he already cut a striking figure in his romantic green robe with his green eyes and golden hair. H. D. herself had, in the words of William Carlos Williams, "a loose-limbed beauty." The relationship between H. D. and Pound, nourished by Pound's suggestions for H. D.'s reading (William Morris, William Blake, Henrik Ibsen), led to their engagement in 1905.

H. D. published short stories in two newspapers between 1901 and 1905, but her account of her relationship with Pound was to come much later: "Mr. Pound it was all wrong," she wrote in *End to Torment*. "You turned into a Satyr, a Lynx, and the girl in your arms (Dryad, you called her), for all her fragile, not yet lost virginity, is Maenad. . . ." In her account, the tone of their encounter is Greek, pagan.

Pound was, almost predictably, less than faithful to his dryad, and his 1908 trip to Europe resulted in a fascination with troubadour lyrics—and with the ideal of adulterous love that they embodied. By 1909, Pound had published *A Lume Spento* and *Personae*, and he was meeting William Butler Yeats, Ford Madox Hueffner (Ford), and other literary lights in London. In 1911, H. D. joined him there.

Since 1908, Pound had been discussing a new style of poetry, one that would cut away trite or stilted language by focusing on the "thing," by using no word that fails to contribute to "the presentation," and by writing "in sequence of the musical phrase," not according to a metronomic beat. The new style was called "Imagisme." H. D. was to be its avatar.

The January, 1913, issue of *Poetry* contained three poems by H. D., which Pound had sent to the editor with a warm commendation, after editing them slightly—and signing them for her "H. D. *Imagiste*." His manifesto for Imagism (written with F. S. Flint) followed two months later. The Modernist era had begun.

Life's Work

Ancient Greece was the magnet of H. D.'s poetic mind: Her first published poem was entitled "Hermes of the Ways," and it is a Greek simplicity that she strives for and that Pound turns to his own purposes by calling it Imagism. People thought that H. D. looked Greek: "her features were Greek, they suggested a hamadryad," Louis Wilkinson wrote in *The Buffoon* (1916), and indeed her leggy beauty was admirably suited to the tastes of a world bent on escaping the confining corsets of its Victorian past. Her "Grecianness" was not, however, merely a myth woven about H. D. within her circle of friends; it was a serious (if not utterly scholarly) pursuit.

After H. D.'s marriage in 1913 to Richard Aldington, the couple spent time in Paris, where they met Henry Slominsky, a young philosopher who had recently published *Heraclit und Parmenides*, and spent many evenings with him ("noctes Atticae," Aldington called them) discussing Homer and Aeschylus, Pythagoras and Plato. In the Diocletian Gallery in Rome, H. D. discovered a little statue of the Hermaphrodite, which she would visit each time she returned to the eternal city; and on a short visit to Capri—her first true taste of the Grecian world—she believed she saw the god Pan.

The result of this immersion in the Greek spirit was the invention or discovery of a peculiarly modern and personal mythic Greece that was to dominate her poems. More directly, she began work on translating some choruses from *Iphigenia in Aulis*. Her Greek was not scholarly: She once commented to a friend on the word "freesia," saying it was an example of a beautiful Greek word, only to be told the flower had been named for F. H. T. Freese. Douglas Bush claims that her "self-conscious, even agonized, pursuit of elusive beauty is quite un-Greek."

If H. D. indulged at times in false etymologies, that has always been the prerogative of a poet, and T. S. Eliot was to say of her translations of Euripides that they were, "allowing for errors and even occasional omissions of difficult passages, much nearer to both Greek and English" than those of Gilbert Murray, the dean of Greek translators. Writing of her poem "Hermes of the Ways," Hugh Kenner would capture to a nicety the curiously Greek yet un-Greek, ancient yet modern tone of so much of H. D.'s work: "We do not mistake the poem for the imagined utterance of some Greek, nor do we hear a modern saying 'I feel as if. . . .'"

Within her Greek matrix, H. D. presented her own struggles and betrayals, her own erotic ambiguities and creative anxieties. H. D. published *Sea Garden*, her first book of verse, and *Choruses from the Iphigenia in Aulis* in 1916: Her early collections all contain translations from—and works inspired by—Sappho, Meleager, and Euripides. *Hymen* (1921), *Heliodora and Other Poems* (1924), and *Red Roses for Bronze* (1929) followed.

H. D. lived in England through World War I. Her marriage to Aldington was virtually over by 1917. In 1918, she met Bryher (Winifred Ellerman), who was to be her lifelong companion, she had a daughter, Perdita, by Cecil Gray, in 1919. Meanwhile, and she had appeared in numerous Imagist anthologies, had formed friendships with D. H. Lawrence and other creative artists, and had traveled in Greece and Egypt. *Collected Poems of H. D.* was published in 1925.

During the 1920's, H. D. began to write prose fiction. *Palimpsest* (1926) is set in classical Rome, London between the wars, and the Egypt of the archaeologists. *Hedylus* (set in ancient Alexandria) followed in 1928. She also wrote several works with specifically lesbian content, which were not published during her lifetime: *Pilate's Wife, Asphodel,* and *Her* (published as *Hermione* in 1981).

In 1933, H. D. went into analysis with Sigmund Freud. If her poetry was of the realm of the gods, dryads, and maenads of Greek myth, his technique of psychoanalysis was no less rooted in Greek mythology—the myth of Oedipus—in language, and in a notion of self-uncovering for which he himself used the metaphor of archaeology. Indeed, H. D.'s title *Palimpsest* could also stand as metaphor for Freud's sense that there are layers upon layers of meaning within human consciousness, inscribed upon one another in the same way that writing is layered upon writing in a palimpsest.

"I am on the fringes or in the penumbra of the light of my father's science and my mother's art—the psychology or philosophy of Sigmund Freud," H. D. would write later. Freud told her she was a perfect example of the bisexual and that she had "two things to hide, one that you were a girl, the other that you were a boy."

Freud and H. D. were in some ways perfectly matched: It is no surprise that her first account of her analysis, *Tribute to Freud* (1956), was described by Freud's biographer Ernest Jones as "surely the most delightful and precious appreciation of Freud's personality that is ever likely to be written." An expanded version was published in 1974.

After her Freudian analysis, World War II was the next major influence on H. D.'s writing—it was also the only time that H. D. and Bryher lived together for an extended period—the two strands coming together in her long poetic sequence *Trilogy* (published posthumously in one volume in 1973), comprising *The Walls Do Not Fall* (1944), *Tribute to the Angels* (1945), and *The Flowering of the Rod* (1946).

The poems of *The Walls Do Not Fall* are remarkable, written in a time of bombs falling, magnesium flares, houses torn open: "there is zrr-hiss,/ lightning in a not-known,// unregistered dimension;/ we are powerless,// dust and powder fill our lungs/ our bodies blunder// through doors twisted on hinges. . . ." Like the *Four Quartets* of T. S. Eliot ("The dove descending breaks the air/ With flame of incandescent terror"), these poems of war carry war into apocalypse. It is the spiritual dimensions, the possibility that H. D. calls "spiritual realism," in which the ancient past merges with the present, that H. D. is after: "possibly we will reach haven,/ heaven." No less remarkable are the poems that make up *Tribute to the Angels*, which H. D. herself called a "premature peace poem."

In December, 1946, aged sixty, H. D. moved to Lausanne, Switzerland, and what was arguably the most fertile period of her life began, in which she published *By Avon*

River (1949), a tribute to Shakespeare; *Bid Me to Live* (1960), a novel; *Helen in Egypt* (1961), a poem about Helen of Troy; and *End to Torment* (1979), a memoir of her long friendship with Ezra Pound.

H. D. died in Zurich on September 27, 1961, having become the first woman to receive the Award of Merit Medal for Poetry of the American Academy of Arts and Letters the year before.

H. D. summed up her life and writings, from "Hermes of the Ways" to her final poetic sequence, in this taut phrase: "H. D.—Hermes—hermeticism and all the rest of it." *Hermetic Definition* (1972), her final sequence of poems, was published posthumously.

Summary

Long thought of as Pound's protégé or as the quintessential early Imagist—and thus a minor figure of note in a largely male poetic history—H. D. can be seen as more in the light of a feminist rewriting of critical history. Imagism itself becomes the cult of H. D., and modern poetics begins with her at least as much as with Pound.

In addition, she brings (as does her friend and colleague Marianne Moore) a uniquely feminine vision to her poetry. Judy Grahn is among those poets who have followed H. D. in the exploration of feminine myth, in such works as *The Queen of Wands* (1982) and *The Queen of Swords* (1987).

Writing in 1993 of Gertrude Stein, Marianne Moore, and H. D., Margaret Dickie noted, "Because they were considered marginal figures even by their friends among the male Modernists, these women were free to experiment long after their male contemporaries were moved to consolidate and conserve. . . . They have waited almost a century for the readers that they have today because they were at least that far ahead of their times."

Bibliography

Dickie, Margaret. "Women Poets and the Emergence of Modernism." In *The Columbia History of American Poetry*, edited by Jay Parini. New York: Columbia University Press, 1993. A sensitive essay offering an extended treatment of H. D., Marianne Moore, and Gertrude Stein.

Guest, Barbara. *Herself Defined: The Poet H. D. and Her World*. Garden City, N.Y.: Doubleday, 1984. An excellent biography of H. D., tracing the many strands that, woven together, constitute the complex life of a woman whose work was always autobiographical, always rooted in the concrete event as it flowered in symbolic and mythic thought. A bibliography and an index are included.

H. D. *Tribute to Freud*. Boston: David R. Godine, 1974. H. D.'s own account of her psychoanalysis with Freud, which provides an entrance into the understanding of her life and mode of work, besides being a fascinating account of both Freud and psychoanalysis. Widely recommended as the first book of H. D.'s to read. An appendix of letters from Freud to H. D. is included.

Robinson, Janice S. *H. D.: The Life and Work of an American Poet*. Boston: Houghton

Mifflin, 1982. Another excellent biography of H. D. Includes notes, a bibliography, and an index.

Stock, Noel. *The Life of Ezra Pound*. New York: Pantheon Books, 1970. A biography of the poet who was H. D.'s first love and mentor in poetry, and from whose shadow she has only recently begun to emerge. Provides essential background on Imagism and early modernism. Index.

Charles Cameron

EDITH HEAD

Born: October 28, 1898(?); Los Angeles, California
Died: October 24, 1981; Hollywood, California
Areas of Achievement: Film and fashion design
Contribution: A prolific designer of film costumes who helped shape Hollywood's image of women for fifty-eight years, Edith Head was a dominant force in a profession largely defined by men.

Early Life

Edith Head was born Edith Claire Posener in Los Angeles, California, sometime around 1898 (some sources list 1907, but later events in Edith's life cast doubt on the accuracy of that date). When her parents divorced and her mother married a mining engineer, she became Edith Spare. She recalled growing up unschooled in a succession of mining camps in Mexico and in the southwestern United States. The most memorable of these camps, according to Head, was in Searchlight, Nevada. Records indicate she was graduated from grammar school in northern California in 1911. Edith attributed many of the characteristics which helped her become one of Hollywood's greatest and most enduring costume designers to growing up as an only child in the desert, where she dressed up family pets to play specific characters at her tea parties.

The family moved to Los Angeles about the time Edith was ready to attend high school, arriving a decade before the film industry would make Hollywood its center of production. Edith was graduated from Los Angeles High School with honors and went on to attend the University of California at Berkeley and Stanford University, where she received a master's degree in French. Few women attended college then, and Edith felt more like a spectator than a participant. While at Berkeley she adopted the habit of hiding behind dark-tinted glasses, which she hoped would camouflage the thick lenses she needed in order to see clearly.

Unsure of what to do after college, Edith agreed to serve as a temporary replacement for the French teacher at Bishop's School, an exclusive girl's school in La Jolla, near San Diego. This position led to a similar appointment at the Hollywood School for Girls, where she was also required to teach art. In order to stay one step ahead of her students, Edith began taking night classes at the Otis Art Institute and later at the Chouinard School of Art. At Chouinard, she met Charles Head, the brother of a classmate, and was married to him shortly thereafter. A salesman who was often on the road, Charles eventually died of the effects of alcoholism. Edith divorced him but kept his name professionally and remained a loyal friend until his death.

Needing supplemental employment in the summer of 1923, Edith responded to an ad for a sketch artist at Paramount Studios. She came to her interview with Howard Greer, Paramount's head designer at that time, carrying a portfolio of sketches borrowed from her fellow art students. Impressed by either her facility or her audacity, Greer hired her on the spot. Teaching her to sketch, Greer discovered that she was a quick study, and he soon began giving her designing duties.

Life's Work

Edith Head approached every assignment with enthusiasm, from counting the beads and buttons in the Paramount inventory to designing the tasseled elephant headdresses in the epic biblical films of director Cecil B. DeMille. She was a careful researcher and tireless worker who shunned the limelight. Greer and his new number two designer, Travis Banton, took Head to all of their fittings and encouraged her to express her opinion. Both men had been successful fashion designers before coming to the fledgling film industry, and the training they provided Head was invaluable.

Film costuming, along with everything that went into filmmaking, was a new art, and Banton and Greer were making it up as they went along. Before 1920, actresses were often hired based on the versatility of their own personal wardrobes. Most of the earliest studio designers were women who had designed for theater or for private salons, but their tenure was brief. By the time Head came to Paramount, most designers were men figuring out how to embellish a film star in a way that served both the demands of the character and the camera, as well as an increasingly glamour-hungry audience.

While Greer and Banton molded the stars, Head was left to assemble wardrobes for the rest of the cast and for the entire populations of the lesser "B" pictures and Westerns Paramount was churning out. After Greer left the studio in 1927, Banton made Head his assistant. Known for his ability to bring out the special qualities in each actress, Banton threw up his hands at the short and increasingly round "It" girl, Clara Bow. Head also struggled to make her first major star look attractive in the military uniform in which Bow was script-bound, but reluctant, to appear. Head eventually won Bow over, as she would nearly everyone with whom she ever worked. To win, Head stated that she had to be "a combination psychiatrist, artist, fashion designer, dressmaker, pincushion, historian, nursemaid and purchasing agent."

She used her fluency in Spanish to gain the confidence of her next big star, Lupe Velez, for whom she designed a spectacular gown and earned her first critical notice—"if there hadn't been so much dress, there would have been more scene." Head learned quickly and was able to use exaggerated design to appropriate advantage with her next star, the curvaceous Mae West. *She Done Him Wrong* (1933) diverted audience attention from the deprivations of the Depression and broke film theater attendance records across the country. Head noted how the studios seemed to appreciate designers who earned publicity, and, when the sarong she designed for Dorothy Lamour in *The Jungle Princess* (1936) launched a fashion trend, she made sure the buying public knew who was behind it.

Despite this recognition and the fact that many major stars had come to trust and demand Head's services, there was little fanfare when she took over for Travis Banton in 1938 and became the first female head designer of a major motion picture studio. She had already been working fifteen hours a day, seven days a week making thirty to forty films a year. This breakneck pace meant that several wardrobes would be in process at one time, from research to sketch pad to seamstress to camera tests and directorial approval to alteration, with fittings scheduled every fifteen minutes throughout the day and a stack of scripts waiting to be read and annotated.

In addition to these demands, the studio moguls wanted their head designers to be fashion trendsetters. In 1929, hemlines had fallen as suddenly as the stock market. Concerned that so many of their films quickly looked outdated, the studios became determined to wrest control of the fashion industry from the French couture houses. They made contracts with garment makers, retail outlets, and even fabric manufacturers. The costume designers were called upon to approve designs and endorse the products. Department stores around the country soon carried the Edith Head signature line. While insisting she never designed for fashion unless the script called for it, Head kept abreast of the latest trends and incorporated contemporary sensibilities into her costumes.

In 1940, Head managed to take a break from her hectic schedule to travel to Las Vegas, where she was married to her longtime friend and Paramount art director, Wiard Boppo "Bill" Ihnen. The entrance of the United States into World War II brought new demands upon Head. While her husband went into the Army as a camouflage expert, Edith Head used her position to urge American women to be thrifty and resourceful in adapting their wartime wardrobes. She was forced to follow her own lead as luxury costume materials ranging from silk to shimmering bugle beads became impossible to find and the amount of fabric alloted for garment construction was limited by law.

With the men at war, women at home were anxious to know how to transform themselves into the sex symbols they saw on the screen. As the head of her own department and as a designer who had outfitted the major stars of three film eras, Edith Head believed she could help the average woman gain control of her image. Her name recognition prompted Art Linkletter to invite her to act as fashion consultant on his weekly radio program, *House Party*. When Linkletter's program moved to television in 1952, women across America looked to Head, a diminutive figure in her trademark tinted glasses, to tell them how to turn their liabilities into assets.

In 1948, the Academy of Motion Picture Arts and Sciences finally recognized costume design as an award category. Edith Head received her first Oscar for her work in *The Heiress* (1949). She was nominated each year throughout the 1950's—receiving thirty-four nominations during her career—and she continued to compile a body of work unrivaled in its depth and its artistic execution. During the 1960's and 1970's, fashion became more androgynous, glamour lost its cachet, and studio designers often bought their clothes at department stores. When Gulf and Western Corporation took over Paramount in 1967, they quietly let Edith Head go after forty-four years. She moved to Universal Studios and continued to design for films and television as well as to lecture, mount fashion shows, and help create a line of sewing patterns. She won her eighth and final Oscar in 1974 for *The Sting* (1973). She died two weeks after completing her 1,131st film, *Dead Men Don't Wear Plaid*, in 1981.

Summary

A successful career woman who worked tirelessly to transform women into glamorous sex objects, Edith Head's life and work were somewhat at odds, although she did not see it that way. She felt, as she stated in her best-selling book, *The Dress Doctor*, "clothes are a practical therapy, and a woman's happiness—her outlook on life, her ability to meet the terrible competition in love and in war, in business and before the eagle eye of her sisters—can be decided by what she wears." Rather than question the premise, Head sought to empower the average woman by giving her the tools to project an alluring image. She prided herself on discovering and enhancing the unique qualities of each actress she designed for and subtly adapting those to the characters they were assigned to play. Detractors have called her designs mediocre, but her professionalism and her ability to get along with her clients have never been questioned. She expressed her own competitiveness by working harder and by learning from others and from her own mistakes. Many producers and directors lauded Head's designs precisely because these designs did not call attention to themselves, believing costumes should serve the story and not the other way around. Although she had dressed many actresses in pants for a part, Head was confused when they started routinely coming to fittings in jeans. As a five-foot-tall designer who worked every day of her long career in heels, Head never could understand the need to be liberated from glamour.

Bibliography
Chierichetti, David. *Hollywood Costume Design*. New York: Harmony Books, 1976. A thorough history of Hollywood costume design with a foreword by Edith Head. Organized by studio, it attributes much of the "Paramount Polish" to Head's long reign there and places her many contributions to the field in historical perspective.
Head, Edith, and Jane Kesner Ardmore. *The Dress Doctor*. Boston: Little, Brown, 1959. Head's first autobiography, it focuses on her self-described role as "dress doctor" to the stars. She describes her many successes with a variety of challenging figures and includes the philosophies she gleaned from her work, and their practical applications for the average woman.
Head, Edith, and Paddy Calistro. *Edith Head's Hollywood*. New York: E. P. Dutton, 1983. A more complete biography based on material provided by Edith but fleshed out by Calistro, who provides insight and counterpoint to Head's oft-told and sometimes apocryphal tales of Hollywood.
LaVine, W. Robert. *In a Glamorous Fashion*. New York: Charles Scribner's Sons, 1980. An excellent history of the rise and fall of glamour in the movies. The chapter on Edith succinctly capsulizes her entire career and contributions.
Leese, Elizabeth. *Costume Design in the Movies*. New York: Frederick Ungar, 1977. An excellent reference of costume designers in Britain and America, this work places Head's work in a larger context.

Susan Chainey

PHOEBE APPERSON HEARST

Born: December 3, 1842; Franklin County, Missouri
Died: April 3, 1919; Pleasanton, California
Area of Achievement: Patronage of the arts
Contribution: Phoebe Hearst was a leading patron in the areas of women's causes, education, and the arts.

Early Life

Phoebe Elizabeth Apperson was born in rural Missouri in 1842. Her father, William Apperson, was one of the wealthiest farmers in the county. Life in rural Missouri for the most part was unexciting for young Phoebe, who was always interested in reading about faraway places and other people's adventures. In a move that was quite unusual for a farm girl, Phoebe learned French and became a schoolteacher.

Phoebe was considered a very gentle and well-mannered young lady, and it surprised everyone when she fell in love with George Hearst, a rough-around-the-edges miner and distant cousin who was eighteen years her senior. Phoebe had been named for George's mother, and he had carried her on his back when she was a little girl but had not seen her for years because he had gone out West to seek his fortune. He returned to Missouri when his mother died, and when he saw the young Phoebe all grown up, he decided to marry her.

Phoebe's parents were concerned that if she married George he would take her out West, and they were right. Phoebe and George were married on June 15, 1862, in Steadman, Missouri, and they set out for the kind of adventure Phoebe, who had never been farther than St. Louis, had always imagined. Later, when she and George were living in San Francisco, she convinced her parents to move to California. They sold their farm and bought a ranch not far from San Francisco to be near their daughter, who had written them frequently to tell them how exciting life was in the Wild West.

The couple's life together began with an extended honeymoon trip. A train ride to New York, a ship to Panama, and another one to San Francisco began what could be called an extraordinary journey for a farmer's daughter. While on board the ship to California, Phoebe became pregnant. She was often quite ill, but she met a kindly woman who befriended the young bride and often brought her tea. The two retained a lifelong friendship, and Phoebe sponsored the woman's son so that he could pursue an art career in Europe. He was Orrin Peck, one of America's leading portrait painters. Once in San Francisco, she would remember the poor people back in rural Missouri and would send money to people whom she believed needed a helping hand. Her charitable nature and concern for serving her community would benefit countless people in the years to come.

Life's Work

Phoebe Apperson Hearst believed that her role in life was to be a good wife. George was often away at the mines in Nevada, South Dakota, and Wyoming. As his fortune grew, he extended his empire to include vast cattle ranches in Mexico and California. He had large swings of fortune, which Phoebe never seemed to mind since she was always optimistic about their future.

Their only son, William Randolph Hearst, the legendary publishing tycoon, was born on April 29, 1863. Because her husband was away for long periods of time, Phoebe had a free hand in raising young Will, and, although some people believed that she overindulged the boy, she had a very clear idea of the man she wanted to mold. Ever the schoolteacher, Phoebe set out to give young Will an exceptional education that would teach him to understand the world around him and revere accomplishment. Phoebe Hearst would often host teas at her home, inviting leading politicians and noted artists. She would encourage young Will to stay, listen, and learn. According to her grandson, William, Jr., she performed the same exercise for the benefit of her grandsons, affording them the extraordinary experiences and memories of having met world-famous artists, musicians, and statesmen. William, Jr., recalls in his memoir that his grandmother had three rules: Be on time, have good manners, and respect older people. Phoebe loved to have an impact on shaping the characters of young people.

She began to influence the people of San Francisco in a small way. She installed a playhouse on her property and presented the first Punch and Judy shows for the neighborhood children. Her largesse grew as her husband's influence grew, and in 1886, George Hearst was appointed senator from the state of California to Washington, D.C., where the family moved and where Phoebe was exposed to the inner workings of politics. By this time, her son was a grown man who had left Harvard University in order to become a journalist and publisher.

George Hearst did not like the idea of his son entering the newspaper business, but Phoebe backed the young man emotionally and financially. Even later, when her son was suffering great financial strains, she would sell the Anaconda mine for $7.5 million so that he could pursue his dream. She believed in him, and William often stated that she was his greatest ally. When he decided to go into politics, she supported his wife and children and would invite the grandchildren out to the family ranch in California so that they could escape the hot New York summers and have a healthy outdoor vacation. Although his political attempts did not succeed, as a newspaper publisher William Randolph Hearst had no equal, and his media empire continues to span the globe, controlling numerous newspapers, magazines, and radio and television properties, as well as the cattle ranches and mines originally purchased by his father.

This quiet and gentle woman stood up to her husband in order to help her son. She also ignored George's distaste for the arts by taking her son abroad to show him castles, museums, and theater. Many of Will's passions grew out of Phoebe's determination to expose her son to the greatness in civilization. When visiting Windsor Castle, Will apparently stated that he wanted to live there. Years later, he hired Julia Morgan to design his famous Shangri-La, San Simeon, in California. Phoebe created her own dream castle in northern California, which she called Wyntoon. Wyntoon was based on romantic storybook castles in Germany. Later, out of respect to his mother, Will expanded her vision and created an entire village in the forest.

In Germany, Will became a collector of *Bilder Bucher* comics, which later inspired him to have his staff create the "Katzenjammer Kids." He was tutored in German and French and closely studied the political systems in Europe. While in Ireland, he saw young women and children doing the work of animals, and he was so horrified by the poverty that he and his mother together began to fund agencies to help the unfortunate.

The two art collectors—mother and son—took painstaking trouble to make their trips unique in order to assemble the best of European culture and bring it home. Phoebe arranged for Will to visit private art collections, an activity that would engender the obsessive acquisitiveness for which William Randolph Hearst became famous. Phoebe was extending her role beyond that of a wife and mother. She was beginning to use her own influence and express her own beliefs with significant results.

In 1887, George Hearst became senator for a full six-year term, and he turned the management of the *San Francisco Examiner*, a failing, unpopular newspaper, over to his son. William made an enormous success out of it. Perhaps because of observing his own mother's capabilities, William became the first publisher to hire women reporters and treat them with the same respect he extended to their male counterparts. His mother, aside from guiding him intellectually, confounded traditionalists when, after her husband's death in the 1890's, she assumed control of his vast conglomerate. She became one of the wealthiest women in America and was a living example for the cause of equality for women.

Phoebe joined in the effort to give women the right to vote. She gave generously to the Young Women's Christian Association (YWCA) and donated so much money to the University of California at Berkeley that she became known as its fairy godmother. She built women's dormitories and a gymnasium, and she funded women's scholarships in medicine, engineering, and the arts. One of her student protegés was a young architect named Julia Morgan, who became the first female to graduate from the École des Beaux-Arts in Paris. Morgan was later the architect of the Hearst Castle at San Simeon.

Her lifelong interest in children's education led Phoebe to sponsor free kindergartens before they became part of the public school system in San Francisco. She was the founder of the first Parent Teachers Association and the largest benefactor of San Francisco's Children's Hospital, Infants' Shelter, and Old People's Home. One of her greatest gifts to the American children was the establishment of the Milk Fund.

While she and her husband were living in Washington, D.C., Phoebe established free kindergartens there, and she was responsible for building both the National Protestant Episcopal Cathedral and the National Cathedral School for Girls. She paid for the restoration of Mount Vernon and provided the funds for the family to donate Abraham Lincoln's sixty-two-acre farm to the state of Illinois.

She never lost her thirst for adventure, and she admired greatly those who fearlessly explored the universe. She was fascinated by archeology and underwrote the costs to excavate missions in California and to undertake digs as far away as Egypt, Russia, Peru, and Greece. Seeing an additional need, Phoebe founded the Travelers' Aid Society to assist other adventure-hungry Americans abroad.

Summary

It is estimated that during her lifetime, which ended at the close of World War I, Phoebe Apperson Hearst gave away as much as $25 million. That sum today would compute to an almost unfathomable amount. She gave these funds at a time when there were no tax deductions for charitable donation. She gave with very little fanfare but great personal satisfaction. It was said that she could be seen chatting with students on the Berkeley campus in a nonimposing and kindly manner. Phoebe was, after all, a lady who believed in the public good and the improvement of humankind. She was a living example of the American dream—a country girl who became a prominent citizen of the world and the founder of a philanthropic dynasty whose work continues today on a significant scale. Many people benefited from Phoebe Apperson Hearst's generosity and dedication. Scholars and dreamers were able to fulfill their goals and complete their tasks because of Hearst's belief in encouraging those who dared to try. Countless women and children received relief and respect because Phoebe Apperson Hearst persisted in believing in a better future for all. Phoebe Apperson Hearst was a resolute woman with a well-defined mission. She leaves behind an impressive legacy and serves as a paradigm for women everywhere.

Bibliography

Chaney, Lindsay, and Michael Cieply. *The Hearsts: Family and Empire: The Later Years*. New York: Simon & Schuster, 1981. A superficial overview of the lives of William Randolph Hearst and his family, Phoebe Apperson Hearst among them. The tone of the work is tabloid-style, and the information on living members of the Hearst Family is now outdated.

Davies, Marion. *The Times We Had*. Edited by Pamela Pfau and Kenneth S. Marx. Indianapolis: Bobbs-Merrill, 1975. Always the bridesmaid and never the bride, Marion Davies describes her life as William Randolph Hearst's mistress with much good humor, as if she were entertaining their guests at a dinner party at San Simeon.

Hearst, William Randolph, Jr., with Jack Casserly. *The Hearsts: Father and Son*. Niwot, Colo.: Roberts Rinehart, 1991. A charming and intimate portrait of an extraordinary family. Although the book demonstrates his fondness for his father, Hearst's experience as a journalist is evident in his even-handed treatment of his subjects. Contains useful information about Phoebe Hearst.

Robinson, Judith. *The Hearsts: An American Dynasty*. Cranbury, N.J.: University of Delaware, 1991. Phoebe Apperson Hearst is discussed at length in this useful family biography.

Swanberg, W. A. *Citizen Hearst*. New York: Charles Scribner's Sons, 1961. The most comprehensive biography of William Randolph Hearst, this work discusses his career successes and failures as well as his political activities. This well-organized book has been well researched and is impressively documented. Phoebe Apperson Hearst is discussed in passing.

Susan Nagel

LILLIAN HELLMAN

Born: June 20, 1905; New Orleans, Louisiana
Died: June 30, 1984; Martha's Vineyard, Massachusetts
Areas of Achievement: Literature and film
Contribution: A leading American playwright and important screenwriter, Hellman published memoirs in the 1960's and 1970's that advanced the growing interest in women's lives and in autobiography.

Early Life

Lillian Florence Hellman was born in New Orleans, Louisiana on June 20, 1905, the daughter of Max Hellman, a shoe salesman, and Julia Newhouse, an Alabama native whose family had succeeded in several business enterprises, including banking. As a child, Lillian was acutely conscious of the power the Newhouses' money gave them; financial speculation and chicanery would become the theme of her most powerful plays. When her father's New Orleans shoe business failed, he moved his family for six months of each year to New York City while he traveled as a salesman. Five-year-old Lillian found it difficult to adjust to two different cultures and school systems; her record as a student was erratic. Nevertheless, she acquired a diversity of experience that stimulated her precocious imagination and provided many of the themes of her plays and memoirs.

Hellman was an only child, doted on by her parents, who indulged her whims and gave her room to experiment in the heady, vibrant atmosphere of New York City in the 1920's. Hellman attended classes at New York University and then at Columbia, but she did not earn a degree. Instead she worked briefly for the innovative New York publisher, Horace Liveright, where she met important writers and celebrities, including her future husband, Arthur Kober, whom she married on December 21, 1925. Kober wrote plays and stories for *The New Yorker*, and he helped Hellman obtain various jobs as a script reader and publicity agent for theatrical producers. She had ambitions to write, but her early attempts at fiction fizzled, and she accompanied her husband to Hollywood, where he had a contract to write screenplays.

Hellman was hired in Hollywood as a script reader. Her job was to summarize books that might make good films. She found her work dull, but she made friends with writers and film actors, eventually meeting Dashiell Hammett, the handsome and successful writer of hardboiled detective stories. With the marriage to Kober failing (they were divorced in 1932), she became romantically involved with Hammett, who suggested that she write for the stage. He even provided the plot, based on a true story, for her first successful play, *The Children's Hour* (1934). Despite many problems, the relationship with Hammett would endure until his death in 1961 and become an important theme in her memoirs.

Life's Work

For *The Children's Hour*, Lillian Hellman updated the story of two teachers who had been accused of lesbianism in nineteenth century Edinburgh. She shifted the setting to twentieth century New England and made the teachers, Karen and Martha, victims of an accusation leveled against them by a malevolent child, Mary, who refuses to be disciplined and who strikes back by suggesting to her grandmother, a powerful member of the community, that her teachers have an "unnatural" love for each other. Karen and Martha are not lovers, but Martha kills herself when she realizes that she does have sexual feelings for Karen. The two teachers are the targets of the blind hysteria of society, which tends to take the word of authority figures and to be swayed by the emotional impact of a shocking accusation. An enormous success (the play ran for more than seven hundred performances on Broadway), *The Children's Hour* established Hellman as a promising playwright with a keen eye for both individual and social psychology.

Hellman's success as a playwright brought an offer from Samuel Goldwyn to write screenplays. Throughout the 1930's, Hellman worked for Goldwyn, producing superior scripts for *The Children's Hour*, retitled *These Three* (1936), and for *Dead End* (1937) as well as working in collaboration on other projects. She had unusual creative control over her own scripts and a reputation in Hollywood for independence. She was instrumental in forming the Screen Writers Guild and became involved in leftist politics, briefly becoming a Communist Party member from 1938 to 1940.

Hellman is perhaps best known for her third play, *The Little Foxes* (1939), a classic of the American theater, set in the South just after the Civil War. The play's main character, Regina Hubbard Giddens, holds her own with her brothers, Ben and Oscar Hubbard, in capitalizing on the family business. Although the play is susceptible to a political reading and can be analyzed as a critique of capitalism, it is equally the story of a family, each member struggling for dominance and individuality. One of the most striking features of this play is its lack of sentimentality, a hardheadedness Hellman herself exemplified in the pursuit of her career and which she attributed to her mother's family in *An Unfinished Woman: A Memoir* (1969) and *Pentimento* (1972).

In *Watch on the Rhine* (1941), Hellman focuses on the innocence of Americans and their blindness to the appeasement of fascism that had gone on throughout the 1930's. In Kurt Müller, a German anti-Fascist fighter seeking momentary refuge in the United States, she creates a vulnerable hero, a fragile man with broken hands who is constrained to strangle a foreign national who threatens to reveal Kurt's presence and to expose the network of anti-Fascist groups Kurt supports. That Fanny Farrelly, the mother of Kurt's American wife, Sarah, must condone this killing in her own household and allow Kurt to escape, accomplishes the playwright's aim in bringing home to Americans the fact that they are implicated in the world's evils and must take some responsibility for combating them, even at the price of losing their innocence.

Although Hellman managed to complete a second successful play on the Hubbards, *Another Part of the Forest* (pr. 1946, pb. 1947), she began to sense that her resources as a playwright were diminishing. Her final plays—*The Autumn Garden* (1951), *Toys in the Attic* (1960), and an adaptation of a novel, *My Mother, My Father, and Me* (1963)—show that she was moving toward the form of the memoir as more flexible and more open than her tightly wound melodramas.

Called on to explain her career in numerous interviews, and energized by the contentious campus life of the 1960's (she taught at Harvard, Yale, and other colleges), it seemed incumbent on Hellman to present some record of herself. In her memoirs, Hellman dedicated herself not only to explaining the origins of her work but also to revealing to a later generation what it was like growing up in the 1920's, making her way among the writers and the politics of the 1930's and 1940's and coping with being blacklisted in the 1950's for her leftist sympathies.

Hellman's first two volumes of memoirs, *An Unfinished Woman* and *Pentimento*, were an enormous success, garnering her the best reviews of her life. She became a cult figure, lionized by young people, especially women, who saw in her a role model who had held her own in a man's world while remaining feminine. There was criticism of her long-term relationship with Hammett—some women viewing Hellman as the subordinate partner—but on the whole she was praised for confronting the temper of her times with magnificent courage and candor. The style of the memoirs, particularly *Pentimento*, was much admired, for her chapters read like short stories, especially her account of her childhood friend, Julia, who had become part of the anti-Fascist underground in Europe and whom Hellman had aided at considerable risk to herself.

When Hellman's third memoir, *Scoundrel Time* (1976), appeared, it was initially greeted with rave reviews. Eventually, however, the tide turned as her enemies of the 1930's and 1940's emerged to dispute her accounts. In an article published in *The Paris Review* in 1981, Martha Gellhorn, Ernest Hemingway's third wife, ridiculed the contradictions and inaccuracies of *An Unfinished Woman* and made a compelling case for Hellman's having lied about many incidents to aggrandize her own life. Other attacks followed, pointing up the self-serving quality of *Scoundrel Time* and its deficiencies as history. The culmination of this criticism came in Mary McCarthy's allegation on national television that every word Hellman wrote was a lie.

Hellman received little sympathy when she decided to sue McCarthy for libel. Having built her reputation on candor, the likelihood that the stories in *Pentimento*, especially Julia's, were fiction came as devastating news to Hellman's readers, and Hellman did not deign to reply to the charges. When she died on June 30, 1984, the suit against McCarthy was still pending, but Hellman's reputation had been significantly damaged.

Summary

Several of Lillian Hellman's plays—*The Children's Hour, The Little Foxes, Another Part of the Forest, The Autumn Garden, Toys in the Attic*—are regularly revived and are likely to remain a part of the American repertory. The quality of the writing in her memoirs is high, although their final place in the canon of American literature remains to be determined, as does the precise nature of her political views and the extent to which those views must be considered in an analysis of her writing.

Hellman's life represents a challenge and an inspiration to women's studies. On the one hand, she was a product of her moment—especially of the 1930's—when her writing reflected the need of many writers to engage in some form of political engagement. She chose to pursue the hardboiled creed of her mentor, Dashiell Hammett, never excusing or rationalizing her actions. On the other hand, her memoirs and plays provide ample criticism not merely of male chauvinism but of her characters and of herself. She knew that she was "unfinished," and that many of her actions were contradictory. The very terms she used—such as pentimento—suggest that she recognized that human identity, and especially a woman's identity, entailed constant revision and remaking—similar to the artistic process of repenting, in which an artist makes changes and paints over his or her work. This dynamic process of self-creation is what accounted for the tremendous success of Hellman's memoirs, and it is what is likely to repay study in considering Hellman's status as a woman of achievement.

Bibliography
Dick, Bernard F. *Hellman in Hollywood*. Rutherford, N.J.: Fairleigh Dickinson University Press, 1982. The only complete study of Hellman's screenwriting career, based not only on archival sources but also on interviews with her coworkers. Notes, bibliography, and index.
Feibleman, Peter. *Lilly: Reminiscences of Lillian Hellman*. New York: William Morrow, 1988. An effective memoir of his close association with Hellman, which provides important details on the last years of her life.
Lederer, Katherine. *Lillian Hellman*. Boston: Twayne, 1979. A sound introductory study, including a chapter on her biography and discussions of her major plays and memoirs. Contains notes, chronology, bibliography, and index.
Newman, Robert P. *The Cold War Romance of Lillian Hellman and John Melby*. Chapel Hill: University of North Carolina Press, 1989. An important contribution to an understanding of Hellman's politics and her personal life, concentrating on her relationship with Melby, an American foreign service officer dismissed from his position in the 1950's because of his love affair with Hellman.
Rollyson, Carl. *Lillian Hellman: Her Legend and Her Legacy*. New York: St. Martin's Press, 1988. A full-length biography that discusses all of Hellman's major work as autobiographer, screenwriter, and playwright. There is also an extensive discussion of her politics and sketches of the main characters in her life. Useful footnotes, bibliography, and index.
Spacks, Patricia Meyer. *The Female Imagination*. New York: Alfred A. Knopf, 1975. Contains a searching and highly critical discussion of Hellman's memoirs.
Triesch, Manfred, comp. *The Lillian Hellman Collection at the University of Texas*. Austin: University of Texas Press, 1966. An important census and discussion of Hellman's manuscripts in the most important depository of her work.
Wright, William. *Lillian Hellman: The Image, The Woman*. New York: Simon & Schuster, 1986. A full-length biography concentrating on Hellman's life. Wright is less concerned with her plays and memoirs than with her politics, which he treats in a fairly objective manner. Notes and index.

Carl Rollyson

BETH HENLEY

Born: May 8, 1952; Jackson, Mississippi

Area of Achievement: Literature

Contribution: Focusing many of her plays on female characters and contemporary women's issues, Beth Henley has broken into the traditional male canon of mainstream American theater, with her plays regularly staged, produced, anthologized, and taught.

Early Life

Elizabeth Becker Henley, daughter of Charles Boyce Henley, an attorney, and Elizabeth Josephine Henley, an actress, was born on May 8, 1952, in Jackson, Mississippi. The second of four daughters born to the couple, Henley was close to her sisters despite their stormy personal relationships as they grew to maturity. The Henley family embraced both the theater and a bit of theatricality. As a child, Beth became enthralled with the glamour of the stage, watching her mother perform in local community theater productions. Although far from Broadway, regional theater captured Henley's imagination, luring her by its promise of excitement and adventure beyond the confines of her small Southern town. Regularly attending her mother's rehearsals and assisting her as she memorized lines, Beth developed an early appreciation for the nuances and rhythms of the stage. The theater not only fulfilled the Henley family's need for entertainment but also extended into their daily routines. When her mother went out to shop for the family's groceries, she often practiced her acting skills by assuming the roles of the characters whom she played, even to the extent of selecting items that her character would likely eat.

While Beth's mother exercised her talent for acting on the theatrical stage, her father Charles chose to exercise his talents in the political arena. Bemusedly, the playwright recalls accompanying her father on his campaign trail as a candidate for the Mississippi state senate. When she noticed that Beth's shoes were spotlessly clean, her mother whimsically suggested that Beth take a moment to muddy them a bit before joining her father on the platform, apparently concurring that a senator's child should not appear totally above blemish if voters are to relate to her.

After completing high school, Beth entered Southern Methodist University (SMU), in Dallas, Texas, with aspirations of becoming an actor, an occupation that she initially considered to be easier than playwriting. As a student, she avidly read many great playwrights, particularly Anton Chekhov, her favorite. While attending SMU, she combined acting with playwriting, penning what eventually became *Crimes of the Heart* (1981) as a course assignment. When she was only a college sophomore, Henley wrote a one-act play *Am I Blue* using a pseudonym; the play was staged during her senior year at SMU in the fall of 1973. College proved an important influence on Henley's career, for she became friends with various aspiring young playwrights, actors, and directors, all of whom encouraged her writing. After graduating from SMU with a bachelor of fine arts degree in 1974, she taught creative dramatics and worked as an actor at the Dallas Minority Repertory Theatre. Henley received a teaching scholarship to attend the University of Illinois at Champaign, where she completed a year of graduate study and teaching. Continuing to pursue her interest in acting, Henley acted in the *Great American People Show*, a historical pageant presented at the New Salem State Park in the summer of 1976.

Life's Work

Eager to launch her professional career, Beth Henley moved to Los Angeles in 1976 to live with actor-director Stephen Tobolowsky, a former colleague from her undergraduate days at SMU. Her pursuit of an acting career proved disheartening, given the fierce competition for jobs. Believing that the struggle to find acting jobs—scraping for work on television commercials and mailing her picture to countless strangers—was tantamount to losing time better spent on writing, Henley turned her attention to screenplays. Despite her fears about writing and challenges posed by her dyslexia, Henley persevered. Her early years in Los Angeles proved difficult as she lacked the services of an agent and had little influence in convincing producers to read her scripts. Her first screenplay, *Nobody's Fool*, was completed during this period, but was not produced until 1986.

A few years after Henley's arrival in Los Angeles, her screenwriter friend Frederick Bailey submitted a script of *Crimes of the Heart* to the Actors Theatre of Louisville. After the play won the Great American Play Contest, enjoying its world premiere in Louisville in February of 1979, it went on to further acclaim on Broadway, winning the 1981 Pulitzer Prize for Drama. As Henley's first full-length play, *Crimes of the Heart* introduces the MaGrath sisters of Hazelhurst, Mississippi, whose reunion is precipitated by the family's efforts to support their youngest sister, who has been accused of attempting to murder her husband. Henley's dramatic style, characterized by the critics as Southern Gothic, incorporates a blend of comic and tragic elements. Even in the midst of tragedy, her characters can see the humor of their situations. Artfully interweaving these themes, Henley exposes various crimes and taboos, both obvious and subtle, including wife battering, attempted murder, extramarital and interracial affairs, and patriarchal subjugation of women.

Lauded by the critics for her vision, warmth, and style, Henley was heralded, at age twenty-nine, as the youngest female playwright to win the Pulitzer Prize. *Crimes of the Heart* also won the 1981 New York Drama Critics Circle Award for best new American play, a Guggenheim Award from *Newsday*, and a Tony Award nomination for best play. Henley was later asked to write the screenplay for the film adaptation of *Crimes of the Heart*, which starred Diane Keaton, Jessica Lange, and Sissy Spacek in the lead roles. Greeted with some skepticism by film critics, the picture received mixed reviews. Some early admirers of the play were disappointed that what had worked as a "kitchen drama" on the stage had somehow gone down the kitchen drain in the film. Unthwarted by the criticism, Henley received an Academy Award nomination for best adapted screenplay for the film adaptation in 1986.

Although her next play did not enjoy the same level of success, Henley premiered *The Miss Firecracker Contest* at the Victory Theatre in Los Angeles in the spring of 1980. As in her earlier effort, Henley based her subject matter, characters, and dialects on her own Southern experience. The play's protagonist, Carnelle Scott, dreams of proving her worth—to herself and to the town—by winning a local beauty contest and being crowned "Miss Firecracker." The play eventually had a 1984 Off-Broadway run. When adapted for film in 1989 with a Hollywood cast that included Holly Hunter, Mary Steenburgen, Alfre Woodard, and Tim Robbins, *Miss Firecracker* received some critical acclaim, but was not a box office success.

Henley's next play, *The Wake of Jamey Foster*, was an autobiographical work first produced by the Hartford Stage Company in 1982 that had a disastrous run in New York. Many critics considered the play to be derivative of the earlier *Crimes of the Heart*, yet Henley maintained that the new play exposed other "ghosts." As before, Henley's female characters are beleaguered with conflicting emotions and experience catharsis in the midst of tragedy. Still, the play provided ample evidence of Henley's artistry as a playwright, highlighting her ability to portray women from various angles and at various stages in their emotional and physical lives.

Despite the dismal reviews she received for *The Wake of Jamey Foster*, Henley continued to write. She introduced her next play, *The Debutante Ball*, in the spring of 1985 at the South Coast Repertory Theater in Costa Mesa, California. *The Lucky Spot*, a tragicomedy that tests the bonds of love and marriage, premiered at the Williamstown Theatre Festival in the summer of 1986. Centered around the opening of a dance saloon, the play chronicles the unexpected and tumultuous homecoming of a long-lost wife, whose husband has—in her absence—promised marriage to his young, pregnant lover. As with Henley's other plays, the characters in *The Lucky Spot* manage to rise above their audacious and outrageous antics to reveal the truth about themselves. Henley's characters also betray decisively Southern roots—in their biting honesty, in the intensity of their loves and hates, and in their collective refusal to accept defeat.

Abundance, which premiered in California in April of 1989, is set in the West of the 1880's and probes themes of friendship and marriage as two mail-order brides test their survival instincts in their encounters with the coarse, maimed, and often brutal men of the new frontier. Neither the harshness of the environment nor the hostility of the local Indian tribes can compare, however, to the psychological cruelties of the marriage bed. One female character, unremarkable and seemingly faint and fragile, rises in stature as the other woman, worldly and confident, loses her soul.

In addition to her fame as a playwright, Henley has achieved success in other media, including television and film. She wrote the script for a television pilot *Morgan's Daughters* (1979) and wrote the screenplay for *The Moon Watcher* (1983), an Embassy Pictures release. Together with Budge Threlkeld, she cowrote a script for *Survival Guides* (1986), a Public Broadcasting System television production, and *Trying Times* (1987). With Stephen Tobolowsky and singer David Byrne, she collaborated on the screenplay of *True Stories* (1986). As noted above, she was also responsible for the screenplays of *Crimes of the Heart* and *Miss Firecracker*. Several other screenplays, including *A Long and Happy Life* (based on a book by Reynolds Price) and her adaptation of *The Lucky Spot*, have been completed and are awaiting production.

Henley's play *Control Freaks*, which opened at the Met Theatre in Los Angeles in July of 1993, marked her directing debut. Coproduced with the play's star, Holly Hunter, *Control Freaks* is a dark comedy, replete with overtones of incest and murder. The play represents something of a departure for Henley, who insists that she has come to love the hostile, desperate characters whom she initially despised. *Revelers*, a comedy about a memorial weekend for a dead acting teacher. debuted as a workshop production at Chicago's Center Theatre in August of 1993.

Summary

Beth Henley was one of several female playwrights who exploded onto the Broadway scene during the 1970's and 1980's. As the first female in decades to win a coveted Pulitzer Prize for Drama, an accolade traditionally claimed by male playwrights, Henley experienced a level of success that helped open doors for other female dramatists, including Marsha Norman, whose *'night Mother* received the Pulitzer Prize in 1983. Celebrated for her bizarre humor and her ability to fuse the comic with the grotesque, Henley was drawn upon her childhood experiences—the images and rhythms of the South. Although critics debate whether her dramas fully reflect feminist issues, all agree that the plays are decidedly southern.

Because of her ability to move from regional theater to Broadway, Henley set a precedent for other promising female playwrights striving to introduce their dramas to mainstream American audiences. Her work represents a break from theater of the past, particularly in her emphasis on women's sense of community. Unlike playwrights who preceded her, such as Susan Glaspell, whose *Trifles* (pr. 1916) also focused on this sense of community, Henley complicates her characters by highlighting their actions through a simultaneously comic and tragic viewpoint. With unflinching honesty, Henley relentlessly pursues the truth beneath the humorous surface of her sometimes bizarre characters. Testing extremes of love and hate, Henley reveals her female characters' muddled identities, guilt, and self-loathing and traces the roots of these conflicts to patriarchal antecedents. While much of her work has been dubbed "kitchen drama" for its focus on women within the traditional environment of home, Henley deftly skewers traditional assumptions by revealing the price women pay either for staying or for leaving home.

Bibliography

Betsko, Kathleen, and Rachel Koenig, comps. *Interviews with Contemporary Women Playwrights.* New York: Beech Tree Books, 1987. The interview with Henley contained in this collection provides readers with insight into Henley's perception of herself as a writer. Contains useful information on the southern influences evident in Henley's themes and characters.

Guerra, Jonnie. "Beth Henley: Female Quest and the Family-Play Tradition." In

Making a Spectacle: Feminist Essays on Contemporary Women's Theatre, edited by Lynda Hart. Ann Arbor: University of Michigan Press, 1989. Critical of Henley for her seeming inability to reinvent or challenge the conventions of the family-play genre, Guerra surmises that Henley's characters fail in their quests to overcome oppressive definitions of their identities.

Jaehne, Karen. "Beth's Beauties." *Film Comment* 25 (May/June, 1989): 9-14. This article argues that the film *Miss Firecracker* aptly captures the essence of the true southern belle, trapped within the confines of the obsession with being beautiful. Jaehne also sheds light on the personal and professional relationship between Henley and the film's protagonist, Holly Hunter. Illustrated.

Jones, John Griffin, ed. "Beth Henley." In *Mississippi Writers Talking*. Vol. 1. Jackson: University Press of Mississippi, 1982. The interview with Henley contains details about her childhood, family background, education, and development as a playwright. Conveys her philosophy on developing characters and story lines and her affection for incorporating her southern roots into her dramatic works.

McDonnell, Lisa J. "Diverse Similitude: Beth Henley and Marsha Norman." *Southern Quarterly* 25 (Spring, 1987): 95-104. Drawing comparisons between Henley's *Crimes of the Heart*, *The Wake of Jamey Foster*, and *The Miss Firecracker Contest* and Norman's *Getting Out* (pr. 1977) and *'night Mother*, the author notes that these plays differ remarkably in their tone and style, with Henley's plays demonstrating a "theatrical" orientation, in contrast to Norman's more "literary" bent. Although both playwrights incorporate gothic humor and family themes, Henley emphasizes serious dimensions within a comedic framework, whereas Norman adds comic overtones to what are essentially serious dramas.

Thompson, Lou. "Feeding the Hungry Heart: Food in Beth Henley's *Crimes of the Heart*." *Southern Quarterly* 30 (Winter/Spring, 1992): 99-102. Examining food as a metaphor for the absence of love, Thompson analyzes the relationships of Henley's female characters with important male figures, present or absent, in the play. Thompson contends that the MaGrath sisters use food as a narcotic, confusing their emotional hunger with physical hunger.

Linda Rohrer Paige

KATHARINE HEPBURN

Born: May 12, 1907; Hartford, Connecticut

Area of Achievement: Film

Contribution: With a career spanning most of the twentieth century, Katharine Hepburn has, from her early career days, embodied wit, independence, and charm to the American public. Hepburn was one of the first actresses to break down Hollywood's stereotype of women, and she has served as a model of grit and beauty throughout her career.

Early Life

Katharine Houghton Hepburn was born on May 12, 1907 (despite conflicting reports that have dogged her since her first Hollywood film), the second of the six children of Katharine "Kit" Hepburn and Thomas Hepburn. Her mother was part of a well-known New England family, the Houghtons. Encouraged by her dying mother to acquire an education for herself and her sisters, Kit Houghton eventually earned a bachelor's degree from Bryn Mawr (1899) and a master's degree from Radcliffe (1900). Houghton's upbringing encouraged her to value independence, education, and social responsibility, three qualities that dominated her life. Because of her mother's interests, Katharine Hepburn had a childhood that was characterized by her family's deep involvement in many social causes of the day: the suffrage movement, the presence of brothels in their home city of Hartford and the associated spread of venereal disease, and the efforts to provide safe birth control to women (the latter cause was ably headed by Margaret Sanger, a friend of the Hepburns.) The Hepburn family's social conscience was not, however, guided solely by Kit Hepburn. Thomas Norval Hepburn was a young medical student when he first met Kit Houghton, and his sense of social awareness was as acute as hers. He chose to specialize in urology, an unmentionable subject in the polite society of that time. His practice led him to understand the horrors of syphilis, which was devastating the populations of all social classes. He chose to speak out about this unmentionable disease, at one point even paying for the printing and distribution of a play (*Damaged Goods*, by French dramatist Eugène Brieux) on the subject.

Another feature of Hepburn's childhood was her family's emphasis on physical activity. From ice cold baths to swinging on a homemade trapeze strung from the trees to playing tennis and golf, the family's active life was the result in large part of Thomas Hepburn's belief that a sluggish body led to a sluggish mind.

This closely knit family did suffer one early tragedy that also shaped Hepburn's growth: the accidental death by hanging of the oldest child, Tom, who was especially close to his sister Katharine. Soon after this time, Hepburn and her four siblings formed the Hepburn Players, an assortment of neighborhood children who put on performances with their own staging and direction. Even here, the family's social consciousness dominated: All proceeds from the production of *Beauty and the Beast* went to benefit the children of the Navajo Indians in New Mexico. (Hepburn herself played the beast.)

Like her mother and grandmother before her, Hepburn attended Bryn Mawr College, where she took part in many of the school theatricals: Her parts ranged from playing a young man in one performance to playing Pandora in *The Woman in the Moone* [sic]. These experiences seem to have led to her decision to become an actress; just before the end of her senior year, she approached Edwin H. Knopf, a director of a local theater company, armed with a letter of introduction and asking for work.

Life's Work

In 1928, just before her graduation from Bryn Mawr, Katharine Hepburn's persistence overrode Knopf's objections, and he hired her to play one of six ladies-in-waiting in a production of *The Czarina* (1928). Hepburn's early years on the stage were marked by many struggles and ups and downs. She was, as she later said, "a quick study": She could read a part wonderfully and impress the director. When she was hired, however, she lacked the training and experience to carry through a full performance.

In 1932, Hepburn played the supporting role of Antiope, an Amazon warrior, in the Broadway production of *The Warrior's Husband*. Her entrance staggered Broadway: Wearing a short tunic, a helmet, a breastplate, and leggings, and carrying a dead stag over her shoulder, Hepburn leapt down a steep ramp and onto a platform, where she hurled the stag at Hippolyta's feet. This performance led to an offer of a screen test for Hepburn. On the basis of this screen test, Hepburn was awarded her first role in Hollywood, playing Hillary Fairfield in the 1932 film *A Bill of Divorcement* with the famous John Barrymore. This role led to Hepburn's instant fame, although her second film in Hollywood, *Christopher Strong*, was neither a popular nor a critical success. Hepburn's popularity returned after her third picture, *Morning Glory* (1933), for which she was awarded her first Academy Award for Best Actress. Hepburn's next film role, Jo in *Little Women* (1933), was critically acclaimed, but she was not to be part of another popular film until *Stage Door* in 1937.

After she received her Academy Award, Hepburn's appeal was so great that she was offered the lead in the stage production of *The Lake* (1934). The play began disastrously, with a hard director apparently trying to browbeat Hepburn into buying out her contract. Hepburn stuck to her work, however, and struggled so hard to improve each performance that, by the time the play closed, she was turning in excellent performances. Soon after this experience, Hepburn returned to Hollywood.

In 1938, Hepburn's second film with the talented Cary Grant, *Bringing up Baby*, was released. Though it was not enormously popular upon first release, *Bringing up Baby* later came to be considered the finest of the "screwball comedies" that were so popular during the 1920's and 1930's.

Despite her successes in dealing with Hollywood on her own terms and her previous difficulty with *The Lake*, Hepburn often returned to the stage. One of her most successful theatrical runs was in *The Philadelphia Story* (1939). As well as starring in the play, Hepburn was involved in all aspects of its production, from writing to casting to arranging financing. Hepburn was as deeply involved in the writing and production of the film version of *The Philadelphia Story* (1940), in which she repeated her role from the stage version.

In 1942, yet another Hepburn film, *Woman of the Year*, was released. This picture marked Katharine Hepburn's first screen work with the superb actor Spencer Tracy, and it initiated what became the longest screen partnership in history as well as a legendary Hollywood romance. Hepburn and Tracy worked together until 1967, when their last film together, *Guess Who's Coming to Dinner*, was completed shortly before Tracy's death. Hepburn's work in this film earned for her a second Academy Award, which she believed must have been meant for both Tracy and herself.

The African Queen (1951), made with Humphrey Bogart on location in Africa, saw the transition in Hepburn's career from a young Hollywood actress whom the studios had tried to portray as a starlet to the mature Hepburn, who was able to show film audiences the confidence and competence she had possessed all along. As one of her biographers, Sheridan Morley, explained, with the role of the missionary Rose Sayer, Hepburn transcended the "battle-of-the-sexes . . . comedies . . . and the old high-society romps" of her early career to become a great dramatic actress. This picture (for which Bogart won the Academy Award for Best Actor) was a critical and financial success for all concerned. Another Hepburn film that received great critical acclaim was *Long Day's Journey into Night* (1962), in which she gave a compelling performance of a woman sinking into the depths of drug addiction. According to many critics, this performance was the pinnacle of her career, a review that seems a bit premature, since Hepburn continued to work. She won her next two Academy Awards for Best Actress for her portrayal of Eleanor of Aquitane in *The Lion in Winter* (1968) and for her portrayal of Ethel Thayer in *On Golden Pond* (1981). These two films clearly demonstrated to the studios and critics that the American public would not only pay to see but also relish quality films starring mature, competent actors.

Summary

Throughout her career, Katharine Hepburn has pushed herself to explore the limits of her ability and of the motion picture medium. Her frequent stage work, from her struggles with *The Lake* to her success in *The Philadelphia Story* to her frequent Shakespeare roles, bears testimony to her determination not to rest on her laurels. Her four Academy Awards for Best Actress attest her talent as an actress and the admiration of her colleagues. Although audiences initially did not know what to make of her early performances (which were far from the typical Hollywood stereotypes of women) and despite more than her share of critical attacks, Hepburn eventually came to epitomize honesty, independence, and intelligence, and she was idolized by millions of filmgoers. Hepburn's biographer, Gary Carey, quoted Richard Watts of the *Herald Tribune* as saying, "Few actresses have been so relentlessly assailed by critics, wits, columnists, magazine editors, and other professional assailers over so long a period of time, and even if you confess that some of the abuse had a certain amount of justification to it, you must admit she faced it gamely and unflinchingly and fought back with courage and gallantry."

Hepburn's work and, more important, her independent, indomitable personality and her integrity continue to delight and inspire film and theater audiences worldwide as they have for most of the twentieth century.

Bibliography

Andersen, Christopher. *Young Kate*. New York: Henry Holt, 1988. Based on conversations with Hepburn, this book chronicles her parents' lives, vividly recounts what it was like to grow up in the Hepburn family, and provides a detailed family chronology as well as a bibliography of supplementary references.

Bryson, John. *The Private World of Katharine Hepburn*. Boston: Little, Brown, 1990. Primarily a fine collection of photographs taken by the author (a professional photographer) of Katharine Hepburn over the years, this work also provides complementary text (based on discussions with Hepburn) that relates many stories about her family, her life, and her career.

Carey, Gary. *Katharine Hepburn: A Hollywood Yankee*. New York: St. Martin's Press, 1983. After a brief discussion of her childhood and college years, this book provides a general survey of Hepburn's career from her first theater job through her work in the early 1980's and a chronology of her films from her first film in 1932 to *On Golden Pond* in 1981.

Edwards, Anne. *A Remarkable Woman: A Biography of Katharine Hepburn*. New York: William Morrow, 1985. Although it seems to relate a romanticized version of Hepburn's life, this biography includes detailed theater, film, radio, and television chronologies, a list of all of Hepburn's Academy Award nominations, and a long bibliography that lists many good references about Hepburn and about Hollywood and the theater in general.

Hepburn, Katharine. *The Making of The African Queen: Or, How I Went to Africa with Bogart, Bacall, and Huston and Almost Lost My Mind*. New York: Alfred A. Knopf, 1987. This is Hepburn's writing at its best as she recalls the making of *The African Queen* from her first awareness of the project through the trials of the location work in Africa, the completion of the film in the studio, and Bogart's Academy Award.

_____ . *Me: Stories of My Life*. New York: Alfred A. Knopf, 1991. This book lives up to its title, providing stories of Hepburn's life from childhood through 1990. Written in a warm, readable, almost telegraphic style, the book discusses her career, her films and plays, and her family in a personal manner. Many photographs are included.

Kanin, Garson. *Tracy and Hepburn*. New York: Viking Press, 1971. This very personal chronicle of the work and lives of Hepburn and Spencer Tracy is based on the author's long friendship with both and tells many stories of their lives together, both privately and professionally.

Morley, Sheridan. *Katharine Hepburn*. Boston: Little, Brown, 1984. This thorough retrospective of Hepburn's career, written by the son of one of Hepburn's former colleagues, provides detailed information about the progress of Hepburn's career and each of her pictures. Fourteen pages are devoted to a filmography, which provides thorough documentation about her films through 1984, her television work, and her stage work.

Katherine Socha

AILEEN CLARKE HERNANDEZ

Born: May 23, 1926; Brooklyn, New York

Areas of Achievement: Labor relations, social reform, and women's rights
Contribution: As president of the National Organization for Women (NOW), director of the International Ladies' Garment Workers Union, and commissioner of the Equal Employment Opportunity Commission, Aileen Hernandez has represented the interests of women and minorities in the forefront of social reform.

Early Life

Aileen Clarke was reared in Brooklyn by her parents Charles and Ethel Clarke, who had emigrated from Jamaica in the British West Indies and eventually became American citizens. Her mother was a costume maker and seamstress in the New York theater district, and her father worked in the art supply business. Aileen and her brothers were taught to cook and sew, since her parents believed that no gender distinctions should be made in employment. They also emphasized people should not be treated differently regardless of race or gender. This family value left an indelible mark on Aileen that would deeply influence her life and career. She was graduated from Bay Ridge Public School as valedictorian, and in 1943 from Bay Ridge High School as class salutatorian. Aileen received a scholarship to attend Howard University in Washington, D.C. She served as editor and writer for the campus paper *The Hilltop*, and wrote a column for the *Washington Tribune*. In 1946, she received honors in Kappa Mu Society, Howard's counterpart to Phi Beta Kappa.

Her political philosophy was molded by her college years in Washington, D.C., during the postwar period. She joined the student chapter of the National Association for the Advancement of Colored People (NAACP) and demonstrated against racial discrimination of the National Theatre, Lisner Auditorium, and the Thompson Restaurant chain. Her decision to participate in these early pickets stemmed largely from living as an African American in the United States. Venturing south for her college years at Howard, she experienced even more distinct discrimination as she traveled by train and waited for the segregated taxis in Washington, D.C., which were always the last in line. Believing that "democratic government requires full participation by all citizens," she supported equal rights for black World War II veterans returning to an unchanged segregated America.

After graduating magna cum laude from Howard University in 1947, with a degree in sociology and political science, Aileen Clark traveled to Norway as part of the International Student Exchange Program and studied comparative government. From 1947 to 1959, she attended New York University, the University of California at Los Angeles, and the University of Southern California. In 1959, she was awarded a master's degree in government, summa cum laude, from Los Angeles State College. In 1979 Southern Vermont College granted her an Honorary Doctorate in Humane Letters.

Life's Work

While attending New York University Graduate school, Aileen Clarke accepted an internship to the International Ladies' Garment Workers Union (ILGWU) Training Institute. She was hired in 1951 and transferred to the ILGWU Pacific Coast Region in California as an organizer. Eventually she served for eleven years in the ILGWU's West Coast office at Los Angeles as education director and public relations director. Her duties ranged from organizing social affairs to mobilizing strikes, pickets, and legislative lobbies. She was also responsible for naturalization classes for foreign-born union employees. In 1957, she married Alfonso Hernandez, a Mexican American garment worker whom she had met in Los Angeles. They were later divorced in 1961.

In 1961, her career shifted from union work to politics, managing a victorious campaign for Alan Cranston, as state controller. She was appointed assistant chief of the California Division of Fair Employment Practice Commission (FEPC), in 1962. In this position she supervised a staff of fifty in four field offices. While serving with the FEPC, she initiated a Technical Advisory Committee (TACT). The TACT report was a comprehensive analysis of industrial testing as it affects the hiring of minorities.

By this time she had acquired experience and recognition for her work in labor relations and fair employment practices. With the recommendation of California Governor Edmund G. "Pat" Brown, President Lyndon B. Johnson appointed her the first woman to the five-member commission of the Equal Employment Opportunity Commission. Her duties included coordinating the activities of state and local commissions with the National EEOC. During her term on the Commission, commercial airlines overturned their traditional policy of terminating female flight attendants when they married. After eighteen months of service, she resigned from the EEOC because she felt that the commission lacked any power to enforce its own policies. In 1966, she established her own consulting firm in San Francisco, Hernandez and Associates, to advise businesses, government, labor, and private groups in urban affairs, and for the purpose of hiring minorities and women.

Aileen was present in 1966 at the Third National Conference of the State Commissions on Women in Washington, D.C. Betty Friedan, author of the 1963 best-seller *The Feminine Mystique*, was also there and they spoke of the necessity to establish a civil rights movement for women. At that conference, the National Organization for Women (NOW) was created and Friedan was chosen as its first president. In 1967, NOW appointed Aileen vice president of the Western region. In 1971 she succeeded Friedan as president of NOW. Her leadership, and articulation of the women's movement were a real asset. Until 1971 many African American women viewed the women's movement as the elitist preserve of white middle-class women with nothing better to do. Aileen Hernandez considered NOW as an extension of the Civil Rights movement for all women. In one interview, Hernandez addressed the issue head on: "Until women, black as well as others, gain a sense of their own identity and feel that they have a real choice in society, nothing is going to happen in civil rights. It's not going to happen for Blacks; it's not going to happen for Mexican-Americans; it's not going to happen for women."

Summary

Aileen Hernandez's contributions to labor relations, the women's movement, equal opportunity, political activism, and community service compose an extensive list of accomplishments. Her dedication to public service has made her both a national and an international figure. She has represented the State Department abroad in Latin America, where she toured six countries, Argentina, Chile, Colombia, Peru, Uruguay, and Venezuela, lecturing in English and Spanish on trade unions, minorities, and the political system of the United States.

As president of NOW in 1973, she chaired the summer meeting in Boston of the International Feminist Planning Conference, bringing together women from thirty countries. At the invitation of the U.S. State Department and the Konrad Adenauer Foundation, in 1975 she attended the International Conference in Bonn, Germany, on *Minorities and the Metropolis*. She traveled to the People's Republic of China with an American Rights group in 1978. That same year, with the National Commission, she made a fact-finding tour of South Africa with the National Commission. The report of that regional study by the Commission published in 1981 entitled, *South Africa: Time Running Out*, received praise for its analysis of apartheid and U.S. policy in South Africa. She has also received international visitors on behalf of the United States from Japan, South Africa, Australia, New Zealand, Norway, Germany, Bangladesh, Belgium, Nigeria, and Sweden.

The numerous awards in recognition of her public service are impressive. She was chosen as Woman of the Year in 1961 by the Community Relations Conference of Southern California. Howard University honored its distinguished alumna in 1968 for Distinguished Postgraduate Achievement in the Fields of Labor and Public Service, and that same year she received the Charter Day Alumni Post Graduate Achievement in Labor and Public Services Award. *The San Francisco Examiner* named her one of the Ten Most Distinguished Women of the San Francisco Bay Area in 1969. The Bicentennial Award was granted to her in 1976 by the Trinity Baptist Church of San Mateo County. Equal Rights advocates commended her in 1981 for her service to the women's movement, and in 1984, the Friends of the San Francisco Commission on the Status of Women honored her. In 1985, The San Francisco League of Women Voters named her among the Ten Women Who Make a Difference, the National Urban Coalition recognized her service to urban communities, and the San Francisco Black Chamber of Commerce presented her with the Parren J. Mitchell Award for dedicated service to the African American community. The Memorial United Methodist Church commended her services to humanity in 1986 and Gamma Phi Delta Sorority made her an honorary member. She has also received awards in appreciation from the National Institute for Women of Color in 1987, and the following year from the Western District Conference on the National Association of Negro Business and Professional Women's Clubs as well as the San Francisco Convention and the Visitor's bureau. The Northern California American Civil Liberties Foundation conferred the Earl Warren Civil Liberties Award in 1989.

Bibliography

Banner, Lois W. *Women in Modern America: A Brief History.* 2d ed. San Diego: Harcourt Brace Jovanovich, 1984. A survey of the women's rights movement from the 1890's to 1984 that places Hernandez in the context of the formation of NOW.

Christmas, Walter. *Negroes in Public Affairs and Government.* Vol. 1. Yonkers, N.Y.: Educational Heritage, 1966. This specialized study, although dated, recognizes the work of Hernandez in the EEOC, labor relations, and NOW.

Dreyfus, Joel. "Civil Rights and the Women's Movement." *Black Enterprise* 8 (September, 1977): 35-37, 45. Includes Hernandez as the first African American woman to hold a national office and her vision of the women's movement as part of the larger Civil Rights movement.

Hartmann, Susan M. *From Margin to Mainstream: American Women and Politics Since 1960.* New York: Alfred A. Knopf, 1989. Hartmann's study of women who emerged on the American political scene between 1960 and 1980 assesses their impact on public policy.

Lewis, Ida. "Conversation: Ida Lewis and Aileen Hernandez." *Essence* 1 (February, 1971): 20-25, 74-75. An interview with Hernandez during her presidency of NOW in which she speaks about her role and the issues of the women's movement, civil rights, and equal opportunity.

Emily Teipe

LORENA HICKOK

Born: March 7, 1893; East Troy, Wisconsin
Died: May 1, 1968; Rhinebeck, New York
Area of Achievement: Journalism
Contribution: One of the first female political analysts in American history, Hickok became perhaps Eleanor Roosevelt's closest friend, the New Deal's primary reporter on Depression conditions, and a leading contributor to the women's movement.

Early Life

Alice Lorena Hickok (she later reversed her first and second names) was born on March 7, 1893, in an apartment above the creamery where her father worked in East Troy, Wisconsin. Her mother, Anna J. Hickok, died from a stroke in 1906, leaving thirteen-year-old Lorena and her two younger sisters at the mercy of an abusive father. Addison Hickok, an ill-tempered butter maker, allegedly raped Lorena (as she later stated privately), resulting in her departure from the family home before she reached the age of fourteen.

Lorena's interest in literature and writing commenced at a very early age. Her mean-spirited father subjected her to frequent harangues because she persistently locked herself in her room with only books to keep her company. He also ridiculed an avid youthful commitment to reform politics his daughter developed when she witnessed Mary Pickford's performance in a theatrical version of Harriet Beecher Stowe's *Uncle Tom's Cabin* (1852). The young girl developed a fascination with news reporting when she was seized by an irrepressible urge to notify hometown residents that an assassin had shot President William McKinley.

As Lorena's remaining family moved from town to town, she followed at a safe distance, usually seeking employment as a domestic servant. Although schoolwork was drudgery for her, her prizewinning essay on Abraham Lincoln impressed a teacher who recognized her intellectual talents and encouraged more serious study habits.

Painfully shy and overweight, Lorena intermittently attended Lawrence University in Appleton, Wisconsin, until she dropped out when no sorority asked her to pledge. She briefly wrote for the Battle Creek, Michigan, *Journal* before becoming society editor for two years at the Milwaukee *Sentinel*. Working at the *Sentinel* proved to be immensely helpful, since it enabled Lorena to perfect the techniques that established her reputation for brilliance.

Lorena's meager salary as a reporter proved to be unsatisfactory, so "Hick" (the nickname friends and colleagues assigned to her) sought a more remunerative career as a press agent. This effort also failed, as did a journalistic attempt in 1917 with the New York *Tribune*. Desperate for money, she briefly became one of New York's first policewomen before moving to Minneapolis in 1918 for one final try at college.

This time she succeeded. Attending the University of Minnesota by day and writing stories for the Minneapolis *Tribune* by night under the byline of Alice L. Hickok, the pudgy, pipe- and cigar-smoking young reporter acquired a large metropolitan following. Standing on the sideline covering the Minnesota Golden Gophers football team, Hick earned the respect of the otherwise all-male sports staff. Her stories ranged in subject from gridiron greats such as Harold "Red" Grange to America's first winner of the Nobel Prize in Literature, Sinclair Lewis.

The Lewis interview convinced Lorena to become a novelist. When the experiment proved disappointing, however, she returned to reporting the news with William Randolph Hearst's New York *Mirror*. So successful were her stories that the Associated Press made her one of its few female reporters. At the age of thirty-five, "Fatty" Hickok had finally arrived. No longer the butt of jokes, she moved in the highest journalistic circles.

Life's Work

Lorena Hickok's first major political assignment took her to Hyde Park and Albany, New York, in 1928 to cover Franklin D. Roosevelt's first gubernatorial campaign. Since male reporters got the choice stories, Hickok found herself covering Franklin's wife Eleanor, who, like Hickok, suffered from deep insecurities. When the two women got to know each other through Malvina "Tommy" Thompson, who simultaneously served as secretary for Eleanor and the New York State Democratic Committee, they quickly became friends. Hickok covered New York's first family for four years following her original interview with Eleanor Roosevelt on November 7, 1928. After FDR soundly defeated Herbert Hoover in the 1932 presidential election, Hickok followed the Roosevelts to the White House.

As the Depression deepened, Hickok moved closer to Eleanor Roosevelt, whom she quickly analyzed as a "woman [basically] unhappy about something." Conversely, as Roosevelt learned about Hickok's difficult life, a close bond of friendship formed between the two women. The Associated Press exploited Hickok's penetration of Eleanor's inner circle of advisers, promoting her to "Mrs. R's personal reporter."

Hickok consequently began spending weekends at Val-Kil, the First Lady's private retreat, miles away from the presidential hubbub surrounding the "big house on the Hudson." Hickok also became close friends with Eleanor Roosevelt's compatriots and business partners, Marion Dickerman and Nancy Cook, who helped to run a private school for disabled children and the furniture factory that was associated with it. When an assassin's bullet narrowly missed President Roosevelt and killed Chicago mayor Anton Cermak, Hickok rushed to Eleanor's side. For the next ten years, the two women were frequent companions.

Since Hickok's relationship with Eleanor Roosevelt made it difficult to write White House news objectively, she left the Associated Press in 1933 to become the New Deal's chief investigative reporter. Specifically, Hickok became Harry L. Hopkins' special investigator. Hopkins, who ran the Federal Emergency Relief Administration, which provided welfare for the 25.2 percent of the population who were unemployed, sent Hickok out into "the field," meaning the country. "Tell me what you see and hear," Hopkins ordered Hickok. "Don't ever pull punches."

Hickok rarely disappointed Hopkins or the president. Traveling to thirty-two states and the Virgin Islands, Hickok poignantly described the misery suffered by "one third of a nation ill-housed, ill-clad and ill-nourished." Her appointment was a nearly perfect choice. Roosevelt wanted to prevent politics and bureaucratic waste from interfering with the vital process of relief, and Hickok gave him an in-depth analysis of the situation. Frequently, she and Eleanor Roosevelt traveled together among the desperately poor, enhancing the First Lady's reputation as the nation's number-one humanitarian.

When Hickok entered a town in Georgia, California, or Massachusetts, she frequently worked under a veil of politically enforced secrecy. Although local officials sometimes knew that she represented Franklin D. Roosevelt and the New Deal, she did not allow interviews, and her reports, which FDR restricted to his cabinet and "brain trust," profoundly influenced the New Deal's shift from pure relief (welfare) toward the creation of jobs through the Civilian Works Administration and the Works Progress Administration. By 1936, Franklin Roosevelt and Harry Hopkins viewed Lorena Hickok as their "voice of the people."

Hickok's years of journalism paid handsome dividends. Her reports to Harry Hopkins were candid, clever, and very effective political analysis. She also persuaded her old newspaper contacts to submit confidentially stories analyzing local relief conditions. Because Hickok abhorred publicity and worked in almost total anonymity, most of her achievements escaped media attention. Knowing that they could trust her, the Roosevelts increasingly relied upon her political judgment. Hickok covered labor disputes, patronage struggles, and the scandalous bureaucratic waste that infiltrated government at all levels.

In 1936, President Roosevelt appointed Hickok as his chief political field reporter for the National Emergency Council—covering all forty-eight states. The task of predicting political outcomes was much more difficult than analyzing Depression conditions. Hickok misjudged Republican strength throughout the country. Her forecast that FDR trailed Kansas Governor Alfred M. Landon looked ridiculous after Roosevelt crushed his Republican opponent 523 to 8 in the Electoral College. Recognizing that she had outlived her political usefulness, Hickok resigned her position in 1937 and worked for the New York World's Fair until 1940.

Despite her departure from the New Deal, Hickok remained Eleanor Roosevelt's very good friend and one of New York's most prominent and powerful Democratic women. She served as Executive Director of the Women's Division of the Democratic National Committee from 1940 to 1945. Eleanor Roosevelt invited Hickok to live in the White House during World War II, and it became Hickok's residence until FDR died in April, 1945. Hickok finished her professional career as an officer of the New York Democratic State Committee from 1947 to 1952.

During the 1950's, Hickok's eating and drinking patterns exacerbated her diabetes, resulting in partial blindness. As her condition worsened, she moved from New York City to Hyde Park, New York, in order to remain close to Eleanor Roosevelt. The two women collaborated on a book entitled *Ladies of Courage* (1954), which focused on women who played prominent roles in American politics. In 1962, Hickok wrote *Reluctant First Lady*, an incisive analysis of Eleanor Roosevelt.

During the 1960's, Hickok descended into poverty, and she depended upon Eleanor Roosevelt's financial support until the former First Lady died in 1962. Hickok finished the final six years of her life living near the Roosevelt estate, where she died on May 1, 1968. Significantly, Hickok's will donated her personal and professional papers to the Franklin D. Roosevelt Presidential Library but stipulated that they remain closed until ten years after her death.

Summary

Lorena Hickok was one of America's first great female reporters. Her stories were witty, tersely analytical, factual, and unbiased. When Eleanor Roosevelt persuaded Harry Hopkins to hire Hickok as the New Deal's chief investigator, Hickok delivered some of the most acute analyses ever written about the Great Depression. Hopkins thought that eventually they would constitute perhaps the best history of the Depression ever written.

In the years following Hickok's death and the opening of her papers at the Roosevelt Library, her relationship with Eleanor Roosevelt became the subject of some controversy. Numerous historians and journalists commented on the fact that the two women spent so much time together. Because Hickok apparently became involved in several lesbian relationships, scholars have speculated about the extent of her involvement with Eleanor Roosevelt. Most historians have concluded that the relationship essentially represented an emotional dependence rather than a sexual alliance. Whatever the nature of their relationship, Hickok and Roosevelt remained friends for life.

Lorena Hickok was much more than Eleanor Roosevelt's close friend. She, perhaps more than any other American, became the country's chief observer of the Great Depression. Because President Roosevelt, out of political necessity, kept Hickok's reports secret, the vital role she played in serving her government and people received very little credit until years after she died. She never became one of the New Deal's "celebrities." Her contributions and accomplishments usually went to others—Harry Hopkins, Eleanor Roosevelt, and the president himself. Yet that was the way Hickok wanted it. She never sought the limelight.

Her principal regret focused on the newspaper career that she sacrificed for Franklin and Eleanor Roosevelt. "I was just about the top gal reporter in the country. . . . God knows," she remembered in her later years. Being in government, however, meant more than reporting the news. It meant making the news.

Because of her closeness to the First Lady, Hickok penetrated FDR's inner circle. Playing her unique role to the hilt, Hickok made many significant contributions. Finishing the job started by Louis M. Howe (FDR's personal secretary), Hickok brought Eleanor Roosevelt out of her shell. If Harry Hopkins was Franklin's alter ego, Lorena Hickok was Eleanor's. She performed a service that was appreciated by many but credited by few. The fact that she labored in obscurity only delayed the acclaim that she deserved. In death, Hickok's public and private papers elevated her to a position of prominence and recognition she never pursued in life.

Bibliography
Chafe, William H. "Eleanor Roosevelt: 1884-1962." In *Portraits of American Women: From Settlement to the Present*, edited by G. J. Barker-Benfield and Catherine Clinton. New York: St. Martin's Press, 1991. This article lent balance to the historical analysis of the relationship between Eleanor Roosevelt and Lorena Hickok. It omits the subjective or prejudicial interpretations that characterized many of the earlier interpretations.

_____ . *The Paradox of Change: American Women in the Twentieth Century.* New York: Oxford University Press, 1991. An objective observation of contributions made by American women, including Eleanor Roosevelt and Lorena Hickok.

Faber, Doris. *The Life of Lorena Hickok.* New York: William Morrow, 1980. This work created a mild sensation in the popular press when it appeared in print because of its allegations of a lesbian relationship between Lorena Hickok and Eleanor Roosevelt.

Hickok, Lorena. *One Third of a Nation: Lorena Hickok Reports on the Great Depression.* Edited by Richard Lowitt and Maurine Beasley. Urbana: University of Illinois Press, 1981. This fine collection of letters from the Lorena Hickok Papers in the Franklin D. Roosevelt Presidential Library offers an excellent insight into the depths of the depression and the quality of Hickok's perceptive analytical essays.

_____ . *Reluctant First Lady.* New York: Dodd, Mead, 1962. This short work constitutes a valuable contribution to understanding Hickok's friendship with Eleanor Roosevelt even though the author went to considerable lengths to downplay their close interdependence.

Olson, James S., ed. *Historical Dictionary of the New Deal.* Westport, Conn.: Greenwood Press, 1985. A good collection of articles written by historians about prominent events, agencies, and persons during the Depression, including a balanced analysis of Lorena Hickok by H. Carleton Marlow.

Roosevelt, Eleanor, and Lorena Hickok. *Ladies of Courage.* New York: G. P. Putnam's Sons, 1954. Hickok wrote the chapter on Roosevelt in this book, which is an excellent survey of political advances made by women during the 1930's and 1940's.

Ross, Ishbel. *Ladies of the Press.* Reprint. New York: Arno Press, 1974. This book provides perhaps the best summary of Lorena Hickok's journalistic career and indicates the great potential she exhibited at the time she sacrificed that career in order to work with Franklin and Eleanor Roosevelt.

J. Christopher Schnell

MARGUERITE HIGGINS

Born: September 3, 1920; Hong Kong, China
Died: January 3, 1966; Washington, D.C.
Area of Achievement: Journalism
Contribution: While covering the Korean War, Higgins became the first woman to win a Pulitzer Prize for international reporting.

Early Life
Marguerite Higgins was born on September 3, 1920, in the British crown colony of Hong Kong. Her Irish American father, Lawrence Daniel Higgins, was a World War I veteran flier who married a French woman, Marguerite Godard, in Paris before taking her to Hong Kong, where their only child was born. As an infant, the young Marguerite was stricken with malaria and was sent to recuperate at a health facility in Vietnam, the start of what would become a life of exotic travels. After a few years working as a freight agent for a shipping line in Hong Kong, Lawrence Higgins moved the family to Oakland, California, in 1923.

Leaving the exotic locales of the Far East for a middle-class existence in Oakland, the family purchased a modest home in the suburbs. Marguerite's father found employment as a stockbroker and then as a bank manager after losing his job in the stock market crash in 1929. His wife supplemented their earnings by teaching French at the Anna Head School in Berkeley, where her multilingual daughter was enrolled on scholarship. Marguerite remembered these years as a dreary interlude as her father sought solace in the bottle and her mother became prone to fainting spells brought on by stress.

In 1937, Marguerite, or Maggie as she later became known, entered the University of California at Berkeley, where she joined the staff of the school newspaper as a freshman. The *Daily Californian* had a reputation as one of the best college newspapers in the country, and it was here in the newsroom that Higgins discovered what would become her life's work. In 1941, she graduated cum laude with a degree in journalism.

After graduation she sought work with a newspaper, the first step in attaining her goal of becoming a foreign correspondent. Rebuffed in her attempts to find employment, she returned to school to hone her journalistic skills by entering the graduate program at the Columbia School of Journalism in New York City. While a student, she worked part-time as a campus correspondent for the *New York Herald Tribune*. Upon graduating in June of 1942 with a master of science degree in journalism, Marguerite began full-time employment with the paper.

Life's Work
Marguerite Higgins sought entry into the largely masculine ranks of professional journalism at an opportune time. With many male reporters joining the armed forces in the 1940's, positions were available that had been formerly closed to most women.

During her tenure at the *Tribune*, her affairs with various male staff members contributed to Higgins' reputation for using her formidable sex appeal to advance her career.

During her first year at the *Tribune*, Higgins was married to Stanley Moore, a professor of philosophy at Harvard University and scion of a wealthy California family. Shortly after their marriage in 1942, Stanley was inducted into the armed forces. Their marriage, however, was short-lived because of the exigencies of wartime separation as well as Marguerite's frequently publicized infidelities.

By 1943, Higgins was one of the few *Tribune* staffers to receive a byline. Her determination and ambition were demonstrated while procuring her first overseas assignment. Unable to secure a position as a foreign correspondent, Higgins violated protocol by bypassing her editors and taking her request directly to the owner's wife, Helen Rogers Reid, who, besides taking an active role in the management of the *Tribune*, was known for her feminist stance on many issues. In 1944, Higgins took her place along with seven other war correspondents on the *Queen Mary* en route to England, where she was first headquartered at the London bureau. Confined to the home front in London, Higgins was determined to report from the battlefield as she saw 1944 draw to a close. War reporting had steadily become an obsession for Higgins, having been reared in a household that celebrated her father's wartime exploits as an aviator. After a bout with jaundice that landed her in a hospital, Higgins finally received the necessary clearance to join her colleagues in Paris.

Assigned to the Berlin bureau in the last year of the war, Higgins was still waiting to see frontline action. Her opportunity arrived in March, 1945, when the Eighth Army Air Force offered to allow journalists to view sections of Germany recently devastated by bombing raids. Although her career as a war correspondent during World War II lasted only six weeks, she managed to cover the liberation of the concentration camps at Buchenwald and Dachau as well as the capture of Munich. Her reporting merited the Army campaign ribbon for outstanding service under difficult conditions and the New York Newspaper Women's Club Award as best foreign correspondent of 1945 for her coverage of the events surrounding the evacuation of Dachau.

It was in this, her first war, that Marguerite Higgins developed her reputation as a war correspondent. Russell Hill, her senior at the Paris bureau, attributed her success more to her courage than her writing skill, admitting "Personally I never thought her a great writer, but few could beat her reporting skill." Higgins went on to report on the Nuremberg Trials, the treason trial of Marshal Philippe Pétain, and the Berlin blockade as well as the developing Cold War.

In 1947, at age twenty-six, Higgins was promoted to Berlin bureau chief for the *Tribune*. Ill-equipped for such a supervisory position, she gained a reputation for pettiness for her refusal to be scooped by other publications, considering it a personal affront if such an instance occurred. In Berlin, Higgins met the love of her life, Major General William "Bill" Hall, director of Army intelligence and married father of four children at home in the United States. Higgins and Hall were eventually married in 1953 and had two children together.

In May, 1950, Higgins was transferred to Tokyo. This was a major blow since she realized that this assignment was out of the journalistic limelight and that her predecessor had been fortunate to get one story a week published. In the words of her fellow correspondent, Keyes Beech, she found her new position "about as exciting as a duck pond." Little did Higgins realize that in her new position as the *Tribune* Far East bureau chief she would cover her greatest story. On June 25, 1950, North Korea crossed the thirty-eighth parallel, inaugurating the Korean War.

Higgins covered the fall of Seoul for the *Tribune*, barely escaping ahead of invading Communist troops. She was soon joined by a much more seasoned war reporter for that paper, Homer Bigart, and their professional rivalry became legendary. The *Tribune* management believed that Higgins should return to Tokyo to resume her position as bureau chief. She refused and was given the ultimatum to either return or be fired. She stayed and reported the first skirmishes of the war until she received orders to leave Korea immediately. Lieutenant General Walton W. Walker, commander of the American forces in Korea, had issued an edict banning all women, claiming that "there are no facilities for ladies at the front." Higgins again enlisted the aid of Helen Rogers Reid to circumvent protocol. Appealing the decision directly to General Douglas MacArthur, Walker's superior, Higgins received permission to return to the battlefront.

During the war, Higgins covered many of the major campaigns, and her exploits included landing with the Marines under enemy fire at Inchon. She gained the respect of her male counterparts as well as the foot soldiers for sharing in their hardships. Her reports on the war regularly appeared in the *Tribune*, sometimes on the same page as her competitor Homer Bigart. In October, 1950, *Life* magazine ran a feature on Higgins accompanied by an array of photographs of her in battle fatigues, which contributed to the legend of this woman war reporter. In 1951, she published *War in Korea*, an account of her combat coverage that went on to become a best-seller. That same year Higgins, along with five other correspondents, was awarded the Pulitzer Prize in the international-reporting category, the first woman to be so honored. Over the next few years she would be the recipient of dozens of awards, including the Overseas Press Club's George Polk Award, the Marine Corps Reserve Officers Award, and the 1951 Woman of the Year Award from the Associated Press.

In 1953, Higgins was in Vietnam covering the French debacle at Dien Bien Phu, when her close friend, photographer Robert Capa, was killed by a land mine only a few feet away. While in Vietnam, she received word that she had been granted a visa to visit the Soviet Union, the first American reporter to be allowed such access since the death of Joseph Stalin. From this excursion came her next book, published in 1955, *Red Plush and Black Bread*, an account of her 13,500-mile journey through the Soviet Union. Her book, *News Is a Singular Thing*, was released the same year. Because she was viewed as an expert on Russian affairs, *U.S. News and World Report* published a lengthy interview with her in 1956, recounting her travels behind the Iron Curtain. Following her journalistic instinct for being in the right place at the right time, Higgins covered the Congo crisis in 1961. She was the first *Tribune* reporter to report from this

African region since Henry Morton Stanley passed through while searching for David Livingstone in 1877. In 1963, Higgins returned to Vietnam. In the prescient *Our Vietnam Nightmare* (1965), she described the dangers of United States involvement in Vietnam.

After leaving the *Tribune* in late 1963, she moved to Long Island, New York, and contributed weekly columns to *Newsday*. Continuing her travels abroad, she made her tenth trip to Vietnam in 1965. During this trip, Higgins contracted the tropical disease, leishmaniasis, and was hospitalized at Walter Reed Hospital upon her return to the United States. Two months later, on January 3, 1966, she died while in a coma. She was buried at Arlington National Cemetery.

Summary

A soldier's daughter and wife, Marguerite Higgins made war reporting her life's work. Although not a standard bearer for feminism, she challenged the traditional female stereotype so prevalent in the 1950's. While she often embellished her accomplishments, the reality of what Higgins actually achieved in her short life is testimony to her heroic career. As witness to the major conflicts of the mid-twentieth century, she had to contend with double standards in the ranks of the male-dominated press corps as well as within the military establishment that she so ardently covered. It is somewhat ironic that although she published six books in between assignments, she would not be remembered primarily for her writing skills but instead for her intelligence and courage. What is certain is that Marguerite Higgins achieved a distinguished record as a war reporter, ultimately losing her life to a tropical disease contracted while in pursuit of the news in the far-flung reaches of the world.

Bibliography

Desmond, Robert W. *Tides of War: World News Reporting, 1940-1945*. Iowa City: University of Iowa Press, 1984. The fourth in a series on international news reporting, this volume reviews coverage of events preceding and including World War II. The experiences of hundreds of journalists are described against the backdrop of the era.

Edwards, Julia. *Women of the World: The Great Foreign Correspondents*. Boston: Houghton Mifflin, 1988. A series of short studies of important female foreign correspondents placed with the historical context of women and international reporting. The author debunks the notion that Higgins was the first woman to receive the Pulitzer Prize for journalism; Higgins was, however, the first to be recognized in the category of international reporting.

Kluger, Richard. *The Paper: The Life and Death of the New York Herald Tribune*. New York: Alfred A. Knopf, 1986. This is a history of the *Tribune* from its inception in 1835 through the early 1980's. An excellent account of Higgins' relationship with the paper and other journalists such as Homer Bigart is given.

Knightly, Phillip. *The First Casualty*. New York: Harcourt Brace Jovanovich, 1975. An overview of the role of the wartime correspondent and how much they should be relied on for accurate news reporting. The author provides a critical look at war journalism dating back to the Crimean War in an attempt to distinguish fact from fiction.

May, Antoinette. *Witness to War: A Biography of Marguerite Higgins.* New York: Beaufort Books, 1983. This extremely readable account is the only comprehensive biography of Higgins' life. Relying on secondary materials, May documents not only Higgins' wartime experiences but also her sexual liaisons.

Mydans, Carl. "Girl War Correspondent." *Life* 29 (October 2, 1950): 51-52. This article was significant in creating Higgins' image of the courageous yet sexy war correspondent. Although informed by prevalent 1950's stereotypes, it does convey a sense of Higgins' accomplishments as a journalist.

Mitchel P. Roth

MARGARET HILLIS

Born: October 1, 1921; Kokomo, Indiana

Area of Achievement: Music

Contribution: One of the twentieth century's leading choral conductors, Margaret Hillis achieved recognition in a field that was one of the last bastions of male domination in the arts.

Early Life

Margaret Hillis, the only daughter (there were three sons) born to Glen R. Hillis and Bernice Haynes Hillis, was reared in her hometown, Kokomo, Indiana. She came from a family of high achievers for whom the aggressive pursuit of excellence was a way of life. Her maternal grandfather, Elwood Haynes, for example, invented the rotary gas-valve engine, Stellite (a cutting-tool alloy), and a practical horseless carriage (preserved in the Smithsonian Institution).

Margaret began taking piano lessons at the age of five, and she attended concerts as far away as Chicago and New York because of her love of music, which was shared by her mother and grandmother. Among the artists she heard as a youngster were the famed Polish pianist and politician Ignace Jan Paderewski and the celebrated Danish opera star Kirsten Flagstad; she heard the latter on many occasions. By the age of eight, Margaret was writing music and, over the next several years, delving into the mysteries of such musical instruments as the saxophone, the French horn, and the double bass, all of which were then considered "unusual" and "unsuitable" for female performers.

Despite her skills as an instrumentalist, Margaret became enamored of conducting when, at the age of nine, she heard the Sousa band. Her interest in conducting was reinforced when, at the age of thirteen, she heard her first symphonic concert in Indianapolis. A year later, she made her first conducting appearance with her high school orchestra; the work she chose was the Overture to Carl Maria von Weber's opera *Der Freischütz.* Her affluent parents believed that she needed the benefits a private school could bestow, so they sent her to Tudor Hall, a girls' school in Indianapolis, for her junior and senior years. The negative aspect of this experience was the school's lack of a band or orchestra. A well-rounded teenager, Margaret occupied herself in such pursuits as horseback riding, swimming, water skiing, and golfing at a championship level.

When she entered the Indiana University (IU) music school in Bloomington in the fall of 1940, she majored in piano because the school did not then offer a major in conducting, her first love. She did, however, gain orchestral experience by playing the double bass in the IU orchestra. In an accelerated wartime program, she completed her junior year in December of 1942. Because she had taken flying lessons during this period, she left college to attend the Navy's ground school in Muncie, Indiana. She quickly became a civilian flight instructor, a position that occupied her for the next year and a half. Her imperfect vision without glasses prevented her from fulfilling her wish to join the Women's Auxiliary Service Pilots (WASP).

Upon her return to the university, Margaret continued to teach flying to private students on a part-time basis while changing her major to composition. This choice was predicated on the reality that such advanced theoretical subjects as counterpoint and fugue, which formed part of the composition program, were essential for a conductor. Her composition teacher, Bernhard Heiden, suggested that she concentrate on choral rather than orchestral conducting, because the choral area would provide fewer obstacles to a woman. She took his advice and went to the Juilliard School in New York City in 1947 to study with Robert Shaw and Julius Hereford. She became Shaw's assistant and, in this role, was able to conduct his Collegiate Chorale.

During the period from 1948 to 1951, Hillis gained further experience by directing the Metropolitan Youth Chorale, an amateur group, in Brooklyn; this ensemble gave two large-scale concerts annually and also performed in schools and churches. The musician had thus completed her apprenticeship and embarked upon what was to become one of the most astonishing musical careers achieved by an American woman.

Life's Work

Margaret Hillis' professional career can be traced to her direction of the Tangle-wood Alumni Chorus, formed in the fall of 1950, with which ensemble she led a full season of concerts in New York, with important performances being broadcast by the radio station WNYC. The following season, under the name Concert Choir, the ensemble was heard at the American Music Festival in Brooklyn and, on May 12 and May 26, 1952, in two Carnegie Hall concerts in which such works as Franz Joseph Haydn's Theresin Mass in B-flat Major, Antonio Vivaldi's *Gloria*, and Paul Hindemith's *Six Chansons* were performed to favorable critical notice. In the 1953-1954 season, Hillis broadened the group's repertoire to include works by Baroque composers Claudio Monteverdi and Giacomo Carissimi as well as such twentieth century masters as Ned Rorem. Her interpretation of Johann Sebastian Bach's colossal Mass in B minor in April of 1954 drew mixed reviews, but her all-Stravinsky program, which included the opera *Mavra*, caused critic-composer Virgil Thomson to declare that she was possessed of "a first-class musical temperament, powerful, relentless, thorough."

With Arnold Gamson's American Chamber Opera Society, the now-quite-visible conductor gave the American premieres of two eighteenth-century operas, Christoph Willibald Gluck's *Paris and Helen* and Jean-Philippe Rameau's *Hippolyte et Aricie*. Her all-Beethoven concert on January 21, 1955, with the New York Concert Choir and Orchestra was lauded by such critics as Paul Henry Lang. Other performances during that year, at Town Hall in New York, included works by Robert Moevs and Jan Meyerowitz, winners of the Fromm Music Foundation's awards, and by Arnold Schoenberg (*Friede auf Erden*, for a capella chorus) and Leoš Janáček (*Children's Rhymes*).

Working in New York until 1962, Hillis did much freelancing in addition to teaching at the Union Theological Seminary. She came into contact with such literary figures as the novelist and playwright Thornton Wilder, the poet Langston Hughes, and the noted opera satirist Anna Russell. A major turning point in her career came when Fritz Reiner, conductor of the Chicago Symphony Orchestra, invited Hillis to establish the Chicago Symphony Chorus in 1957. This she did while commuting from New York for a five-year period; in addition, she continued her otherwise frenetic activities, which included acceptance of an invitation from the U.S. Department of State to represent her country at the Brussels World Fair by conducting the American Concert Choir at that highly visible event. Over the years, the Chicago Symphony Chorus, consisting of a core of professionals and talented amateurs, has been recognized as one of the finest choral ensembles in the world. After settling in the Chicago area, Hillis engaged in teaching at Northwestern University and conducting the Elgin, Illinois, Symphony Orchestra, while accepting guest conducting engagements with the major orchestras of Cleveland, Minneapolis, St. Louis, Baltimore, and Milwaukee, as well as Washington, D.C.'s National Symphony. She has also served frequently as a clinician and workshop director throughout the country. She even managed to handle the duties of choral director for the Cleveland Orchestra from 1969 to 1971.

Margaret Hillis made her debut in a Chicago Symphony subscription concert in 1972 when she substituted for conductor Rafael Kubelik and directed the orchestra and chorus in George Frideric Handel's *Jeptha*. In the bicentennial year, she inaugurated a popular "Do it yourself *Messiah*," in which members of the audience actively participate in performing this beloved oratorio. In the same year, she recorded, with the American Concert Choir, the choral anthem of Ernest Bloch's *America: An Epic Rhapsody*, which concluded a performance conducted by Leopold Stokowski and the Symphony of the Air. In 1977, Hillis made national headlines when she stepped in at the last moment to replace Sir Georg Solti, conductor of the Chicago Symphony Orchestra, in a performance of Gustav Mahler's gargantuan Eighth Symphony in Carnegie Hall. She had proved to herself and to the world that both were ready for a female conductor to be at the helm of a world-class orchestra. One year later to the day, on October 31, she conducted the same work at her alma mater, Indiana University, with that institution's orchestra and chorus, a total of 490 musicians, at the Musical Arts Center in Bloomington.

Numerous awards and honors have been bestowed upon Margaret Hillis. In 1978, for example, she received the Leadership for Freedom Award from the Women's Scholarship Association of Roosevelt University and the Alumni Achievement Award of Kappa Kappa Gamma, and was named "Woman of the Year in Classical Music" by the *Ladies' Home Journal*. Honorary doctorates in music were conferred upon her by such schools as Temple University and Indiana University, and honorary doctorates in fine arts were awarded to her by St. Mary's College at Notre Dame and North Park College, Chicago. From 1977 to 1991, she received Grammy Awards from the National Academy of Recording Arts and Sciences eight times for best classical choral recordings with orchestra in such works as Giuseppe Verdi's *Requiem*, Ludwig van Beethovan's *Missa Solemnis*, Franz Joseph Haydn's *The Creation*, Johannes Brahms's

A German Requiem (twice, once with Georg Solti and once with James Levine), Carl Orff's *Carmina Burana*, Hector Berlioz's *The Damnation of Faust*, and J. S. Bach's Mass in B minor. She also received a Grammy for her work in the best opera recording of 1985, Arnold Schoenberg's *Moses und Aron*.

In 1993, Margaret Hillis stepped down as director of the Chicago Symphony Chorus, as a new era for the orchestra began under the baton of Daniel Barenboim.

Summary

Margaret Hillis has had a profound influence on the world of music, particularly choral music, in the twentieth century. Although her original goal in life was to conduct a symphony orchestra, she came to grips with the reality that women were perceived to be unsuited to command such an ensemble. Undeterred, she achieved this goal later in her career through the back door, so to speak, all the while building her reputation as one of America's foremost choral directors. She recognized and seized opportunities when they arose and, through sheer grit and effort, bolstered by a prodigious talent and a capacity for growth, moved into the top ranks of professional musicians. When the opportunity came to fill in for Georg Solti at Carnegie Hall, she was ready, willing, and decidedly able.

Apart from her achievements in the choral field, Hillis has, over the years, made the transition to orchestral conductor with skill and aplomb; her knowledge of both the choral and orchestral repertories makes her a double threat. Furthermore, her contributions as a teacher of choral conducting and choral singing have brought her to a pinnacle of success that has inspired a new generation of conductors, both male and female. Her thorough knowledge of her craft has made her an outstanding role model, especially for women conductors. Her place in the musical history of her country is secure.

Bibliography

Ericson, Raymond. "Miss Hillis Carries Her Baton Lightly." *The New York Times*, November 2, 1977, p. C17. A detailed account of Hillis' last-minute preparations for her eventful appearance on October 31, 1977, in Carnegie Hall before the Chicago Symphony Orchestra and Chorus in which she replaced Sir Georg Solti on the podium in a performance of Mahler's *Eighth Symphony*. The acclaim accorded this feat was such that it launched Hillis on a secondary career as an orchestral conductor and gained for her access to other major orchestras.

Le Page, Jane Weiner. *Women Composers, Conductors, and Musicians of the Twentieth Century*. 3 vols. Metuchen, N.J.: Scarecrow Press, 1980-1988. Le Page's useful biography examines the career of Margaret Hillis through the 1970's.

McElroy, George, and Jane W. Stedman. "Chorus Lady." *Opera News* 38, no. 15 (February 16, 1974): 10-13. Focuses on the trials and tribulations associated with the early years of Hillis' association with her Chicago Symphony Chorus, and details the qualities for which she looks when she auditions potential singers in her ensemble.

Rhein, John von. "The Active Voice." *Chicago Tribune*, April 12, 1987. Emphasizing Hillis' role in developing the Chicago Symphony Chorus into a world-class ensemble, this article stresses the conductor's rehearsal techniques, musical philosophy, and relationship with her choristers.

Samuelson, Jane. "For the Love of Music." *Chicago*, April, 1980, 192-195, 230, 233-236. A comprehensive account of Margaret Hillis' career, this excellent, well-researched article examines major performances, career highlights, and significant honors and awards. It includes perceptive commentary by musicians with whom she has worked and by critics who have reviewed her performances.

David Z. Kushner

OVETA CULP HOBBY

Born: January 19, 1905; Killeen, Texas

Area of Achievement: Government and politics
Contribution: As army officer, cabinet member, and business leader, Hobby was a pioneer for American women in many areas of public life.

Early Life

Oveta Culp was born on January 19, 1905, to Isaac William Culp and Emma Hoover Culp. Her father was an attorney who was first elected to the Texas state legislature in 1919; her mother was a housewife who was active in the woman suffrage movement. From her earliest childhood, Oveta's father took a personal interest in her training and schooling. Isaac Culp instilled an interest in public life in Oveta and convinced her that her gender did not constitute a barrier to any ambition she might have had. It was still somewhat unusual for a woman of her day, even one of the educated classes, to attend college. Not only did Oveta complete her undergraduate work at Mary Hardin-Baylor College, but she also studied law at the main campus of the University of Texas.

At a very young age and only partly through the influence of her father, Oveta Culp began securing positions in the law, business, and government matrix of Texas. At the age of twenty, she was working as assistant city attorney in Houston. For several years, she served as parliamentarian, or chief clerk, for the lower house of the Texas state legislature, a position that enabled her to make extensive contacts in Texas politics. She made some use of these contacts when she decided to run for the legislature as a Democrat in 1929. Despite her efforts, she was not elected; women in electoral politics were to be more truly a phenomenon of her children's generation. On February 23, 1931, Oveta took a more conventional step when she married William P. Hobby, a man some thirty years her senior who was the publisher of the Houston *Post* and a former governor of Texas.

Life's Work

Marriage, however, did not mean retirement to domesticity and obscurity for Oveta Culp Hobby, as it did for many women of the period. Hobby immediately threw herself into both the business and editorial aspects of her husband's newspaper business. Starting out as a research editor, she moved steadily up the hierarchy of the newspaper until 1938, when she was named executive vice president. These were not ceremonial positions; Hobby's husband, busy managing other sectors of his extensive business interests, delegated much of his responsibility for the *Post* to his wife.

Houston during the 1930's was a much smaller city than it became later in the century, and the *Post* was in many ways a small, regional newspaper. Hobby made efforts to modernize the newspaper and bring it to the level of sophistication achieved by dailies on the East Coast. She placed a premium on intelligent coverage of women's issues, adding a woman editor to the staff to cover the activities and interests of women. Aside from her newspaper work and her devotion to her children, Hobby was particularly active within the Texas chapter of the League of Women Voters.

Hobby first attained national prominence with the beginning of American involvement in World War II. The United States government realized immediately after the onset of the war that this conflict would be more "total" than previous ones. It would affect not only soldiers fighting the war but also civilians living and working on the home front. Realizing that women would be more actively involved in the war effort than before, the government sought the assistance of recognized women leaders to help coordinate this involvement. Hobby was recruited to be the head of the women's division of the War Department's Bureau of Public Relations. This mainly involved liaison work between the army and female family members of servicemen, and therefore fell short of giving women full equality in the war effort. The War Department soon realized the inadequacy of this situation, and, in the spring of 1942, the Women's Auxiliary Army Corps (WAAC) was established to mobilize the talents and energy of women. Because of her work with Army Chief of Staff George C. Marshall to plan the WAAC, Hobby was the natural choice to head this corps and, as such, was given military rank, first as a major, and then, more appropriately considering the status of her role, as colonel.

World War II was one of the great watersheds in the democratization of American society. Most, if not all, of this democratization was unintentional. The government did not set out to use the war to enfranchise women and African Americans. Yet its need for manpower compelled the government to make use of their talents to serve the war efforts. Hobby's tenure at the WAAC saw the most thorough emergence of American women into the public sphere in history. Once it was realized that the contribution of women was indispensable to the war effort, their social marginalization was far less viable. The increasing significance of women was recognized when the "auxiliary" was dropped from the name of the corps in the middle of the war. By 1945, Hobby's efforts with the WAC had become nationally known, and, next to Eleanor Roosevelt, shebecame the second most important woman in the American war effort.

After the war, Hobby returned to her duties at the Houston *Post*, but her interest in Washington affairs continued. In 1948, she advised the commission headed by former President Herbert Hoover on reducing waste in government bureaucracy. Surprisingly, her continuing interest in politics was no longer centered on the Democratic Party. In the Texas of Hobby's girlhood, it had been culturally mandatory for a Texan to be a Democrat, since Texas, like many Southern states, was dominated by a virtual one-party system. During her years in Washington, D.C., however, Hobby was increasingly drawn to the Republican Party, especially after its transformation under the leadership of Thomas E. Dewey. Under Dewey, the Republicans accepted most of Franklin D. Roosevelt's New Deal social policies, while being more friendly to the free market and to capitalist initiative than were the Democrats. Hobby, a business-woman as well as a liberal, was particularly sympathetic to this point of view. In addition, since they did not depend as heavily on the political influence of Southern conservatives and urban party bosses, as did the Democrats, the Republicans could theoretically be more responsive in alleviating the oppression of African Americans. As a result, although she continued to support local Democratic candidates, Hobby actively campaigned on behalf of Republican presidential candidates in 1948 and again in 1952.

Although Dewey suffered an upset loss in his 1948 presidential race against incumbent Harry Truman, the Republicans won in 1952 with the election of former general Dwight D. Eisenhower. By this time, Hobby was solidly in the Republican camp. When it came time for the new president to make his appointments, Eisenhower remembered Hobby's wartime service and asked her to be the director of the Federal Security Agency. This agency coordinated the various government efforts directed at securing the health and comfort of American citizens. Socially concerned Democrats had long wanted to give this agency cabinet-level status, but it was the Eisenhower Administration, often attacked for its conservativism, that presided over the agency's elevation as the Department of Health, Education, and Welfare (HEW). After her appointment as secretary of this department was approved in 1953, Hobby became the second woman to serve in the cabinet. (Frances Perkins, Secretary of Labor in the Roosevelt Administration, was the first.)

Hobby had enormous ambitions for her department, not all of which were realized during her tenure. She considered plans for overhauling the nation's medical insurance system, proposing legislation that would have established a federal corporation to provide financial backing for private low-cost medical plans. Although her proposals were defeated as a result of staunch opposition by the American Medical Association and fiscal conservatives in Congress. many elements of her plan received renewed attention during the 1990's under President Bill Clinton. Hobby also wished to focus more attention on the plight of the disadvantaged and economically subordinated, a highly unpopular cause during the prosperous 1950's. So much of the budget was being spent on Cold War defense projects that funding for the projects Hobby wished to undertake was simply not available.

Despite these difficult challenges, Hobby performed her job with dynamism and diligence. She was particularly instrumental in the widespread distribution of Jonas Salk's polio vaccine. As one of the few highly visible women in public life in the 1950's, she made a decided impression on young women growing up at the time. She seemed responsible, capable, optimistic, someone equipped for the challenges of the political world. Although she had only been in office for two years when she resigned to take care of her ailing husband on July 13, 1955, Hobby had made important contributions during her tenure at the HEW.

Hobby did not rest on her laurels after her retirement from government. Taking over the executive reins at the Houston *Post*, she presided over its development into a large metropolitan daily, acquiring the latest in technological equipment to help the paper keep pace with the exponential growth of Houston itself. She also oversaw the expansion of the *Post* media empire into the new realms of radio and, especially, television. She served as cofounder of the Bank of Texas and was invited to serve on the boards of several corporations, including the Corporation for Public Broadcasting. Hobby also developed more interests in the cultural sphere, accumulating an impressive collection of modern art, including paintings by Pablo Picasso and Amedeo Modigliani. Although Hobby did not pursue public office herself, she did have the satisfaction of seeing her son, William, Jr., elected as lieutenant governor of Texas in 1972 and serve twelve years in that position. In 1978, she became the first woman to receive the George Catlett Marshall Medal for Public Service from the Association of the United States Army in recognition of her contributions during World War II.

Hobby continued to be a prominent and much-beloved figure on the local Houston scene. In the later years of her life, Hobby's business success and family fortune made her one of the richest women in the United States. She could look back on a remarkable and unmistakably American life.

Summary

It is difficult to isolate one specific mark Oveta Culp Hobby made on American history, if only because her long life saw her excel in so many pursuits. Her wartime service helped pave the way for the promotion of women to a position of full equality in the military as well as in civilian society. Her business success proved that women not only could direct a large corporate concern but also could transform and expand that concern at an age when many business executives typically settled into retirement.

Nevertheless, it was arguably in her cabinet role as the first secretary of Health, Education, and Welfare that Hobby made her most enduring contribution. Hobby started her cabinet position off on a good footing, helping institutionalize it so that it (and, more importantly, the concerns it represented) became a Washington fixture. The Eisenhower cabinet of which Hobby was a member was derided at the time as consisting of "eight millionaires and a plumber," but it was in fact composed of many remarkable personalities, four of whom survived well into the 1990's: Attorney General Herbert Brownell, Secretary of Agriculture Ezra Taft Benson, Attorney General William Rogers, and Hobby herself. Perhaps slighted by the Democratic bias of many historians, the Eisenhower cabinet was, especially in terms of domestic policy, a progressive force. Hobby's presence was crucial in shaping this tendency.

Hobby's cabinet service also firmly established the tradition of women being present in the cabinet. Under Roosevelt, the Democratic Party had been most associated with the equality of women. Hobby's presence in a Republican cabinet meant that drawing upon the abilities of Americans of either gender became a bipartisan concern. Every future woman cabinet member owed her position, in a way, to the achievement of Oveta Culp Hobby.

Bibliography

Beasley, Maurine H., and Sheila J. Gibbons. *Taking Their Place: A Documentary History of Women and Journalism.* Washington, D.C.: American University Press,

1993. This book provides an impression of the history of women in journalism before, during, and after Hobby's newspaper years.

Clark, James Anthony. *The Tactful Texan: A Biography of Governor Will Hobby*. New York: Random House, 1958. This biography of Hobby's husband provides information on Hobby's early career.

Eisenhower, Dwight D. *The White House Years: Mandate for Change, 1953-1956*. Garden City, N.Y.: Doubleday, 1963. The first volume of Eisenhower's presidential memoirs makes frequent mention of Hobby in her role as head of the HEW.

Howes, Ruth, and Michael Stevenson, eds. *Women and the Use of Military Force*. Boulder, Colo.: Lynne Rienner, 1993. This book considers the theoretical issues accompanying women's service in the military.

Lyon, Peter. *Eisenhower: Portrait of the Hero*. Boston: Little, Brown, 1974. Emphasizes Hobby's role as the nation's top health-care official.

Margaret Boe Birns

MALVINA HOFFMAN

Born: June 15, 1885; New York, New York
Died: July 10, 1966; New York, New York
Area of Achievement: Art
Contribution: A leading sculptor who achieved international fame in the 1920's and 1930's, Malvina Hoffman ranked among the foremost American women artists. She contributed greatly to the acceptance of women as professionals.

Early Life

Malvina Cornell Hoffman was born in New York City. Her father, Richard Hoffman, came to the United States in 1847 from Manchester, England. He supported the family as a pianist—eventually as a soloist with the New York Philharmonic—and by giving piano lessons. Her mother, Fidelia Lamson, came from a prominent New York family that had descended from colonists who had arrived from England in 1630. The influence of her Lamson relatives later assisted Malvina Hoffman in her artistic career.

Malvina, known as Mallie to her family and friends, was the youngest of five children. She grew up in an atmosphere of kindness, generosity, and encouragement. She received a good upbringing and was at first taught at home by her mother and her oldest sister, Helen. In 1895, Malvina was enrolled in the Chapin School for Girls; later, she attended the Brearley School in New York City. While still at Brearley, she took classes at the Women's School of Applied Design and the Art Students League. Her formal schooling ended in 1904, when she graduated from Brearley.

She began sculpture studies in 1906 at the Veltin School under Herbert Adams and George Grey Barnard. She also studied painting under John W. Alexander. In 1909, she sculpted her first bust, a portrait of her father, done in the last year of his life. When he saw it, he acknowledged her talent and urged her to focus on sculpture as her medium. She was also encouraged by Gutzlon Borglum, the Danish sculptor best known for his carvings of four presidents at Mount Rushmore. He suggested that she carve her father's bust in marble.

Six months after her father's death, Malvina and her mother decided to leave America to promote Malvina's career. They sailed for Naples in March of 1910 and went on a fifteen-month tour that included two months in Italy, travel through Switzerland, and a stay in Paris, where the main part of their visit was spent.

In Paris, Malvina's goal was to study under Auguste Rodin. With greetings from one of Rodin's New York patrons, Mrs. John Simpson, and with a letter of introduction from Borglum, Malvina eventually succeeded in being admitted to Rodin's studio. When he saw photographs of her first bust, the one of her father, and a bust of Sam Grimson, Malvina's future husband, Rodin discerned her talent and gave her permission to work in his studio under his direction. She soon began to receive commissions for portraits of diplomats and socialites.

Life's Work

After spending a couple of months in Paris, Malvina Hoffman made a short visit to London, in July of 1910. There she saw the famous Russian ballerina Anna Pavlova and her partner Mikhail Mordkin perform the ballet *Autumn Bacchanale* to the music of Aleksandr Glazunov. Notes Hoffman made in her diary and sketchbooks of her impressions resulted in several sculptures on the theme of dancing. Her first sculpture, the *Russian Dancers*, was awarded a first prize by the Société Nationale des Beaux-Arts. A second dance sculpture, the *Bacchanale Russe*, was enlarged, cast in bronze, and placed in the Luxembourg Gardens in Paris.

The most important of her dance sculptures, the *Bacchanale Frieze*, throws light on Hoffman's thorough and professional work methods. In twenty-six bas-relief panels, she depicted scenes from *Autumn Bacchanale*. She studied the ballet's poses; to express better its movement in her sculpture, she even learned to dance it herself with Anna Pavlova as her instructor. Pavlova also posed for each panel and allowed Hoffman to take photographs to be used when Pavlova was on tour and not able to pose in person. The *Bacchanale Frieze* was finished in 1924. Because of Pavlova's death in 1931, the frieze remained in Hoffman's studio. She had hoped to exhibit it on Pavlova's last tour in America. It was not shown in its entirety until 1984, when it became part of the exhibition *A Dancer in Relief.*

Hoffman continued to study under Rodin on her return visits to Paris. She was in his studio, in August of 1914, when World War I was declared. After helping Rodin pack and store his sculptures, she returned to the United States, never to see him again. During the war years, she showed her work in several exhibitions, including the Panama-Pacific International Exhibition in San Francisco in 1915.

In 1919, after the war, she returned to Paris with the model of a war memorial. Just before her departure, Robert Bacon, who had seen the model, asked her to carve it in Caen marble. Hoffman knew Bacon from her early years in Paris. She had carved his bust when he was the American ambassador in Paris.

The memorial is known as *The Sacrifice*, although Hoffman's original title was, in translation, *Sorrow is the Mother of Beauty*. The group depicts a woman kneeling at the head of a dead medieval knight in armor. Hoffman arranged to have a ten-ton block of Caen marble shipped from France to the United States, where it was to be carved. When *The Sacrifice* was completed in 1922, it was first placed in a chapel of the Cathedral of St. John the Divine, in New York, and was later moved to the Harvard University Memorial Chapel, in Cambridge, Massachusetts.

After the completion of *The Sacrifice*, Hoffman received another important commission, a group, entitled *To the Friendship of the English-Speaking Peoples*, for the pediment of the Bush House in London. Two male figures stretch out their arms toward each other and hold jointly a flaming torch. The larger-than-life-size figures, together weighing fifty-two tons, were carved in American limestone in the United States and shipped in sections to London. Hoffman oversaw the installation. With a mallet and a chisel in her hands, she made some adjustments on the figures after they had been installed. She was photographed straddling the shoulder of one of the giant figures, a feat that caused excitement and gained her notoriety. The group was unveiled on July 4, 1925.

Hoffman's greatest achievement was the 104 sculptures she was asked to create for the Hall of Man in Chicago's Field Museum. Its president, Stanley Field, and the museum trustees gave her the sole responsibility of modeling men and women representative of several of the world's races. In October of 1930, she signed a contract for twenty-seven life-size sculptures, twenty-seven busts, and fifty heads.

The five-year project involved traveling around the world. Hoffman described her adventures in her 1936 book *Heads and Tales*. With her husband, her secretary, Gretchen Green, and her plaster caster, Jean de Marco, she visited Hawaii, Japan, China, the Philippines, Bali, Java, Singapore, Malay, Burma, India, and Ceylon. A five-foot needlepoint tapestry map in color, created by Ginevra King, showing the continents that Hoffman had covered for the Field Museum, was presented to her upon her return from the world tour.

The sculptures were cast in bronze in Paris. Before they were shipped to Chicago, the first public exhibition of 102 originals and reductions was organized, in November of 1932, at the Ethnographical Museum at the Trocadéro palace in Paris. On June 6, 1933, the Field Museum's Hall of Man was opened to the public. The exhibit became one of the great attractions of the Chicago World's Fair. The Hall of Man sculptures made Hoffman a celebrity.

Portraits were a significant part of Malvina Hoffman's production. She listed almost one hundred busts in plaster, clay, or marble in her autobiography *Yesterday Is Tomorrow: A Personal History* (1965). This book, as well as *Heads and Tales*, is valuable for the background she provided on the persons she modeled. She studied her sitters very closely not only to learn their features but also to understand their personalities.

A typical example of how she worked involves the busts she made of Ignace Jan Paderewski, the Polish statesman and accomplished pianist who had become a trusted friend of Hoffman. To do him justice in all these roles, Hoffman created three busts. The first was entitled *The Statesman*, for which she had made notes and sketches while observing Paderewski in sessions of the League of Nations in Geneva. She discovered an entirely different personality when she attended a piano recital in Carnegie Hall, in New York City. To represent *Paderewski, the Artist*, caught up in the music, she made a second bust. In appreciation of his friendship, she created *Paderewski, the Friend*, because he had encouraged her to write *Heads and Tales*. Ivan Mestrovi, the Yugoslav sculptor, also appeared in *Heads and Tales*. He was not only a friend but also a teacher. He became Hoffman's subject for both a bust and a larger-than-life-size sculpture.

A portrait that she made of the head of the English poet John Keats is interesting because of its mystic background. The bust, which exists in two marble versions, was based on a drawing that Hoffman made in Rome in 1910. She was visiting the room where the poet had died. In *Yesterday Is Tomorrow*, she gave a vivid account of a vision she had of Keats, who was reclining on a couch. She immediately started to draw the poet and continued until the vision disappeared.

As a writer, Malvina Hoffman is very readable. In addition to the two books already mentioned, she wrote a popular college textbook, *Sculpture Inside and Out*, which was published in 1939.

In the 1940's, when realism in art was no longer sought after, Malvina Hoffman received mainly commissions for portraits. Her art, once popular and praised, fell out of favor. In 1967, for example, the year after she died, the *Races of Man*, her main achievement, was dismantled, and most of the figures were placed in storage. The 1980's, with its return to realism in art, generated a renewed interest in her work.

Summary

A highly professional artist, Malvina Hoffman knew both craft and art; she demonstrated that a woman could be an accomplished sculptor. During her lifetime, Hoffman was awarded five honorary degrees. She was named Woman of the Year by the American Association of University Women in 1957. She became a member of the National Institute of Arts and Letters, 1937; a Fellow of the National Sculpture Society, 1958; Academician of the National Academy of Design, 1931; and Chevalier of the Legion of Honor, 1951. In 1964, Malvina Hoffman was awarded the National Sculpture Society's Medal of Honor.

Bibliography

Conner, Janis C. *A Dancer in Relief: Works by Malvina Hoffman*. Yonkers, N.Y.: Hudson River Museum, 1984. This book was published in connection with an exhibition held at the Hudson River Museum in Westchester, New York, from March 25 through May 13, 1984. This catalog shows thirty-one sculptures and sixteen photographs related to the twenty-six bas-relief panel *Bacchanale Frieze*, 1917-1924, which was shown for the first time in its entirety in the exhibition described here. It depicts the Russian ballerina Anna Pavlova and her partner.

Conner, Janis, and Joel Rosenkranz. *Rediscoveries in American Sculpture: Studio Works, 1893-1939*. Austin: University of Texas, 1989. Contains a selection of twenty academic or Beaux-Arts artists who were once famous and successful. Malvina Hoffman is discussed on several pages. The authors' aim is providing information to create interest in bringing the artists back to public attention.

Hill, May Brawley. *Woman Sculptor: Malvina Hoffman and Her Contemporaries*. New York: Paul-Art Press, 1984. This book was published in connection with an exhibition of small bronze sculptures by eleven women sculptors to celebrate the centennial of the Brearley School, which was founded in 1884. Malvina Hoffman was one of the two sculptors who had attended Brearley. Forty-nine pieces were shown, nine of which (nos. 15 to 23) were by Malvina Hoffman.

Hoffman, Malvina. *Heads and Tales*. New York: Charles Scribner's Sons, 1936. Published in Great Britain under the title *A Sculptor's Odyssey*, this autobiographical work was written primarily to discuss Hoffman's most important project, the sculptures for the Field Museum in Chicago.

——————. *Sculpture Inside and Out*. New York: W. W. Norton, 1939. A textbook that gives a brief outline of the history of sculpture, describes techniques and styles of sculpture in all media, and contains the chapter on "Suggestions for a Practical Art Center." The book's 276 illustrations show many of Hoffman's sculptures.

_____ . *Yesterday Is Tomorrow: A Personal History*. New York: Crown, 1965. This autobiography continues the vivid narrative of *Heads and Tales*. An appendix lists the dates and titles of Malvina Hoffman's sculpted works, a total of 312 works of which ninety-four are portraits.

Elvy Setterqvist O'Brien

HELEN HOKINSON

Born: June 29, 1893; Mendota, Illinois
Died: November 1, 1949; Washington, D.C.
Area of Achievement: Art
Contribution: One of the first women to attain outstanding success as a cartoonist, Hokinson inspired other women to enter the field and to focus on feminine themes and characters.

Early Life

Helen Elna Hokinson, the only daughter of Adolph and Mary Hokinson, was born in the small town of Mendota, Illinois in 1893. Helen attended public schools and had a conventional Midwestern childhood. She never traveled much, although she told an interviewer she had spent several months in Paris studying art. Her whole life was devoted to art, and she developed the habit of carrying a sketchbook wherever she went.

Hokinson attended the Academy of Fine Arts in Chicago and later moved to New York with the goal of becoming a fashion illustrator. She did not, however, achieve notable success in that highly competitive field. She then tried producing a comic strip with a collaborator named Alice Harvey. The comic strip was published in the *New York Daily Mirror* for a short time but did not attract sufficient attention to survive.

Hokinson has been described as having "frightened hazel eyes and an untidy hairdo." She was said to be "shy," "retiring," "introverted," and "maidenly." She remained single throughout her life, and her preference for the companionship of women had much to do with the insightful depiction of female characters that was to make her world famous. The reader who examines a collection of Hokinson's cartoons will sense that her naïve, kindly, sexually inhibited, inoffensive, and spunky female characters are all portraits of the artist herself.

"Hoky," as her friends called her, went on to study at the Parsons School of Design under Howard Giles, whose teaching about dynamic symmetry had a lifelong effect on her work. In 1925, while she was still studying with Giles, the one great opportunity of her lifetime presented itself. Harold Ross and Raoul Fleischmann founded *The New Yorker*. The editors conceived of their new publication as a magazine of sophisticated humor, and they were looking for talented writers and artists who could provide the kind of material they wanted. Hokinson submitted one of her sketches. To her surprise, it was accepted, and the editors invited her to bring in fresh material every week for their consideration.

At first, the editorial staff made up captions to go with Hokinson's drawings. Then, in the early 1930's, she met James Reid Parker, a writer who was contributing short stories to *The New Yorker*. The two became friends and collaborators. Parker contributed the captions to most of Hokinson's cartoons and suggested many of the situations she depicted. For the rest of her life, Hokinson's career was linked with that of *The New Yorker*.

Life's Work

As one of the earliest freelance contributors to *The New Yorker*, Helen Hokinson helped to fashion the magazine's distinctive appearance and tone. In addition to contributing cartoons and spot illustrations, she received many assignments for watercolor paintings to be used as *The New Yorker* covers. A famous cover shows a Hokinson woman returning home to the suburbs aboard a commuter train. She has hidden her disgruntled lapdog under a sweater and a big coat and is hoping that the grim conductor will not catch her in flagrant violation of the rule against bringing animals aboard trains.

The magazine became highly profitable because it set the standard for a whole class of Eastern society who were intelligent, educated, sophisticated, and able to buy the expensive items featured in its advertisements. Hokinson began receiving commissions to produce illustrations for advertising and books. This lucrative work enabled her to lead a far more comfortable life than would have been possible if she had had to depend on her income from *The New Yorker* cartoons. Her own books of cartoons added to her income and spread her reputation to a wider audience.

Her life was comfortable and uneventful during the last two decades of her life. She spent her winters in New York City and the rest of the time in rural Connecticut. Like many creative people, she needed to be within commuting range of the big city in order to be able to consult with editors as well as to keep in touch with the intellectual and cultural life of that dynamic city and to observe the parade of humanity that provided material for her cartoons. She liked classical music, backgammon, the French Impressionists, Ray Bolger's dancing, wildflowers, Shakespeare, detective stories, and bridge.

Hokinson's drawings usually featured women. Gradually she realized that her most successful cartoons were those depicting middle-aged females who came to be popularly known as "Hokinson women." Her cartoons always suggest the existence of a whole complex milieu from which her characters have appeared and to which they will shortly return. A typical Hokinson woman is affluent, expensively dressed, and a good thirty to forty pounds overweight. These shapeless women spend a considerable amount of time at beauty parlors and expensive clothing stores, hoping against hope that they can recapture the beauty they once possessed.

Hokinson's women have frequently been described as "dowagers," a term that once meant rich widows but has been broadened by popular usage to refer to affluent women who are past a certain age. They all appear to be in their late forties or early fifties. Some might be widows, but many have long-suffering husbands who are totally indifferent to their physical charms and beyond being surprised by their inanities. It is clear that these women, though wallowing in luxuries, are bored, sexually frustrated, and trying to make the best of essentially empty lives.

Most of Hokinson's cartoons are built around a silly statement made by one of these rather pathetic women. In one, a woman is trying on mink coats while her grim-looking husband is slouching in a nearby chair. The woman says, "Now, don't worry, dear. I'm hoping I won't see anything I like."

Shopping is one of the main activities of Hokinson women. It is a way to kill time as well as a way to get attention. Many of the clerks, beauticians, and masseuses who wait on these affluent dowagers seem to understand perfectly well that they are trying to buy attention and sympathy. With all their money and possessions, these women are not enviable; they are lonely souls who have nothing serious to occupy their minds. They are overweight because they use food to appease their hunger for love.

Most of Hokinson's women appear to have gone to college, usually to Smith, Vassar, or one of the other elite women's institutions of the day. They have acquired an interest in books but have no specialized interests and either read best-sellers or allow themselves to be directed by book dealers or proprietors of lending libraries. It is characteristic of Hokinson women that they are always trying to improve their minds by reading books, visiting art museums, and attending lectures. In one rather touching cartoon, a woman who is holding an open book on her lap is saying to her husband, "Well! I certainly am finding out things about Charles the Second." The husband, a typical Hokinson male, is buried in his newspaper and shows no reaction to his wife's pathetic appeal for attention and communication.

Other favorite activities of Hokinson women are exhibiting their pedigreed lapdogs at dog shows and attending edifying lectures at women's clubs. Hokinson made fun of women, but her humor was always kind and sympathetic. That was the secret of her popularity. In all of her best work there is a sort of hidden dimension of pain that Hokinson undoubtedly experienced herself. During World War II, Hokinson created many cartoons showing her women engaged in such volunteer activities as rolling bandages and selling defense bonds. The war marked the beginning of the end of the kind of world in which these women flourished. Domestic servants went into military service or took defense jobs. Conspicuous luxury became unfashionable. More and more women were choosing to enter careers. No doubt, Hokinson would have found creative ways to depict women in the rapidly changing postwar world if she had lived beyond the 1940's.

Her career, however, was cut short by disaster. On November 1, 1949, while flying to Washington, D.C., to deliver a speech at a charity drive, she was killed in an aircraft collision that still ranks as one of the worst disasters in the history of civil aviation. Her body was returned to Mendota, Illinois, for burial.

Summary

Helen Hokinson was a pioneer in many respects. She was one of the first women to attain outstanding success in the fields of cartooning and illustration, both of which had always been dominated by men. Her example inspired many women to consider cartooning, illustrating, and advertising artwork as viable occupations.

Hokinson was one of the pioneers in creating the distinctive tone and style of *The New Yorker*, which went on to become the most influential magazine of its type in the world. Previously, American humor magazines had tended to be burlesque and even bawdy publications directed to a cigar-smoking, back-slapping male audience. *The New Yorker*'s approach was always light, witty, and urbane, like Hokinson's drawings themselves. To be a regular contributor of cartoons to *The New Yorker* was quite an honor. It required much more than a talent for creating funny drawings: It required intelligence, insight, and especially an ability to see general truths in specific situations. Hokinson was the first to recognize the humorous potential of the class of women she customarily depicted. Many such women were regular subscribers to *The New Yorker*, and, far from being offended by seeing themselves and their friends satirized, they were flattered by the attention.

Hokinson's cartoons set a high standard for artistry and subtlety that other contributors were inspired to emulate. She added a feminine touch to the magazine and thereby paved the way for more women to contribute artwork, short stories, and articles with a distinctively feminine perspective. Hokinson helped *The New Yorker* to become world famous, and in turn the magazine did the same for her. Her name ranks with those of Harold Ross, E. B. White, and James Thurber as one of the creative spirits behind what many people consider the greatest magazine of all time.

Bibliography
Brown, John Mason. "Seeing Things: Helen Hokinson's Dowagers." *Saturday Review of Literature* 32 (December 10, 1949): 30-31. A eulogistic article written by a prominent American author shortly after Hokinson's death.
Hokinson, Helen Elna. *The Hokinson Festival.* New York: E. P. Dutton, 1956. The largest and best collection of Hokinson's cartoons. Contains a memoir by author John Mason Brown and an appreciation by James Reid Mason.
——————. *The Ladies, God Bless 'Em.* New York: E. P. Dutton, 1950. Another collection of Hokinson's *New Yorker* cartoons that was welcomed by her large audience of admirers.
——————. *My Best Girls.* New York: World, 1945. An early collection of cartoons dealing with most of the themes and character types that Hokinson was to exploit throughout her career.
——————. *So You're Going to Buy a Book!* New York: Minton, Balch, 1931. The first collection of Hokinson's cartoons and drawings, published shortly after she began her long association with *The New Yorker.*
——————. *When Were You Built?* New York: E. P. Dutton, 1948. A later collection of Hokinson's cartoons, some of which show her use of wartime themes for morale-boosting humor.
Kramer, Dale. "Those Hokinson Women." *Saturday Evening Post* 223 (April 7, 1951): 24-25, 97-99. An appreciation of Helen Hokinson containing reprints of some of her *New Yorker* cartoons and a photograph of Hokinson. Discusses her life, her likable personality, her career, and her contribution to popular art.
Sochen, June, ed. *Women's Comic Visions.* Detroit: Wayne State University Press, 1991. An interesting collection of essays analyzing women's humor, written from diverse disciplinary perspectives. Helen Hokinson is discussed in the second section.
Thurber, James. *The Years with Ross.* Boston: Little, Brown, 1959. A history of *The*

New Yorker by one of its earliest and most loved contributors, who knew Helen Hokinson, Harold Ross, and all the other creative people associated with the magazine's birth.

Bill Delaney

BILLIE HOLIDAY

Born: April 7, 1915; Philadelphia, Pennsylvania
Died: July 17, 1959; New York, New York
Area of Achievement: Music
Contribution: One of the most influential jazz singers ever recorded, Billie Holiday created the standards by which jazz singers continue to be judged. Her life reflected the racism of a white entertainment industry and the sexism within a male-dominated jazz world.

Early Life

Although she is known as a hometown celebrity in Baltimore, Billie Holiday was actually born in Philadelphia, Pennsylvania, on April 7, 1915. Much about her early life is unknown. Much of what is said about her comes from her autobiography, which is known to be inaccurate in many respects. Her autobiography, *Lady Sings the Blues*, written with the help of author William Dufty, represented Holiday's early years as pitiful and worthy of sympathy. This account has Billie Holiday starting life as Eleanora Fagan, born to thirteen-year-old Sadie Fagan and eighteen-year-old Clarence Holiday. A second, more accurate account by Robert O'Meally, author of *Lady Day*, has established the ages of her mother and father as nineteen and seventeen, respectively. Billie Holiday said that she took on the Holiday name when her parents married three years later and moved to a home on Durham Street in East Baltimore, but O'Meally could never establish that that marriage took place or that her parents had ever lived together. He concluded that the move from Philadelphia to Baltimore was her mother's attempt to start over. In Baltimore, Holiday's mother worked as a maid to support the two of them. The autobiography explained that Eleanora became "Billie," a name she took from her screen idol, Billie Dove. This source also noted that her father was drafted during World War I, was sent to Europe, and suffered lung damage from inhaling poisonous gas. While recovering in Paris, he learned how to play the guitar, and he played professionally when he returned home to the United States, a career that required much traveling and family separation. He toured as a musician with the jazz band of Fletcher Henderson and soon abandoned his family, leaving Sadie struggling to make a living. Eventually, the couple divorced. Whatever the reason, young Holiday lived a solitary life as a child.

Her mother left Holiday with relatives in Baltimore while she went to New York seeking better wages. Holiday stayed with a physically abusive cousin, Ida, her maternal grandparents, her great-grandmother, and Ida's two children, with whom Holiday had to share a bed. The great-grandmother told stories about her life as a slave on the plantation of Charles Fagan, the father of her sixteen children. Holiday was traumatized when her great-grandmother died after lying down with Eleanora for a story and a nap. According to the autobiography, Holiday awoke and could not loosen the dead arms, which had to be broken to remove them from her small body.

According to *Lady Sings the Blues*, Holiday spent her early years in extreme poverty, working at six as a babysitter and a step scrubber. She finished the fifth grade in the Baltimore schools. She performed household chores for Alice Dean, a brothel owner, ran errands for the prostitutes, and listened to the jazz that was played on the record player in the parlor of the brothel. As the records played, she sang along. By 1925, mother and daughter had saved enough money to move to a house on Pennsylvania Avenue in northern Baltimore, where the mother met a dockworker named Philip Gough, who became her husband. Within a short time, his sudden death brought the family to poverty again. An attempted rape of young Holiday by a forty-year-old neighbor led to more terror when she was put in jail to ensure her testimony and then was placed in a home for wayward girls until she reached twenty-one years of age. The judge assumed that her mature appearance had brought on the rape. Robert O'Meally found that Holiday was sent at age ten to the House of the Good Shepherd, a Catholic home for African American girls. Their records indicated that she had no guardian and was on the streets at this time. Her mother, unable to help young Holiday, again went North seeking better wages.

Holiday wanted to be with her mother, who managed to reverse the judge's ruling and bring her daughter to New York to work as a maid in 1927. From that time, Holiday and her mother remained close throughout her lifetime. Holiday boarded in a Harlem apartment owned by Florence Williams, a well-known madam. Billie became a twenty-dollar call girl to earn money. The profession led to arrests and a four-month prison term when her mother testified that her daughter was eighteen (she was thirteen) years old so that she could avoid another term in a home for wayward girls. Holiday returned to prostitution after her release, and both mother and daughter could afford to move to an apartment on 139th Street in 1929. It was not long before the effects of the Great Depression touched the Holiday women.

Life's Work

Not until she received an eviction notice in 1930 did Billie Holiday launch her career as a singer. To avert her forthcoming eviction, she sought work as a dancer at *Pod's and Jerry's*, a Harlem speakeasy. Since she was no dancer, she asked to sing. Jerry Preston, the owner, was so impressed with her presentation that he offered her the job. From that point on, Holiday enjoyed recognition as part of a floor show featuring tap dancer Charles "Honi" Coles and bassist George "Pops" Foster. In 1933, when Prohibition was repealed, the speakeasies became legitimate jazz clubs, and jazz enthusiast John Hammond heard Holiday perform in *Monette's*, a jazz club on 133rd Street. He noticed her exquisite phrasing and manipulation of lyrics, which led him to give her a rave review in the magazine *Melody Maker*. He brought influential musicians and managers to hear her sing, and soon organized her first recording session, which launched her public career. A few days after her twentieth birthday, Billie Holiday appeared for her first performance at the Apollo Theater. That same year, she recorded with some of the finest jazz musicians of the time under the direction of Teddy Wilson. These recordings built Holiday's reputation as a jazz singer. She toured with the bands of Fletcher Henderson, Count Basie, and Artie Shaw.

During the 1930's, she continued to record and perform. She played a small part in a radio soap opera. She appeared briefly in a musical film, *Symphony in Black*, in which she played a prostitute. When she appeared outside Harlem, she was criticized for not being "jazzy" enough or for singing too slowly. She had a bad temper, and stories about her throwing an inkwell at a club manager and similar tantrums spread throughout the business. She used the money she earned to buy a restaurant for her mother, and the two of them lived in the upstairs apartment. She sang and waited on tables. She refused to accept tips unless they were handed to her, a practice that led the other women to call her "a lady." When jazzman Lester Young found a rat in his hotel room, he moved in temporarily with Holiday and her mother. During this time, the tenor saxophonist and the women gave nicknames to each other. He called Billie "Lady Day," a title that remained with her, and her mother "Duchess," the mother of a lady. In turn, they called him "the President," or "Pres," because he was the commander-in-chief of the saxophone players. Together, the two performers produced some of the finest music of Holiday's career.

Holiday was essentially a jazz singer who put the blues feeling into every word she sang. During her entire career, however, she included only a dozen blues songs in her repertoire, preferring instead to use popular songs as the vehicles of her art. She learned her art from blues queen Bessie Smith. One of her best-known songs, "Billie's Blues," was a distinctive, original blues that demonstrated her total control of her music, a control she never had in her life. Holiday strung her songs together in ways characteristic of African speech, and she invested her music with a blues feeling that contained not only sadness but also honesty and directness of expression. Like the best blues artists, she created music that transcended trouble and pain.

She took subtle liberties with melodies, improvising in the same way that jazz musicians improvised with their instruments. Moreover, Holiday could sing mundane lyrics and make them sound significant and urgent. Her sophisticated approach to singing yielded a novel effect. Whereas popular singers only entertained audiences, Holiday both entertained and communicated with her listeners. She conveyed to them in song what she knew about a life of pain and disillusion. The songs she sang lent themselves to improvisation and metaphorical protest. With the release of her song "Strange Fruit" in 1939, Holiday became a celebrity. Her record was based on Lewis Allen's poem, which recounted lynchings in the American South. The "strange fruit" was the bodies of the lynched blacks hanging from the branches of the trees. "Strange Fruit" as sung by Holiday became a powerful condemnation of racism and her signature song. Perhaps the pain expressed in the song replicated her sense of the injustice of her father's death in March of 1937. Her father's weak lungs, inability to find a black hospital to treat his pneumonia, and rejection by white Jim Crow hospitals in the South led to his death in a Dallas veterans' hospital.

As the bands with which Holiday sang toured the South, they experienced Jim Crow segregation at hotels, theaters, restaurants, and public restrooms. Band members survived through mutual support and accommodation to segregation. When she was told that her skin was too light to play with the band, Holiday put on special makeup to darken her face so that the audience would not think she was white under the lights. Her song "God Bless the Child" captured the response of the black community to segregation. When she joined the Artie Shaw Orchestra, an all-white band, the touring problems were worse. In order to avoid finding her a segregated hotel room, Artie Shaw painted a red dot on her forehead, making the hotel management think she was an East Indian. This technique succeeded occasionally. In the North, her performances at *Cafe Society*, the only unsegregated nightclub outside of Harlem, made her a star and broke down racial barriers. By the early 1940's, she was the highest-paid performer in jazz. The versatile Holiday was at home in both the swing and the bebop eras of jazz, a rare feat among jazz musicians. Her subtle phrasing and imagination enabled her to approximate what jazz instrumentalists did with their instruments.

The success of her career was not duplicated in her personal life. In 1941, Holiday married James N. Monroe, whose brother owned the *Uptown House*, a nightclub. She started to use heroin. James Monroe smoked opium, and he soon shared his habit with his wife. Within a year, their marriage disintegrated, and Holiday began a relationship with a heroin addict, Joe Guy. When her mother died in 1945, Holiday felt alone. She was voted best singer in the *Esquire* Jazz Critics Poll (1944), was named *Metronome* Vocalist of the Year (1946), and had a role in the film *New Orleans* (1946), but these successes did not stem the tide of her drug addiction. The addiction sapped her strength, made her late to performances, and created an unending need for more money. In 1947, she checked herself into a sanatorium to beat the habit. When she returned to the stage, however, she started to use heroin again. Arrested several times, she served time in prison rather than undergo rehabilitation. By 1949, she was released but was denied a license to perform in New York; she slowly slipped back into addiction.

Holiday experienced both setbacks and successes during the 1950's. Her contract with Decca records lapsed in 1950. In 1952, she signed with the Verve label and recorded more than a hundred songs. In 1954, she received a special award from *Down Beat* as "one of the all-time great vocalists in jazz," and in 1956, she married Louis McKay, her manager, had her autobiography published by Doubleday, and was again arrested for possession of narcotics. Following her rehabilitation, she turned to alcohol. Ultimately, the drug and alcohol addiction took its toll. McKay and Holiday separated in 1957. The following year, she recorded her last album, *Lady in Satin*, backed by the string arrangements of Ray Ellis. When her longtime friend Lester Young died in 1959, Holiday was hospitalized for cirrhosis of the liver and heart failure. She was arrested in her hospital bed for drug possession. She died on July 17, 1959, of congestion of the lungs and heart failure, leaving a bank account of seventy cents and a small dog as her family. The forty-four-year-old jazz singer was buried in Saint Raymond's Catholic Cemetery in the Bronx, New York City.

Summary

Billie Holiday commands attention because of the unique blues-inspired jazz singing that she contributed to American music. Her renditions, phrasing, pitch, and timing still move audiences and continue to influence singers and instrumentalists. Her career brought jazz from Harlem into cafe society, breaking down racial barriers. Billie Holiday expressed the dynamic tradition of black independence in a unique and powerful voice. In her art, she found the power and control that eluded her in other areas of her life.

Bibliography
Burnett, James. *Billie Holiday*. Spellmount, N.Y.: Hippocrene, 1984. A standard work on Holiday's career which devotes considerable attention to her personal relationships.
Chilton, John. *Billie's Blues: Billie Holiday's Story, 1933-1959*. New York: Stein & Day, 1975. In his biography, Chilton focuses primarily on Holiday's musical career. The work contains an extensive bibliography and a discography.
Holiday, Billie, with William Dufty. *Lady Sings the Blues*. Garden City, N.Y.: Doubleday, 1956. Holiday's autobiography, written with Dufty, provides details but is often chronologically and factually inaccurate.
Kliment, Bud. *Billie Holiday*. New York: Chelsea House, 1992. This biography, written for juvenile readers, provides an introduction to Holiday's career as a singer. Unfortunately, the work repeats many of the inaccuracies included in Holiday's autobiography. It does, however, contain useful appended material, including a selected discography, a chronology, and a bibliography.
O'Meally, Robert. *Lady Day: The Many Faces of Billie Holiday*. New York: Arcade, 1991. This book corrects many of the errors of previous biographical sources and illuminates the various facets of Holiday's personality and career.
White, John. *Billie Holiday: Her Life and Times*. New York: Neal, 1987. White's book does a fine job of placing Holiday within the historical framework that shaped her life and music.

Dorothy C. Salem

HANYA HOLM

Born: 1893; Worms, Germany
Died: November 3, 1992; New York, New York
Area of Achievement: Dance
Contribution: A pioneer in modern dance, Holm was an outstanding dance educator who adapted the spatial, rhythmic, and expressive focus of German modern dance to encompass a distinctly American sensibility.

Early Life

Hanya Holm was born Johanna Eckert in Worms, Germany, to Valentin and Marie Eckert in 1893. Her early convent-based schooling instilled in her a love for all branches of knowledge, creativity, and the desire to strive for perfection in all endeavors. She began piano lessons at the age of ten, and at sixteen continued her studies at the Hoch Conservatory in Frankfurt am Main. When she graduated from the convent, she attended Émile Jacques-Dalcroze's Institute for four years, where she studied music improvisation, theory, analysis, and composition: These experiences developed her understanding of music and rhythm but did not totally satisfy her need for physical expression. In 1921, she saw Mary Wigman perform in Dresden and decided that the next stage in her development would be best served by joining Mary Wigman.

In his 1969 biography of Hanya Holm, Walter Sorell explains Holm's decision. "It was the result of her constant search for the inner experience that brings peace of mind—and with this gratification, new desires for the excitement of new experiences . . . she was gripped by the wish to find out whether one could acquire the knowledge and skill which led to Wigman's art." The modern dance was a very new art form, and Mary Wigman and her group were involved in a process of discovery, finding out what dance meant to them and how to become physically expressive. Holm did not set out to become a dancer, but she found the experience of working with Wigman deeply fulfilling; she had begun her life's work.

Life's Work

Hanya Holm remained with Mary Wigman for ten years, becoming codirector and chief instructor of the Mary Wigman Central Institute in Dresden as well as dancing in Wigman's company from 1923 to 1930. Wigman entrusted her with the company and students when she went on solo tours. According to biographer Walter Sorell, it was during those years that "Hanya realized her own growing strength as a personality; and it was then that it became obvious to her that teaching, if meaningful, was a creative act." Holm's first major role as a dancer came when she was chosen to choreograph and dance the lead role of the princess in Igor Stravinsky's *L'Histoire du Soldat* in 1929 for a staging of that opera in Dresden. This success was followed by her appearance in Wigman's antiwar dance *Das Totenmal*, performed in Munich in 1930. Holm had the difficult role of leading the women's chorus while assisting

Wigman in directing and overseeing the production. A pivotal experience, it led Holm to the conclusion that she had indeed found her métier. The question that remained was whether her contribution in dance would be as a teacher, choreographer, or performer. Circumstances and instinct led her to New York in 1931, where she opened the Mary Wigman School in America.

German modern dance predated American modern dance by about ten years. When Holm came to the United States to found and operate the Mary Wigman School, only the German dancers had established a technical and pedagogical base and a full choreographic repertoire. American modern dance pioneers such as Martha Graham, Doris Humphrey, and Helen Tamiris had just begun to present their own works. Students flocked to the Wigman school that first year to experience Holm's teaching and to understand at firsthand what the Wigman technique was like. The novelty soon wore off, however, and Holm was faced with the reality of an American culture that was extremely different from the climate to which she was accustomed.

Describing her experience in the United States in the 1930's, Holm stated: "At first, I was taken aback by their points of view, by their philosophy of life. The feeling that nothing is impossible, that everything goes . . . their idea so often expressed in their gestures: I pay for my class, so you go and show me." She discovered that the American temperament and mentality demanded a different approach to modern dance, and in 1936 she wrote to Mary Wigman for advice. Anti-German sentiment was high in the United States, and Wigman suggested changing the name of the studio to the Hanya Holm School, freeing Holm to develop her own style of expression.

In 1939, Holm became a U.S. citizen. Never content to experience only one aspect of America, Holm traveled extensively, and her love of the open spaces of the West led her to establish a summer dance school in Colorado Springs, Colorado, in 1941. The Center of the Dance was at Colorado College, where Holm worked with dance students in an atmosphere that was entirely different from that of hectic New York City, and her summer intensive workshops brought students and dance professionals from all across the United States. She returned every summer to teach there until her retirement in 1983.

Forced by economic restrictions in 1946 to give up her company, Holm retired from performing a few years later. Fortunately, her choreographic impulses found another outlet: the Broadway stage. Between 1948 and 1965, Holm choreographed thirteen musicals, two operas, two plays, and dance works for film and television. Among her major triumphs as a Broadway choreographer are the unforgettable *Kiss Me, Kate* (New Century Theatre, New York City, 1948), *The Golden Apple* (The Phoenix Theatre, New York City, 1954), *My Fair Lady* (Mark Hellinger Theatre, New York City, 1956), *Camelot* (The Majestic Theatre, New York City, 1960), and *Anya* (Ziegfeld Theatre, New York City, 1965).

Holm's choreography for the Broadway stage was notable for its range of dance styles, its inventiveness, and its artistic integration. Holm's dances connected with the expression, style, and spirit of the play, forming an artistic gestalt that enhanced every aspect of the theatrical performance. In 1952, Holm became the first choreographer to register a complete dance score for copyright in Washington, D.C. The choreography in *Kiss Me, Kate*, notated in Labanotation by Ann Hutchinson, established a precedent for choreographers, putting them on an equal level with composers. Choreographers could now formally be recognized as the owners of their work, and the choreography itself could be seen as a specific entity, separate from the music and the play.

A shortened version of Holm's *Metropolitan Daily* was broadcast on television by TV-W2XBS in New York City on May 31, 1939, the first instance of live dance adapted for the television medium. As a result of her Broadway successes, Holm was invited to Hollywood in 1956 to choreograph *The Vagabond King*. The film was a flop, but Holm's choreography was praised as being imaginative and memorable.

Holm's dedication to the modern dance as an educator and choreographer continued until her death. Her innovations in teaching directly influenced generations of younger dancers, choreographers, and future dance educators. In recognition of her achievements, she received an honorary degree of Doctor of Fine Arts from Colorado College in 1960, the Capezio Award and the Samuel H. Scripps American Dance Festival Award in 1984, and the Astaire Award in 1987. An eloquent writer, she is also remembered for the numerous essays she published in periodicals and books. She died on November 3, 1992, leaving a legacy of words, dances, and inspiration.

Summary

Hanya Holm's contributions to the field of dance were numerous. Her choreography for the concert stage as well as Broadway theaters places her among the most respected pioneers of American modern dance. Her *Trend*, a choreographic masterwork, defined a new level of accomplishment for group choreography. Holm's choreography in the late 1930's addressed powerful social issues and demonstrated to generations of future choreographers that dance could portray serious themes. From the 1940's through the 1960's, Holm's choreography for the musical theater helped to establish the American musical as an indigenous and innovative artistic expression, setting new standards for Broadway choreography; her ability to reflect and complement the stylistic aesthetic of each show was renowned.

It was as a dance educator that Holm's greatest gifts were most apparent. This first to introduce improvisation as an adjunct to dance training, Holm also is credited with several other pedagogical innovations: an emphasis on the interconnectedness of knowledge of anatomy and dance technique, special training in percussion and rhythms, and development of a spatial awareness in movement that stemmed from her study with Mary Wigman but was uniquely her own. As a teacher she was demanding, blunt, and often witty. She emphasized the importance of understanding where and how a movement originates, why one is performing it, and why it should be done in a particular way. Her students included later prominent dancers and choreographers Lucinda Childs, Murray Louis, Alwin Nikolais, Don Redlich, and Glen Tetley.

It is as a teacher that Holm was most influential. As she said, "If there is anything in life I am proud of having achieved it is being a dance educator."

Bibliography

Brown, Jean Morrison, ed. *The Vision of Modern Dance*. Princeton, N.J.: Princeton Book, 1979. A collection of essays by pioneer figures in dance history. Holm's essay "Hanya Speaks" is a wonderfully pithy amalgam of advice and instruction to would-be dancers; her comments reflect her personality and teaching style.

Martin, John. *America Dancing: The Background and Personalities of the Modern Dance*. New York: Dodge, 1936. Martin discusses the emergence and early development of the modern dance in the United States through 1938. His section on Holm is informative regarding her teaching practices and how they descend from her work with Wigman.

Rogers, Frederick Rand, ed. *Dance: A Basic Educational Technique*. New York: Dance Horizons, 1980. Rogers' collection contains essays by the leading figures in dance education, choreography, and criticism in the 1940's. Holm's "The Attainment of Conscious, Controlled Movement" clearly presents her philosophy and teaching techniques.

Sorell, Walter, ed. *The Dance Has Many Faces*. 3d rev. ed. Chicago: A Capella, Books, 1992. Sorell's book contains essays by many leading ballet and modern dance choreographers, performers, critics, and educators from the 1940's through the 1990's. Holm's essay "The Mary Wigman I Knew" reveals the extent to which Holm incorporated Wigman's aesthetics and pedagogy, while finding her own personal expression and methodology.

——————. *Hanya Holm: The Biography of an Artist*. Middletown, Conn.: Wesleyan University Press, 1969. A detailed and informative biography of Holm, from her early training in Germany through the 1960's. The book is well organized and offers insight into Holm's personality and beliefs. It contains photographs, a choreographic chronology, and an abbreviated bibliography.

Cynthia J. Williams

GRACE MURRAY HOPPER

Born: December 9, 1906; New York, New York
Died: January 1, 1992; Arlington, Virginia
Area of Achievement: Invention and technology
Contribution: A pioneer in programming languages, Hopper developed FLOW-MATIC, the foundation of COBOL, and then standardized all Navy versions.

Early Life

Grace Brewster Murray was the eldest of three children born to Walter Murray, an insurance broker, and his wife Mary Campbell Van Horne Murray. In reflecting on her childhood, Grace later said, "I was born with curiosity." When she was seven years old, Grace wandered into the bedrooms of the family's large summer cottage and, out of curiosity, deconstructed seven alarm clocks. Her hobbies included reading and playing the piano. She eventually became expert at knitting, a pastime she would continue all of her life.

Grace attended the Graham School and later Schoonmakers School, two private schools in New York City where she played basketball, field hockey, and water polo. When she flunked a crucial Latin exam, Vassar College told her she would have to wait a year to enter. For remediation, Grace became a boarding student at Hartridge School in Plainfield, New Jersey, and continued her record of active participation. The quotation selected to describe her in the yearbook proclaimed: "In action faithful and in honor clear."

During all of her schooling, Grace loved mathematics, especially geometry. She remembered, "I used to draw pretty pictures with it." When she entered Vassar College in 1924, her interests in mathematics combined with those in physics and engineering. A gifted student, Grace also audited all the beginning courses in botany, physiology, and geology. She continued to play basketball and sought out adventure, once flying in a barnstorming biplane over the campus.

A Phi Beta Kappa graduate from Vassar in 1928 with a bachelor of arts degree in mathematics and physics, Grace undertook graduate studies at Yale University, where she was invited to join Sigma Xi, an honor society that recognizes scientists for their outstanding research achievements. After receiving her master's degree from Yale in 1930, Grace was married to Vincent Foster Hopper on June 15, 1930.

Because jobs were scarce during the Great Depression, Grace seized the opportunity to teach at Vassar in 1931 at a salary of $800 a year. As an assistant professor in mathematics, she taught algebra, trigonometry, and calculus. The Hoppers built a house in Poughkeepsie, New York, near the Vassar campus, and Vincent commuted to his teaching position in New York City until they were divorced in 1945. Grace earned her Ph.D. in mathematics and mathematical physics from Yale in 1934, a significant accomplishment for that era. Her doctoral thesis was entitled "A New Criterion for Reduceability of Algebraic Equations."

Highly patriotic, Grace yearned to serve her country during World War II. After threatening to quit her post at Vassar, she obtained a leave of absence in order to enter the United States Naval Reserve. Her admission to the reserve was nearly denied because she weighed only 105 pounds, not the requisite 121 pounds. After obtaining a waiver, in 1943 Grace entered the USNR Midshipman's School for Women in Northampton, Massachusetts. Despite early errors in identifying carriers and submarines, Grace graduated first in her class and was commissioned lieutenant, junior grade, on June 27, 1944. She was immediately assigned to the Bureau of Ships Computation Project in Cruft Laboratory at Harvard University with Howard Aiken as director. This assignment, unique because there were fewer than six computer projects underway in the United States, would change the course of her career.

Life's Work

When Grace Hopper reported to work on July 2, 1944, Commander Aiken waved his hand at the Mark I installation and introduced her to this "computing engine," the first programmable digital computer in the United States. He gave her a code book and asked to have the coefficients for the interpolation of the arc tangent ready by the following Thursday.

Mark I, also known as the Automatic Sequence Controlled Calculator, could do three additions every second—important because rapid computations were needed for the new weapons systems. Mark I was a monster of a machine: 51 feet long, 8 feet deep, 8 feet high, and approximately 5 tons in weight. It had 800,000 parts and contained more than 500 miles of wire. Mark I was fed instructions and data punched out on four long paper tapes: one control tape for instructions and three tapes for data input.

To program the Mark I, instructions had to be written in a machine code that told the computer exactly what operations to perform and their precise sequence. The instructions detailed which switches were to be set at either the on or off position, and a new program representing a different pattern of codes had to be written for each task or problem. Because it was easy to make errors, Hopper and her colleagues collected correct programs in a notebook with a routine for the sine, cosine, and the arc tangent. As one of her first challenging tasks, Hopper wrote an operating manual for the computer that eventually became one of the most famous documents in the literature of computers. In this manner, Hopper became the third programmer on the first large-scale digital computer in the United States.

The Navy leased the Mark I for the remainder of the war to compute quickly the complex calculations necessary to aim new Navy guns with precision. Hopper and her staff of three other officers and four enlisted men operated around the clock, providing critical information about ballistic trajectories. She later said, "I slept nights on a desk to see if my program was going to get running."

Hopper stayed on at Harvard after the war and joined the faculty as a research fellow in 1946. The Mark II, a multiprocessor, had been designed, built, and tested for the Navy Bureau of Ordnance since Hopper's arrival at Harvard and was five times faster than the Mark I. In the summer of 1947, a moth was found in the computer, beaten by a relay which then stopped functioning well, causing erroneous information. The two-inch moth was taped into a notebook and described as "first actual bug found." Later, when little work was being accomplished, Hopper and others would use the handy excuse that they were "debugging" the machine.

In 1949, she joined the Eckert-Mauchly Corporation, a Philadelphia firm run by John W. Mauchly and J. Presper Eckert, coinventors and developers of the world's first electronic computer known as ENIAC (Electronic Numerical Integrator and Calculator). The company had also built EDVAC and BINAC, binary automatic computers, and was building UNIVAC I (Universal Automatic Computer), the first commercial electronic computer. This new smaller computer had many memory devices, including storage tubes and a magnetic core, and was 1,000 times faster than the Mark I. Hopper joined the company as senior mathematician.

Hopper reasoned that if computers could be used to write their own programs, they would be used for business purposes. Accordingly, she developed a compiler to alleviate the problem of mistakes in code writing that developed when programs had to be written in octal code (base 8 instead of 10). The compiler translated the programmer's mathematical notations into the machine's binary language and performed the calculations. Her first compiler in 1952 was the A-0 System, standing for algebraic codes starting with routines at zero. By 1955, she had developed A-2, the first compiler to use mathematical computations extensively.

Next, Hopper developed the B-0 compiler for business, the first computer language employing English words rather than mathematical symbols. Earlier called MATH-MATIC, B-0 or FLOW-MATIC was an enormous advance in the development of programming languages. To create FLOW-MATIC, Hopper wrote 500 typical programs and identified 30 verbs common to all programs including words such as *count*, *divide*, *subtract*, *move*, *replace*, and *multiply*. She later claimed that she wrote this language because she was lazy: While other programmers wanted to play with the bits, she wanted to get the job done.

By 1959, there were three major computer languages, each requiring one specific computer. That year, a committee was authorized to develop a common business-oriented language to be used with any kind of computer. Heavily influenced by Hopper's FLOW-MATIC, the resulting product, COBOL, uses syntax and terms close to natural English, is easy to understand, and is efficient at processing large quantities of information. Because the Defense Department urged businesses to adopt COBOL if they wanted to continue selling their products to the government, COBOL eventually became the most widely used business computer language.

Hopper retired from the Naval Reserve when she reached the age of sixty in 1966 with the rank of commander. Much to her delight, however, the Navy discovered that it could not get along without her. Its payroll program had to be rewritten 823 times. Seven months later on August 1, 1967, she was called out of retirement to standardize the high level languages and get the entire Navy to use them. Specifically, Hopper was asked to develop a COBOL certifier, a set of programs that would tell the user whether a compiler labeled COBOL was legitimate for use. Hopper was initially recalled for six months, but the orders were changed to "indefinite"—allowing her to work for nearly twenty additional years. During the years she served as director of the Navy Programming Languages Group, Hopper developed a manual called *Fundamentals of COBOL* to train people on its use as well as a catalog with user hints and an index of sample statements.

In a ceremony held in August of 1986, on "Old Ironsides," the oldest commissioned warship, Hopper retired from the Navy at the age of seventy-nine with the rank of rear admiral. As the oldest commissioned naval officer on active duty, she said, "I love this ship. We belong together." The only woman admiral in the history of the U.S. Navy, Hopper telephoned her friends in Philadelphia to watch the grave of her great-grandfather Russell, who had also been a rear admiral, humorously warning them that he might rise from the dead. Never one to rest, Hopper immediately began working as a senior consultant for Digital Equipment Corporation.

Hopper received many prestigious honors, among them the Man of the Year award from the Data Processing Management Association (1969) and induction into the Engineering and Science Hall of Fame in Dayton, Ohio (1984). In recognition of her extraordinary contributions, the Navy dedicated the Grace Murray Hopper Service Center of the Navy Regional Data Automation Center in San Diego, California, in 1985. In 1991, when President George Bush awarded Hopper the National Medal of Technology, she was the first woman to receive it individually.

Witty, unorthodox, and sometimes combative—a self-described "boat rocker"—Hopper died at age eighty-five of natural causes.

Summary

Known as the "grand old lady of software," Grace Murray Hopper is considered a primary leader in developing compilers and standardizing computer languages. Cynics scoffed at the idea that computer programs could be written in English, but Hopper confidently proved otherwise.

An innovator, she accomplished many things: She helped to lift computing out of the mechanical age and into the era of electronics, she also helped to modernize the Navy by standardizing its use of the computer, and played a major role in building COBOL, thus making computers accessible to nonmathematicians.

Later in her life, not satisfied to rest on her laurels, Hopper became an ardent spokesperson for education and a public relations asset for the Navy. "Amazing Grace," as her associates called her, traveled all over the country, encouraging risk-taking and innovation. She spoke as many as 200 times a year, especially to young audiences. A lover of possibilities, she shared her philosophy with them: "Go ahead and do it. You can always apologize later."

As an educator, she worried that computers might create a new kind of gender discrimination: Men would be thinkists, women typists. Hopper insisted that females must study computer science, engineering, and business and gain confidence in their abilities as individuals. She believed women are as capable as men of doing programming and that computing is a good field for career mobility. "Women turn out to be very good programmers for one very good reason: They tend to finish up things, and men don't very often," she stated. Despite her obvious support of women, Hopper once called the women's movement "tommyrot and nonsense." She firmly believed that skilled, ambitious women would not be held back.

The mother of COBOL, Hopper was a pioneer in developing computer technology and leading the country into the information age.

Bibliography
Billings, Charlene W. *Grace Hopper: Navy Admiral and Computer Pioneer*. Hillside, N.J.: Enslow Publishers, 1989. A biography for adolescents with a thorough assessment of Hopper's life. Clear explanations of Hopper's groundbreaking work with compilers. Excellent photographs.
Gilbert, Lynn, and Gaylen Moore. "Grace Murray Hopper." In *Particular Passions: Talks with Women Who Have Shaped Our Times*. New York: Clarkson N. Potter, 1981. Lively interviews with thirty-nine celebrated women. Hopper was a spunky seventy-three-year-old at the time of her firsthand account.
Hopper, Grace Murray, and Steven L. Mandell. "Man the Thinkist, Woman the Typist?" In *Understanding Computers*. 2d ed. St. Paul, Minn.: West Publishing Co., 1987. A provocative essay in her now classic textbook.
Slater, Robert. "Grace Murray Hopper: Bugs, Compilers, and COBOL." In *Portraits in Silicon*. Cambridge, Mass.: MIT Press, 1987. A portrait focusing on Hopper as a software specialist.
Smith, William D. "Pioneer in Computers: Navy Officer Likes to Rock Boat." *The New York Times*, September 5, 1971, Section III, p. 5. A frank interview with Hopper regarding her scientific career.
Tropp, Henry S. "Grace Murray Hopper." In *Encyclopedia on Computer Science*, edited by Anthony Ralston and Edwin D. Reilly. 3d ed. New York: Van Nostrand Reinhold, 1993. A chronological listing of Hopper's achievements as a computer professional.

Deborah Elwell Arfken

MARILYN HORNE

Born: January 16, 1934; Bradford, Pennsylvania

Area of Achievement: Music

Contribution: An internationally famous American trained mezzo-soprano, Marilyn Horne is best known for her performances and revivals of nineteenth century bel canto operatic and recital repertoire, especially the works of Gioacchino Rossini.

Early Life

Marilyn Horne was born on January 16, 1934, in Bradford, Pennsylvania, to Bentz and Berneice Hokanson Horne. The third of four children in a musical family, Marilyn was a precocious child and already singing at the age of two. Her father, a trained tenor, recognized that his daughter showed an extraordinary musical talent and became a driving force behind Marilyn's musical development. When Marilyn was just five, her father found a voice teacher who would accept the child. It was Edna Luce, one of her first teachers in Pennsylvania, that Horne credits with the initial training in breath support upon which she was able to build throughout her career. Piano lessons were also part of Marilyn's early studies, and it was her father who supervised her practice time.

In 1945, the Horne family moved to Long Beach, California. The West Coast afforded Marilyn numerous opportunities during her formative years that were valuable stepping stones in her evolving singing career. As a young girl, she sang with the Roger Wagner Concert Youth Chorale, and in 1952 she toured Europe with Wagner's professional group as one of the soloists. Her major vocal studies in California were with William Vennard, one of America's best-known teachers and author of one of the first textbooks of its kind on vocal production, *Singing: The Mechanism and the Technic* (rev. ed. 1967). Vennard assumed guardianship of Marilyn's voice—a responsibility that had primarily been her father's. In 1952, she entered the University of Southern California, where Vennard was on the faculty, and she had her first operatic experiences there under Carl Ebert. Other advantages of being in California at that time were the relationships that resulted for Horne with world-famous musicians. One of the most important was with composer and conductor Igor Stravinsky. Because of her high degree of musical intelligence, Horne was able to learn Stravinsky's difficult scores quickly and was often chosen to perform his works. Another major influence on the singer's work was her contact with Lotte Lehmann, the operatic diva and unequaled German lieder singer. Lehmann's vocal master classes were attended by singers from all over the world, and Marilyn was a frequent student in these classes.

In 1954, Horne's professional life received some important boosts. The soprano gave her first major recital at the Hollywood Bowl. She also made her operatic debut, as Hata in *The Bartered Bride* (1866) by Bedřich Smetana, with the Los Angeles Guild Opera. In the same year, she was hired to dub the voice of Dorothy Dandridge in the film *Carmen Jones*. This activity led to a trip to Europe in 1956, the year of her father's death. Her association with Stravinsky made possible Horne's participation in the 1956 Venice Festival. After a year in Vienna, she signed a contract with the Municipal Opera of Gelsenkirchen, Germany. Thus far, all of her training had been as a soprano rather than a mezzo-soprano, and she spent three years in the repertory company singing mostly soprano roles. Her assignments included Mimi in Giacomo Puccini's *La Bohème* (1896), Tatiana in Peter Tchaikovsky's *Eugene Onegin* (1879), Minnie in Puccini's *The Girl of the Golden West* (1910), and Marie in Alban Berg's *Wozzeck* (1925).

Life's Work

The turning point in Marilyn Horne's singing career occurred when, upon her return from Germany, she was available to sing the role of Marie in *Wozzeck* as a substitute on short notice for the San Francisco Opera. One of those who took note of the young American was Ann Colbert, a New York-based performing arts manager with whom Marilyn soon signed a management contract.

Events of major importance were also taking place in her personal life. Prior to her trip to Europe, Marilyn had met conductor and string bass player Henry Lewis. Lewis was to become the first black musician to achieve status as a conductor of a major orchestra in the United States with his appointment to the New Jersey Symphony in 1968. It so happened that Horne and Lewis were both working in Europe at the same time. The interracial relationship with Lewis thrived against all odds, and the two were married in 1960. The marriage lasted until 1976 but was not without conflict. Emotional and professional pressures finally caused the marriage to break up after efforts on both their parts to salvage it. The Lewises had one daughter, Angela, who was born in 1965. During their years together, however, the conductor took over the role formerly played first by Marilyn's father and then by Vennard—that of guiding her vocal development. It was he who began to encourage the singer to make different use of the vocal registers, especially her lower voice, which had always been strong. In working with Lewis, Marilyn centered her vocal range a bit lower than she had in the past and began to work in the lyric mezzo-soprano range. In so doing, she found that she no longer experienced the vocal fatigue that had often been a problem for her.

The exploration of different roles opened many new possibilities for the singer. In fact, not long after Horne signed with Colbert, the manager arranged an audition for Horne with soprano Joan Sutherland and her pianist/conductor husband Richard Bonynge, who were looking for a mezzo partner for Sutherland in the florid nineteenth century (bel canto) repertoire. This audition brought Marilyn a Town Hall debut in 1961 as Agnese in Bellini's *Beatrice di Tenda* with Sutherland, for which she received high praise. Horne became a permanent member of the Sutherland-Bonynge team. It was as if her voice had found its home. From her vocal coaching with Bonynge and intensive study on her own, she began to acquire knowledge of the bel canto roles, and her musical focus shifted almost solely to the bel canto literature. It was in that repertoire that Horne's performances both in opera and recital were most highly acclaimed. Horne developed a love for the music of Gioacchino Rossini during this time, and she made the coloratura mezzo roles such as Rosina in *Il barbiere di Siviglia* (1816), Isabella in *L'Italiana in Algeri* (1813), and the title role in *Tancredi* (1813), her special property in the operatic world. No other mezzo-soprano since the nineteenth century had so intensely explored that portion of the repertoire.

Horne began to be in demand in opera houses all over the world, and performances from this period include her 1964 Covent Garden debut in London as Marie in *Wozzeck*, another round of appearances with Sutherland in Boston and internationally as Arsace in Rossini's *Semiramide* (1823), Adalgisa to Sutherland's Norma (in *Norma*, by Vincenzo Bellini, 1831) in Covent Garden (1967), and a 1969 La Scala debut as Neocles in Rossini's *Le siège de Corinth* (1827). After she had sung in most of the world's major opera houses, in 1979 the Metropolitan Opera in New York hired Horne to make her debut in *Norma* in the proven role of Adalgisa with her familiar partner Joan Sutherland. She went on to sing many other roles at the Met, ranging from her fun-loving Rosina in *Il barbiere di Siviglia* (in 1971) to the spirited Carmen (in *Carmen*, Georges Bizet, 1875) with Leonard Bernstein conducting (in 1972), and Isabella in *L'Italiana in Algeri* (in 1973). She is well known for her revival of the title roles in Handel's *Rinaldo* (1711) and Rossini's *Tancredi* (1813), which Houston Opera mounted for her in 1975. She sang Rinaldo again in 1984 at the Metropolitan.

Horne's professional work was not restricted to opera. Her deep affection for the art song and German lieder is vividly expressed in her many outstanding recital performances. Martin Katz was for many years her friend and accompanist. Their musical collaboration produced magnetic performances, and Horne credits Katz with valuable vocal coaching. The versatility of Horne's vocal technique was apparent in her selection of recital material. Her repertoire ranged from traditional lyric recital fare to Rossini songs, works by her favorite lieder composer Hugo Wolf, simple American songs arranged by Stephen Foster and Aaron Copland, and even to the "Immolation Scene" of Brünhilde from Richard Wagner's music drama *Götterdämmerung* (1874). A 1979 recital at the Salzburg Festival with Martin Katz has been referred to by the singer several times as one of the highlights of her career.

Summary

Marilyn Horne, known as "Jackie" to her friends, is appreciated as much by the public and her colleagues for her personal warmth and sense of humor as for her musical accomplishments. As an American-born and American-trained singer, she was somewhat unusual at a time when many operatic performers felt the need to spend much of their early careers in Europe in order to be successful. Her work conveyed an energetic spirit, directness, and independence that carried her through many stages of professional and personal development to achieve worldwide acclaim. Endowed with remarkable natural talent and the intelligence to cultivate it, she made use of the resources around her at each plateau in order to learn as much as possible and to perform with integrity. Her enthusiastic cooperation with fellow musicians yielded marvelous results. She is celebrated for the rich, resonant timbre of her voice, which, although it is labeled mezzo-soprano, has the brightness and range of a soprano. The warm yet extremely flexible instrument is well suited to the demands of the rhythmically charged nineteenth century bel canto repertoire on which Horne leaves her most indelible mark. Her devotion to researching the original intentions of the composers and traditional performance styles has made her performances of the music of composers such as Bellini and Rossini some of the most authentic of the twentieth century. In fact, her work was so admired by the Italians that in 1983 the Rossini Foundation in Pesaro named her the first-time winner of the prize given in honor of Teresa Belloc, the nineteenth century soprano for whom Rossini wrote the opera *La gazza ladra* (1817). Horne's many recordings of operatic and concert material demonstrate the beauty and power of her singing.

As a mature musician, although continuing to perform and record on a selective basis, she has made efforts through adjudication of auditions and sponsoring of master classes and musical competitions to pass on her knowledge to young musicians. Her resolve always to work with discipline and to develop her musical and artistic gifts to the fullest make Marilyn Horne an important example for future musicians as well as for aspiring professionals in any field.

Bibliography

Hines, Jerome. *Great Singers on Great Singing*. New York: Limelight Editions, 1984. Horne is among forty opera stars interviewed by Metropolitan Opera bass Jerome Hines. She discusses in detail her technique of singing and the training responsible for her vocal development, and she offers advice for young singers.

Horne, Marilyn, with Jane Scovell. *Marilyn Horne: My Life*. New York: Atheneum, 1983. Horne's autobiography is a lively, intimate account of her personal and professional development. Experiences with other artists, details of concert tours, and insight into personal and family relationships are included, along with a discography that is complete up to 1983.

Jacobson, Robert. "At the Zenith." Parts 1-2. *Opera News* 45 nos. 12 and 15 (1981). Jacobson interviewed Horne just after she had begun to receive critical acclaim for Metropolitan performances and work with stars such as Joan Sutherland and tenor Luciano Pavarotti. Horne discussed the slow, although steady, progress of her career and the difficult choices she made along the way.

Mayer, Martin. "Musician of the Month: Marilyn Horne." *High Fidelity/Musical America* 33 (1983): 1, 4-5, 10. Mayer discusses the enviable beginnings of Horne's career and her recognition as a world-famous diva. Attention is also given to her research and performance of Rossini's works and the acknowledgment received from the Italians for her performances and revivals of pieces from the bel canto repertoire.

Newman, Edwin. "In Her Glory." *Opera News* 55, no. 7 (1990): 10-14, 43. In one of the latest interviews with Horne, the singer talks about her past career choices and experiences as well as her future plans for performing and tapering her engagements toward retirement.

Pleasants, Henry. *The Great Singers*. New York: Simon & Schuster, 1966. Pleasants discusses Horne's contributions to the contemporary performance practices of nineteenth century opera within the context of other major singers who have specialized in bel canto.

Sargeant, Winthrop. *Divas*. New York: Coward, McCann & Geoghegan, 1973. One chapter is devoted to Horne's life. Other international singers discussed are Eileen Farrell, Birgit Nilsson, Leontyne Price, Beverly Sills, and Joan Sutherland.

Sandra C. McClain

KAREN HORNEY

Born: September 16, 1885; Eilbek, near Hamburg, Germany
Died: December 4, 1952; New York, New York
Area of Achievement: Psychology
Contribution: Horney was a leading psychologist who contributed to understanding the psychology of women, emphasized the role of sociocultural factors in producing neurosis, and developed a new noninstinctivist psychoanalytic theory.

Early Life

Karen Clementina Theodora Danielsen was born in Eilbek, Germany, on September 16, 1885. She was the daughter of Berndt Henrik Wackels Danielsen, a sea captain with the Hamburg-American Lines, who was a Norwegian by birth but later became a naturalized German, and Clothilde Marie Van Ronzelen Danielsen, of Dutch background. Clothilde, or "Sonni," was sixteen years younger than her husband when she married him. Danielsen had four grown children from a previous marriage who did not like his new wife and the new children that came later. Berndt Danielsen, an intensely religious man, believed in a patriarchal family structure with women in subservient roles. His emotional presence in the home was felt by everyone. Sonni was a religious freethinker, was more educated, liberal, and cultured than her husband, and advocated a greater independence for women.

Karen Danielsen was born as Hamburg was coming into the industrial age. Just ten years after her birth, Hamburg Harbor became the third largest international port in the world. Karen traveled with her father and experienced life in different cultures, which added to her understanding of human nature. She was an avid reader, and her life was greatly augmented and embellished by her own imagination. It may have been her imagination that led her to envision a path for herself that was not common for any German female of her time. In her imagination, she thought of herself as Doctor Karen Danielsen, even though, in 1899, there was not one university in Germany that admitted women. Germany was, however, changing quickly enough to accommodate her. She attended the first Gymnasium for Girls in Hamburg in 1900. In the spring of 1906, Karen graduated from the Gymnasium, and on Easter Sunday of the same year, she boarded a train bound for the University of Freiburg to begin university life and her medical studies. The University of Freiburg became the first university in Germany to graduate a woman, even though female professionalism was considered unnatural. On October 30, 1909, while still a medical student, Karen married Oskar Horney, a student of political science and economics. Oskar was that rare man in Berlin who was able to tolerate ambition in a wife. They had three daughters, Brigitte (born in 1911), Marianne (born in 1913), and Renate (born in 1915). Karen received her M.D. from the University of Berlin in 1915.

Life's Work

After passing her medical exams, Karen Horney worked for the influential Berlin psychiatrist Hermann Oppenheim, as an assistant in his clinic. It was there that she learned of psychoanalysis and began analysis with Karl Abraham, the only trained Freudian analyst in Berlin. Once Horney had discovered psychoanalysis, it became the intellectual and emotional focal point of her life. Unfortunately, psychoanalysis was frowned upon by the medical establishment. Understanding the stigma associated with psychoanalysis, Horney continued to specialize in psychiatry during the day, but after hours she pursued Freudian psychoanalysis as a patient and a student. She was decidedly cautious about discussing Freud's ideas in and around Berlin and in the psychiatric clinics where she trained. While writing her doctoral dissertation, she was extremely careful not to discuss Freudian ideas. Everything about her dissertation suggests that she was a faithful and serious disciple of her psychiatric profession. Upon receiving her medical degree in 1915, she was from that point on a psychoanalyst. She was no longer hesitant to discuss Freudian ideas. She became more controversial and even more convinced of the therapeutic value of psychoanalysis. She took her first patients in psychoanalysis in 1919 and became actively involved with the Berlin Psychoanalytic Clinic and Institute for the next twelve years.

The relationship between Karen Horney and her husband became strained and began deteriorating. Their lifestyle had been prosperous, but with the economic crisis of 1923, Oskar was forced to declare personal bankruptcy. He later developed a severe neurological illness that caused a radical change in his personality. The Horneys separated in 1926 and were divorced in 1937. After her divorce, Karen channeled most of her energy into professional writing. Over the next six years, she was to publish a total of fourteen professional papers. The years between 1926 and 1932 were among the most productive of her life. Her friends, busy practice, and active involvement in institute affairs made Karen Horney a central figure in the beginnings of the Berlin Institute. Her most important contribution to the future of psychoanalysis grew out of her teaching role. She was a member of the education committee at the institute and a member of the education committee of the International Psychoanalytic Association beginning in 1928.

Horney made contributions to feminine psychology over a thirteen-year period from 1923 to 1936. She did not like the tenets of Freudian psychology, which described female development from a male-oriented, phallocentric viewpoint and made it appear that women had an inferior status. She put emphasis on interpersonal attitudes and on social influences in determining women's feelings, relations, and roles. Six of her papers on marital problems were published between 1927 and 1932.

In 1932, Horney accepted the position of associate director of the new Chicago Institute for Psychoanalysis, offered to her by its director, Franz Alexander, a former Berlin colleague. She looked forward to the United States and greater freedom of expression than she was allowed in Berlin. She remained in Chicago for only two years because she clashed with Alexander and the practices he was introducing at the institute. She had already begun to emphasize cultural factors in female psychology, which departed from Freud's original ideas. Alexander regarded her departure from orthodox Freudianism as revolutionary. In 1934, she moved to New York City, built an analytic practice, and taught at the New York Psychoanalytic Institute and the New School for Social Research. During this time, she produced her major theoretical works, *The Neurotic Personality of Our Time* (1937), which discussed the role of social practices in causing neuroses, and *New Ways in Psychoanalysis* (1939), spelling out her differences with Freudian theory. Horney had a strong personality, and she tended to resist all attempts at control and regulation. These traits, combined with her expressed desire that the New York Psychoanalytic Institute should become a progressive institution instead of a rigid teaching institution, caused friction between her and the institute's president, Lawrence Kubie. He did not like her departure from Freud's original ideas, and in the end he and others required that she return to Freud or teach her ideas elsewhere. She was singled out as a troublemaker and demoted from instructor to lecturer.

Shortly after this demotion, in April of 1941, she and four other analysts offered their letters of resignation to the secretary of the New York Psychoanalytic Society. These five then started their own organization, the Association for the Advancement of Psychoanalysis. The first volume of the organization's journal, the *American Journal of Psychoanalysis*, listed fifteen "charter members" in New York and a handful in other cities. The organization offered thirteen courses for students and interested physicians. The curriculum was to train psychiatrists for clinical practice in psychoanalysis. Horney's third book, *Self-Analysis*, was published in 1942. After her break from the New York Psychoanalytic Institute and Freudian orthodoxy, she found herself in enormous demand as a psychoanalyst. *Self-Analysis* was ignored or reviled by every popular and psychoanalytic publication. Many did not review it at all, an indication of the power of the New York Psychoanalytic Society. Her last two books, *Our Inner Conflicts* (1945) and *Neurosis and Human Growth* (1950), were also not reviewed. Karen Horney's new alternative institution never gained official national recognition. Her work continued to be overlooked and minimized within psychoanalysis because of this split.

In her later years, Horney took to religion, especially Zen Buddhism. She met with D. T. Suzuki, the author of *Zen Buddhism and Its Influence on Japanese Culture* (1949). She, Suzuki, and some of her friends planned a trip to Japan to experience Zen life at first hand. The trip to Japan was to be one of the happiest adventures in Karen Horney's life. Suzuki led Horney and her friends for a month on a tour of some of the most important Zen monasteries in Japan. Within two months after her return, she suddenly became ill and was admitted to Columbia Presbyterian Hospital. She was diagnosed as having cancer of the gall bladder. During her second week in the hospital, her condition rapidly worsened. On December 4, 1952, Karen Horney died. She was buried in Ferncliff Cemetery in Ardsley, a quiet suburb of Westchester, north of New York City.

Summary

Karen Horney disputed the basic principles of Sigmund Freud, his psychoanalysis theories, and the therapeutic results of the application of these theories. She believed that neuroses and personality disorders were the results of environmental and social conditions, not of biological drives. She challenged Freud's libido theory and his theories of psychosexual development. She also contended that feminine psychology could not be understood unless the masculine bias in psychoanalysis and other fields were lifted. There was a clear need to formulate a masculine and feminine psychology to prepare the way for her whole-person philosophy. Horney was considered an early feminist, although she was not allied with any political movement. She fought for the equality of the sexes and praised women for being homemakers and mothers. She also stated that women should have the freedom to have careers. Since her death, many of her followers have continued to praise her theories and to apply them to new problems and conditions. Her ideas have entered the mainstream of psychology and some have been rediscovered and appropriated by other schools. Her theories regarding the causes and dynamics of neurosis and her later revision of Freud's theory of personality have remained influential. Her analysis of humankind allowed for a broader scope of development and coping than did the determinism of Freud. Her influence on American readers has been far-reaching.

Bibliography

Alexander, Franz, Samuel Eisenstein, and Martin Grotjohn, eds. "Karen Horney: The Cultural Emphasis." In *Psychoanalytic Pioneers*. New York: Basic Books, 1966. This work tells the histories of the pioneers in psychoanalysis and describes their work and its influence.

Kelman, Harold, ed. *Feminine Psychology*. London: Routledge & Kegan Paul, 1967. A collection of Karen Horney's papers on women, many of which were previously unavailable in English.

Quinn, Susan. *A Mind of Her Own: The Life of Karen Horney*. New York: Summit Books, 1987. The first full-scale biography of Karen Horney, this is a fine source that covers the full range of Horney's life and work.

Rubins, Jack L. *Karen Horney: Gentle Rebel of Psychoanalysis*. New York: Dial Press, 1978. Examines the life story of Karen Horney from the persecution of the Jewish psychoanalysts during the early Nazi period to the analytic classes in Chicago and New York.

Sayers, Janet. *Mothers of Psychoanalysis: Helene Deutsch, Karen Horney, Anna Freud, Melanie Klein*. New York: W. W. Norton, 1991. The mother-centered view of psychoanalysis constituted a direct challenge to the discipline, which was once patriarchal and phallocentric. The story of the revolution in psychoanalysis is told here through the biographies of its first women architects.

Westkott, Marcia. *The Feminist Legacy of Karen Horney*. New Haven, Conn.: Yale University Press, 1986. Westkott presents a social-psychological theory that explains women's personality development as a consequence of growing up in a social setting in which they are devalued.

Darlene Mary Suarez

HARRIET HOSMER

Born: October 9, 1830; Watertown, Massachusetts
Died: February 21, 1908; Watertown, Massachusetts
Area of Achievement: Art
Contribution: America's first and best neoclassical female sculptor, Hosmer was successful in Europe and the United States, and she inspired other female artists to follow her example.

Early Life

Harriet Goodhue Hosmer's father was Hiram Hosmer, a successful family physician in Watertown, Massachusetts. Her mother was Sarah Grant Hosmer. They had two daughters and then two sons. "Hatty," as Harriet was called, was the second child. By 1836, tuberculosis had killed both brothers and her mother. Six years later Hatty's sister died. To make Hatty healthier, her father prescribed outdoor activity, including horseback riding, rowing, swimming, skating, running, climbing trees and hills, and shooting with pistols and bow and arrow. She also stuffed birds and modeled animals out of clay.

When Harriet Hosmer was a tomboyish sixteen, her father sent her to the excellent boarding school in Lenox, Massachusetts, run by Elizabeth Sedgwick, sister-in-law of the novelist Catharine Sedgwick. The girl enjoyed her three years both in and out of class there, and gained as a life-long friend Cornelia Crow, a fellow pupil whose father was a rich St. Louis businessman and civic leader. Hosmer also became friendly with the Lenox resident Fanny Kemble, the well-known English actress.

Deciding to become a sculptor, Hosmer took art classes in Boston. When her father asked the Boston Medical Society if she could study anatomy there and was refused, he let her go to the more enlightened Missouri Medical School (later part of Washington University) in St. Louis, where she lived with Cornelia Crow and her family from 1850 to 1851. Early in 1851, Hosmer took two unescorted steamboat trips on the Mississippi River, then returned to Watertown, did sculptural work in a backyard studio, became friendly with the writer Lydia Maria Child, and met and disliked the sensational dancer Lola Montez. Then she met the actress Charlotte Cushman, who so admired the young woman's ambition to compete in the male-dominated field of sculpture that she encouraged her to go to Rome with her. Accompanied by her father, Hosmer embarked for Italy, armed with her anatomy-school diploma and daguerreotypes of her first art work, an idealized bust called *Hespera* (1852).

Hosmer fell at once under the spell of Rome, its art, its expatriate artists, and, above all, its professional opportunities. Through friends she met John Gibson, a renowned British sculptor who lived in Rome. Approving her credentials, he began tutoring her. Soon, she was on amiable terms with many Americans and their families in Rome— including the sculptor-writer William Wetmore Story; the sculptors Paul Akers, Thomas Crawford, and Joseph Mozier; and the painters Luther Terry and Cephas Giovanni Thompson—as well as Robert and Elizabeth Browning (whose hands she memorably cast in bronze c. 1853), the painter-sculptor Frederic Leighton, Fanny Kemble's socially prominent sister Adelaide Sartoris, and other Britishers. Assured that his daughter was safe and happy, Hiram Hosmer returned home in 1853, promising Harriet a moderate stipend and vainly hoping she would finish her foreign lessons soon and follow him back. The spell of Rome, however, endured.

Life's Work

Harriet Hosmer devoted herself wholeheartedly to sculpture. Doing so meant, in her view, remaining indefinitely in Rome to learn what Gibson could offer, after which she would establish a studio of her own, gain commissions, and work hard. Gibson, who had studied under Antonia Canova and Bertel Thorvaldsen, passed on to Hosmer his neoclassical ideals. After drawing antique statues and copying classical works, she carved two marble busts—*Daphne* (1853) and *Medusa* (1854)—and gained publicity in the United States by sending copies home. Crow was so impressed that he commissioned a life-size marble statue on any subject the sculptor might select. The result was the attractive marble *Oenone* (c. 1855); this nymph, abandoned by Paris, is seated, with her right hand on the ground, nude down to hips. Hosmer followed this work with the delightful marble *Puck* (1855). Her mischievous creature, out of William Shakespeare's *A Midsummer Night's Dream*, sits on a toadstool, winged and with his legs crossed, scowling impishly, holding a scorpion in his right hand. Hosmer sold about fifty copies of *Puck* for $1,000 or so apiece—one to the Prince of Wales. Then came *Beatrice Cenci* (1856). This tragic subject of history and legend, a young woman raped by her vicious father, whom she then killed, is represented as awaiting execution. Hosmer poses her sleeping subject brilliantly: her sensitive face, her classically coiffed head and upper torso pillowed on a short couch, her right hand loosely holding a rosary, and her flowing garments revealing and concealing her legs, one straight, one bent.

Three commissions followed—for the life-size marble *Judith Falconnet* (1858), the larger-than-life marble *Zenobia in Chains* (1859), and the bronze *Thomas Hart Benton* (begun c. 1862). When the teenaged Judith Falconnet died in Rome, her mother engaged Hosmer to create a sarcophagus statue, which, when completed, was installed in the Church of Sant' Andrea delle Fratte—the first work by an American artist to be placed in a Roman church. The simply garbed, sweet-faced effigy lies full-length on a legged couch, a chaplet in her right hand, with her left hand at her side. The standing figure of Queen Zenobia, taken captive in exotic Palmyra, is portrayed heavily robed, with her head still crowned but bowed in disgrace. *Zenobia* was exhibited in England and toured the United States for sizable fees. Of the many copies made and sold, Mrs. Potter Palmer, the Chicago art patron, bought one for her lavish home. The original has since been lost. When her father suffered a stroke in 1860, Hosmer returned home, found him improving, and went on to St. Louis to see old friends. After conferring with a committee about the statue of Thomas Hart Benton, the distinguished Missouri senator, she returned to Rome and, after completing some other works, turned to her ten-foot model of Benton in clay, a plaster cast of which was sent to Munich. It was cast in bronze, shipped to St. Louis, and unveiled in Lafayette Park before an applauding crowd of 40,000 people in 1868. Hosmer's Benton has a sensitive face and fine hands; he is depicted unrolling a map of the West and wearing a togalike cloak and sandals. Hosmer received $10,000 for her part in the lavishly expensive work.

When her father suddenly died in 1862, Hosmer inherited means sufficient to make her even more independent. She was disappointed when she was invited to compete for an Abraham Lincoln monument for Springfield, Illinois, only to have her over-elaborate design rejected in favor of one by Larkin Mead (1867). She had begun to take working summer vacations in England, regularly visiting the estates of titled friends. Works from this period include a seven-foot marble *Fountain of the Siren* for her friend Lady Marian Alford's London house (1861), a *Sleeping Faun* (1865), so charming that when it was shown in Dublin the Irish aristocrat Sir Benjamin Guinness bought it for a thousand pounds, and a marble chimney piece called *The Death of the Dryads* (c. 1868) for her friend Lady Louisa Ashburton's mansion at Romney, in Hampshire.

Hosmer modeled relatively few outstanding works after about 1875. Instead, she spent much time and energy trying to invent a perpetual-motion machine and experimenting with synthetic marble. She returned a few times to the United States to be with friends, travel, and lecture to admiring audiences. She competed for a monument to Lincoln in Chicago but lost out to Augustus Saint-Gaudens, who completed his work there in 1887. She returned to America for good in 1900, where she died eight years later in Watertown, Massachusetts.

Summary

In 1869, Harriet Hosmer wrote the following to Phebe A. Hanaford, a pioneer American clergywoman whom she had heard preach:

> I honor every woman who has strength enough to step out of the beaten path when she feels that her walk lies in another; strength enough to stand up and be laughed at if necessary. That is a bitter pill we must all swallow at the beginning; but I regard those pills as tonics quite essential to one's mental salvation. . . . [I]n a few years it will not be thought strange that women should be preachers and sculptors, and everyone who comes after us will have to bear fewer and fewer blows. Therefore I say, I honor all those who step boldly forward, and, in spite of ridicule and criticism, pave a broader path for the women of the next generation.

Hosmer was criticized for becoming an artist at a time when "respectable" women were expected to marry, have children, and be subservient to men. She soberly studied anatomy, showed casts of body parts to art students of both sexes, outraced and outclimbed many men her own age, rode horses with zest and skill through the Roman streets and out of town, and became a sculptor of international acclaim. She never seriously wished to be a wife and mother, since she believed that marriage would siphon time, energy, and emotions away from her art, and she often called her statues her children. Once her reputation was established, she became a role model for other female artists—Margaret Foley, Louisa Lander, Emma Stebbins, and Anne Whitney being the most successful. These women also suffered from gender prejudice, but they fought to greater degrees of success than they would have otherwise because of Hosmer's inspiring example. Hosmer also numbered among her friends such progressive females as Charlotte Cushman and Fanny Kemble, and she called many goodhearted men her friends. Royalty, male as well as female, also beat a path to her Roman studio—most notably, the Czar of Russia, but also the Empress of Austria and her sister, the former Queen of Naples, both of whom she celebrated in statues. Hosmer's sculpture may be criticized today because of the dominance of sometimes effete neoclassical works in her era, but it would surely be too much to expect that this spirited woman should have broken the way to vital naturalism in sculpture. She accomplished far more than might have been expected of her as it was.

Bibliography
Carr, Cornelia Crow, ed. *Harriet Hosmer: Letters and Memories*. New York: Moffat, Yard, 1912. Contains letters to and from Hosmer, lovingly edited by her closest nonprofessional friend, and informative commentary.
Craven, Wayne. *Sculpture in America*. Rev. ed. New York: Cornwall Books, 1984. This work places Hosmer in the tradition of American sculpture and contains astute criticism of her works.
Kasson, Joy S. *Marble Queens and Captives: Women in Nineteenth-Century American Sculpture*. New York: Yale University Press, 1990. Considers Hosmer's works in relation to aesthetic traditions of the nineteenth century, during which attitudes about women's nature and their role in society changed. As they did so, traditional narrative statues of powerful women and helpless women were subjected to new analyses.
Rubinstein, Charlotte Streifer. *American Women Sculptors: A History of Women Working in Three Dimensions*. Boston: G. K. Hall, 1990. This useful encyclopedia has a twenty-six column entry on Hosmer and is excellently illustrated and annotated.
Sherwood, Dolly. *Harriet Hosmer, American Sculptor, 1830-1908*. Columbia: University of Missouri Press, 1991. Making use of all available published and unpublished materials and magnificently documented, this definitive biography details Hosmer's early years, her lively relationships with fellow expatriates in Rome, her professional successes, and her direct and indirect encouragement of other likeminded women.

Robert L. Gale

JULIA WARD HOWE

Born: May 27, 1819; New York, New York
Died: October 17, 1910; Newport, Rhode Island
Areas of Achievement: Literature, women's rights, and social reform
Contribution: In addition to proving that a woman could become a top-ranking poet, Julia Ward Howe set an example as an early crusader for women's rights. Her inspiring "Battle Hymn of the Republic" helped the North win the Civil War and free the slaves.

Early Life

Julia Ward was born on May 27, 1819, in New York City. Her father, Samuel Ward, was a partner in a prestigious Wall Street banking firm and provided a comfortable life for his family. Her mother, Julia Cutler Ward, was a sensitive woman who suffered from poor health mainly because she bore seven children and had one miscarriage in a ten-year period. She died of tuberculosis when Julia was only five. Julia and her siblings were reared by their Aunt Eliza Cutler, who wrote poetry, cultivated the arts, and invited many like-minded friends to soirees at the Ward home.

Samuel Ward, however, was a strict disciplinarian who frightened his children with tales of damnation and hellfire. The combination of family influences was to shape Julia's character. She was taught at home by governesses and attended young ladies' schools run by pious spinsters. Her principal interests were literature and Romance languages. Like many upper-middle-class young ladies, she had limited formal education but picked up a great deal of education by utilizing her abundant leisure for self-improvement. She taught herself to read German and studied German philosophy. At an early age, she published essays on Johann Wolfgang von Goethe, Johann Schiller, and Alphonse Lamartine in the *New York Review* and *Theological Review*, giving proof of her self-discipline and literary inclinations.

Julia was married at the age of twenty-three. Her husband, Samuel Gridley Howe, a wealthy philanthropist and social activist, was in his early forties. They settled in South Boston, where Julia tried to occupy her time with housekeeping and child care, while her husband pursued his many philanthropic interests.

The couple had six children over the next sixteen years. The youngest died of diphtheria at the age of three. Julia became disenchanted with her husband and with the dependent, confined condition of middle-class married women. On the day of their marriage, she had written: "I am perfectly happy to sacrifice to one so noble and so earnest, the daydreams of my youth." In an entry in her journal twenty years later, she wrote: "In the course of that time I have never known my husband to approve of any act of mine which I myself valued."

Her first book of poetry, titled *Passion-flowers*, was published anonymously in 1854. It contained many poems expressing her frustrations. Her second book of poems, *Words for the Hour* (1857), also published anonymously, contained poems in a similar vein, as in the following example:

> Between us, a silence of torment,
> That each is disdainful to break,
> That fretteth the soul as a garment,
> That stingeth the heart, like a snake—

Her husband was furious over her exposure of their marital problems, since many people guessed the identity of the author of both books. The Howes came close to divorce on several occasions, but remained under the same roof until Samuel's death in 1876.

Life's Work

As a writer, Julia Ward Howe enjoyed only local fame and did not expect more. She wrote two plays that enjoyed little success. It was not until the *Atlantic Monthly* published her "Battle Hymn of the Republic" in February, 1862, that she achieved national recognition. The lines, which were set to the tune of "John Brown's Body," quickly became known throughout the North because the song seemed to capture the emotions of a country at war. President Abraham Lincoln heard it sung in Washington shortly after the Battle of Gettysburg and, with tears in his eyes, called out: "Sing it again!"

Howe created the work in a single sitting. It consists of five verses, the first of which is the best known:

> Mine eyes have seen the glory of the coming of the Lord;
> He is trampling out the vintage where the grapes of wrath are stored;
> He hath loosed the fateful lightning of His terrible swift sword:
> His truth is marching on.

"The Battle Hymn of the Republic" remains Julia Ward Howe's best-known work. It continues to inspire people in other crusades for justice. One of America's greatest writers, John Steinbeck, used the phrase "The Grapes of Wrath" as the title of his most famous novel, published in 1939, which was a heartfelt cry for social reform on behalf of dispossessed Oklahoma sharecroppers.

After the war, Howe used her fame to champion worthy causes. She was primarily interested in the women's movement. She was a founder of the New England Women's Club and the New England Woman Suffrage Association. She was a popular speaker at conventions and legislative hearings. In 1870, she founded the weekly *Woman's Journal* and served as its editor and a contributor for twenty years.

Her interest in the women's movement was not limited to the suffrage cause. She was active in founding or supporting many organizations devoted to the advancement of women in such areas as education, artistic endeavors, and the professions. Like many feminists of her time, she believed that women could have a civilizing effect if they obtained political power. She did not want women to have power purely for the sake of power, but for the good that women could do.

Howe was extremely active in promoting international peace. She believed that if women around the world could gain political power, they could temper male militancy. In 1870 she published "Appeal to Womanhood Throughout the World," agitating for a peaceful settlement of the Franco-Prussian War, and in 1872 she tried unsuccessfully to organize a Woman's Peace Congress in London. Later, she was director and vice president of the American Peace Society.

Howe had a strong religious faith that each human life had meaning and purpose. She was very much concerned about the deterioration of traditional values during the Gilded Age following the Civil War and called on women to defend marriage, family, and religion. In lectures and essays, she ridiculed the gaudy mansions, ostentatious parties, and cultural poverty of the nouveau riche, comparing them unfavorably with the dedicated social leaders of her own generation. She especially deplored the decline in religious faith, which was partly a result of the growing prestige of science.

After her husband's death, financial difficulties forced Howe to travel as a paid lecturer. In 1876 she toured the Midwest, and in 1888 she traveled to the Pacific Coast. She also preached at Unitarian and Universalist churches. Two of her books, *Modern Society* and *Is Polite Society Polite?*, are collections of lectures. She founded women's clubs all over the United States, including the Wisconsin Woman's Club (1876) and the Century Club of San Francisco (1888).

During her lifetime, Howe was one of America's best-loved writers. In old age, she had become a sort of national institution, America's unofficial poet laureate. Her funeral was held in the Church of the Disciples, with the governor of Massachusetts and many other dignitaries attending. After her death in 1910, she was buried beside her husband in Mount Auburn Cemetery in Cambridge, Massachusetts.

Summary

Julia Ward Howe was the first American woman to rival America's most distinguished male writers. Before her time, writing by women had been confined to domestic topics and romantic sentiments, much as women themselves were confined to home and family by tradition and economic necessity. She devoted her life to breaking down the barriers that confined women and prevented them from developing to their full potential.

Her greatest impact was in the crusade for woman suffrage, in which she was a leading figure until her death. American women did not receive enfranchisement until August 26, 1920, when Congress passed the Nineteenth Amendment. Howe had been dead for ten years, but her work had contributed greatly to that momentous event.

Howe was the first woman to be elected to the American Academy of Arts and Letters. She proved to the world that women could write as well as men in any literary form. She wrote not only poetry but also plays, travel books, biographies, memoirs, essays, political tracts, and innumerable letters. She used her writing and speaking skills to fight for worthy causes, setting an example for many younger women to follow.

Bibliography

Clifford, Deborah Pickman. *Mine Eyes Have Seen the Glory: A Biography of Julia Ward Howe*. Boston: Little, Brown, 1979. This is the definitive biography of Howe, exhaustively researched and thoroughly documented. Written in an interesting, anecdotal style, it discusses her marital problems in detail. Contains a comprehensive bibliography and extensive chapter endnotes.

Elliott, Maud Howe. *The Eleventh Hour in the Life of Julia Ward Howe*. Boston: Little, Brown, 1911. A record of Julia Ward Howe's activities during the last five years of her long life, written by her daughter. Quotes many bits of practical wisdom the famous poet passed on in epigrammatical form.

Hall, Florence H. *Memories Grave and Gay*. New York: Harper & Brothers, 1918. This book of the reminiscences of Howe's eldest surviving daughter contains interesting chapters on Howe's involvement in the antislavery movement and the Civil War.

Howe, Julia Ward. *Reminiscences, 1819-1899*. New York: Houghton, Mifflin, 1899. The author's autobiography is full of interesting anecdotes about her travels and recollections of important personalities of her time. It captures the flavor of nineteenth century America. Illustrated with many old photographs.

Ream, Debbie Williams. "Mine Eyes Have Seen the Glory (J. W. Howe)." *American History Illustrated* 27 (January/February, 1993): 60-64. This beautifully illustrated article covers the complete history of Howe's creation of her most famous poem, "The Battle Hymn of the Republic," and the inspirational effect of that work during the Civil War.

Richards, Laura E. H., and Maud Howe Elliott. *Julia Ward Howe, 1819-1910*. 2 vols. Boston: Houghton Mifflin, 1916. This early biography of Julia Ward Howe was written by two of her daughters. The work received a Pulitzer Prize. Contains numerous excerpts from Howe's poetry and letters. Liberally illustrated with old photographs.

Schreiber, Mary Suzanne. "Julia Ward Howe and the Travel Book." *New England Quarterly* 62 (June, 1989): 264-279. Discusses Howe as one of the first women to break into the male-dominated area of travel writing, a popular literary form in the nineteenth century. Describes Howe's empathy for women in foreign lands because of their condition as second-class citizens.

Tharp, Louise Hall, *Three Saints and a Sinner: Julia Ward Howe, Louisa, Annie, and Sam Ward*. Boston: Little, Brown, 1956. A composite biography of four members of the prominent Ward family of Boston and New York. The three "saints" are Julia Ward Howe and her two sisters; the "sinner" is their flamboyant brother Sam.

Wallace, James D. "Hawthorne and the Scribbling Women Reconsidered." *American Literature* 62 (June, 1990): 201-222. Discusses Nathaniel Hawthorne's views on contemporary American women writers, including his mixed feelings about Howe's poems published anonymously in *Passion-flowers*. Hawthorne objected to her revealing family secrets.

Bill Delaney

TINA HOWE

Born: November 21, 1937; New York, New York

Area of Achievement: Literature
Contribution: Since 1969, Tina Howe has written plays that use comic absurdity to show the pain underlying domestic life.

Early Life

Tina Howe was born in New York City on November 21, 1937 into an intimidatingly artistic, blue-blooded New England family. Her father was Quincy Howe, an eminent radio and television newscaster for CBS. Tina Howe later asserted that her father was, "not only famous, but intelligent. . . . He felt it was through work that you find yourself and make a contribution. 'You have to use yourself,' was his constant refrain." Howe states that she has always preferred men to women because her father was "very gentle and mild." Mary Howe, a painter, was "a large, often cruel mother," according to her daughter. Although she was five feet, eleven inches tall, Mary Howe insisted on increasing her stature by wearing outrageously big hats. Her manner was dramatic and domineering. "[M]y mother towered a good foot above my father in size and in volume," Tina Howe remarked in a 1989 interview.

Howe maintains that, in her family, the highest value was placed on achievement, not money. She felt that she could never live up to their rarefied expectations. "I've never felt successful," she explained. "I have periods when I feel so inferior and homely I can't even go out. I just stay home and hide under the furniture."

Howe received her elementary school education at the Brearley School and the Chapin School, two New York City private academies for girls. Just as she felt out of place in her overachieving family, she was profoundly uncomfortable in the "narrow, suffocating social world" of school. Howe spoke with a lisp and was tall and shy, characteristics which caused the other girls in her class to taunt her mercilessly. "So I assumed the role of class clown, just to get them to laugh with me instead of at me," she recalled.

Quincy Howe's liberal sympathies came under suspicion in the McCarthy era of the 1950's. Consequently, he left CBS and took a job teaching journalism at the University of Illinois in Urbana. There, Tina Howe and her older brother enrolled in the experimental University High School, where she was informed that she had a low IQ and spent her years there feeling oppressed, cowed, and humiliated.

Two disagreeable years at Bucknell University in Lewisburg, Pennsylvania, followed high school. Then, Howe transferred to Sarah Lawrence College in Bronxville, New York. There, in her senior year, she took a creative writing class that changed her life.

It was a short story class. Although Howe later recalled that she had difficulty in mastering the short story form, she eventually found her writing niche. "My work was just so self-conscious and purple and hopeless that out of frustration I began writing this little one-act play . . . called *Closing Time*, and I showed it to my buddy Jane Alexander. And she loved it and said, 'Tina, we've got to put this on.' It was this great hit. And everyone was yelling 'Author!' 'Author!'" That moment of acclaim convinced Howe to spend the rest of her life writing plays.

Life's Work

After graduating from Sarah Lawrence in 1959, Tina Howe traveled to Paris, where she rented a little room overlooking the Seine and focused all of her energies on writing. In 1960, Howe witnessed the Paris production of Eugène Ionesco's *The Bald Soprano*. "It was as if I had been struck by lightning," she later remembered. Ionesco became her idol. "He is often called an absurdist," she remarks. "To me, he is the ultimate realist. He shows us the laxness of reality and what a pathetic time we have getting through the day."

Howe returned to New York City and met Norman Levy, later a novelist, but at that time an acting student. They married in 1961 and later had two children, Eben and Dara. Howe supported her husband's graduate studies by teaching high school English in Maine and Wisconsin. She also coached drama at both schools, under the condition that she could produce her own plays. "I learned the craft in those years of writing plays for students," she recalls.

When she moved with her family to upstate New York, Howe wrote her first professionally produced play, *The Nest*. In it, a young woman hopes to entice a man to marry her by jumping into an enormous wedding cake and having him lick the icing off her nude body. The play opened in 1969 at the Act IV Theatre in Provincetown, Massachusetts. It did well there, but it closed after one performance Off-Broadway at the Mercury Theatre in 1970.

In that same year, the second of her two children was born, and she began to write her next play, *Birth and Afterbirth*. The play concerns a suburban couple who are controlled by their four-year-old-son, played by a grown man. They clash with a childless couple who graphically describe the savage birth rituals they have witnessed during the course of their careers as anthropologists.

When she finished the play in 1973, Howe recalls, "everyone was appalled by it." Although it was never professionally produced, Vintage Books published it in 1977, in a collection called *The New Women's Theatre*, edited by Honor Moore.

Howe decided to moderate her absurdist style to make her plays more commercially viable. "I paid attention to the plays that were successful. They all tended to be escape plays, set in these fantastic settings. . . . So I tried to think of exotic settings— the last place on earth one would expect a play to be set—and I came up with a museum."

Museum is considered Howe's first major play. It chronicles the reactions of museum-goers as they view contemporary art. Instead of having a traditional plot, the play features a series of conversations and reactions. It was first performed in 1976 at the Los Angeles Actor's Theatre. It had a workshop production in the 1976-1977 season at Joseph Papp's Public Theater in New York before opening Off-Broadway on February 7, 1978. It ran for seventy-eight performances and was later published in 1979.

Howe grappled with one of her neuroses in her next play *The Art of Dining*, which is set in a small gourmet restaurant run by a woman whose husband is constantly eating the food meant for customers. "I find eating terrifying, especially in public," she confesses. "I turned my own fear and distaste for food into [its] opposite." The play premiered at the Public Theater in New York on December 6, 1979, but closed three days later. It subsequently played for five weeks, beginning on December 20, at the John F. Kennedy Center for the Performing Arts in Washington, D.C. Dianne Wiest won an Obie award for her performance in the role of an awkward, myopic writer. *The Art of Dining* was published in 1980.

In 1976 and 1977, Howe's parents died. She explored her relationship with them in her most successful play to date, *Painting Churches*. It took her three years to write this story of a thirty-something artist who returns home to paint a portrait of her elderly parents and to win their blessing for her work.

Painting Churches opened in January, 1983, at the Off-Off-Broadway South Street Theatre and ran for five weeks. On November 23, 1983, it moved Off-Broadway to the Lambs Theatre, where it ran until May 24 of the next year. This play, along with *Museum* and *The Art of Dining*, earned Howe an Obie award in 1983 for distinguished playwriting. She also won a Rosamond Gilder award for creative achievement and a playwriting grant from the Rockefeller Foundation. *Painting Churches* was voted best Off-Broadway play of 1983-1984 by the Outer Critics Circle, and was televised on the *American Playhouse* series on PBS in a version starring Gregory Peck and Lauren Bacall.

Painting Churches was the first of Howe's works to be directed by Carole Rothman, who has directed all of her plays since 1983. "For me it's been crucial to have Carole," Howe asserts. "To have a woman who's not only sensitive to my point of view but who is also completely workmanlike is astonishing." Although Howe's feminist friends had previously urged her to work with a female director, Howe's memories of her tyrannical mother and sadistic schoolmates caused her to demur. Working with Rothman and the Second Stage theater company, however, helped to change Howe's mind.

Second Stage produced Howe's next play, *Coastal Disturbances*, which premiered Off-Broadway in November, 1986, then moved to Broadway at Circle in the Square, where it opened in February, 1987. The play, which explores summer romance against a backdrop of twenty tons of real sand on the stage, ran longer than any other play at Circle in the Square up to that time. *Coastal Disturbances*, which was published in 1987, was nominated for Tony awards in writing and directing and earned an Obie award for director Carole Rothman.

Approaching Zanzibar, Howe and Rothman's third collaboration, ran from May 4 to May 28, 1989, at the Second Stage Theatre Off-Broadway. It starred Howe's college friend Jane Alexander as the mother of a family of four who take a car trip halfway across the country to visit a dying great-aunt. Howe commented, "It's the internal journey that interests me—how [they] come to terms with their own problems, their fears, their mortality."

Howe's next work, *One Shoe Off*, opened in April, 1993, at The Joseph Papp Public Theater (renamed in honor of the late producer). It was produced once again by Second Stage and directed by Carole Rothman. In the play, five people come together for a dinner party in a house that is being invaded by plant life, representing the forces that creep into a marriage to tear commitment apart. The absurd style of the play, which was published in 1993, was condemned by many critics, but others found it imaginative and refreshing.

Summary

Tina Howe has noted that women's writing has only just begun to be accepted in the theater, attributing this delayed recognition to the perception that women are still in their "infancy as playwrights." She observes that many powerful dramatic characters, although written by men, are female: Clytemnestra, Medea, Lady Macbeth, Hedda Gabler, and Blanche Dubois. In addition to recognizing women's power to create and nurture, Howe is very sensitive to women's power to destroy. She says, "Part of how I've gotten by is by playing the clown, . . . but I know there's the 'Tina the Destroyer' part of me and that that's part of being a woman."

Howe covered her antic style with a veneer of realism in order to make her plays more acceptable to New York theater critics. Yet, in *One Shoe Off*, Howe returned to the expressionistic, absurd style of her earliest work, and that of the European writers she admires: Eugène Ionesco, Samuel Beckett, and Luigi Pirandello. She is, perhaps, growing into her natural voice, one that makes her, in the words of one writer, "the natural heir of Beckett and Ionesco, a daring female voice speaking in the idiom of . . . Metaphysical Farce."

Bibliography

Barlow, Judith E. "An Interview with Tina Howe." *Studies in American Drama, 1945-Present* 4 (1989): 159-175. Howe explains the importance of having a director who understands her work. She discusses her fear of her own femininity, which she associates with her ferocious mother and her brutal schoolmates.

Betsko, Kathleen, and Rachel Koenig, eds. *Interviews with Contemporary Women Playwrights*. New York: Beech Tree Books, 1987. In this revealing interview, Howe describes her upbringing and how it affected her development as a playwright. She explains that, like herself, her main characters are not anorexic, merely neurasthenic.

Blaney, Retta. "Gone to Seed." *American Theatre* 10 (May-June, 1993): 8-9. Blaney offers a detailed description of the production of the play *One Shoe Off*. She highlights Howe's return to a larger-than-life style after a decade of writing under a façade of realism.

Byers-Pevitts, Beverly. "Tina Howe." In *Notable Women in the American Theatre: A Biographical Dictionary*, edited by Alice M. Robinson, Vera Mowry Roberts, and

Milly S. Barranger. New York: Greenwood Press, 1989 Byers-Pevitts brings Howe's career up through 1989, shortly after her play *Approaching Zanzibar* was produced.

Lamont, Rosette C. "Tina Howe's Secret Surrealism: Walking a Tightrope." *Modern Drama* 36 (March, 1993): 27-37. Lamont favorably compares Howe to such European surrealists as René Magritte, Marcel Duchamp, Tristan Tzara, and Alfred Jarry. She postulates that if Howe had remained in Europe, her absurdist works would have been embraced rather than reviled, as they were by New York critics "reared on Stanislavsky realism."

Walker, Lou Ann. "Comedies with a Dash of Menace." *The New York Times*, April 30, 1989, p. H7. Walker skillfully condenses Howe's biography through 1989, just before *Approaching Zanzibar* opened. Howe explains that this bittersweet work was written in response to her reaching the age of fifty and witnessing the toll that AIDS had taken on the theatrical world.

Irene E. McDermott

DOLORES HUERTA

Born: April 10, 1930; Dawson, New Mexico

Area of Achievement: Trade unionism

Contributions: Cofounder of the United Farm Workers Association with César Chávez, Huerta became renowned throughout the labor movement as a tireless and effective negotiator and organizer. Her role as a Chicana labor leader in the male-dominated culture of southwestern farmworkers has made her a champion of the woman's movement in the 1970's and beyond.

Early Life

Dolores Huerta was born Dolores Fernández in the mining community of Dawson, New Mexico, in 1930. Her father, Juan Fernández, was of Native American and Mexican heritage; her mother, Alicia Chávez Hernández, was a second-generation New Mexican. Dolores' parents were divorced while she was quite young, and she was reared by her mother in Stockton, California. Her mother worked in a cannery and saved enough to buy a small hotel and restaurant while establishing her household in an integrated working-class community. Dolores, along with her two brothers, grew up assuming that women and men were equal, drawing on the example of her mother, who never favored her sons above her daughter and who became a business entrepreneur on her own. Dolores grew up in a racially mixed neighborhood of farmworkers and other laborers of Chinese, Latino, Native American, Filipino, African American, Japanese, and Italian descent. As a result, she learned to appreciate the rich diversity of a range of ethnic cultures at a young age. This absence of sexual or cultural discrimination, in combination with her egalitarian family background, contributed to Dolores' leadership style in later life. Because she suffered no sense of inferiority at home and subsequently no acceptance of a secondary role in life or in her later career, Dolores came to maturity convinced that she was not required to accept the traditional feminine role of women as submissive domestic partners. Instead, she rebelled against conventional restraints upon women and competed directly with her male colleagues.

After graduating from an integrated high school in Stockton, Dolores married her high-school sweetheart, Ralph Head, in 1950. The marriage ended in divorce after the birth of their daughters Celeste and Lori. Dolores' mother took care of the children while Dolores studied for a teaching degree at Stockton College. Although she eventually received a provisional teaching credential, she became dissatisfied with a career as a teacher. A dawning awareness of the pervasiveness of social injustice confronting the Mexican American community and other ethnic minorities led Dolores in a new direction in 1955.

In that year, Dolores met Fred Ross, an organizer for Saul Alinsky's Industrial Areas Foundation who was trying to encourage the growing political consciousness of members of Mexican American communities throughout California. Ross started the Community Service Organization (CSO), a self-help association that led voter registration drives, pushed for more Chicanos on the police forces, lobbied for Spanish-speaking staff at hospitals and government offices, and campaigned for sewers and community centers in the barrios. Because of her newfound civic activism and devotion to the work of the CSO, Dolores' marriage to her second husband, Ventura Huerta, also ended in divorce.

Life's Work

It was through her activities with the CSO that Dolores Huerta eventually became active as a labor organizer among migrant workers in California's San Joaquin Valley. She first came in contact with César Chávez when she was introduced to him by Fred Ross in 1955 when both were working for the CSO. By that time, Huerta was a full-time lobbyist for the CSO in Sacramento, pressuring the legislature for disability insurance, unemployment insurance, and minimum wage bills for farmworkers. Although she was instrumental in securing the passage of bills that extended social insurance and welfare benefits to farmworkers and aliens, she was convinced that these workers could never escape poverty through the CSO strategy of pressure-group politics. What they needed was a union. At approximately the same time, César Chávez was reaching the same conclusion. By 1962, Chávez had presented the CSO with a program outlining strategy for the unionization of farmworkers. When this program was rejected, he left the organization. While his wife Helen worked in the fields to support their family of eight children, Chávez organized small meetings of workers sympathetic to the idea of a union of agricultural laborers. The Farm Workers Association (FWA), a precursor of the United Farm Workers (UFW) union, was founded in Fresno, California, in September, 1962, at a convention attended by about three hundred delegates—practically the entire membership. It was organized primarily by César Chávez, but the first person he called upon to work with him organizing the Mexican American farmworkers into a union was Dolores Huerta, who promptly left her post with the CSO to help Chávez.

When Dolores Huerta began her labor organizing efforts, she was pregnant with the seventh of her eleven children (she had two by her first husband, five by her second, and four by her live-in lover, Richard Chávez, the brother of César). Because of the demands of her work, Huerta was frequently absent from home, and her children spent much of their childhood in the care of her friends or family. Her union work was always her first priority, to the consternation and outrage of the more traditional adherents to Latin culture. Huerta clearly loved her children and was loved by them in return, but she refused to allow motherhood to deter her from her work. Even her colleague César Chávez disapproved of Huerta's divorces, her decision to live with his brother, and her seemingly chaotic way of raising her children. Nevertheless, he understood that the union was the center of her life—just as it was for him.

The foundation of the United Farm Workers union was laid during the bitter Delano Grape Strike of 1965-1970. The farmworkers of the 1960's often lived in mind-numbing poverty and toiled under inhumane conditions. The bulk of the workforce spoke little English, was often of illegal residency status, could not vote, and was poorly educated. As a result, they were easily exploited by the powerful growers in the agribusiness industry of California. The growers often used deadly pesticides, primarily DDT, in the fields, ignoring the devastating health effects these chemicals had on both the workers and their unborn children. Pickers were paid by the bushel or basket rather than the hour. A field over-staffed with pickers, therefore, could result in a day's labor with little or no pay for the worker. There were no health and welfare benefits, no medical insurance, and no low-cost housing for the mainly transient workforce. Workers were forced to live in cars, shacks, and tents; many workers had no other place to sleep than the chemical-laden fields in which they had worked earlier in the day.

The grape-growing industry was perhaps the worst offender in terms of working conditions and pesticide use in all of California. Because of this, it became the logical site of the 1965 United Farm Workers (UFW) battle known as the Delano Grape Strike with César Chávez and Dolores Huerta at the forefront. The strike began at dawn, when the workers moved out into the fields around Delano. The pickets met them carrying NFWA banners with the union's symbol of a black Aztec eagle on a red flag with the single Spanish word "Huelga" (strike). The pickets led the workers off the fields of Delano and the five-year battle began. Before the strike ended in 1970, Huerta was arrested eighteen times.

As quickly as the UFW pickets pulled work crews out, these laborers were replaced by scabs, or strikebreakers, trucked in from Mexico and Texas by the growers. The union's pickets and organizers were harassed and arrested continually by local police, under the influence of the powerful growers. Support for the farmworkers was growing, both within the labor movement and on a national level. Senator Robert Kennedy embraced their cause and became their champion. Powerful unions, including the United Auto Workers (UAW), Amalgamated Clothing Workers, and the Packinghouse Workers rallied behind the striking grape pickers and provided relief in the form of fresh pickets, food, and money. It was against this backdrop of national labor and political support that Chávez and Huerta made the decision to escalate the strike to a nationwide struggle by declaring a universal consumer boycott. This boycott initially targeted individual growers and products, but eventually led to the boycott of all California-grown grapes. Hundreds of workers were delegated throughout the country to promote and organize the boycott, while Huerta herself organized in New York City. She was an eloquent and powerful public speaker, and her speeches expressed the deep desires and struggles of all poor and dispossessed peoples, not just those who worked the fields.

The UFW boycott was successful. Trade unionists across the country joined forces with the farmworkers, and a new consciousness of the Chicano in the United States was born as a result of the Huelga, as the strike was commonly known. On May 30, 1970, the first table grapes bearing a union label—a black eagle on a red flag—were shipped to market. The grapes came from seven growers who, unable to withstand the effects of the boycott, had signed contracts with the UFW. On July 29, twenty-six Delano growers filed into the UFW union hall to sign the contracts that ended the bitter five-year battle. As negotiated by Huerta, the workers received an hourly wage of $1.76, a guaranteed yearly increase of fifteen cents per hour, and a twenty-five-cent bonus per box picked. In addition, the growers were required to contribute to a health and welfare plan and to low-cost housing for their workers. Most importantly, the growers agreed not to use certain pesticides, and DDT was banned forever from California vineyards. Huerta's skills as a negotiator were entirely self-taught. In fact, before the strike she had never even read a union contract. Besides negotiating the UFW's first contracts, Huerta had organized for the strike in the fields, in boycott offices, and in union election halls as well as serving as a picket herself. In retrospect, however, it was her skill, tenacity, combativeness, and cunning as a negotiator that truly separated Dolores Huerta from her peers in the labor movement. Her contract negotiations with the California growers was the crowning achievement of one of the greatest victories ever in the history of American workers.

Dolores Huerta continued to serve in the UFW as negotiator and vice president into the 1990's. She became notorious in the union for her fervor and tenacity; stories are told of growers begging to face anyone at the negotiating table except Huerta. Huerta and Chávez continued their aggressive style of Chicano trade unionism through periodic use of the consumer boycott, most notably against Gallo Wine, the Dole Company, and California table grapes. In the wake of Chávez's death in 1993, Huerta, in her sixties, continues to be an eloquent and frequent speaker and organizer on behalf of workers, Mexican Americans, and women.

Summary

As a leading figure in the Chicano trade union movement, Dolores Huerta has found union organizing to be an enjoyable, creative process that has provided her personal and intellectual fulfillment. All of her work has been based on four philosophical axioms: first, to establish a strong sense of identity; second, to develop a sense of pride; third, to maintain always the value of services to others; and fourth, to be effective and true to oneself. Huerta was convinced of the necessity to lead others through persuasion and personal example, rather than by intimidation. Ideas are vital and criticism is necessary, but for Huerta, action through responsible commitment and moral choice is the key to creating a just society. More than a liberal, ethnic unionist, Huerta has taken additional pride in her stance as a feminist, a Chicano activist, and, above all, a humanist. Huerta's cause has transcended the narrow scope of unionism. As Huerta herself stated at an organizing rally at Santa Clara University in 1990: "I would like to be remembered as a woman who cares for all fellow humans. We must use our lives to make the world a better and just place to live, not just a world to acquire things. That is what we are put on the earth for."

Bibliography

Coburn, Judith. "Dolores Huerta: La Passionaria of the Farmworkers." *Ms.* 5 (November, 1976): 10-16. An interview with Dolores Huerta during a union election dispute in Sacramento, California, in 1975.

Fink, Gary M. *Biographical Dictionary of American Labor*. 2d ed. Westport, Conn.: Greenwood Press, 1984. A listing of biographical data on important people in the history of the American labor movement.

Foner, Philip. *Women and the American Labor Movement: From World War I to the Present*. New York: Free Press, 1980. A historical overview of the entire American labor movement since World War I with an emphasis on the roles of women, both as labor leaders and as workers.

Garcia, Richard A. "Dolores Huerta: Woman, Organizer and Symbol." *California History* 71 (Spring, 1993): 57-71. This article, appearing in the journal of the California Historical Society, explores the philosophical and ethical underpinnings of Dolores Huerta's activism.

Meier, Matt S. *Mexican American Biographies: A Historical Dictionary, 1836-1987*. New York: Greenwood Press, 1988. Meier, an expert on Mexican American history, includes a profile on Huerta in this biographical dictionary. Although brief, the sketch on Huerta does provide a fine summary of her activities on behalf of "la causa."

Rose, Margaret. "Dolores Huerta." In *Notable Hispanic American Women*, edited by Diane Telgen and Jim Kamp. Detroit: Gale Research, 1993. A thorough biographical profile of Huerta that traces her activism from the 1950's up through her injury at a 1988 demonstration in San Francisco protesting various Bush Administration policies.

Derrick Harper West

CHARLAYNE HUNTER-GAULT

Born: February 27, 1942; Due West, South Carolina

Area of Achievement: Journalism

Contribution: The first African American woman to earn a bachelor's degree from the University of Georgia (1963), Hunter-Gault has had a distinguished career in national broadcast journalism.

Early Life

Charlayne Alberta Hunter was born on February 27, 1942, in a village in northwestern South Carolina. Her father, Charles S. H. Hunter, Jr., an African Methodist Episcopal minister, rose to the rank of lieutenant colonel as an Army chaplain. Her mother, Althea Ruth Brown Hunter, the granddaughter of a white landowner, worked as a manager in a black-owned real estate company after the family moved in 1951 from Covington to Atlanta, Georgia. An only child until she was eight, Charlayne was joined by two younger brothers, Charles and Franklin Hunter. In 1954, she entered the all-black Henry McNeal Turner High School, but she finished the eighth grade in an all-white school near Anchorage, Alaska, when the family joined her father, who was stationed there. Charlayne's recreational outlet was playing the piano. In 1955, her mother moved the children back to Atlanta to live with their maternal grandmother. This separation led to her parents' eventual divorce.

Charlayne admired her mother's intelligence, strength, and femininity. From her father, who expected her to earn straight A's, she gained self-discipline and a desire to succeed. Whites might be "different," she learned, but they "were not superior" to blacks. At age sixteen, Charlayne broke with her parents by converting, together with two girlfriends, to Catholicism. She was attracted by Catholicism's rituals and by the Atlanta Catholic hospital's acceptance of black patients.

Encouraged by her English teachers at Turner High School, Charlayne became editor-in-chief of the student newspaper, *The Green Light*, and assistant yearbook editor. These were significant steps toward achieving her childhood dream of becoming a journalist, like the comic-strip reporter "Brenda Starr." Tall and slim, with hazel eyes, Charlayne was elected Miss Turner, the homecoming queen, and graduated third in the class of 1959.

Supported by the Atlanta Committee for Cooperative Action, an African American business and professional group, Charlayne applied to the University of Georgia, together with Hamilton Holmes, Turner senior class president, valedictorian, and football team cocaptain. They were denied admission, in August, 1959, on the grounds that all dormitories were full. Had they been white, they would have been welcomed enthusiastically. Charlayne and Hamilton enrolled, respectively, at Wayne State University in Detroit, Michigan, and at Morehouse College in Atlanta. Meanwhile, their attorneys, Donald Hollowell of the National Association for the Advancement of Colored People (NAACP) and Constance Baker Motley of the Legal Defense Fund in New York City, began a legal challenge. Because her participation might have jeopardized the suit, Charlayne was told not to join the 1960 student sit-ins in Atlanta.

In November, 1960, Charlayne and Hamilton were interviewed at the University of Georgia in Athens. Registrar and Admissions Director Walter Danner found Charlayne acceptable but said that there was no room for her category of transfer student until the fall of 1961. After asking whether Holmes had visited a red light district, Danner rejected him as unsuitable. In December, 1960, *Holmes and Hunter v. Danner* came to trial in Athens. On January 6, 1961, Federal District Judge William A. Bootle ruled that they had been excluded by an unspoken racial policy and ordered them admitted immediately.

Life's Work

Charlayne Hunter walked onto campus on Monday, January 9, 1961, "loving myself a lot and demanding respect." Those steps would influence her career as a journalist. It was a historic movement, she wrote in her autobiography, *In My Place* (1992), with Georgia's "white sons and daughters facing their most apocalyptic moment since Sherman marched to the sea" and "Black sons and daughters their most liberating moment since the Emancipation Proclamation." After some delay and a car-rocking attempt by white students, Dean of Men William Tate drove them around campus to register at the various departments.

The evening after the first day of classes, January 11, segregationist students rioted in front of Hunter's dormitory. When the state patrol failed to arrive, the Athens police used tear gas. For their own safety, Hunter and Holmes were driven to their homes in Atlanta. Judge Bootle, however, ordered their readmission. Protected by government escorts, they safely returned to classes. Faculty members patrolled the campus, and student rioters faced suspension or expulsion.

To pay the $1,500 annual university expenses, Hunter received some financial assistance from the Elks, the United Packinghouse Workers, her Delta Sigma Theta sorority, and last-minute contributors. She received no money from the NAACP—only a plaque. For Hunter's protection on the large campus, her mother borrowed money to buy her a car.

Surprised by their admission, Hunter and Holmes were also surprised by continuing white resentment. Segregated in a freshman dormitory, Hunter later had black roommates. While Hunter pressed for her student rights, including eating in university dining halls, she was willing to eat alone and actually enjoyed solitude. Holmes, who often felt threatened on campus, lived with a black family in Athens and returned home every weekend. He concentrated intensely on his premedical studies, graduated Phi Beta Kappa, and was the first black to enroll in the Emory University Medical School. Holmes, a successful orthopedic surgeon in Atlanta, is the medical director of Grady Memorial Hospital and the associate dean of Emory's medical school.

The outgoing Hunter, who did most of the public speaking, remained the focus of media attention and received a thousand letters from the United States and abroad. She maintained a B+ average in journalism courses but was on academic probation her junior year because of difficulties with mathematics and science courses. Hunter admitted that in comparison with other people, including Holmes, "maybe in some things I am inferior, but it has nothing to do with race or gender."

Hunter found the School of Journalism friendly but the student newspaper, *Red and Black*, hostile. She had an internship with the Louisville *Times* during the summer of 1961 and worked on weekends for the Atlanta *Inquirer*, founded by Georgia college students. Keenly observing the journalists who reported on the university's desegregation, she resolved to emulate those, such as Calvin Trillin, who wrote with sensitivity.

She was thrilled when Robert F. Kennedy said, in his May, 1961, Law Day address at the Law School, that their graduation would help the United States fight communism abroad. On June 1, 1963, Hunter and Holmes became the first blacks to earn bachelor's degrees from a historically white university in the deep South. Hunter, however, was determined to win recognition for her achievements as a journalist rather than for having integrated the University of Georgia. She also showed her independence by secretly marrying before graduation Walter Stovall, a white southern journalism student. They had a daughter, Susan. They subsequently divorced, and in 1971, she married Ronald Gault, a black Chicagoan and a vice president of First Boston Corporation. They have a son, Chuma Gault.

Charlayne Hunter-Gault has developed a distinguished career in journalism, beginning as a staff writer at *The New Yorker*. In 1967, she was awarded a Russell Sage Fellowship to study social science at Washington University in St. Louis, Missouri. There she edited articles for *Trans-Action* and reported on the Poor People's Campaign in Washington, D.C. She then joined Washington's WRC-TV as an investigative reporter and local evening news anchor. From 1986 to 1978, she was on the *New York Times*'s metropolitan staff, reporting primarily on Harlem. During a year's leave of absence, she codirected the Michele Clark Fellowship program for minority journalism students at Columbia University. She effected a change in the *Times* editorial board's policy of describing African Americans as "Negroes," promoting the term "blacks," and received three *New York Times* Publishers Awards. In 1970, she was cowinner with Joseph Lelyveld for reporting on a twelve-year-old child who died of a heroin overdose. She also won that award for her 1974 story on Mayor Abraham Beame's selection of New York City's first black deputy mayor and for her 1976 reports on crime among blacks and the renaming of Harlem's Muslim Mosque to honor Malcolm X.

In 1978, Hunter-Gault joined public television's *The MacNeil/Lehrer Report*, serving as a third correspondent and "swing anchor." Her 1979 documentary "A Matter of Dignity," which examined the 1954 *Brown v. Board of Education* decree desegregating public schools, highlighted the University of Georgia's integration and the persistence of all-black high schools such as Turner. After becoming national correspondent for *The MacNeil/Lehrer News Hour* in 1983, she won two National News and Documentary Awards for reporting on the 1983 United States invasion of Grenada and for "Zumwalt: Agent Orange" in 1985. Elmo Zumwalt III died of cancer caused by contact with that defoliant in Vietnam when he served under his father, Admiral Elmo Zumwalt, Jr. Her five-part documentary "Apartheid's People," about the situation in South Africa, won her the 1986 George Foster Peabody Award for Excellence in Broadcast Journalism, given by the University of Georgia's Henry W. Grady School of Journalism. Her many other honors include the 1986 Journalist of the Year Award from the National Association of Black Journalists, the American Women in Radio and Television Award for Excellence in Journalism, and the Lincoln University Unity Award, for reporting on teenage unemployment.

Summary

On June 11, 1988, Charlayne Hunter-Gault became the first black to deliver a commencement address—it was entitled "In Our Place"—at the University of Georgia. By then, the university had established in her and Holmes's honor a chair supporting an annual lecture on civil rights or race relations. Discussing her university experiences, she emphasized what the South had accomplished as a melting pot and what it still needed to do. She noted that the number of black graduating seniors had risen from two to three hundred but pointed out that there were only twelve hundred blacks among the university's twenty-six thousand students. The president's hiring of fifteen new black faculty members would serve as a magnet for additional black students. Together, they "will move this place—our place—to a new phase in its pioneering history." The University of Georgia can "be a model for a more perfect union." Since by century's end every third American "will be a person of color," she believed that "It really is our turn."

Charlayne Hunter-Gault is a role model for black students of both genders and for women of all races. She has earned widespread professional recognition for her sensitive reporting of complex events. Voicing independent judgment when necessary, she brings her own perspectives into stories on racism. During the early 1990's, she reported in sympathetic detail on famine in Somalia and the U.S. mission there and on the renewed prospects for peace in the Middle East.

Bibliography

Dyer, Thomas G. *University of Georgia: A Bicentennial History, 1785-1985*. Athens: University of Georgia Press, 1985. Provides a detailed chapter on the University of Georgia's desegregation and suggests that it opened up new educational opportunities for both races.

Hine, Darlene Clark, ed. *Black Women in America: An Historical Encyclopedia*. 2 vols. New York: Carlson, 1993. A valuable collection of biographies, including one of Hunter-Gault, and entries treating such topics as the Civil Rights movement and black women's organizations.

Hosley, David H., and Gayle K. Yamada. *Hard News: Women in Broadcast Journalism*. Contributions in Women's Studies Number 85. New York: Greenwood Press, 1987. Concentrates on women who work at the major networks or their affiliates. Although it does not include Hunter-Gault at PBS, this work discusses the problems faced by women in broadcast journalism: the equal pay issue, their limited access to decision-making positions, and their age and looks.

Hunter-Gault, Charlayne. *In My Place*. New York: Farrar, Straus & Giroux, 1992. Contributes many insights about Hunter-Gault's family life and personal development before the desegregation suit. The final chapter is based on her 1988 commencement address at the University of Georgia.

Raines, Howell. *My Soul Is Rested: Movement Days in the Deep South Remembered*. New York: Penguin Books, 1983. Provides a collection of personal perspectives on the Civil Rights movement, including views of other black students such as Hamilton Holmes.

Trillin, Calvin. *An Education In Georgia: Charlayne Hunter, Hamilton Holmes, and the Integration of the University of Georgia*. Foreword by Charlayne Hunter-Gault. Athens: The University of Georgia Press, 1991. The first thorough account of the University of Georgia's desegregation, this book captures the personalties and experiences of Holmes and Hunter as student heroes.

Marcia G. Synnott

ZORA NEALE HURSTON

Born: January 7, 1891; Eatonville, Florida
Died: January 28, 1960; Fort Pierce, Florida
Area of Achievement: Literature
Contribution: The most accomplished African American woman writing in the first half of the twentieth century, Zora Neale Hurston was a major writer of the Harlem Renaissance and an important influence on later generations of women writers.

Early Life

Zora Neale Hurston's hometown was Eatonville, Florida, a self-governing all-black town that allowed her to develop a sense of individuality. One of eight children, she was urged to "jump at de sun" by her mother, who tried to preserve her high spirits so that she would not become, in Zora's words, " a mealy-mouthed rag doll." Her father, however, feared that her audacious spirit would not be tolerated by white America and often punished her for impudence. A minister and three-term mayor of Eatonville, John Hurston was something of a hero among the townsfolk, and Zora would devote a novel (*Jonah's Gourd Vine*, 1934) largely to his life story. Yet she was also fascinated by her mother, who molded John Hurston into the successful public man that he became. Lucy Ann Potts Hurston was perhaps the only person in town who did not regard her husband with awe. As Zora described their relationship in her autobiography, "the one who makes the idols never worships them, however tenderly he might have molded the clay." Zora observed with keen interest how Lucy Ann, with a few simple words, could confound the very arguments for which townsfolk or church members praised John.

Zora read widely, preferring adventure stories such as *Gulliver's Travels*, Norse mythology, and the Greek myth of Hercules to stories that urged little girls to become dutiful and domesticated. Eatonville gave her a strong sense of herself, but she was also impatient with small town restrictions. "My soul was with the gods and my body in the village. People just would not act like gods. . . . Raking back yards and carrying out chamber-pots, were not the tasks of Thor. I wanted to be away from drabness and to stretch my limbs in some mighty struggle."

Hurston's world fell apart when her mother died. When John Hurston remarried, Zora's stepmother had no use for her and her siblings, and Zora had to leave home. She was passed from relative to relative, was unable to attend school, and badly missed the close family environment in which she had grown up. She was also poor and had to work as a nanny and housekeeper, although she really wanted to read and dream. Tired of poverty and dependence, she was hired as a wardrobe girl by a young actress in a traveling troupe who performed Gilbert and Sullivan musicals. She was well-liked and, in turn, she enjoyed the camaraderie and adventure of traveling.

Life's Work

Zora Neale Hurston's writing career began not long after she left home. After graduating from night school at Morgan Academy in Baltimore in 1918, she attended Howard University. While there, she wrote a story that caught the attention of the founder of *Opportunity* magazine, Charles S. Johnson, who sponsored literary contests and was instrumental in the development of the black arts movement of the 1920's known as the Harlem Renaissance. Johnson published her next two stories, "Drenched in Light" (1924) and "Spunk" (1925), and she suddenly found herself among the Harlem Renaissance's prominent writers.

Both these stories and her play *Color Struck* (1926) were based on the folk life she had observed in Eatonville. In her autobiography *Dust Tracks on a Road* (1942), Hurston describes the importance of Joe Clarke's general store, a repository of the rich African American oral tradition. There she heard the "lying sessions"—that is, exaggerated folk tales featuring talking animals such as Brer Rabbit, Brer Fox, and Buzzard—that she eventually used in her finest writings. In an age in which many blacks believed that fitting into America meant showing that they could conform to middle-class values just as well as whites, Hurston concentrated on the black masses and their values. Far from being ashamed of the lower classes, she knew that their expressions—black folklore, blues, and spirituals—were those of a people who were healthy minded and who had survived slavery through their own creative ingenuity.

Hurston's talent as a writer attracted the interest and friendship of several benefactors, including Fannie Hurst, a best-selling white author who befriended Hurston and hired her as a secretary, and Annie Nathan Meyer, who secured a scholarship to Barnard College for Hurston.

Two other benefactors helped to show Hurston that the folk culture of Eatonville had anthropological, as well as literary, interest. A paper she wrote at Barnard caught the eye of Franz Boas, the noted Columbia University anthropologist, and she was invited to study with him. He urged her to regard the Eatonville folklore as a continuation of African oral storytelling and suggested that she return to the South and collect it. Another person who encouraged her to do so was Charlotte Osgood Mason, who was nicknamed "Godmother" for her maternal characteristics and perhaps also because of her godlike behavior (she liked to sit on a thronelike chair when her "godchildren" visited her). She was a wealthy white patron of the arts who wished to preserve "primitive" minority cultures—in other words, cultures free of the civilized pretensions of modern life. She provided Hurston with money, a movie camera, and an automobile with which to collect folklore in the South. *Mules and Men* (1935), a masterly collection of southern black folktales, was the eventual result of Hurston's efforts in that area.

Although Hurston was pressured to adapt her novels to a prescribed theme about struggles against racism, she believed that such a theme would be a limitation. She preferred to concentrate on those indigenous elements of black community life that survived racism intact.

Her first novel, *Jonah's Gourd Vine* (1934), is the story of a Baptist minister who delivers powerful sermons but who upsets his congregation by following his own natural impulses and entering into adulterous relationships that his parishioners cannot reconcile with his role as minister. *Their Eyes Were Watching God* (1937), Hurston's masterpiece, explores a black woman's three marriages, her frustrations, and her aspiration to become a fully autonomous human being. *Moses, Man of the Mountain* (1939) is an ambitious allegory about the "hoodoo man" Moses, who tries to inspire in an enslaved people a group identity. To dispel the idea that black writers were limited to black subjects, Hurston devoted her last novel, *Seraph on the Suwanee* (1948), to the subject of poor southern whites.

Richard Wright criticized *Their Eyes Were Watching God* because it did not protest racial oppression, but Hurston disagreed with the attitudes of protesters, whom she called "the sobbing school of Negrohood." In *Dust Tracks on a Road*, she insisted that all individuals had it in their power to determine their fates and that an appeal to racial uniqueness was the refuge of the weak. Believing that "skins were no measure of what was inside people," Hurston ridiculed anyone "who claimed special blessings on the basis of race." In spite of the fact that it was criticized—most notably by Arna Bontemps—her autobiography won the Anisfield-Wolf Award for its contribution to better race relations.

Hurston's devotion to writing and collecting left her little time for sustained relationships. She states in her autobiography that *Their Eyes Were Watching God* was written in Haiti in an attempt to come to terms with a love affair she had had in New York with a young college student of West Indian descent. She left him for the same reason that she had divorced her first husband, Herbert Sheen, in 1931. She wished to be free to pursue her career, and her relationships with men did not allow her that freedom. As she writes about her young lover: "My work was one thing, and he was all the rest"; to him, however, it was "all, or nothing." A second attempt at marriage, with Albert Price III in 1939, ended in divorce a year later.

In 1948, Hurston was arrested and charged with molesting the ten-year-old son of a woman from whom she had rented an apartment in New York. Although she proved that she could not have committed the act because she was out of the country at the time, the story was sensationalized in the African American press. She felt betrayed and wrote, "My race has seen fit to destroy me without reason."

After the 1948 publication of *Seraph on the Suwanee*, Hurston never published another book. In her last decade, she worked as teacher, librarian, reporter, and maid. She also became active as a political conservative. She supported the 1946 campaign of Republican Grant Reynolds against Adam Clayton Powell, Jr., in Harlem, and in the primary elections of 1950, she opposed the liberal Claude Pepper. In "I Saw Negro Votes Peddled" (1950), she attributed to a lack of self-esteem black complicity in vote-buying schemes perpetrated by the Pepper campaign. In 1954, she opposed the Supreme Court's decision in *Brown v. Board of Education*, which ordered school desegregation. She viewed it as a matter of self-respect. She could get little satisfaction from a law that forced associations between persons who did not want to associate and that assumed that blacks could not develop properly unless they associated with whites.

After suffering a stroke in 1959, she died on January 28, 1960, in a nursing home in Fort Pierce, Florida. Her grave remained unmarked until the 1970's, when Alice Walker located it and erected a stone that reads, in part:

Zora Neale Hurston
"A Genius of the South"
Novelist, Folklorist, Anthropologist

Summary

To Alice Walker, who documented her discovery of Zora Neale Hurston in the collection of feminist essays *In Search of Our Mothers' Gardens*, Hurston represented an artistic foremother whose achievements and defiance of conventional roles for women were inspiring. Hurston's efforts to preserve, nurture, and transmit African American folk culture were based on her belief that folklore was the common person's art form and that black folklore provided America with its greatest cultural wealth. Her ability to capture the sounds of folk speech and to retell the imaginative stories of African Americans was the foundation of her talent as a writer of fiction. Living most of her life in obscurity and buried in an unmarked grave, Hurston lived and wrote with a confidence and self-acceptance that made her a favorite model for later generations of writers.

Bibliography

Bloom, Harold, ed. *Modern Critical Views: Zora Neale Hurston*. New York: Chelsea House, 1986. This book of essays about Hurston includes contemporary accounts by those who knew her, as well as modern critical appraisals.

Glassman, Steve, and Kathryn Lee Seidel, eds. *Zora in Florida*. Orlando: University of Central Florida Press, 1991. This book of critical essays examines Hurston's lesser-known works and is particularly concerned with the influence of her native Florida on her work.

Hemenway, Robert E. *Zora Neale Hurston: A Literary Biography*. Urbana: University of Illinois Press, 1977. The strength of this scholarly biography is its placing of Hurston's literary achievements in the context of American and African American literary history.

_____ , ed. "Introduction." In *Dust Tracks on a Road: An Autobiography*, by Zora Neale Hurston. 2d ed. Urbana: University of Illinois Press, 1984. Despite its unfortunate attempt to discredit the conservative views expressed in Hurston's autobiography, this essay does provide useful information about the political context in which the book was written and confirms that Hurston's birth year was more likely 1891 than the oft-cited 1901.

Holloway, Karla F. C. *The Character of the Word: The Texts of Zora Neale Hurston*. New York: Greenwood Press, 1987. An analysis of Hurston's use of language in her writings.

Howard, Lillie P. *Zora Neale Hurston*. Boston: Twayne, 1980. A useful overview of Hurston's life and works in an accessible format including a bibliography.

Hurston, Zora Neale. *Dust Tracks on a Road: An Autobiography*. 2d ed. Urbana: University of Illinois Press, 1984. Hurston's autobiography is a chronicle of an independent woman. She discusses her earliest childhood impressions, her involvement in the Harlem Renaissance, and her thoughts on the racial problem in the United States.
_____. *Their Eyes Were Watching God*. Reprint. Urbana: University of Illinois Press, 1978. Hurston's compelling novel about a woman's search for love and self-actualization is a masterpiece of African American literature. Hurston states that it had an autobiographical basis.
Walker, Alice. "Zora Neale Hurston—A Cautionary Tale and a Partisan View." Foreword to *Zora Neale Hurston: A Literary Biography*, by Robert E. Hemenway. Urbana: University of Illinois Press, 1977. This partisan defense of Hurston's work is written by the person most responsible for engineering a revival of interest in Hurston. The essay emphasizes Hurston's value to feminists and views her poverty as a cautionary story from which other women writers can learn.

William L. Howard

ANNE HUTCHINSON

Born: July 17, 1591; Alford, Lincolnshire, England
Died: August or September, 1643; Pelham Bay, New Amsterdam (later Bronx, New York)
Area of Achievement: Religion
Contribution: An early advocate of equality of the sexes, Hutchinson devoted her life to the promotion of humane treatment of all persons under God's covenant of grace.

Early Life

On July 17, 1591, Anne Marbury was born to Francis Marbury and Bridget Dryden Marbury in the small town of Alford in Lincolnshire, England. Francis, at various times a schoolmaster and preacher, had lost his license to preach because of his insistence on religious reform. Having nothing to occupy himself except for minor tasks around a very small house, he devoted himself to his daughter's education. Among Anne's early readings was one composed by Francis himself, a drama recording his own public trial at the age of twenty-three. His unrepentant ridicule of the bishop of London was not lost on this impressionable young reader.

When Anne was fourteen, her father managed to redeem himself sufficiently to receive an appointment to a prestigious church in London. Many people prominent in church and politics attended Marbury's services, and they often found their way to the parsonage dinner table, where Anne was permitted to sit as a silent spectator. It was here that religion and politics became a part of her ordinary discourse.

It was during the London years that Anne, now the eldest daughter at home, became the primary assistant to her mother in cooking and caring for the younger children. She also received her first experience as midwife, being present to deliver two of her younger brothers and one sister. Here, too, Anne came in contact with the Familists, a sect that stressed the equality of the sexes as well as direct communication between the individual and God.

In 1611, when Anne was nineteen, her father died, leaving her financially secure but intellectually without anchor. Devastated by her loss, Anne yielded to social expectations in 1612 and married William Hutchinson, a childhood friend who had become a wealthy textile merchant. The two left London shortly after the wedding to set up housekeeping in Alford.

Life's Work

Back in Alford, Anne Hutchinson commenced her role as wife and homemaker and in a little more than nine months bore Edward, the first of fifteen children. Pregnancy awakened in Anne an intense interest in the mysteries of her own body; always deeply religious, she now came more and more to rely on prayer to preserve herself and her infant. Her meditations enhanced her belief in the immanence of God, and soon, like the Familist preachers who dominated the area around Alford, Anne believed that she was led by the spirit to interpret the Scriptures for herself.

Anne Hutchinson knew that there were others who shared her beliefs, and she was encouraged by the news that the Reverend John Cotton, who had strong Puritan inclinations, had taken a church at Boston, only twenty-four miles from Alford. She became an avid disciple of Cotton's, traveling to Boston to hear his sermons at every available opportunity. Cotton was such a superb orator and attracted such a following that he had to begin giving sermons on weekdays to accommodate the crowds.

The Hutchinson family continued to grow, with a child appearing about every eighteen months. Anne could not look at a newborn infant and accept the church position that all infants were born in sin. She also could not accept the dictum that Eve was fully responsible for bringing sin into the world and that women and evil were therefore synonymous. Encouraged by her association with John Cotton, Hutchinson began inviting women to her home for meetings at which she presented her own interpretation of Scripture.

Hutchinson was playing a more and more important role in the community in other ways as well. She had learned much about herbal medicine from her mother, and she was an accomplished midwife. Her services as nurse and midwife were constantly in demand, and those activities, along with the requirements of her growing family, left her little time for herself. She nevertheless continued to take every opportunity to ride to Boston with her husband to listen to John Cotton, who was now experiencing increasing conflicts with authority.

When Cotton was finally forced to flee to New England for religious sanctuary, the Hutchinsons made the decision to follow. By this time, Anne was very vocal about revelations she received from God, and some of the Puritan divines were taking offense. Nevertheless, when she and William and ten of their children set sail on the *Griffin* in 1634, Anne was fully expecting to realize her dream of a society in which she could freely follow where the spirit led without fear of retribution and in which women and men would be equal partners before God.

Because her reputation preceded her, Anne Hutchinson was not accepted at the Boston, Massachusetts, church until she had been subjected to intense interrogation. She must have experienced disappointment to find that the situation in the colonies was much like that in England. Women were nonpersons. They had no political rights and were segregated from the men in church.

Anne Hutchinson was further dismayed because John Cotton devoted himself to study and was not available for theological discussion. For her own edification, as well as that of the other women, she once again began to hold meetings in her own home. First, they were held to discuss Cotton's sermons, and only women attended. Eventually, however, she began to present her own interpretations of Scripture. She preached individual responsibility and initiative, which appealed to the commercial interests of Boston, and she insisted that all people should be guided by their own consciences and need not be supervised by the church or the state. Soon, the women were joined by numerous men, sometimes as many as eighty or ninety in all, meeting in the Hutchinson home.

Hutchinson's popularity frightened the local clergy, and John Winthrop, governor of the colony, feared that she would develop such a large following of women that they could subjugate the men. Winthrop believed that the disunity in the colony was the result of evil, and evil was associated with women. Therefore, he concluded, Hutchinson must be an agent of the devil. The more she attacked the legalism of the Puritan preachers in favor of her doctrine of grace, the more the authorities determined that they must put an end to her activities.

For a time, Hutchinson's supporters gained controlling positions in the colony and she was left alone, but in 1637 John Winthrop once again was elected governor, and the tables turned. He had been back in power for less than two weeks when the Pequot War broke out. The colonists easily slaughtered the natives, but Winthrop was incensed because Hutchinson and her followers, being pacifists, would not support the war. This event resulted in the calling of the first religious synod in New England. There a decision was made to bring Hutchinson's case to the General Court in November.

When Anne Hutchinson was called before the court, she had to stand for hours before forty-nine men who continuously questioned her. John Winthrop tried to convince her to agree to his position of a Covenant of Works, but she would have none of it. She was particularly angered by his insistence that what she was doing was not "befitting" for her sex. Because she was permitted to answer all questions posed during the trial, her position was recorded for posterity. She gave excellent responses to all charges, but her last hope was extinguished when her longtime friend and mentor John Cotton felt compelled to join those who voted against her.

The sentence that Anne Hutchinson received was banishment from Massachusetts. She would be allowed to remain until good weather in the spring but would be placed under house arrest until then. In March of 1638, she was excommunicated from the New England church. Shortly thereafter, Hutchinson and several of her followers left Massachusetts for Rhode Island. In Rhode Island, her following increased, but she was still continually plagued by tormentors from Massachusetts.

When her husband died in 1642, Anne Hutchinson decided to leave the English colonies altogether and seek a more peaceful existence in New Amsterdam. There she settled at Pelham Bay. Tragically, in late summer of 1643, Hutchinson and all of the children still at home, except her young daughter Susanna, were massacred by Indians. The Reverend Thomas Weld reported to England that the Lord had finally freed the New England church of this sore affliction.

Summary

Anne Hutchinson was a woman well ahead of her time. Her desire for religious freedom, political equality, and recognition of the rights and capabilities of women would not be realized for several centuries. With her death in 1643, it seemed to many of her contemporaries that her cause had been crushed. The irony was that her attackers were American Indian youths who were unaware that she was among their greatest advocates in the colonies.

Hutchinson had been born a witness to social injustice. Having watched her father suffer for following his conscience, she became determined to work for a more humane world for all people. Her conviction that salvation was a gift from God brought much-needed relief to many New Englanders, and one noted that as a result of Hutchinson's efforts the heavy burden of Puritanism began to lift.

Anne Hutchinson was survived by five children, and the Hutchinson family continued to provide New England with the impetus for reform. Her family and followers relentlessly pursued their advocacy of peace, antislavery, and human rights and gave to the future a belief in the possibility of a free society that would draw its sustenance from the grace of God. The best efforts of the leaders of Puritan Massachusetts could not permanently obliterate her memory or her beliefs.

Bibliography

Battis, Emery. *Saints and Sectaries: Anne Hutchinson and the Antinomian Controversy in the Massachusetts Bay Colony*. Chapel Hill: University of North Carolina Press, 1962. Battis claims to be presenting a balanced interpretation of Hutchinson's life but actually returns to the more traditional position of supporting those who oppressed her. The volume is interesting and well researched but speculative.

Bolton, Reginald Pelham. *A Woman Misunderstood: Anne, Wife of William Hutchinson*. New York: Schoen, 1931. Bolton notes the manner in which Hutchinson was misinterpreted and misused by those who opposed her and attempts to construct an account that includes the positive side of her character.

Crawford, Deborah. *Four Women in a Violent Time*. New York: Crown, 1970. Hutchinson is included in this study along with three other colonial women. Crawford describes their misfortunes, their protests, the manner in which their lives intertwined, and the ways in which they changed their world.

Curtis, Edith Roelker. *Anne Hutchinson: A Biography*. Cambridge, Mass.: Washburn & Thomas, 1930. One of the first biographies of Hutchinson written by a woman, this work is brief and somewhat superficial. Curtis begins with Hutchinson's arrival in New England, omitting the first forty-three years of her life.

Hall, David D., ed. *The Antinomian Controversy, 1636-1638*. Middletown, Conn.: Wesleyan University Press, 1968. A collection of documents relating to the antinomian controversy in Massachusetts between 1636 and 1638. The introduction provides a definition of antinomianism and a brief description of the issues. The examination of Anne Hutchinson and the report on her trial are included.

Lang, Amy Schrager. *Prophetic Woman: Anne Hutchinson and the Problem of Dissent in the Literature of New England*. Berkeley: University of California Press, 1987. This book is not about Hutchinson's life. Its focus is the view of Hutchinson that was promulgated in Puritan tracts and histories, a view that was thoroughly antiwoman in nature. *Prophetic Woman* is useful because of its analysis of the religious views that Hutchinson opposed and because of its portrayal of the society in which she lived.

Rugg, Winnifred King. *Unafraid: A Life of Anne Hutchinson*. Reprint. Freeport, N.Y.: Books for Libraries Press, 1970. In this biography, first published in 1930, Rugg presents Hutchinson as an individualist, a fearless feminist, an early advocate of freedom, and a woman who shook New England in the 1600's.

Williams, Selma R. *Divine Rebel: The Life of Anne Marbury Hutchinson.* New York: Holt, Rinehart and Winston, 1981. A well-researched and historically accurate biography. Williams considers Anne's life in England, transcripts from her trial in America, and accounts of her activities on both sides of the Atlantic.

Nancy Erickson

HELEN HUNT JACKSON

Born: October 15, 1830; Amherst, Massachusetts
Died: August 12, 1885; San Francisco, California
Areas of Achievement: Literature and social reform
Contribution: Jackson received the first government commission on behalf of American Indians and fought vehemently for their civil rights and liberties.

Early Life

Helen Maria Fiske was born on October 15, 1830, to Nathan Wiley Fiske and Deborah Vinal Fiske. Nathan Fiske was a Congregational clergyman and a professor of philosophy and language at Amherst College who brought his children up under strict Calvinistic authority. Helen's mother Deborah was a quiet, demure woman whose influence on the young vivacious Helen was minimal. Indeed, Helen's father's only real influence occurred when he either punished her physically or derided her in front of her friends. Although her home in Amherst provided her with stability and a strict code of ethics, little affection or warmth was conveyed to the young and impressionable Helen. For friendship and companionship, Helen would turn to her friend Emily Dickinson, who lived down the road from her house. Helen's friendship with the reclusive Emily proved to be a sustaining relationship throughout her life.

Illness was a common feature of New England life in the middle of the nineteenth century. Deborah contracted tuberculosis and died a few months after Helen's twelfth birthday—the year was 1844. Helen had been a devoted daughter and had received all of her education from her mother up to that point. By the summer of 1846, Nathan had also contracted tuberculosis, but he was set on traveling to the Holy Land. Since the death of Deborah, Helen had been separated from her younger sister Ann and had been attending various seminaries. A year after leaving Amherst, Nathan died, and he was buried on Mount Zion. Helen was nearly fifteen when she was faced with being separated from her only sister and living in seminaries with virtual strangers.

These early years of personal hardship and grief were formative in how Helen lived her life and clearly forged many of her later moral and political values. Despite such hardship, Helen maintained her somewhat carefree and unstructured lifestyle. From these early years as a young girl until she finally came to live in San Francisco, Helen remained true to her own ideals rather than those of other people. Corresponding with Emily Dickinson was the one unaltered joy that sustained her through many personal and family hardships.

From this period in her life until her death in San Francisco, Helen was a traveler whose trunks and cases seemed to be permanently packed. These formative years gave the young, headstrong Helen a yearning to travel and to experience new and different places, becoming a part of society wherever she found herself.

Life's Work

Although Helen Hunt Jackson's novel *Ramona* (1884) made a lasting contribution to American literature, her literary and political endeavors had a rather inauspicious beginning. After the death of her first husband, Lieutenant Edward Bissel Hunt, in 1863 and the tragic death of her nine-year-old son two years later, Jackson turned to writing as a form of solace. (She became Helen Hunt Jackson when she later married William S. Jackson, a wealthy Quaker financier, in 1875.) Recognizing that she had an ability to write, she set out to become a well-known and respected writer. Helen undertook a life dedicated to writing. Articles, poems, sketches, and novels became her life-blood. Outwardly, at least, Helen Jackson remained vivacious and ebullient, seemingly undaunted by the tragic life that had been hers in only thirty-five years.

In the summer of 1865, Parke Godwin, the assistant publisher of the *New York Evening Post*, published Helen's poem "The Key to the Casket." This unexpected acceptance of her work inspired Helen to move to the writing community of Newport, Rhode Island. Thomas Wentworth Higginson, a respected writer and critic, soon became Helen's writing mentor, friend, and confidant. Newport allowed Helen the freedom to write even though woman writers were at that time far from being accepted. Because women writers were still an enigma, Jackson was forced to publish her works anonymously. Only when *Ramona* was published in 1884 did Jackson believe that her true identity was no longer an issue.

Because of the phenomenal success of *Ramona*, many people have the impression that Jackson was really only the author of a solitary novel. This could not be further from the truth. From her early years at Newport and continuously throughout her life, Jackson wrote in many different subject areas.

Jackson's early writing, however, reveals little of the passion and conviction that the cause of the American Indians would eventually evoke in her. The seed for her later and most famous writing was planted during a trip to California in May of 1872. After crossing the Platte River, Helen was given her first close-up experience of what Indians looked like and how they lived. This singular encounter caused Helen a certain degree of heartache as she witnessed for herself the abject poverty in which this disenfranchised people lived.

Bits of Travel appeared in 1870, and *Bits of Travel at Home* was finally published in 1878. During the period between writing these complementary pieces, Jackson's very successful "No Name" novels were hailed as drawing-room masterpieces. Jackson published *Mercy Philbrick's Choice* in 1876 and *Hetty's Strange History* in 1877. Up to this point in her writing career, Helen Hunt Jackson had published under the name H.H.

When *Century of Dishonor* appeared in 1881, Helen received all the criticism and vindictive press that was associated with writing about the plight of American Indians. Jackson's hope was that this laboriously researched work, which told the history of how badly the Indians had been treated, would spark some sympathy for them. In fact, the opposite proved to be the case. At her expense, she mailed a copy of *Century of Dishonor* to every congressman, again to little avail.

A woman who was no stranger to tragedy and who was relentless in pursuing what she believed to be right, Jackson continued to badger members of Congress. In particular, she focused on getting the attention of the secretary of the interior, Henry Teller, as well as appealing to Hiram Price, commissioner of Indian affairs. Both thought that Jackson was raising the controversial question of Indian land rights as a means of gaining publicity, but eventually the constant letter writing and appeals paid off. Jackson's singular efforts gained for her the position of special commissioner of Indian affairs in Southern California. This was a major breakthrough, particularly because Jackson was the first woman to hold such a government position.

Abbot Kinney was her choice for coagent and interpreter—a traveler and visionary like herself. They met while she was on an assignment for *Century* magazine in California. Two years after *Century of Dishonor* had been published, Jackson and Kinney began their travels of the Southern California missions. What had originally begun as a crusade to gain land rights for the Ponca Indians in Nebraska turned into a full-scale investigation into how mission Indians were being treated under government laws.

By now, Jackson had become very familiar with all of the missions in Southern California, and she undertook her commission with passion and zeal. Much of her traveling in Southern California in 1883 was done by carriage. With old stagecoach routes as their only means of traveling from one mission site to the next, Jackson and her troupe crisscrossed the sand plains and traversed the rugged mountains of the three most southerly counties of California.

Even though theirs was a fact-finding trip, Jackson's party continually came upon violations of Indian rights by white land settlers. Helen's passion for writing was now being used to record facts, figures, and names that she hoped would indict those early landowners.

To her dismay, Jackson's fifty-six-page report, which was appended to *Century of Dishonor*, created little stir. Perhaps the government hoped that the task would be more than one person could bear and that the society lady from New England would return to writing children's books and homilies. Realizing that the plight of the Indians was still in the balance, she took the advice of her close friend J. B. Gilder and began to write a novel.

When Gilder had first suggested that a novel might be the way to prick the conscience of a nation, Jackson balked at the immensity of such a project. Now, however, Jackson saw the need for such a book and was prepared to write her best. The many trips to California had steeped her in Indian culture and lifestyle. Despite the fact that *Ramona* forcefully portrays injustices toward the Indians, the novel quickly became a classic because it paints an exquisite, romantic portrait of mission life in old California.

Summary

Helen Hunt Jackson was a woman who took up the cause of a people that had little or no voice in society. Like many other pioneering women of the nineteenth century, she contributed greatly to both literature and social reform.

Jackson's untimely death meant that she did not see the full effect of her efforts, but other individuals and groups took up where Jackson's work and unfailing devotion to the Indian people left off. The Women's National Indian Association quickly recognized Jackson's contribution and hailed *Ramona* as a strong voice for Indian reform. Members of Congress, the commissioner of Indian affairs, members of various Christian organizations, and Indian reformers gathered at Lake Mohonk to discuss ways of dealing with Indian land rights. Many of the reforms that were later implemented by the government came directly as a result of these meetings. Jackson's message had little impact while she was alive, but soon after her death, groups and individuals were to carry that message throughout America.

While Jackson's contribution to the American Indian cause has etched her name in American history, her personality and life also attest this same vision. Ralph Waldo Emerson considered Jackson one of America's greatest poets. Such an accolade only draws attention to Jackson as a woman who was forced to live in anonymity for much of her literary life. Helen Hunt Jackson provided the leadership and courage that would inspire many more American women to turn their dreams into reality.

Bibliography

Banning, Evelyn. *Helen Hunt Jackson*. New York: Vanguard Press, 1973. Relying heavily on the work of Ruth Odell's 1939 biography, this work takes a painstaking look at Jackson's lesser writings. Indian rights are not a central theme, yet its scholarly approach makes this a useful reference.

Garner, Van H. *The Broken Ring: The Destruction of the California Indians*. Tucson, Ariz.: Westernlore Press, 1982. Thorough and well researched, this work covers the period from the 1840's to the 1980's. There are a number of useful entries concerning Jackson's specific dealings with various Indian tribes.

Jackson, Helen Hunt. *A Century of Dishonor*. Boston: Roberts Brothers, 1885. A thorough and meticulously researched document that became the backbone of Indian land reform. Much of the book resembles a legal brief, yet it manages to communicate the passion of Jackson's quest for reform.

Mathes, Valerie Sherer. *Helen Hunt Jackson and Her Indian Reform Legacy*. Austin: University of Texas Press, 1990. The purpose of this work was to reestablish Jackson as a prominent author and reformer. With thoughtfulness and sound research, this work offers an excellent insight into American Indian history.

May, Antoinette. *Helen Hunt Jackson: A Lonely Voice of Conscience*. San Francisco, Chronicle Press, 1987. This is a complete bibliography of Helen Hunt Jackson's life from early childhood to her death. May's writing is based primarily on anecdotal sources, and she embellishes much of Jackson's life with an almost fictional style.

Richard G. Cormack

MAHALIA JACKSON

Born: October 26, 1911; New Orleans, Louisiana
Died: January 27, 1972; Evergreen Park, Illinois (near Chicago)
Area of Achievement: Music
Contribution: One of the greatest American singers, Mahalia Jackson introduced black gospel music to an international audience and was a leading figure in the Civil Rights movement.

Early Life

Mahalia Jackson was born in an impoverished black ghetto in New Orleans, Louisiana, on October 26, 1911. She was the third of six children. Her father, John A. Jackson, a part-time preacher, worked as a stevedore along the Mississippi riverfront and supplemented his meager wages by working as a barber at night. Her mother, Charity Clark, died at the age of twenty-five when Mahalia was only four years old. Mahalia and an older brother were reared by Mahalia "Aunt Duke" Paul, a self-righteous woman who often beat the two children with a cat-o'-nine-tails.

Mahalia Jackson was a veritable Cinderella, working as a household drudge for her aunt after school. She owned only one dress and had no shoes. By the time she was in the eighth grade, she was also working five hours a day as a laundress, trying to save money so that she could escape from her aunt's tyranny and from the near-slavery that was the condition of most African Americans in the South.

Mahalia's ticket to freedom was her magnificent voice, which was recognized at an early age when she sang in the choir of her father's church. At the age of twelve, she was invited to join the famous blues singer Ma Rainey's traveling show, the same show that had discovered the blues star Bessie Smith. Aunt Duke, however, refused to let her niece leave home because of the bad influence such an itinerant life inevitably entailed. In later years, Mahalia acknowledged that her aunt had probably saved her from a dissolute life of drinking, drugs, and promiscuity. Her love-hate relationship with Aunt Duke was the most important influence in her formative years.

Mahalia loved to listen to phonograph records, and her favorite recordings were those by the great blues singer Bessie Smith. Although Mahalia refused to become a blues singer, she was deeply influenced by Bessie's style, which included a powerful delivery, great originality of phrasing, and a flawless sense of rhythm. Like Bessie Smith, Mahalia Jackson was to influence many of the popular singers who followed her, both black and white, male and female.

In 1928, Jackson escaped to Chicago, promising to study to become a nurse. In Chicago, the lonely young woman joined the Greater Salem Baptist Church and began singing in the choir. She soon became a semi-professional singer, traveling around the country with a group called the Johnson Gospel Singers.

In 1935, she married Isaac Hockenhull, a mail carrier. Because he objected to her traveling, their marriage did not last. Her reputation as a singer continued to grow, but her income during the Depression years remained paltry because the people who appreciated her music were living on the brink of starvation. They often had to choose between buying food for the stomach or phonograph recordings that would provide food for the soul.

Life's Work

Mahalia Jackson began recording for the Apollo label in 1945 but made little money with the second-rate firm. The early audience for gospel music on records was confined almost exclusively to blacks, who had little extra money to spend on such luxuries. It was not until she began recording for the giant Columbia Records in 1954 that she reaped big financial rewards. Columbia had the financial resources to advertise her recordings and bring her to the attention of a multiracial audience. By that time, she was in her forties. She sang in hundreds of concerts every year and made many public appearances in behalf of the Civil Rights movement of the turbulent 1960's.

Mahalia Jackson started to become internationally famous during the 1950's. Her greatest triumph occurred when she appeared at Carnegie Hall in New York, the most important showcase for musical talent in America. She toured Denmark, England, and France, where she sang for white audiences. She sang for the empress of Japan, for President Dwight D. Eisenhower and President John F. Kennedy, and for other dignitaries. It was mainly because of Mahalia Jackson that black gospel became as well known to international music lovers as jazz and blues.

In the later years of her career, she began singing other types of music as well as gospel. This brought her to the attention of a still wider audience, although some of her purist followers objected to her experimentation. Many music critics have maintained that Jackson's best recordings were made with Mildred Falls, who accompanied her on the piano for many years and contributed greatly to the irresistible rhythm that is Mahalia's trademark. Among her biggest hits were "Move on up a Little Higher," which had sold more than eight million records at the time of her death.

As Jackson became more and more famous, she experimented by singing popular songs, hymns, anthems, and even Christmas carols, but she steadfastly refused to be a blues singer, for religious reasons. "Anybody singing the blues is in a deep pit yelling for help," she once said, "and I'm simply not in that position." She recorded with some of the greatest orchestras of her time, including that of the famous Duke Ellington.

Jackson was a devoted follower of the Reverend Martin Luther King, Jr., and helped to attract crowds to his speeches during the 1960's with her inspirational singing. She not only sang for political gatherings but also spoke persuasively in support of King's crusade for racial justice and human brotherhood. Because she was loved by people of all races, she influenced many people—including many African Americans who might have taken the violent path advocated by radical leaders such as Malcolm X—to pay heed to King's plea for nonviolent social action.

Jackson was married for a second time in 1965 to a builder and part-time musician named Sigmund Galloway. Their relationship was stormy. They were divorced and then remarried a few years later. Her travels and hectic work schedule put a strain on her domestic relations throughout her life.

Ironically, although Jackson was a deeply spiritual woman, she was very much concerned about making and keeping money. Her early years of bitter poverty had given her an abiding respect for financial security. She usually insisted on being paid in cash for her concert appearances, and she often carried huge amounts of cash in her brassiere. In later life, she invested in real estate and such successful franchise operations as Mahalia's Chicken Dinners, Mahalia's Beauty Salon, and Mahalia's Flower Shop.

Mahalia Jackson was a large woman who weighed approximately 260 pounds. She loved to cook and loved to eat, and her tastes in food included fried chicken, pork chops, and other southern dishes. Although she suffered from heart trouble for many years, she refused to slow down. The strain of her many personal appearances, together with the stressful traveling they entailed, shortened her life. Jackson was only sixty years old when she died, and her voice had lost none of its remarkable power.

Her death was front-page news all over the world. New Orleans, where she was born, and Chicago, where her career began, both held impressive civic ceremonies in her honor. Among the prominent entertainers who attended the Chicago ceremony were the singers Aretha Franklin, Sammy Davis, and Ella Fitzgerald; in New Orleans the ceremony featured the singer Lou Rawls and the comedian-activist Dick Gregory. Jackson's estate was valued at more than a million dollars, and her records continued to generate lucrative royalties for her heirs.

Her personality was a strange mixture of selfishness and generosity, of acquisitiveness and altruism, of hard business sense and emotional self-sacrifice. Even at the peak of her career, when she was being paid as much as ten thousand dollars for a single concert appearance, she would often sing at black churches without charging a fee. "I don't work for money," she once said. "I sing because I love to sing."

Summary

Mahalia Jackson's main contribution to culture was introducing black gospel music to a worldwide audience. The public was already familiar with the other two major types of African American music, jazz and the blues, but knew little about gospel music because it was mainly confined to African American churches and black music lovers who listened to gospel music on records.

Jackson always refused to be tempted to sing blues, even though it was obvious that she could have been as great a blues singer as Bessie Smith. Her strong religious convictions persuaded her that her voice was a gift from God and that it was her duty to use it in God's service. It is her unwavering religious faith that makes her singing so compelling on the many recordings she left behind. She was a great artist, and it is impossible for anyone to listen to her records without being infected by the powerful emotions she put into her singing. She inspired many people to look for solutions to their life problems in traditional religion. She made gospel music popular with a vast audience and thereby paved the way for vocalists such as Aretha Franklin to obtain widespread recognition.

Mahalia Jackson is also regarded as one of the leading personalities in the Civil Rights movement. By bringing gospel music into the service of a political movement, she contributed a spiritual, religious, and artistic element that had a powerful emotional effect on people of all races. Having suffered all of her life from racial injustice, she understood the message of Martin Luther King, Jr., and helped him bring his crusade for understanding and brotherhood to a wider multiracial audience. Art has the power to unite people, and through her many recordings, which are still widely available, Mahalia Jackson continues to have that impact on people of all races and religions throughout the world.

Bibliography

Goreau, Laurraine. *Just Mahalia, Baby.* Waco, Tex.: Word Books, 1975. This excellent full-length biography uses various styles, including journalistic reconstruction and direct quotations. It traces the roots of African American music into the realms of voodoo and the supernatural. Full of interesting anecdotes about Mahalia and all the famous people she knew. Contains many photographs.

Hughes, Langston. *Famous Negro Music Makers.* New York: Dodd, Mead, 1955. A collection of short biographical sketches by a famous African American poet, scholar, and educator. Includes sketches of Bessie Smith and Mahalia Jackson.

Jackson, Mahalia, with Evan McLeod Wylie. *Movin' on Up.* New York: Hawthorn Books, 1966. An autobiography based on Mahalia Jackson's personal recollections of her early struggles and her rise to fame as a professional singer. Captures her dynamic, optimistic spirit and focuses on the hardships and joys of her childhood years.

Jones, Hettie. *Big Star Fallin' Mama: Five Women in Black Music.* New York: Viking Press, 1974. This interesting small volume contains chapters on five of the most important African American singers: Ma Rainey, Bessie Smith, Mahalia Jackson, Billie Holiday, and Aretha Franklin. It tells how each of them influenced the others. Contains good photographs of all five of these great musical artists.

Lincoln, Eric, and Lawrence H. Mamiya. *The Black Church in the African-American Experience.* Durham, N.C.: Duke University Press, 1990. This large, scholarly book contains an in-depth discussion of the history of African American Christian churches and makes many references to religious music as it evolved in those churches over the centuries. Thoroughly researched and documented.

Schwerin, Jules. *Got to Tell It: Mahalia Jackson, Queen of Gospel.* New York: Oxford University Press, 1992. This author describes his book as an "impressionistic biography" based on many personal meetings with Jackson over a period of approximately eighteen years. He portrays Jackson as a strange mixture of contrasting characteristics: proud, suspicious, generous, selfish, competitive, spiritual, and materialistic.

"Two Cities Pay Tribute to Mahalia Jackson." *Ebony* 27 (April, 1972): 62-72. Published shortly after Mahalia's death, this long article describes the ceremonies held in her honor by the cities of Chicago and New Orleans. It summarizes her lifetime achievements and is full of excellent color photographs.

Wolfe, Charles. *Mahalia Jackson.* New York: Chelsea House, 1990. Part of Chelsea House's American Women of Achievement series. Written for juvenile readers, this is a good basic biographical work containing most of the essential information about Mahalia Jackson's career and personal life. Includes a bibliography, a discography, a chronology, and an index.

Bill Delaney

ALICE JAMES

Born: August 7, 1848; New York, New York
Died: March 6, 1892; London, England
Area of Achievement: Literature
Contribution: During the last three years of her life, Alice James, invalid sister of
novelist Henry James and psychologist William James, kept a diary in which she
recorded her impressions of British and American society and provided revealing
and intimate portraits of her famous brothers.

Early Life

Alice James was born August 7, 1848, in New York City, the youngest child and
only daughter of Henry James, Sr., and Mary Walsh James. Her father, the son of a
wealthy Irish immigrant who lived in Albany, New York, spent his adult life in
lecturing and writing on social and religious philosophy and exchanging ideas with
an intellectual circle of friends that included Horace Greeley and Ralph Waldo
Emerson. In July, 1840, the elder Henry James married Mary Robertson Walsh, who
came from a well-to-do family who lived in New York City. The Jameses' first son,
William, was born in 1842, followed by Henry, Jr., in 1843, Garth Wilkinson in 1845,
Robertson in 1846, and Alice in 1848.

Henry James, Sr., took his young family to Europe in 1843 for an extended stay.
While in England, he formed friendships with such intellectual leaders as Thomas
Carlyle, George Henry Lewes, John Stuart Mill, and Alfred, Lord Tennyson. Though
the Jameses returned to New York in 1845, the family seldom stayed in one place for
long. In 1855, and again in 1859, the family traveled to Europe, where they remained
for extended periods. In 1860, the James family settled in Newport, Rhode Island; in
1864, they moved to Boston; and in 1866, they moved to Cambridge, Massachusetts.

Henry James, Sr., had theories on education that were quite unusual for the
nineteenth century. He believed that spontaneity was the most important element in
learning and that the best education included exposure to art galleries, theaters, and
experiences that excited the "sensibilities," or senses. As a result of their father's
unorthodox views on education, the James sons experienced an erratic assortment of
tutors and experimental schools in Europe and the United States. Surprisingly, Henry
James, Sr., held more traditional views on the education of females, believing that
formal education for women was not advisable; therefore, Alice was educated primarily at home by a series of governesses and tutors.

Alice began to suffer from mysterious ailments early in her adolescence. Unable to
make a more specific diagnosis, various physicians attributed her fainting spells,
headaches, and depression to "neuralgia," "neurasthenia," or "hysteria," vague categories of illness in frequent use at the time. Alice's poor health was not, however,
unusual in her family; her father and her brothers were subject to nervous and physical
breakdowns, and with the exception of Mary James, all family members apparently
suffered almost continuous bouts of poor digestion, depression, and other maladies.

Before Alice's twentieth birthday, her continued pattern of ill health without apparent physical cause had become a permanent source of attention and concern for her family. Any exertion or excitement brought on a fainting spell or a violent outburst, and she became increasingly depressed.

Life's Work

Though Alice James enjoyed brief periods of relative health, she was never entirely well. Throughout her adult life, her physical and emotional well-being remained precarious. As William and Henry left home to attend college, and Garth Wilkinson and Robertson enlisted to fight in the Civil War, Alice's outside activities were restricted, by her illnesses, to brief intervals spent doing charity work in Boston and New York.

Alice grew increasingly doubtful that any permanent cure could be found, while various physicians prescribed rest cures, exercises, massages, or ice or electricity treatments. In 1872, she was well enough to travel to Europe, accompanied by her brother Henry and their maternal aunt Catharine Walsh. Henry was able to write encouragingly to his parents, reporting that Alice remained well when she was surrounded by the activity of the cities they visited. By the end of the trip, Henry had decided that Europe would provide more stimulus for his writing career, so he remained there. Alice returned to Cambridge and the care of her parents.

In 1875, Alice became a volunteer history instructor for Miss Anna Ticknor's Society to Encourage Studies at Home, a charitable organization that ran correspondence courses for women across the country. Though Alice's work with the organization ended before 1880, it was this brief association that led to her devoted and abiding friendship with Katherine Peabody Loring, a young woman from Beverly, Massachusetts, who was active in social and charitable works. Throughout the balance of her life, Alice James relied upon Katherine Loring for companionship and, when she became permanently bedridden, for nursing care.

In 1878, Alice had a severe nervous breakdown. During one period of prolonged depression, she told her father that she was strongly tempted to commit suicide, asking him if such an act would be a sin. Henry James, Sr., responded that he would not consider suicide a sin if her aim was to end her own suffering, as long as she ended her life in such a way as to cause as little distress as possible to her family and friends. By giving Alice permission to end her life, Henry James, Sr., shrewdly acknowledged his daughter's right to choose death and thereby countered her impulse for immediate action. As Alice explained to her father, while she knew that the option remained open to her, she had no immediate need to act upon it.

As her brothers, notably William and Henry, began to forge careers for themselves, Alice lived in Cambridge with her parents. After her mother died in early 1882, Alice and Henry James, Sr., moved to a smaller house in Boston. Alice took over the management of the household and devotedly cared for her bereaved father. Sadly, this period of activity, which provided Alice with a sense of purpose and an unusual amount of independent responsibility, lasted only a few months. Henry James, Sr., was in declining health; he died later in the same year, having chosen to starve himself rather than continue to live.

Her father's death left Alice with enough money to ensure that she could live comfortably. After spending three months at the Adams Nervine Asylum near Boston, following a crisis of nerves early in 1883, Alice tried living alone in the house she had shared with her father, but she felt depressed and isolated there. In November, 1884, she traveled to England, accompanied by Katherine Loring. Alice James would spend the rest of her life in England.

After a difficult crossing during which she stayed in her cabin, Alice had to be carried ashore at Liverpool. When she was stronger, Henry James, Jr., arranged for her to move into rooms in London. As Alice's health deteriorated, Katherine Loring finally moved in to care for her, and the two spent the remaining years in lodgings in Leamington or in London, finally settling in a house on Campden Hill. Henry frequently arranged to take rooms near his sister's house so that he could spend time with her.

In May, 1889, Alice began to keep a diary, hoping that the activity would provide respite from "the sense of loneliness and desolation which abides with me." Like the other members of her family, Alice was a prolific writer, but unlike her famous brothers, she had confined her own efforts to her correspondence and her common-place book. Except for rare excursions, when she was taken into the countryside in a wheelchair, Alice's circumscribed world was limited to Katherine and a series of nurses, with regular visits from Henry and occasional calls by acquaintances. She did, however, read the London newspapers, taking an avid interest in society, contemporary manners, and political events on both sides of the Atlantic, with all the alert and self-confident analysis of a more active participant.

Alice's diary became an important outlet for her share of the family's literary talents. Limited in opportunity by the time in which she lived and by the societal expectations for women of the period, Alice may have adopted illness as a substitute for the sort of achievements that made Henry James, Jr., and William James prominent intellectual and literary figures. In her own narrow world, however, Alice recorded the activities of her family and friends, interjecting witty and often biting commentary about the foolish behavior of "society." In addition, her journal entries provided closer, more intimate images of the remarkable members of her family than might otherwise have been available. As Katherine Loring looked after and protected her, often taking down journal entries in dictation when Alice was too ill to write, the invalid composed her diary in relative secrecy.

In May, 1891, Alice's physician informed her that she had a terminal condition—a cancerous breast tumor. Alice jubilantly recorded the event in her diary, writing, "To him who waits, all things come!" Having spent so many years in illness, she wrote of her "enormous relief" at having, at last, "some palpable disease." While subsequent journal entries included frequent mentions of her illness and coming death, Alice continued her accustomed commentary upon people and politics.

Alice James died March 6, 1892. She had continued to dictate her diary entries to

Katherine Loring through March 4. After her ashes were returned to Cambridge, Massachusetts, her loyal companion edited the manuscript and had four copies printed, one for each of Alice's surviving brothers and one for herself. Katherine Loring's initial intention was to publish the diary, but the project was put aside at the urging of Henry James. Not having known that his sister was keeping a journal, he was distressed at the idea that his private conversations with his sister should be revealed to the public. The diary was not published until 1934.

Summary

Alice James has come to epitomize the tragedy of nineteenth century women who, possessing talents of their own, were limited by societal expectations to the traditional roles of middle- and upper-middle-class women. In life, she led a private existence, surrounded by family and friends, her activities curtailed by her continuous illnesses. Since the publication of her diary, scholars have frequently suggested that psychosomatic illness was Alice James's conscious or subconscious response to the denial of opportunities for achievement, which, though open to her remarkable brothers, were denied to her. The diary she began toward the end of her life proves that, like her more prominent father and siblings, Alice James was a gifted writer and an insightful social critic.

Bibliography

James, Alice. *Alice James: Her Brothers—Her Journal.* Edited by Anna Robeson Burr. New York: Dodd, Mead, 1934. A dated and rather sentimental work combining a short collective biography of Alice James's four brothers with her own diary. This edition of the diary lacks explanatory footnotes, leaving many passages incomprehensible to the modern reader.

_____ . *The Death and Letters of Alice James.* Edited by Ruth Bernard Yeazell. Berkeley: University of California Press, 1981. A perceptive examination of James's role as invalid at the center of a remarkable family of intellectuals, as illustrated by her selected correspondence with family and friends from 1860 until her death in 1892.

_____ . *The Diary of Alice James.* Edited by Leon Edel. New York: Dodd, Mead, 1964. The complete text of James's diary, with a useful introduction by the editor and helpful explanatory footnotes identifying people and contemporary events mentioned in the entries.

Lewis, R. W. B. *The Jameses: A Family Narrative.* New York: Farrar, Straus & Giroux, 1991. A rich, comprehensive family biography that provides much information about Alice James not available in earlier works.

Matthiessen, F. O. *The James Family: Including Selections from the Writings of Henry James, Senior, William, Henry, and Alice James.* New York: Alfred A. Knopf, 1961. An insightful biographical treatment of the James family, incorporating letters, journal entries, and essays to illustrate the family's role as intellectual circle.

Sontag, Susan. *Alice in Bed: A Play in Eight Scenes.* New York: Farrar, Straus &

Giroux, 1993. A feminist fantasy portraying James as a tragic figure whose intellectual and literary gifts were incompatible with nineteenth century expectations for women, a conflict that led her to a life of depression and psychosomatic illness.

Jan Jenkins

SARAH ORNE JEWETT

Born: September 3, 1849; South Berwick, Maine
Died: June 24, 1909; South Berwick, Maine
Area of Achievement: Literature
Contribution: Author of twenty books, Jewett was the most accomplished of the American writers associated with literary regionalism and a major force in the creation and development of an American women's literary tradition.

Early Life

The second of three sisters, Theodora Sarah Orne Jewett was born into an established and wealthy family in South Berwick, Maine, on September 3, 1849. Her grandfather, Captain Theodore Furber Jewett, had prospered in the West Indies trade in the early part of the century, leaving the family financially independent.

Although Sarah received her formal education at Miss Raynes's School and at Berwick Academy in South Berwick, much of her true education came from her father, a country doctor. She was her father's frequent companion on his house calls, especially when bouts of ill health kept her out of school. As they moved from house to house, he shared with her his close observations of the surrounding landscape as well as his thoughts on life and literature. Later, Sarah, by now an accomplished writer, would credit her father with pointing out to her that really great writers do not write *about* people and things, but describe them just as they are.

Young Sarah read widely in her parents' substantial library, and when, at the age of seventeen, she read Harriet Beecher Stowe's *The Pearl of Orr's Island* (1862), she found in Stowe's portrayal of scenes from Maine life a hint of the possibilities of the regionalist fiction in which Sarah herself would excel.

Sarah's first published story, "Jenny Garrow's Ghost," appeared in *The Flag of Our Union*, a Boston weekly, on January 18, 1868. The nineteen-year-old author, unwilling at this point that others should know of her literary activities, used the pen name "Alice Eliot." In December of the following year, after two polite rejections, the prestigious *Atlantic Monthly* published her story "Mr. Bruce," confirming Sarah's conviction that she was at least an apprentice writer.

She continued to write for the *Atlantic* and other publications. Finally, William Dean Howells, the novelist and editor, suggested to Sarah that she organize some of her sketches and short stories into a book. Sarah found this work painfully difficult, but the result, *Deephaven* (1877), marked her arrival at maturity as a writer.

Life's Work

The death of her father in 1878 was a difficult blow for Sarah Orne Jewett. Until his death, her relationship with him had been the most important of her life. Her closest adult emotional relationships were her friendships with women. The most important of these was with Annie Fields, whom Sarah met in the 1870's, when Annie was married to the publisher James T. Fields, Annie's senior by some seventeen years.

After Fields's death in 1881, Sarah and Annie's friendship flowered into a "Boston marriage." The term denotes a virtually spousal—although not necessarily, or even usually, sexual—relationship between two women. Sarah and Annie lived together for part of each year, they traveled together, and, when physically separated, kept in touch by letter. To their friends, it became natural to think of them as a couple.

In the years following *Deephaven*, Sarah continued to develop as a writer. She enjoyed her greatest success in the sketches and short stories set in her native Maine. That her life as an adult involved long periods of residence in Boston and of foreign travel seemed to strengthen her imaginative possession of the Maine setting. Her own experience justified the advice she later gave the younger novelist Willa Cather, that to know the parish one must first know the world.

She was mastering a form that was very much her own: a short narrative devoid of plot in terms of dramatic event and linear structure. The form allows for patient observation of the gradual unfolding of human relationships and the interrelationship of the human and the natural in places Sarah had known since childhood. Many of her stories have a conversational quality: a speaker, usually a woman, moves, by what seems superficially like random association, toward a clarification of emotional, spiritual, or moral truth that is the heart of the story.

She had less success with the more conventional sort of novel. Most readers find *The Country Doctor* (1884) her most interesting work in the novel form because of its content, the relationship of Nan Prince and Doctor Leslie, with its intriguing autobiographical resonance, and Nan's determination to enter the medical profession, which was regarded by her contemporaries as a male preserve. Yet the novel achieves only limited dramatic power.

Still, Sarah continued to develop as a literary artist. Her progress was dramatically displayed in the collection *A White Heron and Other Stories*, published in 1886. The title story of the collection, perhaps Jewett's most famous short story, exemplifies its author's respect for the reader's share in the literary experience. She credited her father for pointing out to her the importance in fiction of leaving readers some work to do, rather than bullying them into a passive acceptance of predigested motives and meanings. In this story, indirection in presenting the moment of decision involves the reader centrally in the process of making meaning. This is an art based on process rather than product, on cooperation rather than conquest. Some readers have suggested that it is very much a woman's sort of art, although appreciation of this art is by no means denied to men. In this case, any attentive reader must admire the delicacy and force (the two easily coexist in Jewett's work) with which the author brings into play within the reader's active mind many of the themes central to her fiction. She includes meditations on innocence and experience, on continuity and change, on the city and the country, on nature and culture, on masculine and feminine, on the imagination's power to soar, and on the reaching of the mind toward an androgyny of the spirit that may obviate the need for the sexual union of man and woman. This is much to build on a moment in the life of a nine-year-old girl, but Jewett (who, in a letter written when she was forty-eight, stated that she always felt nine years old) makes it all work.

The collections of stories and sketches published in the decade following *A White Heron and Other Stories* contain much of Jewett's best work in these forms. By now a fully mature artist, she published in 1896 *The Country of the Pointed Firs*, generally regarded as her masterpiece and the finest work of literary regionalism produced by any American writer. Like *Deephaven*, the new book consisted of a sequence of related short narratives unified by setting, characters, and, most powerfully, by the development of the narrator's involvement in the fictional community of Dunnet Landing. An important part of this development is the narrator's relationship with Almira Todd, a native of Dunnet Landing and one of Jewett's greatest triumphs of characterization. Structurally similar to *Deephaven*, *The Country of the Pointed Firs* is, because of its formal control and thematic depth, a much richer work. Writing in 1925, Willa Cather suggested that the work stands with Hawthorne's *The Scarlet Letter* (1850) and Mark Twain's *The Adventures of Huckleberry Finn* (1884) as one of the three American literary works of its century likely to achieve immortality.

Jewett would publish only two more books in her lifetime, *The Queen's Twin and Other Stories* in 1899 and *The Tory Lover*, an attempt at a historical novel, in 1901. In 1901, she was awarded an honorary degree by Maine's Bowdoin College, an all-male institution. She was delighted, she said, to be the only sister of so many brothers. Then, in September, 1902, she suffered a severe spinal injury from which she would never fully recover. Writing fiction became increasingly difficult and, finally, impossible. On June 24, 1909, she died in the Jewett family home in South Berwick, Maine.

Summary

Sarah Orne Jewett was inspired by Plato's maxim that the noblest service that can be done for the people of a state is to acquaint them with one another. The regionalist's literary vocation is precisely to acquaint the people of the larger society—ultimately, perhaps, of the world—with the life of a single region, often one remote from any cosmopolitan center. This vocation was realized by Sarah Orne Jewett more fully than by any other American writer. The stature of *The Country of the Pointed Firs* has been recognized since its first publication. Although there is always the danger that this book will dominate Jewett's posthumous reputation to the extent of reducing her to the status of the "one-book author," the last quarter of the twentieth century has seen a resurgence of interest in the totality of her work. This resurgence has in part been fueled by feminist concerns. That Jewett was a woman who wrote most powerfully about women and whose deepest emotional relationships were with women lends her an undeniable interest. Yet her audience has never been limited to women.

Jewett enjoyed considerable critical recognition in her lifetime. Among the writers who came to be associated with the regionalist movement, she was quickly and widely recognized as preeminent, as was the value of her sort of realism, even if it was a qualified sort. Although she tended to keep the grimmest of realities at the margins of her fiction, she did not expel them completely. For some of her characters, life in the country of the pointed firs follows a pattern of frustration and despair. Certainly, Jewett leaves her readers in little doubt that economic decline is the fundamental condition within which her characters live out their lives.

Jewett was an inspiration to such younger writers as Kate Chopin and Willa Cather, the latter of whom dedicated to Jewett the novel *O Pioneers!* (1913) and in 1925 edited and introduced a collection of Jewett's best fiction. Although Edith Wharton claimed to reject Sarah Orne Jewett's influence, many critics who are familiar with both writers find that the truth of the matter is more complicated.

Her stories continue to be published separately and in anthologies. Her work has been translated into German, Japanese, Spanish, and French. Critical interest in Sarah Orne Jewett's work has never been higher. Narrow though her range may have been, her work within that range reveals clarity, compassion, and the courage of an artist who developed the forms that her imagination demanded. What Willa Cather said of *The Country of the Pointed Firs* may be said of its author: She confronts time and change securely.

Bibliography

Cary, Richard, ed. *Appreciation of Sarah Orne Jewett: Twenty-nine Interpretive Essays.* Waterville, Maine: Colby College Press, 1973. This selection of criticism published prior to 1973 reflects the critical formalism dominant at the time of the book's publication. Supplemented by Nagel's collection.

——————. *Sarah Orne Jewett.* New York: Twayne, 1962. This book, the earliest full critical review of Jewett's work, analyzes her materials, methods, and forms, examining each work in relation to the long maturation of her genius. The organization is, for the most part, topical rather than chronological, and the case for Jewett as more than a one-book author is made convincingly.

Donovan, Josephine. *Sarah Orne Jewett.* New York: Frederick Ungar, 1980. The author explores the themes of city versus country and isolation versus community in Jewett's mature fiction and finds in *The Country of the Pointed Firs* the consummation of her thematic and formal concerns.

Mobley, Marilyn Sanders. *Folk Roots and Mythic Wings in Sarah Orne Jewett and Toni Morrison.* Baton Rouge: Louisiana State University Press, 1991. A critical study that asserts the importance of myth and folklore in the work of two women of different races and generations who draw on the cultural roots of their people.

Nagel, Gwen L. *Critical Essays on Sarah Orne Jewett.* Boston: G. K. Hall, 1984. A collection that supplements Cary's *Appreciation* and reflects later tendencies in Jewett criticism, including feminist perspectives.

Roman, Margaret. *Sarah Orne Jewett: Reconstructing Gender.* Tuscaloosa: University of Alabama Press, 1992. Argues that Jewett consciously collapses gender dichotomies, dissolving binary oppositions of gender.

Sherman, Sarah Way. *Sarah Orne Jewett: An American Persephone.* Hanover, N.H.: University Press of New England, 1989. Explores the growth of Jewett's art out of nineteenth century American culture and the terms in which that culture defined womanhood.

Silverthorne, Elizabeth. *Sarah Orne Jewett: A Writer's Life.* Woodstock, N.Y.: Overlook Press, 1993. This biography emphasizes the relationships between its subject's life and work and places her clearly within the literary and cultural life of her time.

W. P. Kenney

RUTH PRAWER JHABVALA

Born: May 7, 1927; Cologne, Germany

Areas of Achievement: Literature and film
Contribution: Ruth Prawer Jhabvala has demonstrated remarkable staying power as a screenwriter in the film industry, not generally regarded for sustaining careers, particularly for women. At the same time, she continues to be a well-respected novelist and short-story writer.

Early Life
"They should have been my formative years," Ruth Prawer Jhabvala later said of the period between 1933 and 1939, when she was between the ages of six and twelve, "and maybe they were." They were, she recognized, "the beginning of my disinheritance—the way they are for other writers of their inheritance." For Ruth, the year 1933, marking Adolf Hitler's rise to the chancellorship of Germany, changed everything.

Born May 7, 1927, to Marcus and Eleanora Prawer, Ruth Prawer grew up in a Jewish family in Cologne, Germany. She later recalled early memories of a cultured, comfortable home life, with an abundance of aunts and uncles "all well-settled German patriots, full of bourgeois virtues and pleasures." The Prawers' spacious apartment overlooked Cologne's main avenue. Ruth's maternal grandfather, cantor of the city's major synagogue, prided himself on his friendship with pastors.

None of this protected Ruth and her family from the shocks and indignities that were daily occurrences for Jews in Hitler's Germany. In November, 1938, Ruth witnessed *Kristallnacht*, the "Night of Broken Glass," during which Nazi stormtroopers rampaged through Jewish neighborhoods, terrorizing homes and businesses. In April of 1939, she, her father, mother, and brother escaped to England, among the last to leave.

Upon arriving, the Prawers faced further dislocation. Ruth and her brother Siegbert, older by two years, were relocated to Coventry as part of the British plan to evacuate children during the blitzkrieg. Eventually, they rejoined their parents in Hendon, a suburb of London. Ruth enrolled in Hendon County School, where, in her own words, she turned out stories, plays, and unfinished novels "in a relentless stream." She took up the English language unhesitantly, along with its literature, and later claimed that she "made up for [her] disinheritance by absorbing others."

From 1945 to 1955, Ruth attended Queen Mary College, London University, earning a master's degree with a thesis titled, "The Short Story in England, 1700-1750." Critics would find in her own later work the stamp of that period's literature: wit and appeal to reason.

In 1948, the year Ruth turned twenty-one, her father committed suicide. News of the Nazis' liquidation of at least forty members of the Prawers' family had reached England and claimed another casualty.

Life's Work

Ruth Prawer's next dislocation inspired the fictional world that established her literary reputation. In 1951, she arrived in New Delhi, India, the bride of an Indian architect, C. H. S. Jhabvala, whom she had met two years earlier when both were studying at London University.

Ruth Prawer Jhabvala's first five novels from *Amrita* (1956) to *A Backward Place* (1965), probed the domestic lives of middle-class Hindus in post-Independence India. The author lampoons her characters' preoccupation with the arrangement of marriages to achieve business advantage and social stability. Their acquisitive schemes and, ultimately, their self-delusions are the targets of Jhabvala's satire.

These novels have been categorized as "comedies of manners" for their ridicule of romantic excess and unmasking of hypocrisy. Jhabvala's novels of this period are often compared with those of Jane Austen, whose heroines' highly critical intelligence is tempered by sincerity and common sense. Writing in the twentieth century, Jhabvala, while honoring these virtues, refrains from guaranteeing their success.

Jhabvala's perspective as what writer and critic John Updike has called an "initiated outsider" has lent a characteristic irony to her work. Socializing with the families of her husband's Hindu business partners, she readily absorbed the colors and rhythms of their households. Nevertheless, her life remained insulated from India's harsher political and social realities. Sharply rendering the domestic habits and cherished snobberies of a culture in uneasy transition, Jhabvala's fiction was both applauded as Chekhovian tragicomedy and condemned as caricature. While some critics expressed disappointment over a lack of serious "ideas" in her work, others questioned her ability to give unconscious life to her fictional world, not being herself an Indian.

Jhabvala eventually underwent a crisis regarding her life in India. The nation's pervasive poverty began to weigh on her. In an essay entitled "Myself in India," she describes a cycle of emotions affecting Westerners who spend any length of time in India:

> It goes like this: first stage, tremendous enthusiasm—everything Indian is marvelous; second stage, everything Indian not so marvelous; third stage, everything Indian abominable. For some people, it ends there, for others the cycle renews itself and goes on. I have been through it so many times that now I think of myself as strapped to a wheel that goes round and round.

Jhabvala's focus in her stories and novels shifted in the late 1960's from the beehive of Indian family life to the wrenching turns of this cycle, on which Westerners are "strapped." The tone of her fiction darkened as the self-deceptions of her characters deepened. Critics noted a chilling in her work, from a cool appraisal of human folly to a dissection of the complicity between victim and victimizer. Her theme became the willing seduction of spiritually impoverished Westerners—usually women—by charismatic gurus offering initiation into the ecstatic mysteries of the East. The pilgrimages of naïve young Europeans and Americans in the 1960's to the ashrams of India supplied Jhabvala with much of her subject matter.

Another phenomenon of that decade, a growing international film industry, added a new dimension to Jhabvala's career. The newly fledged production team of Ismail Merchant and James Ivory approached her to script her 1960 novel *The Householder* for the screen. Wary at first, Jhabvala answered their phone call, pretending to be her mother-in-law. Finally persuaded, Jhabvala wrote her first screenplay in ten days. (Masses of dialogue would need to be cut.) The film's premiere in New Delhi in 1963 was hosted by the American ambassador, John Kenneth Galbraith, and attended by India's prime minister, Jawaharlal Nehru.

Jhabvala's film work considerably expanded her professional horizons. She finally had the resources to leave India, where she had reared three daughters and spent most of her adult life. The summer she spent writing her Booker Prize-winning novel *Heat and Dust* (1975)—its title serving as her metaphor for India's disease and squalor— was the last she spent in India.

In 1974, Jhabvala moved to New York City, taking an apartment above one shared by her collaborators, Ismail Merchant and James Ivory. Their creative association has provided Jhabvala not only with a sense of personal and professional camaraderie but also with a repertoire of techniques to experiment with in her fiction. Literary critics have noted an increasingly cinematic feel to her novels, based on the dissolves, cross-cutting, and flashbacks she introduces for narrative effect.

At the same time, film critics highlight the "literary" quality of her screenplays— particularly her adaptations of novels by Henry James and E. M. Forster, including *A Room with a View*, which was released in 1986 and for which she won the Academy Award for best screenplay in 1987. With characteristic self-deprecation, in accepting the Writers Guild's 1993 Screen Laurel Award, Jhabvala acknowledged this label as "opprobrium" among "true cineastes," yet she remains "unregenerate" in placing her faith in "interesting characters intersecting with each other in interesting situations thereby producing what I hope will turn into an interesting story." In 1994, Jhabvala received the Writers Guild Foundation's career achievement award.

Jhabvala has maintained her career as a novelist and short story writer alongside that of a screenwriter. The move to America prompted a new phase in her fiction, in which she acidly etches a portrait of decline among generations of German and Austrian émigrés to New York City—among whose number she could have been. Clearly, Jhabvala bears the survivor's twin marks of guilt and detachment. Thus, she includes herself in her observations of humankind's flounderings in the constraints it creates and calls "society."

Summary

If statelessness characterizes the twentieth century, and the capacity to reinvent oneself the American myth, Ruth Prawer Jhabvala's life and accomplishments may be considered representative. Born of a Polish Jewish father, reared in Germany and England, married to a Parsi Indian, and naturalized as a U.S. citizen, Jhabvala has known exile both forced and self-imposed.

Critics agree in identifying Jhabvala's rootlessness as key to her work. Admirers credit her for illuminating the increasing alienation of individuals—particularly women—from the world in which they find themselves. Her fiction has been described by feminist critics as alternative versions of genres generally popular with women: the Gothic romance and the generational epic. In Jhabvala's version of the former, a heroine's passion for a mysterious, charismatic male ruins her rather than redeems him. In the latter, subsequent generations dissipate their forebears' ardor and vitality rather than justify their sacrifices.

By simultaneously acknowledging and demystifying their fantasies, Jhabvala implies that her readers can achieve greater self-awareness. Similarly, her elegant and witty screenplays are more likely to inspire reflection than dreams of romance.

Jhabvala presents the process of shedding illusions and gaining a sharper, clearer vision as painful, and offers no hope that it will not repeat throughout one's life. The message of Jhabvala's work—that growth exacts a price—is one that can be argued reverberates through America's immigrant literature.

Both Jhabvala's novel and screenplay of *Heat and Dust* present the parallel stories of two women, fifty years apart. The modern-day protagonist's re-creation in narrative of events in her predecessor's life invariably reflects back on her and her own, current experiences. Past and present incessantly shape each other. America, still young among the world's civilizations, does well to remember this.

Bibliography

Gooneratne, Yasmine. *Silence, Exile and Cunning: The Fiction of Ruth Prawer Jhabvala*. New Delhi: Orient Longman, 1983. An Indian admirer of Jhabvala's work, Gooneratne analyzes both her fiction and screenplays and examines their mutual influence. Bibliography, index, and notes are provided. Cited are personal conversations with Jhabvala and her husband.

Jhabvala, Ruth Prawer. "Myself in India." Introduction to *Out of India: Selected Stories*. New York: William Morrow, 1986. First appearing in *London Magazine*, this essay reveals Jhabvala's ambivalent feelings about being a European in India. Jhabvala here demonstrates her tendency toward self-analysis.

Long, Robert Emmet. *The Films of Merchant Ivory*. New York: Harry N. Abrams, 1991. Admittedly a fan, Long reviews the career of this long-lasting team chronologically, up to *Mr. and Mrs. Bridge* (1990). Generous with anecdotes and photographs, Long also provides a filmography, a selected bibliography, and an index.

Pritchett, V. S. "Ruth Prawer Jhabvala: Snares and Delusions." In *The Tale Bearers*. New York: Random House, 1980. This chapter is included in the "Exotics" section of a collection of essays about writers by Pritchett, himself an author of fiction as well as nonfiction. Pritchett is among the critics who sees Jhabvala's work as Chekhovian.

Pym, John. *The Wandering Company: Twenty-one Years of Merchant Ivory Films*. New York: The Museum of Modern Art, 1983. This chronological account of the team's career is distinguished by extensive commentary by director James Ivory. The ratio of photographs to text is large.

Shahane, Vasant A. "Ruth Prawer Jhabvala's *A New Dominion.*" *The Journal of Commonwealth Literature* 12 (August, 1977): 45-55. Shahane sees in this novel a new phase in Jhabvala's fiction, its fragmentary style deliberately reflective of its subject, India. Nevertheless, Shahane determines that Jhabvala, failing to identify herself at the deepest level with India, falls short of achieving a convincing artistic vision.

Sucher, Laura. *The Fiction of Ruth Prawer Jhabvala: The Politics of Passion.* New York: St. Martin's Press, 1989. This feminist reading of Jhabvala's fiction focuses on four of her later novels, including two written in the United States, *In Search of Love and Beauty* (1983) and *Three Continents* (1987), as well as several related short stories. In the introduction, Sucher acknowledges that her perspective is probably more politically feminist than Jhabvala's. Notes, a selected bibliography, and an index are included.

Williams, H. Moore. "The Yogi and the Babbitt: Themes and Characters of the New India in the Novels of Ruth Prawer Jhabvala." *Twentieth Century Literature* 15 (July, 1969): 81-91. Moore analyzes Jhabvala's novels of manners in the tradition of Sinclair Lewis' *Babbitt* (1922), the classic American satire of bourgeois life.

Amy Adelstein

FRANCES BENJAMIN JOHNSTON

Born: January 15, 1864; Grafton, West Virginia
Died: May 16, 1952; New Orleans, Louisiana
Area of Achievement: Photography
Contribution: A leading portrait photographer, recorder of American life, and chroni-
cler of pre-Civil War southern architecture, Johnston pioneered in a field where
women had a chance to establish their own careers. Her pictures provide a valuable
record of American life at the beginning of the twentieth century.

Early Life

Frances Benjamin Johnston was born on January 15, 1864, in Grafton, West
Virginia, the only child of Anderson D. Johnston and Frances Antoinette Benjamin
Johnston. Her father worked as lead bookkeeper in the Treasury Department in
Washington. Her mother had family ties to Frances Folsom Cleveland, the wife of
President Grover Cleveland, a connection that helped Frances establish herself as a
favorite photographer of the famous personages in the nation's capital during the
1890's.

Educated at the Notre Dame Convent in Maryland, Johnston spent two years at the
Académie Julien in Paris as an art student. Her interest gradually shifted to photography during the late 1880's. She said that it was a more accurate medium than painting.
After studying with Thomas William Smillie, who directed the Division of Photography at the Smithsonian Institution, she embarked on a career as a professional
photographer. She wrote to George Eastman, who had just developed the Kodak
camera, and asked him to recommend a good camera. He sent her a free camera in
return.

Photography offered women an opportunity to build their own careers at the turn
of the twentieth century. There was a growing market for photographs of family life,
pets, and outdoor scenes. Johnston was one of a number of female photographers who
flourished at this time, including Lillian Griffin and Jessie Tarbox Beals. Johnston's
skill enabled her to become the preeminent figure among these women photographers.
Describing Johnston's photography, a critic said that she belonged to no particular
school and made her own rules about her new profession.

Life's Work

By the early 1890's, Frances Benjamin Johnston had become a fashionable photographer of Washington's upper classes. She believed that to be a success in the field, a
woman must possess common sense, patience with the process of working with her
subjects, good taste, an eye for detail, and a willingness to work hard at her craft.
Johnston's photographs appeared in the *Ladies' Home Journal* and other popular
magazines. At first, she wrote the articles that she illustrated, but soon she concentrated only on her photography. Her pictures of the interior of the White House
appeared in *The White House* (1893). Johnston's ties to Frances Folsom Cleveland

gave her access to all of Washington, and she took striking photographs of President Theodore Roosevelt, his daughter Alice, General Leonard Wood, and bandleader John Philip Sousa. Her pictures of President Roosevelt and his family give a good sense of the popular fascination with the young chief executive who came into office after William McKinley's assassination in 1901. For these excellent portraits, Johnston became recognized as the photographer of the American Court, as official Washington was known at that time.

Johnston was a small, attractive woman who operated in constant motion. She never married, but she had a circle called "The Push," a group of close friends who gathered in her Washington studio on Wednesday afternoons for parties and entertainment. She lived in two worlds. To the people she photographed in Washington, she was very much a woman who embodied the conventional values of that late Victorian time. Among her artistic friends, however, she carried on a less structured and more bohemian existence. She smoked, which conventional women did not do at that time, and gave elaborate costume parties.

Johnston did more than make studio portraits of the famous and powerful of Washington during this phase of her career. While traveling in Europe during the summer of 1899, she took pictures of Admiral George Dewey and his sailors as they made their way back to the United States after defeating the Spanish Navy at Manila Bay at the start of the Spanish American War. She was also at the Pan-American Exposition in Buffalo, New York, in September, 1901, when President William McKinley was assassinated. Johnston's picture of McKinley in his carriage minutes before he was shot was regarded as the last photograph taken of the president before he was killed.

A notable feature of Johnston's photography during the years before 1910 was her interest in the role of industrial workers and the efforts to educate African Americans and American Indians. She went to coalfields in Pennsylvania and iron mines in Minnesota, captured women workers in a shoe factory in Lynn, Massachusetts, in 1895, and visited a cigar box factory in 1910. Her pictures recorded the workers as human beings and emphasized their dignity amid the difficult circumstances of their workplaces. Johnston's work was part of the general ferment of political and social reform that marked the twenty years after 1900.

Johnston's interest in education took her to the public schools of Washington, D.C., in 1899, when she was commissioned to make a series of photographs for inclusion with the United States exhibit at the Paris Exposition the following year. The work was difficult. She had to carry her unwieldy equipment to the schools and persuade lively children to remain still long enough for her to make the necessary exposures. Her efforts did not benefit her financially, because the pamphlets derived from her photographs did not sell. She did, however, win the Palmes Académique at the Third International Photographic Congress in Paris in 1900 for the Washington school photographic series.

As soon as Johnston finished her assignment with the Washington schools, she turned to the photographic documentation of the lives of African American students at the Hampton Institute in Virginia. Reflecting the aims of the school's leadership, Johnston's photographs showed poor black families in the Virginia countryside and then contrasted these scenes with pictures of the middle-class surroundings at the Institute. Her goal was to show the progress that African Americans could make even during a time of limited opportunity for blacks. Her pictures of rural life in Virginia, however, preserved traces of the squalor and trials that blacks faced during that segregated era.

Following up on her work at the Hampton Institute, Johnston did photographic studies of the Carlisle (Pennsylvania) Indian School and the Tuskegee Institute in Alabama, where Booker T. Washington educated African Americans. The photographs that Johnston took at Tuskegee were published in 1903 to illustrate an article that Washington had written about his school's operation.

Johnston encountered personal danger during her trip to Tuskegee. She went to a nearby Alabama town to photograph another black school that had been modeled on what Washington had accomplished. Her traveling escort was George Washington Carver, a famous African American scientist, and they were met by the principal of the school that Johnston was to visit. Circumstances brought them into the town of Ramer at 11:00 P.M. Whites regarded the sight of a white woman traveling with black men in the evening as an intolerable violation of the customs of racial segregation. Shots were fired at Johnston's party before they could make their escape. One of her companions called Johnston the pluckiest woman he had ever seen.

Johnston's work achieved artistic recognition as well as praise from the general public. The innovative photographer Alfred Stieglitz praised her work and hoped to see more of it. She saw herself as working in the tradition of the great painting masters of portraiture, and observed that it was wrong to regard photography as a purely mechanical process. Johnston was selected as a member of the jury for the Philadelphia Photographic Society in 1899, and she collaborated with Stieglitz and other artistic photographers in what became known as the Photo-Secession Movement.

By 1910, her interest turned from photographic portraits and photojournalism to pictures of gardens and houses. She worked in New York City with her business partner Mattie Edward Hewitt. They made photographs of the estates, architecture, and gardens of the upper classes of the East. Johnston's clients included the wealthy Astor, Whitney and Vanderbilt families. Her lectures on gardens became nationally popular, and she toured the country speaking on the subject. She promised her audiences that she would give them the widest possible range of information about the gardens and houses that she described.

During the late 1920's, Johnston was commissioned to make photographs of an estate in Virginia. The experience aroused her interest in photographing the buildings and scenes of the plantation South, which were fading away. She obtained an assignment to conduct a photographic survey of the countryside around Fredericksburg, Virginia, and neighboring towns. Her goal was to preserve as much as possible of the old Virginia towns that she visited.

Recording southern architecture before it vanished, a project she began in her early sixties, became the final phase of Johnston's notable career as a photographer. The pictures she made of Fredericksburg were exhibited at the Library of Congress in 1929. Popular reaction was so positive that she received similar assignments for other southern states. From 1933 to 1940, she traveled through nine states in the South and produced more than seven thousand negatives. It was said that she had a nose for the location of an old southern plantation five miles off the main highway. She became an honorary member of the American Institute of Architects in 1945, and the citation she received praised her for having made a significant contribution to the architectural profession in the United States. Johnston lived out her final years in New Orleans, where she died on May 16, 1952. When someone asked her whether she was a noted photographer, she described herself as the greatest woman photographer in the world. Her photographs and personal papers were given to the Library of Congress.

Summary

The photographs of the United States that Frances Benjamin Johnston made between 1890 and 1910 are an invaluable record of the nation as it moved into the twentieth century. Her pictures of Theodore Roosevelt, Alice Roosevelt, William McKinley, and Mark Twain are superb studies of character. She was a professional who approached photography as a career, and she remained true to her personal standards during all the phases of her long and productive life. She was an important pioneer during the early years of photojournalism and a significant figure in the field of architectural photography as well.

Johnston was not a feminist per se, but she worked during a period when women found new opportunities to establish careers in such new fields as photojournalism and portrait photography. The example of her accomplishments and liberated personal lifestyle reveal the early stages of the development of greater independence for American women that occurred between 1890 and 1920.

Bibliography

Daniel, Pete, and Raymond Smock. *A Talent for Detail: The Photographs of Miss Frances Benjamin Johnston, 1889-1910.* New York: Harmony Books, 1974. The best single book on Johnston and an excellent introduction to her life and career.

Gould, Lewis L., and Richard Greffe. *Photojournalist: The Career of Jimmy Hare.* Austin: University of Texas Press, 1977. Hare was a contemporary of Johnston's, and his career provides an instructive contrast to hers.

Johnston, Frances Benjamin. *The Hampton Album: Forty-four Photographs from an Album of Hampton Institute.* New York: Museum of Modern Art, 1966. A selection of photographs from Johnston's series on the Hampton Institute in 1900.

Nichols, Frederick Doveton. *The Architecture of Georgia.* Savannah, Ga.: Beehive Press, 1976. A book based on the photographs that Johnston took during the 1920's and 1930's.

Lewis L. Gould

MARY HARRIS "MOTHER" JONES

Born: May 1, 1830; Cork, Ireland
Died: November 30, 1930; Silver Spring, Maryland
Areas of Achievement: Social reform and trade unionism
Contribution: As a labor organizer and fiery orator, Mother Jones inspired workers
and breathed life into union organizing efforts in the early twentieth century.

Early Life

The birth date of Mary Harris "Mother" Jones is in dispute as are other critical facts about her early life. This uncertainty is not unusual for poor and working-class people whose lives are often not recorded in traditional ways. Even births, deaths, marriages, and work history may not be documented.

In her autobiography, Jones herself gave 1830 as her birth year, but she gave other dates in interviews throughout her life. Most historians agree on 1830, although one cites 1839 and another 1843. Her father migrated to the United States from Ireland and worked as a laborer building canals and railroads. The family followed and settled initially in Toronto, Canada, where young Mary Harris went to school, graduating in 1858 or 1859. Little is known of her father and mother or her siblings.

Mary Harris taught school in Michigan in 1859, worked as a dressmaker in Chicago in 1860, and again taught school in Memphis, Tennessee. In Memphis, she met George Jones, a member of the Iron Workers' Union, and in 1861 they were married. George Jones and all the couple's children died in the yellow fever epidemic of 1867. In her autobiography, Mother Jones claims to have had four children, but some evidence exists to suggest it may have been one or three. No one disputes the fact that Jones was alone after 1867 with no family and no permanent home.

Mother Jones left Memphis in 1867 to return to Chicago, where she resumed working as a dressmaker for the wealthy. In 1871, she was burned out of her home and lost all of her possessions in the great Chicago Fire. Following the fire, she began attending nightly lectures at the Knights of Labor building, which was located near the place where many homeless refugees from the fire were camping out. Records of these years of her life are scarce, but it is known that Mother Jones traveled during the 1870's and 1880's from one industrial area to another speaking and organizing, usually in connection with the Knights of Labor. In 1877, she was in Pittsburgh for the first nationwide industrial strike, that of the railroad workers. In 1886, she was in Chicago, active in organizing for the eight-hour work day. In 1890, when the Knights of Labor District 135 and the National Union of Miners and Mine Laborers merged to form the United Mine Workers of America (UMWA), Mary Harris Jones became a paid organizer for the union. She was approximately sixty years old and about to enter the national stage. She was thought of as "the Miner's Angel," the most dangerous woman in the country, or America's most patriotic citizen, depending upon the point of view of the different people who encountered her.

Life's Work

Until her health failed in the late 1920's, Mother Jones traveled the nation speaking and organizing not only for coal miners but also for textile, railway, and steel workers. She figured in most major strikes in the United States in the early 1900's, but was repeatedly drawn to the coalfields of Pennsylvania, Colorado, and West Virginia. For a time, she was active in Socialist Party politics, particularly in the campaigns of Eugene V. Debs. She supported Mexican revolutionary Francisco "Pancho" Villa in his fight for better wages and living conditions for Mexican workers, who were often used as strike breakers, particularly in Western mines. She did not support woman's suffrage or other social reform efforts of her era that were not founded solely on working-class rights.

Her speeches reveal that Mother Jones saw herself as an agitator and educator charged with the tasks of teaching the American working class about the nature of capitalism and mobilizing an international working-class movement. In 1909, she told the national convention of the UMWA that she was there to "wake you up." At a UMWA district convention in 1914 she explained, "I hold no office only that of disturbing." In 1920, near the end of her public speaking career, she summarized her mission: "I am busy getting this working man to understand what belongs to him, and his power to take possession of it."

Mother Jones was so effective at "disturbing" workers that corporate and government officials often went to great extremes to keep her from speaking. She was arrested many times, imprisoned, and forcefully escorted out of strike zones where she had been called to help organize. Her success as an educator is less easily documented, but her speeches and audience responses reveal a talented, tireless woman who was able to move people to action while instructing them about the nature of their conflicts and their place in history.

Conditions in mines and mining communities in the early 1900's were stark. Wages were low; mines were unsafe; rates of deaths and disabling injuries were very high; children were often employed. Miners lived in company-owned housing and were often paid in scrip, a substitute currency that could be redeemed only at company stores. If miners tried to improve their conditions through union organizing, they and their families were evicted from houses, and armed guards (often from the Baldwin-Felts detective agency) were hired by the companies to fight the organizing efforts.

In the face of these conditions Mother Jones devised a wide array of organizing strategies, as the 1897 UMWA strike at Turtle Creek near Pittsburgh illustrates. She spoke to ten thousand miners and sympathizers urging them to fight. Then she organized farmers in the region to provide food to strikers and escorted the farmers and their wagons to strike headquarters where the food was distributed. She called on neighborhood women to donate a "pound" of something to the cause and urged factory workers to come to miners' meetings and donate. As in many other strikes, Mother Jones made certain that women and children were actively involved and featured in national news coverage of the conflicts. At Turtle Creek, she organized wives of miners into groups of pickets and demonstrators and positioned the children of miners at the front of parades. In one parade fifty little girls marched with homemade banners, one of which read "Our Papas Aren't Scared."

Mother Jones was often in West Virginia in these early years of the twentieth century. In 1902, she worked in the southern coalfields, but she was successful in organizing only in the Paint Creek and Cabin Creek areas near Charleston, the state capital. While trying to organize the northern part of the state, she was arrested and briefly imprisoned. For several years she traveled across the country to protest child labor, organize miners in the West, and support striking brewery workers, textile workers, copper miners, and smelter workers. Then in 1912 and 1913, once again working as a UMWA organizer, Mother Jones returned to West Virginia's southern coalfields. She faced down armed mine guards in order to allow union meetings and threatened to encourage West Virginia miners to arm themselves and fight back. She was imprisoned again, tried by a state military militia court, convicted of a charge of conspiracy to commit murder, and sentenced to prison for twenty years. She served eighty-five days, passing her eighty-fourth birthday in jail, before national public outcry and the promise of a congressional investigation prompted that state's newly elected governor to free her.

In her final organizing effort with West Virginia miners, Mother Jones attempted to halt the spontaneous 1921 march of thousands of miners on Logan. It was an unusual role for the aging firebrand, and she was not able to stop the march, later known as the "Battle of Blair Mountain." That bloody confrontation left many dead and injured. The determined coal miners proved powerless in the face of armed Baldwin-Felts detectives, the state militia, and the six thousand federal troops and twenty military airplanes sent by President Warren Harding to support the coal operators and prevent the union men from marching into nonunion territory. The battle halted organizing efforts in West Virginia until national legislation authorized collective bargaining in 1932.

Organizing miners in Colorado was as difficult as in West Virginia. Mother Jones made her first visits there in 1903 soon after John D. Rockefeller, Sr., bought control of Colorado Iron and Fuel Company and the Victor Fuel Company. These early organizing efforts were not successful and led to a split between Jones and the UMWA leadership over organizing strategy. She did not return to the UMWA payroll until 1911.

In 1913, miners in southern Colorado went on strike for higher wages; an eight-hour day; coal weighing to be monitored by miners; free choice of stores, schools, doctors and boarding houses; enforcement of Colorado laws; and abolition of the mine guard system. Although most of these provisions were already law in Colorado, the state did not implement them in the southern fields. When the miners went on strike, they were evicted and lived in tent cities through the bitter cold Colorado winter.

Mother Jones joined the striking miners there in the fall of 1913, and returned in December and again in January. Between January and March of 1914, Jones, then in her early eighties, was arrested many times and spent more than a month in basement jail cells in Colorado. Refusing to be silenced, she smuggled out an open letter to the

American people that was read and published across the country. She was not in Colorado in April when the state militia attacked the family tent camp, killing thirty-two, including many women and children. Subsequent state and national investigations into this incident, known as the Ludlow Massacre, were extremely critical of the actions of the governor, the state militia, and Colorado Iron and Fuel Company.

When Mother Jones wrote about her life she always identified her cause with the miners. After her death on November 30, 1930, she was buried as she had requested at the Miners Cemetery in Mount Olive, Illinois. A choir of coal miners sang her final tribute.

Summary

Mother Jones is remembered as a great labor agitator and a tremendously effective public speaker. Stories of her visits to coal camps, leadership at rallies and demonstrations, and confrontations with company and government officials are part of a living oral history of resistance in mining communities. Her memory continues to inspire the labor movement. When women mobilized in a 1989 UMWA strike against the Pittston Coal Group, they identified themselves as the "Daughters of Mother Jones" as they carried out actions in her name, such as occupying company headquarters and holding vigils outside jails where union officials were imprisoned.

The message of Mother Jones's life is that ordinary people, indeed unlikely people, can make important contributions to improving workers' lives. She was homeless and alone; she was poor and sometimes in prison; yet Mary Harris Jones used the resources she had—mind, voice, wit, spirit, and energy—to influence conditions for workers in America.

Bibliography

Fetherling, Dale. *Mother Jones, the Miners' Angel: A Portrait.* Carbondale: Southern Illinois University Press, 1974. This first full-scale biography on Jones presents a sympathetic yet balanced portrait.

Jones, Mother. *The Autobiography of Mother Jones.* Edited by Mary Field Parton. Chicago: Charles Kerr, 1974. First published in 1925; later editions (1972, 1974) add useful introductions. Insights into coal strikes, early twentieth century labor leadership, and Jones's spirit and personality; marred by inaccuracies and serious omissions.

——————— . *The Correspondence of Mother Jones.* Edited by Edward M. Steel. Pittsburgh: University of Pittsburgh Press, 1985. A collection of all known letters, notes, and telegrams (eight communications are added in Steel's 1988 collection of Jones's speeches and writings). Illustrates development of her political views over the course of her life.

——————— . *Mother Jones Speaks: Collected Writings and Speeches.* Edited by Philip S. Foner. New York: Monad Press, 1983. The most comprehensive work and best reference source in conveying the full range of Jones's intellect and activities.

Includes speeches, testimony before congressional committees, articles, interviews, letters, an extensive bibliography, and historical background information.

_____ . *The Speeches and Writings of Mother Jones*. Edited by Edward M. Steel. Pittsburgh: University of Pittsburgh Press, 1988. Collection of thirty-one speeches believed to have been accurately recorded and transcribed in their entirety; also includes seventeen articles Jones penned for newspapers and socialist periodicals. A helpful "Biographical Notes" section identifies people in her speeches. A good introduction to her life with historical context for her speeches and activities.

Long, Priscilla. *Mother Jones, Woman Organizer: And Her Relations with Miners' Wives, Working Women, and the Suffrage Movement*. Boston: South End Press, 1976. Examines Jones's position as a female leader in the labor movement and her relationships with working class women and with women's rights organizations of her era.

Sally Ward Maggard

JANIS JOPLIN

Born: January 19, 1943; Port Arthur, Texas
Died: October 3, 1970; Hollywood, California
Area of Achievement: Music
Contribution: Janis Joplin, one of the prime movers in the evolution of rock 'n' roll, demonstrated that white women were capable of singing with as much emotional intensity as that of great black singers such as Bessie Smith.

Early Life

Janis Joplin was born in Port Arthur, Texas, on January 19, 1943. Her father worked as a mechanical engineer and her mother was a registrar at a business college. In spite of her conventional family background, Janis was a rebel from an early age. As a teenager, she withdrew from high-school social life and spent much of her time listening to the music of black artists such as Leadbelly, Bessie Smith, and Odetta. Her taste in reading, like her taste in music, set her apart from her peers.

Port Arthur is in the heart of the Texas Bible Belt. Janis acquired such a reputation in this ultraconservative community that the citizens were still speaking of her in horrified whispers years after her death. Even while still in junior high school, she scandalized the townspeople with her sexual promiscuity. Her classmates rejected her and called her filthy names; they threw pennies at her as a way of symbolizing that they considered her a whore. Janis felt badly hurt by this rejection, but she built a façade of individualism and indifference which was to remain her outstanding characteristic.

It is evident that Janis was overcompensating for feelings of inferiority resulting in part from being overweight, feeling physically unattractive, and being harshly criticized by her mother. Janis had an insatiable craving for love and belonging which was partly responsible for her legendary sexual promiscuity in later life as well as her consumption of liquor, marijuana, and heroin.

At seventeen, she left home with the intention of earning a living with her voice. She hitchhiked around the country, scraping up money by getting short-term jobs as a folksinger. Eventually, she made it to California, where she attended several colleges but was never graduated. In California, she lived in hippie communes, indulged in group sex, and was introduced to new kinds of drugs.

This was the very beginning of the 1960's, which will always have a place in American history as a period of youthful rebellion against the beliefs and traditions of older generations. At first, Janis found the undisciplined lifestyle of California too much for her, and she returned to Texas to try to live a conventional life. She realized, however, that she had outgrown Port Arthur completely, and she went back to the West Coast.

The most important event in her life occurred when she was asked to become the "chick singer" with a new San Francisco rock 'n' roll group called Big Brother and the Holding Company.

Life's Work

Big Brother and the Holding Company has its place in popular music history because of its connection with the dynamic Janis Joplin. Her first public appearance with this group was at the Avalon Ballroom in San Francisco on June 10, 1966. She was twenty-three years old but had done more living than many people do in their lifetimes.

Partly because of her early adulation of the great Bessie Smith, Joplin had developed the ability to put her heart and soul into her singing. She was also gifted with a voice that had an enormous range and variety of tones. Big Brother and the Holding Company's instrumentalists helped her to discover her true niche as a singer, and in turn she helped the musicians to define themselves as a group.

Joplin's performance at the Monterey Pop Festival in the summer of 1967 is legendary. She electrified the huge audience with the intensity of her performance. Older, much better known groups were totally overshadowed by the dynamic new sound. Music critics were unanimous in their enthusiastic praise of this new female vocalist.

Joplin attained national stardom in 1968 with the release of *Cheap Thrills*, her second album with Big Brother and the Holding Company. The album hit number one on the best-seller charts and stayed there for eight weeks. Janis made a clean sweep of *Jazz and Pop* magazine's awards, winning the International Critics Poll for Best Female Vocal Album and Best Female Pop Singer as well as the magazine's Reader's Poll for Best Female Pop Singer. Yet Joplin had developed an insatiable lust for success. She was no longer satisfied with the musicians who were backing her up, and she announced that she was leaving them to form her own backup group.

Janis was a victim of a scourge that has destroyed the lives of many popular musicians. When musicians speak of the rigors of the "music scene," they are referring not only to the music but also to the destructive lifestyle that goes with it, including drinking, drugs, and association with a criminal element that is attracted to nightclubs and bars. Among these criminals are those who make their living selling illicit drugs, and they are forever trying to recruit new customers. At first, Janis used heroin because she thought it inspired her to be more creative and uninhibited. Ultimately, she was killed by her use of the same drug that destroyed the lives of such great musicians as Charlie Parker and Elvis Presley.

Joplin was one of the star attractions of the Woodstock Music and Art Fair in 1969, and she had a huge success when she toured Europe. At the end of 1969, she won *Jazz and Pop* magazine's International Critics Poll, which named her Best Female Pop Singer for the year. Ironically, as her career skyrocketed, she became more and more depressed and self-destructive.

Just a few days before her death, Joplin attended a reunion of her high-school class at Port Arthur. She expected to return in triumph to the people who had made her so unhappy as a teenager; however, she found that most of the narrow-minded townspeople were unimpressed by her success and still despised her for her hedonistic lifestyle. This disappointment had a powerful impact on the singer and may have led to her death. On Sunday, October 3, 1970, her body was discovered in the Landmark Hotel in Hollywood. The autopsy confirmed the story that was already apparent from the hypodermic needle marks all over both of her arms: She had died of an overdose of heroin.

Janis Joplin's best and most successful record album, *Pearl* (her nickname), was released shortly after her death. It immediately placed number one on the *Billboard* chart. Her rendition of "Me and Bobby McGee," written by Kris Kristofferson, was also released as a single and reached number one in that category as well. It remains her most famous song. The royalties from those two records would have made her a millionaire if she had lived.

Eighteen years after Joplin's death, her picture appeared on the cover of *Time* magazine. The *Time* article states, "Janis Joplin expressed one side of 1968 fairly well: ecstatic and self-destructive simultaneously, wailing to the edges of the universe." Janis was to become the symbol of the "sixties generation" in her music, her lifestyle, her language, her clothing and hairstyle, and unfortunately in her self-destructive use of drugs and alcohol.

Summary

In her short lifetime, Janis Joplin was one of the foremost personalities in defining the so-called sixties generation, a generation that made a more powerful impact on popular culture than has any other generation before or since. She was one of a very few women to make it to superstardom in the male-dominated world of popular music. Called "the high priestess of the rock scene," Joplin was a leader in asserting women's right to sexual freedom. She helped to popularize a new kind of liberated music—a fusion of blues, country-western, and other styles—that has since become the leading wave of popular music around the world. Millions of young women imitated her behavior and her highly individualistic clothing styles, outraging their parents and forcing the older generation to reexamine its traditional attitudes.

Joplin, like many of her youthful contemporaries, was opposed to the undeclared war the United States was waging in Vietnam because it involved ecological devastation and indiscriminate slaughter of women and children. She hated racial discrimination and regarded American involvement in Vietnam as a form of neocolonialism.

The unrest of the 1960's was largely a result of the feeling that the world was doomed to inevitable destruction by atomic holocaust and that the war in Vietnam was only a prelude to the final disaster. The United States and the Soviet Union continued adding to their atomic arsenals until both nations possessed enough of the weapons to destroy humanity several times over. As one of the leaders of the so-called youth rebellion of the 1960's, Joplin was instrumental in forcing the federal government to look for a way out of a conflict that was tearing the country apart.

One of Joplin's greatest contributions to the cause of women was that she demonstrated that women not only could be electrifying performers but also could lead bands, create new and innovative styles, and generate huge incomes, all while living the lifestyles they wished to live. After Joplin's tremendous success, record companies became more willing to give promising women the opportunity to achieve a high level of commercial success and artistic control.

Unfortunately, the fun-loving, high-spirited young singer also set a bad example for millions of young women with her use of drugs and alcohol. This bad influence went all the way down through high school and even affected junior high school students, who erroneously believed that the drinking and drug abuse were somehow connected with the music they loved.

Joplin's death from an overdose of heroin served as an object lesson to many of her admirers; the consumption of heroin in the United States decreased dramatically after her death. Like the deaths of other folk heroes of the period, including comedian Lenny Bruce, Janis Joplin's death served as a grim reminder that substance abuse destroys youth and talent without pity. "If you think you need stuff to play music or sing, you're crazy," said Billie Holiday, one of America's greatest singers. "It can fix you so you can't play nothing or sing nothing."

Bibliography

Amburn, Ellis. *Pearl: The Obsessions and Passions of Janis Joplin.* New York: Warner Books, 1992. This is the best available full-length biography of Joplin. Discusses her early childhood, her development as a vocalist, her numerous love affairs with both men and women, and her self-destructive lifestyle. Contains an excellent bibliography. Thoroughly indexed. Contains many photographic illustrations of Joplin and friends, including one famous picture of Joplin in the nude.

Caserta, Peggy, as told to Dan Knapp. *Going Down with Janis.* Secaucus, N.J.: Lyle Stuart, 1973. An intentionally shocking book about Janis Joplin's private life, especially her use of drugs and her lesbian sexual activities, written by a woman with whom she had a long-term relationship.

Dalton, David. *Piece of My Heart: The Life, Times and Legend of Janis Joplin.* New York: St. Martin's Press, 1985. A collection of interviews and personal impressions by a friend who accompanied Joplin on many of her tours. Written in the informal, expressionistic style characteristic of "New Journalism."

Freidman, Myra. *Buried Alive.* New York: William Morrow, 1973. An early biography written by a woman who was Joplin's press agent and close personal friend. This deeply moving work explains Joplin's manic, self-destructive behavior as a compensation for the fact that the singer believed she was ugly and unlovable (she had been nominated for "Ugliest Man on Campus" at the University of Texas).

Joplin, Laura. "Love, Janis." *Rolling Stone,* no. 638 (September 3, 1992): 55-57. An article based on a collection of letters written by Janis Joplin to members of her family during the 1960's. Laura Joplin is Janis' sister.

Wakefield, Dan. "Kosmic Blues." *Atlantic* 232 (September, 1973): 108-113. A highly intelligent, eulogistic article about Janis Joplin based on a review of two published biographies: *Going Down with Janis* and *Buried Alive.*

Wolf, Mark. "The Uninhibited Janis Joplin." *Down Beat* 56 (September, 1989): 65-66. A good profile of Janis Joplin that covers her life from her childhood in Port Arthur up to the time she joined Big Brother and the Holding Company in San Francisco. Contains illustrations of historical interest.

Bill Delaney

BARBARA JORDAN

Born: February 21, 1936; Houston, Texas

Areas of Achievement: Government and politics, law, and education
Contribution: The first African American elected to the Texas Senate since Reconstruction, Barbara Jordan went on to become a member of the U.S. House of Representatives. She mesmerized the nation during televised coverage of the House Judiciary Committee's investigation considering the impeachment of President Richard Nixon.

Early Life

On February 21, 1936, Barbara Charline Jordan was born to Benjamin Jordan, a warehouse clerk and part-time clergyman, and his wife, Arlyne Patten Jordan, in Houston, Texas. Barbara was raised in a time of segregation and Jim Crow laws. She lived with her parents, her two older sisters, Bennie and Rose Marie, and her grandfathers, John Ed Patten and Charles Jordan.

Barbara's outlook on life as well as her strength and determination can be attributed to the influence of her maternal grandfather, John Ed Patten, a former minister who was also a businessman. While assisting him in his junk business, Barbara learned to be self-sufficient, strong-willed, and independent, and she was encouraged not to settle for mediocrity. Her determination to achieve superiority was quickly demonstrated in her early years.

Barbara spent most of her free time with her grandfather Patten, who served as her mentor. They would converse about all kinds of subjects. His advice was followed and appreciated by the young girl, who adoringly followed him every Sunday as he conducted his business. He instilled in her a belief in the importance of education. Every action, every aspect of life, he stated, was to be learned from and experienced.

With her grandfather's advice in mind, Barbara embraced life and education. She showed herself to be an exemplary student while attending Phillis Wheatley High School in Houston. A typical teenager, Barbara was active in school clubs and other extracurricular activities. She also led an active social life during her years at Phillis Wheatley. It was during her high school years that Barbara was inspired to become a lawyer. She was drawn to the legal profession during a career day presentation by the prominent African American attorney Edith Sampson. Moved by Sampson's speech, Barbara became determined to investigate law as a possible area of study.

Barbara received many awards during her high school years, particularly for her talent as an orator. Her skill in this area was rewarded in 1952, when she won first place in the Texas State Ushers Oratorical Contest. As part of her victory package, she was sent to Illinois to compete in the national championships. She won the national oration contest in Chicago that same year.

The year 1952 began a new stage in Barbara Jordan's education. She was admitted to Texas Southern University after her graduation from high school. It was here that she truly excelled in oration. She joined the Texas Southern debate team and won many tournaments under the guidance and tutelage of her debate coach, Tom Freeman. He was also influential in urging her to attend Boston University Law School. At law school, she was one of two African American women in the graduating class of 1959; they were the only women to be graduated that year. Before 1960, Jordan managed to pass the Massachusetts and Texas Bar examinations. Such a feat was an enviable one. She was offered a law position in the state of Massachusetts, but she declined the offer.

Jordan's impoverished background seemed far behind her. With the continued support of her parents and grandfathers, she opened a private law practice in Houston, Texas, in 1960. She volunteered her services to the Kennedy-Johnson presidential campaign. She organized the black constituents in the black precincts of her county. Her efforts were successful. The voter turnout was the largest Harris County had ever experienced. Jordan's participation in such a history-making event demonstrated her talents for persuasion and organization. These skills, coupled with her education and intellect, were to become her assets in all her future endeavors. The political career of Barbara Jordan was born as a result of the Kennedy-Johnson victory of 1960.

Life's Work

The decade of the 1960's witnessed Barbara Jordan's emergence in the political arena. The 1960's were a period of transition and hope in American history. With the election of the first Catholic president and the epic changes brought on by the Civil Rights movement, it was a time of change. Jordan was determined to be part of that change. After becoming the speaker for the Harris County Democratic Party, she ran for the Texas House of Representatives in 1962 and 1964. She lost on both occasions. Undeterred, Jordan ran for a third time in the newly reapportioned Harris County. She became one of two African Americans elected to the newly reapportioned eleventh district. Jordan was elected to the Texas state senate. She became the first black since 1883 and the first woman ever to hold the position.

Jordan impressed the state senate members with her intelligence, oration, and ability to fit in with the "old boys' club." She remained in the state senate for six years, until 1972. During her tenure, she worked on legislation dealing with the environment, establishing minimum wage standards, and eliminating discrimination in business contracts. She was encouraged to run for a congressional seat. She waged a campaign in 1971 for the U.S. Congress. While completing her term of office on the state level, Jordan achieved another first: In 1972, she was elected to the U.S. House of Representatives. Jordan served briefly as acting governor of Texas on June 10, 1972, when both the governor and lieutenant governor were out of the state. As president pro tem of the Texas senate, it was one of her duties to act as governor when the situation warranted. Despite his being present for all of her earlier achievements, Jordan's father did not live to see her take office as a member of the U.S. House of Representatives. He died on June 11, 1972, in Austin, Texas. His demise spurred Jordan to continue her work.

Having already caught the attention of Lyndon B. Johnson while a member of the Texas state senate, Jordan sought his advice on the type of committees to join. She became a member of the Judiciary and the Ways and Means committees. Little did she know that the Judiciary Committee would evolve into a major undertaking. Jordan's membership in the House of Representatives was to be one of the many highlights of her political career.

The 1974 Watergate scandal gave Jordan national prominence. Her speech in favor of President Richard Nixon's impeachment was nothing short of oratorical brilliance. Her eloquence was considered memorable and thought-provoking. Her expertise as an attorney was demonstrated in 1974 when she spoke about the duty of elected officials to their constituents and the United States Constitution. Despite her personal distaste for an impeachment, Jordan insisted that President Nixon be held accountable for the Watergate fiasco. A Senate investigation, she believed, was warranted. Her televised speech was the center of media attention and critique for days to come. She sustained her reputation for eloquence during the 1976 Democratic National Convention. During her tenure in the House, she introduced bills dealing with civil rights, crime, business, and free competition as well as an unprecedented plan of payment for housewives for the labor and services they provide. Jordan's popularity was at its zenith when talk of her running for the vice presidency was rampant among her supporters. She shrugged off the suggestion, stating that the time was not right.

It was discovered in 1976 that Jordan suffered from knee problems. The ailment was visible during her keynote address when she was helped to the podium to give her speech. She admitted that she was having problems with her patella. The cartilage in one knee made it difficult and painful for her to walk or stand for long. Her brilliant oration was not hampered by her muscle weakness during the delivery of her speech in 1976. She opted not to run for reelection in 1978 and entered the educational field.

During his presidency, Jimmy Carter offered Jordan a post in his cabinet. Political rumor persists that she would have preferred the position of attorney general to Carter's suggestion of the post of secretary of the Department of Health, Education, and Welfare. Since Carter was firm in his offer, Jordan opted to refuse the offer rather than settle for something she did not want. Such an attitude is indicative of her childhood training and upbringing.

Jordan was offered and took a teaching post at the University of Texas in Austin. She taught at the Lyndon Baines Johnson School of Public Affairs. In addition to her instructional duties, she also held the positions of faculty adviser and recruiter for minority students. She continued to hold these positions into the early 1990's. In addition, Governor Ann Richards of Texas appointed her to serve as an adviser on ethics in government.

Barbara Jordan has received innumerable honorary degrees. Universities such as Princeton and Harvard have bestowed honorary doctorates upon her. She has received awards touting her as the best living orator. She is one of the most influential women in the world as well as one of the most admired. She is a member of the Texas Women's Hall of Fame and has hosted her own television show. At the 1988 Democratic National Convention, Jordan gave a speech nominating Senator Lloyd Bentsen as the party's vice presidential candidate. She delivered the speech from the wheelchair she used as a result of her battle with multiple sclerosis. In 1992, she received the prized Spingarn Medal, which is awarded by the National Association for the Advancement of Colored People (NAACP) for service to the African American community.

Summary

Barbara Jordan continues to be an inspiration for all people. Her rise from poverty to prominence through diligence and perseverance in the fields of law, politics, and education is a model for others to follow. During an interview on the Black Entertainment Television channel in February of 1993, Jordan maintained that circumstances of birth, race, or creed should not inhibit an individual from succeeding if he or she wishes to achieve greatness. As an individual who was born poor, black, and female, Jordan demonstrated the truth of her assertion, and her life is a portrait of success highlighted by a series of significant "firsts" and breakthroughs.

In 1984, Jordan was voted "Best Living Orator" and elected to the Texas Women's Hall of Fame. Her honorary doctorates from Princeton and Harvard substantiate her dedication to education and excellence. As a black female from the South, Jordan broke one barrier after the other. She has maintained her integrity and dignity while in political office. Her defense of the U.S. Constitution during the Watergate era as well as her dedication to the field of education continues to be an example to those entering the field of law and education.

Jordan continues to deny that her life's achievements are extraordinary. Her modesty is part of her upbringing. She endeavors to live a life that she believes will benefit the country. One of the reasons she refused to run for reelection in 1978 was her need to serve more than a "few" constituents in her district. She wished to serve them in addition to the masses. As she stated in her resignation: "I feel more of a responsibility to the country as a whole, as contrasted with the duty of representing the half-million in the Eighteenth Congressional District." She continues to maintain that anyone may succeed with the proper attitude. Early in her political career, she made a conscious choice not to marry. Like Susan B. Anthony, Jordan believed that marriage would be a distraction from the cause to which she was drawn. In 1978, Jordan believed that her legislative role and effectiveness had ceased and that her most effective role in the global community was in the field of instruction. A new challenge presented itself, and Jordan was eager to confront it.

In Barbara Jordan, individuals are able to observe that race, socioeconomic status, and societal barriers may be overcome and dispelled as roadblocks to success. She continues to give interviews, lectures, and commencement addresses whenever her schedule permits.

Bibliography

Browne, Ray B. *Contemporary Heroes and Heroines*. Detroit: Gale Research, 1990.

A collection of biographical profiles on men and women who have made major contributions to American life. Includes a fine piece on Barbara Jordan and her career.

Famous Blacks Give Secrets of Success. Vol. 2 in *Ebony Success Library*. Chicago: Johnson, 1973. A collection documenting the lives and achievements of black luminaries. The excerpt on Barbara Jordan traces her political achievements through 1973.

Jordan, Barbara, and Shelby Hearn. *Barbara Jordan: A Self-Portrait*. Garden City, N.Y.: Doubleday, 1979. Jordan's autobiography traces her life from childhood to her political career in the U.S. House of Representatives.

Ries, Paula, and Anne J. Stone, eds. *The American Woman: 1992-93*. New York: W. W. Norton, 1992. This book is one in a series of reports documenting the social, economic, and political status of American women. Includes profiles and articles on Jordan as well as female political contemporaries such as Governor Ann Richards of Texas and Senator Nancy Kassebaum of Kansas.

United States House of Representatives. Commission on the Bicentenary. *Women in Congress, 1917-1990*. Washington, D.C.: Government Printing Office, 1991. Compiled to honor the bicentennial of the U.S. House of Representatives, this work provides biographical sketches of the various women who have served in Congress, beginning with Jeannette Rankin in 1917 and continuing through the women serving in 1990.

Annette Marks-Ellis

DONNA KARAN

Born: October 2, 1948; New York, New York

Areas of Achievement: Fashion and business and industry

Contribution: By combining her talent for designing clothes with her sharp marketing skills, Donna Karan has built her Donna Karan Company into a multimillion dollar international business.

Early Life

Donna Faske was born on October 2, 1948, in Forest Hills in the New York City borough of Queens, and from the very beginning, fashion played a large role in her life. Her father was Gabby Faske, a custom tailor on New York's West Thirty-eighth Street whose clients included many show business personalities. Her mother was Helen Richie Faske, a showroom model and sales representative. When Donna was three, her father died in an automobile accident. Reared by her mother, who maintained a difficult schedule, Donna remembers her childhood as painful, but she describes her mother as a gutsy, wonderful person whose work introduced Karan to the world of fashion.

From the age of seven, Donna, her older sister Gail, and her mother lived in the New York suburb of Woodmere, Long Island. At Hewlett High School, Donna played basketball, volleyball, and softball, and she spent most of her free time in the art department fashioning her first "collection" while dreaming of becoming a famous designer. When she was fourteen, she lied about her age and got her first job, selling in a boutique. There she learned what clothes looked good on people, and she began to realize that her career path would lead to something in fashion, whether designing or selling or both. Her stepfather, Harold Flaxman, who sold women's apparel on Broadway, encouraged her.

In 1966, after completing an undistinguished high school career, Donna was accepted into the prestigious Parsons School of Design in Manhattan on the recommendation of designer Chester Weinberg, her mother's employer. Commuting from Long Island, she met Louis Dell'Olio, another commuter student, with whom she would later form a long-lasting partnership. The two worked together on designs. After class, she sometimes sketched clothing for designers Liz Claiborne and Chuck Howard, both of whom viewed Donna as a future force in the fashion industry. In Donna's second year at Parsons, Howard encouraged her to apply for a summer job with designer Anne Klein. When the summer was over, she decided to remain with Klein full-time; she left school, thus beginning her fashion career. Parsons awarded her an honorary degree in 1987.

Life's Work

Donna Faske worked for Anne Klein for nine months, during which time she was trying to resolve the conflict between the demands of the job and her relationship with

Mark Karan, a Miami boutique owner she had met as a teenager. This preoccupation led to her being fired from Anne Klein and Company. For the following nine months, until 1968, she worked for Patti Cappalli, head designer of Addenda Sportswear, who, in addition to training her in sportswear design, taught Karan to think as a business-person. During that year she married Mark Karan, and with the skills she learned from Cappalli and with her life in order, she returned to Anne Klein.

This time things went well. In 1971, Klein promoted her to associate designer, and in 1974, several days before Donna Karan's daughter Gabby was born, Klein suc-cumbed to cancer and Karan took over the business. The choice of Karan for the position was influenced by Tamio Taki, chairman of Takihyo, the American branch of a Japanese textile firm and largest partner in the Anne Klein Company. He spotted her as the best of several candidates after Karan unveiled her fall, 1974, collection to a standing ovation and rave reviews in *The New York Times*.

In 1976, Karan brought her old friend Louis Dell'Olio to the company as her associate. Building on the Anne Klein sportswear reputation, they began to replace Klein's conservative flowered dresses with sportswear separates that could be mixed and matched to create sophisticated dramatic outfits. Their designs were aimed not at showroom models but at professional working women such as Karan herself. During this period, Karan's personal life also underwent some changes. She divorced Karan and moved in with Stephan Weiss, a sculptor and head of his family's theater supplies company. They were married in 1983.

Each season's collection brought greater successes. In 1977, both Karan and Dell'Olio were awarded the Oscar of the fashion industry, the Coty American Fashion Critics Award. In 1981, they won another Critics Award, and the following year they were inducted into the Coty Hall of Fame. In 1983, continuing to transform Klein's traditional tailored clothing into more dramatic flowing designs, Karan created Anne Klein II. These designs, whose prices were half those of the Anne Klein collection pieces, appealed to the growing number of affluent professional women who wanted to dress quickly but look elegant. Karan's ability to respond to societal changes with designs that were flattering and affordable brought the Anne Klein Company tremen-dous profits.

After completing several successful collections, Karan decided that the company's sportswear design was not moving in any particular direction, and she began to consider launching her own smaller private label. She was hesitant, however, to leave the company with which she had so much success. The decision dragged on into 1984, when Taki's partner in the Anne Klein Company, Frank Mori, made the decision for her by firing her. This action, which was not really a firing in the traditional sense, gave Karan the impetus to go ahead on her own.

Soon after she and Dell'Olio presented their final Anne Klein collection in the fall of 1984, Karan launched her own company, Donna Karan New York. She received $3 million in financial backing from Takihyo and became chief executive officer and head designer of the company. With Donna Karan New York came a new concept of dressing that originated, as did her designs at Anne Klein, in Karan's concepts of what she herself, as a professional woman, wanted to wear. She noted, in an interview for the premiere issue of American *Elle*, that she looked in her own closets each morning and saw lots of clothes but nothing to wear. She needed something that went beyond outfits, pieces that were more conceptual and that could be put together in many different ways.

Her first collection in the fall of 1985 featured soft black and white fabrics. It was an immediate success. Karan combined the basic piece, the bodysuit, with dark tights, wraparound scarf skirts, pants, and sculptural jackets. Chunky gold jewelry completed the outfit. The look is aggressive yet sophisticated. It combines the comfortable interchangeable pieces characteristic of masculine fashions with the feminine look of glamour.

Karan was named designer of the year in 1985 and 1986 by the Council of Fashion Designers of America, and riding on these successes, she expanded into using new colors and shapes, always looking for simpler ways of dressing and designing clothes that she herself would wear. By 1987, the Donna Karan Company was in the black with revenues of $40 million, and by 1989 the company had gone from four employees to more than 200.

In 1988, Karan decided to try yet another market, a second line of separates priced more affordably than her signature collection. In the fall of 1988, she launched the DKNY line, featuring denim jeans, faded khaki pants and trenchcoats, bomber jackets, and white shirts. These clothes could be worn with sneakers and accessorized with whimsical jewelry. Popularized by movie and television personalities such as Barbra Streisand and Candice Bergen, these "fun" clothes were aimed at the same market, the professional woman, but were intended for off-hours. With $58 million in sales in the first year alone, the DKNY line was a remarkable success.

Successful collections followed season after season. Karan is now one of the world's most popular designers and most successful businesspeople. With her husband, she has developed her company into a full-line conglomerate. She has top-of-the-line designs for both men and women, a hosiery line of opaque tights licensed to Hanes, and the popular DKNY line, which now includes clothing for children and men. Her men's clothes, like those for women, are known for comfort and style. Her vests, crewneck sweaters, and bomber jackets reflect the lifestyle of the urban professional man. They too won awards. In 1991, Karan won the Fashion Designers of America Award for the best men's designer of the year.

In 1992, Karan and her husband decided to enter the perfume market, hoping it would lead to a full line of cosmetics. Rather than licensing her name to one of the perfume companies, she developed it on her own. She markets it in the same way she does her clothing, in DKNY boutiques in large department stores.

Karan is also adding to this marketing strategy. Her plans include opening fifty to seventy-five free-standing stores in the United States and expanding the market abroad. Karan already has a store in Hong Kong, where her sales rival those of other international designers. To finance this expansion, the Donna Karan company plans to reduce the involvement of Takihyo, the founding investor, and to go public with their stock. This method of financing would also be another first in the American fashion industry.

Summary

Donna Karan's status as the foremost American designer and the first woman to reach this pinnacle resulted not only from her ability to design clothes but also from her attention to detail, insatiable drive, and uncanny ability to gauge the temper of the market. Her systematic dressing for the busy urban professional woman began with five interchangeable pieces, which look comfortable and feminine on any occasion. Each season she adds new designs. Her clothes are for the typical American working woman, not unlike herself, and she designs to "accentuate the positive" parts of the female figure. The style of these clothes never overpowers the personality of the wearer, as do the styles of some designers. Thus, the wearer, rather than dressing in a business "uniform," retains her individuality in the business world while looking and feeling feminine.

Karan publicizes her attitude toward fashion and lifestyle by making frequent television appearances and giving magazine interviews about her fashions and her position as the owner of a multimillion dollar business. A hard worker, she is as demanding of her employees as she is of herself. Despite her success internationally, she does not let her ego get in the way, never presenting herself as the perfect fashion figure or dresser to famous people. Her advertising appears not only in high-priced fashion magazines but also in subways and bus stops. She attracts many talented young people who not only want to be a part of her expanding business but also want to achieve her look and style. Dubbed by journalists the "Empress of Seventh Avenue," she is the first American woman to achieve international success and fame in what was, until she entered the field, a man's world, dominated by names such as Ralph Lauren and Calvin Klein.

Bibliography

Agins, Teri. "Woman on the Verge." *Working Woman* 18 (May, 1993): 66-69, 96-98. A cover story that profiles Karan from childhood through her success with the DKNY fashion collection. Although somewhat breezy in its tone, the article does provide serious analysis of Karan's shrewd design decisions and her ability to work with management executives who oversee the financial dealings of her flourishing business.

Calasibetta, Charlotte M. "Donna Karan." In *Fairfield's Dictionary of Fashion Design*. New York: Fairchild, 1988. A short entry covering Karan's basic biographical information and giving some brief descriptions of design features in her work.

Mansfield, Stephanie. "Prima Donna." *Vogue* 179 (August 1, 1989): 290. An interview conducted shortly after Karan launched her casual line of DKNY separates, this article discusses Karan's meteoric rise from her origins in the borough of Queens to become one of the hottest young fashion designers on New York City's Seventh Avenue.

Tippins, Sherill. *Donna Karan: Designing an American Dream.* New York: Garrett Educational Corp., 1992. A work in a series on American entrepreneurs aimed at younger readers, this biography focuses on the work and skills that Karan developed in order to succeed in the fashion industry. Includes photographs.

Walz, Barbra, and Jill Barber. *Starring Mothers: Thirty Portraits of Accomplished Women.* New York: Doubleday, 1987. A compilation of sketches on several notable American women. The selection on Karan highlights conflicts between work and parenthood and the way in which Karan resolved them. Tells more about her personal life than about her career.

Louise M. Stone

GERTRUDE KÄSEBIER

Born: May 18, 1852; Des Moines, Iowa
Died: October 13, 1934; New York, New York
Area of Achievement: Photography
Contribution: Käsebier, a celebrated pictorial photographer, was chosen by Alfred
Stieglitz to be one of the founding members of the Photo-Secession, the most
famous group of art photographers in the United States at the turn of the century.

Early Life

Gertrude was born Gertrude Stanton in Des Moines, Iowa, in 1852. At the age of
eight, she moved to the Colorado Territory, where her father, John W. Stanton, first
mayor of Golden, Colorado, ran first a lumber mill and then a mineral refining
business. In 1864, the Stantons moved to Brooklyn, New York, where Gertrude's
father continued to work in the refining business and her mother took in boarders. In
the late 1860's, Gertrude was sent to stay with her grandmother in Bethlehem,
Pennsylvania, where she attended the Moravian Seminary for Women.

Gertrude married twenty-eight-year-old Eduard Käsebier on her twenty-second
birthday; he had been a boarder in the Stanton home. A successful businessman,
Eduard came from a well-connected German family. For about ten years, Gertrude
and Eduard lived in Brooklyn near Gertrude's family; then they moved to a farmhouse
in New Durham, New Jersey. They had three children: Frederick William (born 1875),
Gertrude Elizabeth (1878), and Hermine Mathilde (1880). Yet Gertrude never took to
domesticity. Her impressions of marriage are suggested in a photograph of two oxen
which she made sometime prior to 1915; it is titled *Yoked and Muzzled—Marriage*.

At age thirty-seven, Gertrude Käsebier convinced her husband to move back to
Brooklyn, and she entered art school at the recently established Pratt Institute. Pratt
was progressive, coeducational, and had women artists on the faculty. Käsebier
completed Pratt's Regular Art Course in 1893, receiving a sound academic training
with a strong emphasis on drawing and design. Käsebier continued to study at Pratt
until 1896, including a period in France in 1894 and classes with Arthur Wesley Dow
in 1895 and 1896. Dow, who later taught painter Georgia O'Keeffe, introduced
Käsebier to innovative compositional ideas based on Asian art.

Life's Work

In the 1890's, Pratt Institute did not offer classes in photography, although some
faculty members were proficient in the relatively new medium. The school's art
reference library, however, included numerous photographs of famous works of art,
many by top European photographic firms. Gertrude Käsebier would have been quite
familiar with these images.

Käsebier had begun taking photographs, mainly family snapshots of her children,
in the mid-1880's, when the advent of "dry plates" encouraged many amateurs to take
up the art. She was winning prizes in photo contests and having her work reproduced

in magazines by the spring of 1894, when she left to spend a year in Europe. Her daughters accompanied her overseas and stayed with relatives in Germany; her husband and son remained in New York. She spent the summer in Crécy-en-Brie, France, studying painting with Frank DuMond and chaperoning the younger students from Pratt and the Art Students League. She began to experiment with portrait photography while abroad and also documented the customs of the local peasants. These latter images, along with her explanatory text, appeared in *The Monthly Illustrator* in March and April of 1895. They echo the subject matter and mood of mid-nineteenth century paintings by the French master Jean-François Millet. It was also during this year in Europe that Käsebier received her first formal training in photography, briefly apprenticing herself to a German chemist who was interested in photography.

After returning to America, Käsebier became a professional photographer. In part, she was propelled to make this change in 1896 as a result of her husband's declining health. Her now-widowed mother, Muncy Stanton, joined the household to free Gertrude from domestic chores.

Many women photographers were gaining success as portraitists in the 1890's, and photographic journals particularly extolled their aptitude for photographing mothers and children. Yet the world of commercial studio portraiture was still dominated by men, making Käsebier a real pioneer. She arranged an apprenticeship with a commercial portrait photographer in Brooklyn, Samuel H. Lifshey, from whom she learned how to develop, print, tone, mount, and retouch photographs. She also began to exhibit her work more widely. Increasingly, she was praised for her ability to capture a sitter's personality as well as his or her likeness.

Käsebier's first New York studio, which opened in late 1897 or early 1898, was located in the Woman's Exchange Building on East 30th Street, a stone's throw from the Fifth Avenue studios of the most fashionable portrait photographers of the day. Most of her established rivals utilized elaborate painted backdrops and props; Käsebier rejected this approach in favor of simplicity and individuality. Among her early portraits are a remarkable group of photographs of Sioux Indians, members of Buffalo Bill's Wild West Show. These images depict the sitters as individuals, not as stereotypes.

In June of 1898, Käsebier introduced herself to Alfred Stieglitz, the editor of *Camera Notes* and the leader in the United States of the fight for the recognition of photography as a fine art. She soon became part of Stieglitz's inner circle. She had ten works (the maximum) accepted for exhibition at the first Philadelphia Photographic Salon, for which Stieglitz was a juror. The following February, Stieglitz gave her a solo exhibit at the Camera Club of New York. In 1899 and 1900, Käsebier was a juror for the prestigious Philadelphia Photographic Salons.

By this time, Käsebier's photographic style had matured. Influenced by both aestheticism and the Arts and Crafts movement, she became best known for evocative images of women and children such as the Whistlerian *Blessed Art Thou Among Women* (1899), a platinum print on Japanese tissue which explores white tones set against a white background. Her simple but sensitive style soon gained her international acclaim. In 1900, her work was included in the collection of photographs by American women exhibited by Washington, D.C., photographer Frances Benjamin Johnston at the Paris Exposition. The same year, Boston pictorialist F. Holland Day included a selection of Käsebier's prints in his "New School of American Photography" exhibit at the Royal Photographic Society in London.

In February of 1902, disputes with traditionalists in the Camera Club of New York led Alfred Stieglitz to found the Photo-Secession. Its first exhibition was held that March at the National Arts Club in New York. Under Stieglitz's strong leadership, the group—which included such notable photographers as Edward Steichen, Clarence White, and Joseph Keiley as well as Käsebier—quickly set the standard for modern artistic photography in America. The first issue of Stieglitz's publication *Camera Work* (1903-1917) featured Käsebier. Six of her photographs were meticulously reproduced, and two articles and an editorial were devoted to her work.

By April of 1905, however, when Stieglitz again featured Käsebier in *Camera Work*, their relationship had begun to sour; Käsebier was displeased by the commentary accompanying her images. Yet in February of 1906, she and Clarence White had a joint exhibit at the Little Galleries of the Photo-Secession, which had been opened by Stieglitz at 291 Fifth Avenue in November of 1905. On this occasion Käsebier first exhibited one of her portraits of sculptor Auguste Rodin, taken in France the previous summer.

In 1907, tensions between Käsebier and Stieglitz reached a new peak. Käsebier joined the Professional Photographers of New York, an organization that the high-minded Stieglitz saw as blatantly commercial. The straw that broke the camel's back, however, was a mocking parody of Käsebier by the influential art critic Charles Caffin, which Stieglitz published in the October, 1907, issue of *Camera Work*. Käsebier believed that the article insulted her and posthumously libeled her old friend the architect Stanford White. She was furious.

Increasingly, in exhibitions at "291," as Stieglitz's gallery had come to be known, Käsebier's work was taking a back seat to Steichen's and White's. She began to feel marginalized within the Photo-Secession. She and Stieglitz, both strong willed, reached an impasse when she began to cast her lot with professional photographers and he, who had a private "income" and never had to earn a living as a photographer, criticized her commercialism. When the Photo-Secession was reorganized in 1909, Käsebier was not among those named "Fellows of the Directorate."

Käsebier's husband died on December 17, 1909, after years of poor health. That winter, she began to offer courses in composition to other women photographers through the Women's Federation of the Photographers' Association of America.

In 1910, Käsebier collaborated one last time with Alfred Stieglitz by exhibiting twenty-two prints in what turned out to be the Photo-Secession's "grand finale," the photographic exhibit held at the Albright Art Gallery (later the Albright-Knox) in Buffalo, New York. Yet by 1910, Käsebier and Stieglitz had grown far apart. She continued to make painterly, hand-manipulated prints using the gum bichromate process, while Stieglitz's tastes moved to the "straight" photographic print and to modern painting and sculpture.

The 1910 exhibit at the Albright Art Gallery marked the end of the Photo-Secession's activities as a group. Stieglitz had achieved his long-held goal: to have photography recognized by a major art museum. A dues notice was sent out in 1911, but many Photo-Secessionists had become disenchanted by Stieglitz's dictatorial manner. Käsebier officially resigned from the Photo-Secession in January of 1912; she was the first member to do so.

Käsebier continued her portrait business after her break with Stieglitz. She also took on new photographic challenges, including a series of unmanipulated platinum prints made of the rugged coast of Newfoundland. Her friendship with Clarence White grew as he took up the mantle of leadership for the pictorialist movement, organizing photographic exhibits after Stieglitz began to exhibit modern art. White also became renowned as a teacher, operating a school of photography in Maine in 1910 and, four years later, another in New York. He had many women students who went on to become successful photographers, among them Laura Gilpin, Dorothea Lange, Margaret Bourke-White, and Doris Ulmann. Käsebier occasionally taught at the Clarence White School, and she was a mentor to the younger women. In 1916, White formed the Pictorial Photographers of America. Käsebier was named honorary vice president.

Käsebier continued to operate a New York studio where, in 1924, she was joined in business by her daughter, Hermine Turner. In her last years, she suffered from failing eyesight and financial setbacks resulting from the stock market crash of 1929, the year in which the Brooklyn Institute of Arts and Sciences (later the Brooklyn Museum) gave her a retrospective show. She died at home on October 13, 1934.

Summary

Gertrude Käsebier was among those at the forefront of the pictorial movement in photography, which emphasized aesthetics and artistic vision over clarity and sharpness. She earned a reputation for her work some years before Alfred Stieglitz founded the Photo-Secession, and she quickly became one of the leaders of the new movement. Among the women Secessionists, she was the most celebrated. Yet unlike Stieglitz, who was a dedicated amateur, Käsebier was a consummate professional. She forged her own path and successfully merged photographic artistry with the business of commercial portraiture. As a pioneer in this aspect of photography, Käsebier became an important role model to several generations of women photographers.

Bibliography

Buerger, Janet E. *The Last Decade: The Emergence of Art Photography in the 1890s.* Rochester, N.Y.: International Museum of Photography at George Eastman House, 1984. An excellent and scholarly overview of the rise of pictorial photography.

Bunnell, Peter, ed. *A Photographic Vision: Pictorial Photography, 1889-1923.* Salt Lake City: Peregrine Smith, 1980. A general study of pictorialism by one of the leading scholars of the movement.

Doty, Robert. *Photo-Secession: Photography as a Fine Art*. Rochester, N.Y.: George Eastman House, 1960. The first major study of the Photo-Secession, this work was reissued as *Photo-Secession: Stieglitz and the Fine-Art Movement in Photography* by Dover in 1978.

Green, Jonathan, ed. *Camera Work: A Critical Anthology*. Millerton, N.Y.: Aperture, 1973. This well-indexed volume provides a good overview of the scope of Stieglitz's seminal journal.

Greenough, Sarah, and Juan Hamilton. *Alfred Stieglitz Photographs and Writings*. Washington, D.C.: National Gallery of Art, 1983. A well-documented and richly illustrated volume containing much primary source material relevant to Stieglitz and the Photo-Secession.

Homer, William Innes. *Alfred Stieglitz and the Photo-Secession*. Boston: Little, Brown, 1983. The standard text for studying Stieglitz's movement.

Margolis, Marianne Fulton, ed. *Camera Work: A Pictorial Guide*. New York: Dover, 1978. This volume reproduces, in small format, all the illustrations published in *Camera Work*. Indexed.

Michaels, Barbara. *Gertrude Käsebier: The Photographer and Her Photographs*. New York: Harry N. Abrams, 1992. The most complete and up-to-date biographical study of Käsebier, this monograph is lavishly illustrated and well documented with an extensive bibliography and excellent notes.

Gillian Greenhill Hannum

HELEN KELLER

Born: June 27, 1880; Tuscumbia, Alabama
Died: June 1, 1968; Westport, Connecticut
Areas of Achievement: Social reform and education
Contribution: Blind and deaf since early childhood, Keller exemplified by her life of activism the full empowerment potential of disabled persons who receive appropriate adaptive education. She served as a spokesperson and fund-raiser for the benefit of deaf and blind people.

Early Life

Helen Adams Keller was born in a small town in northern Alabama to Kate Adams Keller and Captain Arthur Keller, a Confederate Civil War veteran. At nineteen months, Helen suffered an illness that left her blind, deaf, and eventually mute. She remained locked in this lonely state of sensory deprivation until she reached the age of six, when her family employed Anne Sullivan, the twenty-year-old daughter of working-class Irish immigrants, as her tutor. Sullivan herself was visually impaired.

With Sullivan's devoted, creative, and stubborn help, Helen soon rediscovered the concept that concrete things are associated with linguistic symbols—in her case, the letters of the manual alphabet spelled into her hand. Once that breakthrough was made and communication was reestablished, the young girl worked quickly to master manual lip-reading, handwriting, typewriting, Braille, and basic vocal speech. Helen's recovery of communication was aided by the residue of language skills that had developed before she went deaf, by a stimulus-rich home environment, by the early age at which her adaptive education began, and by her own remarkable intelligence and perseverance. Accompanied and assisted by her tutor, Helen attended the Perkins Institution for the Blind (Boston), the Horace Mann School of the Deaf (New York), the Wright-Humason School for the Deaf (New York), and, eventually, Gilman's preparatory Cambridge School for Young Ladies and Radcliffe College (both in Cambridge, Massachusetts), from which she was graduated with honors.

While she was still a schoolgirl, Keller began her lifelong career of philanthropic fund-raising, collecting contributions for the education of a destitute blind and deaf boy when she was eleven, giving a tea to benefit the kindergarten for the blind when she was twelve, and campaigning for money to start a public library in Tuscumbia when she was thirteen.

She also began her career as a writer early. In her childhood, she published several short pieces, but those early successes were also accompanied by what she later referred to as "the one cloud in my childhood's bright sky." In 1892, she wrote a short story called "The Frost King," which she sent as a birthday present to Michael Anagnos at the Perkins Institution for the Blind, who published it in one of the Institution reports. The story was discovered to be remarkably similar to Margaret T. Canby's "The Frost Fairies." The twelve-year-old child was accused of willful plagiarism and was interrogated for many hours. The experience traumatized her so deeply that, although she loved stories, she never wrote fiction again, remaining anxious and uncertain about which were her own ideas and which were impressions she had gathered from other writers. Helen's literary creativity turned toward autobiography.

When she was a sophomore at Radcliffe, she was asked by the editors of *Ladies' Home Journal* to write her life story in monthly installments. With the help of John Macy, a Harvard English instructor, and Sullivan (who eventually married Macy), Keller completed the project, which was later published in 1902 as *The Story of My Life*.

Life's Work

After her 1904 graduation from Radcliffe with honors in German and English, Helen Keller continued to write. *The World I Live In* was published in 1908; *The Song of the Stone Wall*, in 1910; and *Out of the Dark*, in 1913. She also wrote a number of magazine articles, primarily inspirational pieces. Some critics objected to the visual and auditory imagery in her work, criticizing it as mere "hearsay" or even offering it as evidence of outright fraud. As time went by, however, the disbelief with which some people greeted Keller's accomplishments gradually faded. This widening public estimation of what was possible for the deaf and blind significantly enlarged the field of opportunities available to all disabled people after Keller.

Sullivan married Macy soon after Keller's graduation, but the partnership between the two women continued into Keller's adulthood. (Keller never married; her engagement at age thirty-six to Peter Fagan was thwarted by her family.) The two women began to lecture together. Keller would speak her lectures and, because Keller's voice was still very difficult for strangers to understand, Sullivan would interpret. Their lectures served to increase public comprehension of the life of the perceptually impaired.

As Keller gained experience, moving through the world on Sullivan's arm, her scope of interest enlarged from human limitations caused by visual and auditory impairment to include human limitations caused by gender, by class, and by nationalism. She began to see the welfare of all people as being interdependent. She worked for woman suffrage. A pacifist to the core, she spoke against the vast amount of money her country poured into military expenditures. She read Marx and Engels, and in 1909 she joined the Socialist Party, of which John Macy was also a member. At the advent of World War I, she became a member of the Industrial Workers of the World. She wrote and lectured in defense of socialism, supported the union movement, and opposed the United States' entry into World War I. She remained sympathetic toward socialist causes all of her life, but in 1921 she decided to focus her energies on raising money for the American Foundation for the Blind.

Around the time of World War I, the advent of modernism in literature caused Keller's sentimental, rather flowery prose to seem less fashionable. An assertive and political single woman in her middle years, Keller was less comprehensible to the American public than she had been as a child. Her income from her writing diminished, and, after years of refusing it, she finally accepted a yearly stipend from the great archcapitalist Andrew Carnegie. Financial issues became more and more important as Sullivan's health deteriorated and Macy descended into alcoholism.

Financial pressure prompted Keller and Sullivan to venture into vaudeville. Between 1920 and 1924, their lectures were a great success on Harry and Herman Weber's variety circuit. Besides further deepening public understanding of blindness and deafness, their years of vaudeville gave them the opportunity to meet and develop friendships with many of the famous people of the day, including Sophie Tucker, Enrico Caruso, Jascha Heifetz, and Harpo Marx. Throughout her life, Keller's extensive acquaintance with influential people was part of the power she wielded in the world. (She was received in the White House by every American president from Grover Cleveland to John F. Kennedy.)

During the 1920's, Keller and Sullivan also traveled frequently on fund-raising tours for the American Foundation for the Blind, an agency that Keller supported until her death. She also continued to write. In 1927, she published *My Religion*, an explanation of her understanding of the alternative reality described by the eighteenth century visionary Emanuel Swedenborg. In 1930, *Midstream: My Later Life* appeared as well.

The 1930's saw more of Keller's books produced: *Peace at Eventide* was brought out in 1932, and *Helen Keller's Journal* was published in 1938. Keller deplored the rise of the Nazis and supported John L. Lewis' union strikes. Anne Sullivan died in 1936. After the death of her primary life-partner, Keller relied mainly on Polly Thompson, a Scots immigrant who had been assisting her since 1915. They remained together until Thompson's death in 1960.

In 1955, Keller published *Teacher*, a biography of Anne Sullivan Macy. She continued to be active on behalf of the blind and deaf until around 1962. In 1964, Keller was awarded the Presidential Medal of Freedom, the country's highest civilian honor. She died quietly in her sleep at the age of eighty-seven.

Keller's life was filled with activity: writing, lecturing, studying, and traveling. Her significance was not simply based on her untiring work on behalf of the constituency that a childhood misfortune and her own choice selected for her. By all accounts, she was a woman of great spiritual authority. Religious faith, the self-mastery needed to overcome tragedy, and a powerful and loving teacher produced in Keller one of the spiritually radiant figures of her time, whose power was not simply based on what she did or who she knew, but also on who she was and the direct effect of her presence on those whose lives she touched.

Summary

Helen Keller worked her entire life for the betterment of the disabled. She wrote. She lectured. She exerted her considerable influence over public institutions and powerful people. She raised funds for a number of agencies serving the disabled. She acted as a catalyst for the organization of state commissions for the blind. She helped to educate the American public about the prevention of gonorrheal blindness in newborn babies. The work that she did earned for her numerous humanitarian awards and citations.

The fruits of Keller's work were important, but what is even more important is that she did that work at all. She came into a world that had extremely limiting ideas about what was possible for a deaf and blind woman to accomplish. The disabled were seen as less than fully human; deaf and blind people were still being locked away in mental asylums in the world into which Helen Keller was born. In that world, the mere existence of a powerful, educated, assertive figure such as Keller was profoundly significant. Each lecture she gave, each article she wrote defied stereotypes and served to change the attitudes and expectations of her society. Her public life as an active deaf and blind woman truly altered the intellectual horizons around her. When she died, she left a world that had been radically changed by her life.

Bibliography

Gibson, William. *The Miracle Worker*. New York: Bantam, 1965. The original play that examined the early years of the relationship between Helen Keller and Anne Sullivan.

Houston, Jean. *Public Like a Frog: Entering the Lives of Three Great Americans*. Wheaton, Ill.: Theosophical Publishing, 1993. Concise biographical sketches of Emily Dickinson, Thomas Jefferson, and Helen Keller, highlighting their spirituality. This work is unique in that the biographies are interspersed with personal growth exercises that invite the reader's imaginative participation in crucial moments of the subjects' lives.

Keller, Helen. *Midstream: My Later Life*. New York: Greenwood, 1968. The story of Keller's life from around 1904 until 1927. Describes her work for the blind, her lecturing and writing career, her experiences in Hollywood, and her relationships with some well-known public figures, including Mark Twain, Alexander Graham Bell, and the Carnegie family.

_____ . *The Story of My Life*. New York: Collier Macmillan International, 1972. The best-known of Keller's autobiographical works, this book tells the story of her first two decades and includes a selection of letters that illustrate the development of her language skills from the age of seven to adulthood. Contains a useful short introduction by Lou Ann Walker.

_____ . *Teacher: Anne Sullivan Macy*. Garden City, N.Y.: Doubleday, 1955. Keller's respectful and loving account of Anne Sullivan's life. Seeks to redress what Keller saw as an imbalance between excessive public attention on herself and neglect of Sullivan's accomplishments.

Lash, Joseph P. *Helen and Teacher: The Story of Helen Keller and Anne Sullivan Macy*. Radcliffe Biography Series. New York: Delacorte, 1980. This long dual biography acknowledges the long, fruitful relationship between Keller and Anne Sullivan.

Donna Glee Williams

FLORENCE KELLEY

Born: September 12, 1859; Philadelphia, Pennsylvania
Died: February 17, 1932; Philadelphia, Pennsylvania
Areas of Achievement: Social reform and women's rights
Contribution: A longtime campaigner for maximum-hour and minimum-wage legislation, Florence Kelley served as chief factory inspector of Illinois and as general secretary of the National Consumers' League.

Early Life

Florence Kelley was born on September 12, 1859, in Philadelphia, Pennsylvania, the daughter of William Darrow Kelley and his second wife, Caroline Bastram Kelley. Her father's opposition to slavery led him into the Republican Party during the 1850's and to a twenty-year career as a U.S. congressman; he was a friend of Susan B. Anthony and a sponsor of the woman suffrage amendment. As a young woman, Kelley also had her great aunt, Sarah Pugh, as a role model; Pugh, of Quaker background, was active in the Female Anti-Slavery Society, established by Lucretia Mott, and in the women's rights movement both before and after the Civil War.

Kelley's early education was intermittently interrupted by illness; she attended for a time the Friend's Central School in Philadelphia, and in 1873 she attended a school for young women organized by Mary Anna and Susan Longstreth. Three years later, she entered Cornell University. Courses in law, economics. politics, French, German, Latin, and American history broadened her intellectual horizons and steered her in the direction she would take during her career. She was graduated from Cornell in 1882, taught evening classes for working women in Philadelphia, and a year later went to the University of Zurich for graduate study. There she met a young Russian medical student, Lazare Wischnewetzky, and she married him on June 4, 1884. She had also come in contact with a number of European socialists, and she received permission from Friedrich Engels to translate into English his book *Die Lage der arbeitenden Klasse in England* (1845; *The Condition of the Working Class in England in 1844*, 1887). Her association with Engels began a long correspondence between the young American and the friend and colleague of Karl Marx.

Kelley, with her husband and her son Nicholas, born in 1885, returned to the United States in 1886. They took up residence in New York City, and Kelley became an active member of the Socialist Labor Party. A controversy between the party leadership and Edward Aveling, translator of Marx's *Das Kapital* (1867, 1885, 1894; *Capital: A Critique of Political Economy*, 1886, 1907, 1909), who had come to the United States with his wife, Eleanor Marx Aveling, on a lecture tour, led in 1887 to Kelley's and her husband's expulsion from the socialist organization. In the meantime, she had written "The Need for Theoretical Preparation for Philanthropic Work" (1887), a primer of Marxian socialism, and, a year after her separation from the party, "Our Toiling Children" (1889), a pamphlet that presaged her life's work in campaigning for the abolition of child labor. She also gave birth to a daughter, Margaret, in 1886 and another son, John Bartram, a year later.

Her marriage, however, was foundering. Wischnewetzky's medical practice was unsuccessful, there were large debts, and in 1891 the couple separated and were divorced. Kelley and her three children went to Chicago, where she took up residence in Hull House and began her long association with Jane Addams and Julia Lathrop. Addams was the founder of the settlement house, and Lathrop later became the head of the United States Children's Bureau.

Life's Work

In Chicago, living at Hull House and participating in its program, Florence Kelley worked as a special agent for the Illinois Bureau of Labor Statistics, inspecting sweatshops in the clothing industry. Then, in 1893, after the election of John Peter Altgeld as governor and the passage of an Illinois statute establishing a state factory inspection department, abolishing child labor under the age of fourteen, and setting an eight-hour day for women and children, Kelley was appointed Illinois' chief factory inspector. With an annual budget of $12,000 and a salary for its chief inspector of $1,500, the department, under Kelley's supervision, established a free medical examination center for working children, recommended in its 1894 report an amendment to the Factory Act that would cover the inspection of dangerous machinery, and examined more than one thousand shops during a smallpox epidemic in Chicago in order to locate contaminated garments.

In 1897, Altgeld was defeated for reelection and Kelley was dismissed as chief factory inspector. There were other setbacks. The eight-hour provision of the Illinois Factory Act was declared unconstitutional by the state supreme court in 1895. Kelley's book *Hull-House Maps and Papers* (1895), a study of Chicago's working class, was not reprinted after the sale of its first edition. Kelley did not give up. In 1899, she became general secretary of the National Consumers' League and held that position for the remainder of her life. Traveling extensively, organizing leagues throughout the United States, Kelley continued to speak out against child labor and for new factory legislation. She promoted the use of the Consumers' League label as a device to obliterate the labor of children under sixteen, to abolish the use of tenements as working sites, and to ensure that all state laws regarding the regulation of factories were obeyed. Those employers who subscribed to the standards received the label for their factories, and the consuming public was encouraged to limit its purchases to conforming companies. Kelley also campaigned for the establishment of the United States Children's Bureau; her book *Some Ethical Gains Through Legislation* (1905) emphasized the need for the extension of the ballot to women and for wage and hour laws that would ameliorate the lives of workers and abolish child labor. Along with Josephine Goldmark, she secured the services of the Boston attorney and later United States Supreme Court justice Louis D. Brandeis to submit a brief in support of the constitutionality of the Oregon ten-hour law for women. The "Brandeis Brief," an innovation in the law, contained two pages of legal precedents and almost two hundred pages of medical reports and scientific data, derived from studies in the

United States and abroad, documenting the deleterious effect of long working hours on the physical health of women. The brief contributed to the successful defense of the Oregon law in the U.S. Supreme Court case of *Muller v. Oregon* in 1907. Most of the research for the brief and its compilation were accomplished in a few weeks by Kelley and Goldmark.

Kelley's campaign for maximum-hour and minimum-wage legislation met with opposition from an unexpected source during the 1920's. After more than a half-century of agitation, American women were finally granted suffrage by the 1920 ratification of the Nineteenth Amendment to the Constitution. The National Woman's Party, under the leadership of Alice Paul, had captured national attention by picketing the White House and by engaging in hunger strikes on behalf of the cause of women's suffrage. Kelley, in fact, had been a member of the party, but in 1921 the National Woman's Party took up the sponsorship of an Equal Rights Amendment. Introduced by Daniel Anthony, the nephew of Susan B. Anthony, in the House of Representatives in December of 1923, the proposed addition to the Constitution guaranteed that "men and women shall have equal rights throughout the United States and every place subject to its jurisdiction."

Florence Kelley was aghast. It was clear to her that all of the progress in enacting protective labor legislation for women was jeopardized by an Equal Rights Amendment. The leadership of the National Woman's Party believed that one-sex protective legislation had the effect of discriminating against women and deterring the advancement of their careers. Kelley and other women in the Women's Trade Union League, the League of Women Voters, and the National Consumers' League argued that the National Woman's Party represented almost exclusively middle-class professionals and that it had no interest in and did not understand the conditions under which women worked in factories. Women who labored in laundries and other manufacturing establishments were almost always unorganized and were not attracted to union membership. The only protection from exploitation they enjoyed was through the passage of state labor legislation setting minimum-wage and maximum-hour standards. The Equal Rights Amendment, Kelley contended, would destroy the improvements of thirty years and make factory women vulnerable to an erosion of the terms and conditions of their employment. Why else, Kelley asked rhetorically, was the National Association of Manufacturers aligned with the National Woman's Party in promoting the passage of an Equal Rights Amendment?

Florence Kelley faced other frustrations during the 1920's. The progressive social reforms of the decade prior to World War I had been replaced during the 1920's by a conservative reaction that viewed social welfare programs as the vehicles of a communist conspiracy. It was not uncommon for Kelley, Jane Addams, and other feminists to be accused of radical proclivities. The Sheppard-Towner legislation, which represented the first time that the federal government appropriated monies for maternity and infant benefits, and for which Kelley spoke eloquently at a Senate hearing in December, 1920, although initially funded, was discontinued in 1929. After the Supreme Court nullified the Keating-Owen Child Labor law in 1918 and a second congressional statute abolishing work by children four years later, in 1923 it disposed of the District of Columbia minimum-wage statute for women. The Child Labor Amendment to the U.S. Constitution that Kelley espoused, although it was passed by Congress in 1924, languished in the state legislatures and failed to be ratified.

Summary

Despite the defeats of the 1920's, Florence Kelley's effect on social reform in the United States was immeasurable. Her long and tireless agitation to improve the health and living standards of millions of American workers, both men and women, came to fruition in the Supreme Court's reversal of its 1923 precedent, upholding minimum wages for women in 1937 in *West Coast Hotel v. Parrish*, and in the passage by Congress of the Fair Labor Standards Act the following year. Child labor was finally abolished, maximum hours and a minimum wage, regardless of gender, were established. Although Kelley did not live to witness the accomplishment of her vision, she was surely responsible for laying the foundations for the judicial and legislative reforms of the Great Depression.

On February 17, 1932, Florence Kelley died in Philadelphia at the age of seventy-two. "She was," wrote the New York lawyer George Alger, "a passionate soldier . . . a great advocate . . . a tremendous driving force for good."

Bibliography

Blumberg, Dorothy Rose. *Florence Kelley: The Making of a Social Pioneer*. New York: Augustus M. Kelley, 1966. An adequate but largely uncritical study of Kelley's early life from her birth to the beginning of her career as the general secretary of the National Consumers' League. Concentrates on her family background and education and on her correspondence with Friedrich Engels.

Forbath, William E. *Law and the Shaping of the American Labor Movement*. Cambridge, Mass.: Harvard University Press, 1991. An analysis of the federal and state court responses to protective labor legislation during the post-Civil War period and their impact on the development and strategies of American unions.

Goldmark, Josephine. *Impatient Crusader: Florence Kelley's Life Story*. Urbana: University of Illinois Press, 1953. An affectionate but sometimes anecdotal biography written by a friend and collaborator in the National Consumers' League. Highlights Kelley's campaign for protective labor legislation and her record as the league's general secretary.

Lemons, J. Stanley. *The Woman Citizen: Social Feminism in the 1920's*. Urbana: University of Illinois Press, 1973. A detailed examination of the Sheppard-Towner bill, the aftermath of its passage, and other causes that motivated politically active women. Discusses the reasons for the attack on and decline of social feminism. Contains a particularly good section on the background of the Equal Rights Amendment and the opposition of Florence Kelley and other women to its passage.

Tentler, Leslie, W. *Wage-Earning Women: Industrial Work and Family Life in the United States, 1900-1930*. New York: Oxford University Press, 1979. A graphic description of the trials and vicissitudes suffered and benefits derived by single and married women who worked in the factories and sweatshops of the United States. A testament to the need for maximum-hour and minimum-wage standards, for which Florence Kelley campaigned.

David L. Sterling

FANNY KEMBLE

Born: November 27, 1809; London, England
Died: January 15, 1893; London, England
Areas of Achievement: Theater and drama and social reform
Contribution: Kemble was one of the finest actresses on the British and American
stage. Her *Journal of a Residence on a Georgian Plantation in 1838-1839* is one of
the best firsthand accounts of slavery in the United States.

Early Life

Frances Anne Kemble was born on November 27, 1809, into the most famous
acting family in Great Britain. Her father, Charles Kemble, had succeeded his brother
John as the manager of the Covent Garden theater in London, and two of her aunts
were well-known actresses. Her mother, Maria Therese De Camp, was an actress who
appeared on the London stage with her husband.

Frances, known as Fanny, was largely reared by her aunt, Adelaide ("Dall")
De Camp, but because of her excitable temperament she was sent to France for her
elementary schooling. Her antics soon caused the school's neighbors to refer to her as
"*cette diable* Kemble" (that devil Kemble). She returned to France for a finishing-
school education in Paris. She became fluent in French, developed a lifelong interest
in religion, and began to read Lord Byron and Sir Walter Scott. She was a natural
bookworm despite her excitable nature. During her years in Paris, Fanny also discovered her histrionic ability when acting in a school production.

Aside from singing and piano lessons, she spent the next three years in England
pondering the question of a career, finding herself drawn to writing except for the
uncertainness of the income. Perhaps a career on the stage would provide the income
for her to pursue her literary aspirations. Her enthusiasm for the theater evaporated,
however, when she pondered how much it had cost other members of the Kemble
family.

Life's Work

Fanny Kemble's return to London in 1829 marked a dramatic change in her life's
work. She found her family in dire financial circumstances because of the burden of
managing Covent Garden, which was covered with bills of sale. Although Kemble
disliked the theater and had never had any dramatic training, her mother enlisted her
to learn the role of Juliet in William Shakespeare's *Romeo and Juliet* (c. 1595-1596).
On October 5, 1829, Kemble made her debut, was an overnight success, and soon
became the darling of the British theater crowd. Two other important events happened
in this two-year period: Kemble's play *Francis I* was published, and Kemble met the
woman who would be her lifelong friend and correspondent, Harriet St. Leger of
Ireland. For two years, Kemble performed in London and the provinces and made
enough money to keep the Covent Garden in business. The great economic and
political crisis of the 1830's, however, finally caused Charles Kemble to abandon the

Covent Garden and to take Fanny Kemble and her Aunt Dall to America in the hope of recouping the family fortunes.

Fanny Kemble determined to keep a journal of her sea voyage and the tour of America. She was a good writer and a keen observer of the American scene, which she recorded in what others would later see as very blunt and unkind language that was unsuitable for a lady.

The tour of America was all that they had hoped it would be. She was as popular in the United States as she had been in Great Britain, and American dollars flowed into the family purse. Although Kemble found being an actress distasteful, she believed that it was her duty to help her parents, and that was the only way that she could do so. As she had in Great Britain, Kemble met in the United States famous and about-to-be famous people, including John Quincy Adams, Dolley Madison, Andrew Jackson, Nathaniel Hawthorne, and Charles Sumner, to list but a few. She also came under the influence of William Ellery Channing, the spiritual leader of the Unitarians and abolitionists in New England.

During this two-year tour of the United States, two important changes in her life occurred: She met and was ardently pursued by Pierce Mease Butler of Philadelphia, and her beloved Aunt Dall died as a result of a coach accident. Some of Kemble's biographers opine that if her Aunt Dall had not died in April of 1834, Kemble might not have been so quick to marry Pierce Butler that June. Her marriage meant that Kemble was saying goodbye to both her father and her country. Her last act of filial duty was to arrange to turn over to her father the monies she expected to receive from the publication of her travel journal.

Although Pierce Butler was well aware of Kemble's independent ways, he soon endeavored to make her over into the submissive wife that he wanted, a wife who would not embarrass him or his family by expressing her own ideas. His attempts resulted in failure and ultimately in the end of the marriage.

At the time of his marriage, Butler was heir, along with his brother, to a Georgia plantation that grew sea-island cotton tended by approximately seven hundred slaves. The Butler family had become one of the wealthiest Philadelphia families with the riches acquired from the absentee ownership of the very lucrative slave property.

At the time of her marriage, Fanny Kemble knew nothing of the source of the Butler wealth—a circumstance which was not at all unusual. By the same token, Pierce Butler was unaware that his new wife had decidedly antislavery views that had been formed in the agitation that had only recently resulted in the abolition of slavery in England. To Fanny, to be anything but antislavery would have been a disowning of her English heritage.

Once Kemble was aware of the source of the Butler money, the overwhelming concern of her life was slavery and how she could convince her husband to free the slaves. During these early days of her marriage, Kemble devoted herself to reading, writing, and elaborating her thoughts on slavery, which soon caused disagreements between husband and wife. The first battle was over the travel journal, which was published in 1835 as the *Journal*. Kemble proposed to include in this travel journal a treatise against Negro slavery. Although Butler was unsuccessful in convincing the publisher to suppress the *Journal*, he did succeed in keeping Kemble from including the tirade against slavery by throwing the offending manuscript into the flames.

Fanny Kemble's opinions about slavery were strengthened when she read William Ellery Channing's *Slavery* (1835) in 1836 and adopted his idea that the slave owner must be won to repentance. Kemble accepted that her duty was to become Pierce Butler's conscience and mentor. In order to accomplish this goal, she needed to go to the Butlers' Georgia plantation. After much resistance, Butler took her there in 1838 when he had to assume the running of the plantation. As she was accustomed to do, Kemble kept a journal of her experiences while living in Georgia for fifteen weeks.

The state of Georgia had one of the densest slave populations of any state. When Kemble arrived, the residences for both the Butler family and the slaves were in wretched condition. The slaves were in poor physical condition, especially the women, who were sent back to the fields immediately after giving birth. This resulted in high infant mortality as well as many gynecological problems that were not treated. Kemble soon sought to remedy some of these conditions. Despite the fact that the slave owner's wife traditionally served as a "doctor" to the slaves, Butler interpreted his wife's interest as female meddling. Anyone who complained to Kemble was promptly flogged. Although Butler sometimes showed compassion—for example, by buying a slave's children from another owner so that the family could remain together—he soon tired of Kemble's complaints. In retaliation, she began to teach slaves to read, which was a serious crime, and to pay them for doing tasks for her.

When the couple returned to Philadelphia, their marriage was already breaking apart, although it would be almost ten years before Pierce secured a divorce. In 1849, the marriage formally ended, and the two Butler children, Sarah and Fan (Fanny), were given into the custody of their father.

For some years, Kemble spent her time between the United States and Europe; eventually, she found herself back in England during the American Civil War. There was much interest in England in the war because of the question of the recognition of the Confederacy as an independent nation. The one thing that might prevent that recognition was slavery. She tried to give an accurate picture of slavery to British authorities she knew, such as Charles Grenville, the diarist, and Lord Clarendon, a liberal peer. Her lack of success led Kemble to publish her journal of the time spent in Georgia. *Journal of a Residence on a Georgian Plantation in 1838-1839* appeared in May of 1863, when recognition of the Confederacy was being debated in Parliament. There is no indication that it had any effect. It was brought out in the United States in July of 1863, shortly after the dual Union victories of Gettysburg and Vicksburg. The book did serve to fan the antislavery fire in what by then were war-weary Northerners.

During her years as a divorcée, Fanny Kemble earned her living by doing dramatic readings, which had become more popular than plays. She was very successful at this and toured both the British Isles and the United States. Upon the death of her husband in 1867, Kemble was able to reestablish contact with her two daughters. As she entered old age, she wrote her autobiographies based on the letters that she had sent to St. Leger and that St. Leger now returned to her. She died at her daughter Sarah's home in England in 1893.

Summary

Fanny Kemble's impact on her time rests on two factors: her acting and her writing. Despite the fact that she did not like acting, she is acknowledged as one of the finest actresses that England has ever produced. Her craft, whether acting or doing dramatic readings, brought the pleasures of Shakespeare and other writers to people throughout the British Isles and the United States. Her most significant written work, *Journal of a Residence on a Georgian Plantation in 1838-1839*, effectively gave the lie to the southern claim that slavery had been a benign institution. Its publication ensured that Northerners would not lose heart in the struggle to end the Civil War and see that the slaves would be freed by the Thirteenth Amendment. Despite efforts to discredit it in the post-Civil War period, it remains the best available firsthand account of slavery in the United States. Kemble had indeed accomplished her goal of being a writer.

Bibliography

Driver, Leota Stultz. *Fanny Kemble.* New York: Negro Universities Press, 1969. Provides portraits, pictures from Butler's island, a bibliography, notes, and an index. Contains interesting facts not recorded in other biographies, but the reader must beware of the author's opinions and her use of emotional terms.

Furnas, J. C. *Fanny Kemble: Leading Lady of the Nineteenth-Century Stage.* New York: Dial Press, 1982. Well illustrated with copious notes and a good bibliography. Provides in-depth coverage of Kemble's life up to the publication of *Journal of a Residence on a Georgian Plantation in 1838-1839.* At times, the author exhibits a male bias.

Kemble, Frances Anne. *Journal of a Residence on a Georgian Plantation in 1838-1839.* Edited by John A. Scott. Athens: University of Georgia Press, 1984. Scott's introduction provides a short biography of Kemble up to the publication of the journal in 1863. Evaluates the importance of the journal.

Marshall, Dorothy. *Fanny Kemble.* New York: St. Martin's Press, 1978. Written from an English viewpoint. Includes many illustrations of family and friends not found in other biographies. Accepts as fact that Kemble was mentally imbalanced.

Wise, Winifred E. *Fanny Kemble: Actress, Author, Abolitionist.* New York: G.P. Putnam's Sons, 1967. Places Kemble's life in historical context by identifying persons whom other biographers simply name. Provides little information about the second half of her life.

Wright, Constance. *Fanny Kemble and the Lovely Land.* New York: Dodd, Mead, 1972. The best of the Kemble biographies. Places Kemble in her historical setting by explaining the historical importance of the various people in Kemble's life. A good bibliography and many illustrations are included.

Anne Kearney

BILLIE JEAN KING

Born: November 22, 1943; Long Beach, California

Area of Achievement: Sports

Contribution: In addition to being a superb tennis player, Billie Jean King has been a driving force for the recognition and improvement of women's tennis. Her victory over Bobby Riggs in September, 1973, established her as the preeminent advocate of equity for women tennis players in every phase of their sport.

Early Life

Billie Jean Moffitt was born in Long Beach, California, on November 22, 1943. Her father, Willard J. Moffitt, was an engineer with the city's fire department, and her mother, Betty Moffitt, was a housewife and receptionist at a medical center. Her parents were not affluent, but they encouraged Billie Jean and her younger brother Randy to take part in sports. Randy Moffitt became a major league pitcher with the San Francisco Giants and other teams.

Billie Jean's tennis career began at the age of eleven, when her father allowed her to take tennis classes. She immediately displayed an aptitude for the game and a burning desire to excel. She told her parents that she wanted to compete in the Wimbledon tournament. She worked at odd jobs to buy a tennis racquet and devoted long hours daily to exercise and practice.

When Billie Jean was fifteen, Alice Marble, the great women's player of the 1930's and early 1940's, became her coach. Billie Jean stood only five feet, three inches tall at that stage of her life, and Alice Marble remembered that her student was "short, fat, and aggressive." It was also evident that Billie Jean had the clear makings of a champion because of her positive attitude toward the sport.

Billie Jean's first tournament victory came in the Southern California championship, when she was fourteen, and she made steady progress in junior girls' tournaments for the next several years. By the time she was eighteen, she and Karen Hantze won the women's doubles title at Wimbledon, the youngest pair ever to do so. In 1962, she and Hantze won again. In the singles, Billie Jean defeated top-seeded Margaret Smith of Australia, 1-6, 6-3, 7-5, in one of the most stunning upsets in the history of the British grass-court classic. Billie Jean lost in the quarterfinals, but the victory over Smith signaled that she was on her way to the top of women's tennis. During these years, she also attended Los Angeles State College (later known as the California State University at Los Angeles).

She returned to Wimbledon in 1963 and reached the finals before losing to Margaret Smith. Her game improved during 1964 and 1965, but she was not successful in the Grand Slam tournaments that she entered. In 1964, she became engaged to Larry King, and they were married on September 17, 1965. By the end of the year, she was the number-one-ranked women's player in the United States. Her breakthrough to the top of women's tennis would come in 1966.

Life's Work

Billie Jean King achieved impressive international triumphs in 1966, when she led the Americans to victory over the British in the Wightman Cup competition and three weeks later defeated Maria Bueno in the Wimbledon final, 6-3, 3-6, 6-1. She faltered at the U.S. Open later in the summer but came back in 1967 to win Wimbledon for the second time. She beat Ann Jones of Great Britain, 6-3, 6-4, in the final, and she also captured the women's doubles and mixed doubles crowns. She triumphed at the U.S. Open without losing a single set in the competition. She bested Ann Jones, 11-9, 6-4, in an exciting final.

For the next sixteen years, Billie Jean King was a major star in women's tennis. She became a professional in 1968 and won seventy-one tournaments during her career. She was the first woman to win more than $100,000 in a single year of competition. Her prize money totaled $1,966,487. She won the Australian and French Opens each on one occasion, but won the United States Open singles title four times and the Wimbledon singles title six times. She won twenty Wimbledon titles in singles, doubles, and mixed doubles.

The grass courts of Wimbledon were the scene for many of Billie Jean's most memorable matches. She lost in the final in 1970 to Margaret Court, 14-12, 11-9, in a contest that both players called one of their all-time best. In 1973, she beat Chris Evert, 6-0, 7-5, for her fifth title. Two years later, King won her last Wimbledon singles crown with a 6-0, 6-1, victory over Evonne Goolagong Cawley. King played her final match at Wimbledon in 1983, when she lost in the semifinals to Andrea Jaeger.

King's success as a tennis player rested on her absolute unwillingness to lose. Standing five feet, four inches tall, with knees that often ached and several times required surgery, she drove herself around the court. She talked to herself during matches, exhorting her body to the athletic extremes that she demanded of herself. She would say, "Oh, Billie, think!" or "You've got the touch of an ox." She resented those who wanted to keep tennis a clubby sport, and she sought to "get it off the society pages and onto the sports pages." She attacked the ball, the net, and her opponents with relentless energy and a shrewd brain for the fine points of the game. Spectators and foes never knew what Billie Jean King might do on the court, but her energy and fiery spirit made her fascinating to watch.

Her sense of outrage at obvious unfairness in her sport made her a leader for the cause of women's tennis during the 1960's and 1970's. After open tennis came along in 1968, Billie Jean could not understand why men should receive more prize money and attention than their female counterparts did. She was instrumental in organizing the women players to start their own tour and to challenge the supremacy of the United States Lawn Tennis Association. She helped to found the Women's Tennis Association, and she served as its president from 1973 to 1975 and from 1980 to 1981.

The event that made Billie Jean King an international celebrity and forever identified her with the cause of rights for women athletes was her match with the male tennis player Bobby Riggs in 1973. Riggs had been an excellent tennis star during the 1930's and 1940's. By the 1970's, he had a well-deserved reputation as a "hustler" on the court who could win even when giving his opponents an advantage in advance. In 1973, Riggs loudly claimed that he could easily defeat any of the star women players of that day, even though he was fifty-eight years old. He challenged Billie Jean King and other women to televised matches on that basis. At first, Billie Jean ignored his sexist taunts lest she give him free publicity.

In May of 1973, however, Riggs defeated Margaret Court in a nationally televised match on Mother's Day. Riggs renewed his challenge to Billie Jean King and said that he wanted to play her as the "Women's Libber Leader." King agreed to meet Riggs. The match was held at the Houston Astrodome on September 20, 1973. The event drew a crowd of almost 31,000 spectators, and the television audience was estimated to be more than thirty million. The match was seen in thirty-six foreign countries via satellite. A circuslike atmosphere prevailed. Billie Jean King came into the stadium on a gold litter that four male athletes carried. Tickets for courtside seats sold for $100.

The match was a total victory for Billie Jean King. She outplayed Riggs in every phase of the game on her way to a three-set victory, 6-4, 6-3, 6-3. Rather than rely on her usual attacking game, Billie Jean kept the ball in play, mixed up the speed of her strokes, and relied on her accuracy and stamina to wear down the older and slower Riggs. After the first set, she was in total command of the match, and the result was in the end no contest at all. For all his bravado, Riggs did not have the shots or the talent to keep up with Billie Jean King at the top of her form.

Since her retirement in 1984, Billie Jean King has been active as a tennis coach, television commentator, and organizer of Team Tennis. She has written her autobiography and an engrossing history of women's tennis. During the early 1990's, she was active in charitable events that raised money for AIDS research. Billie Jean King will be a significant presence in the sport of women's tennis for many years and a continuing inspiration to the younger players who have followed her.

Summary

Billie Jean King was a great champion on the tennis court, especially at Wimbledon, where she dominated for so many years. Her aggressive, attacking style helped popularize women's tennis in the 1960's and 1970's. Off the court, she established the structure of women's tennis that brought the sport to great heights of popularity and international appeal. Without her energy and resourcefulness, it would have taken much longer for women's tennis to have made the gains that it did. The match with Bobby Riggs, although it was a media event rather than a serious athletic contest, had great symbolic and cultural importance in providing credibility for women's athletics at a time when restrictive male attitudes still predominated. As a result of that match, Billie Jean King became more than a famous athlete. She emerged as one of the leaders in the movement for equal rights for women that transformed American society during the last quarter of the twentieth century.

Bibliography
Brown, Gene, ed. *The Complete Book of Tennis*. Indianapolis: Bobbs-Merrill, 1980.

A compilation of stories from *The New York Times*, this book contains accounts of most of the significant matches of Billie Jean King's career.

Danzig, Allison, and Peter Schwed, eds. *The Fireside Book of Tennis*. New York: Simon & Schuster, 1972. This compilation of newspaper and magazine accounts of important tennis players and matches has several important essays that deal with Billie Jean King's rise to prominence in tennis during the 1960's.

King, Billie Jean, with Frank Deford. *Billie Jean*. New York: Viking Press, 1982. A candid autobiography in which King discusses the controversial aspects of her career as an athlete and public figure.

King, Billie Jean, with Cynthia Starr. *We Have Come a Long Way: The Story of Women's Tennis*. New York: McGraw-Hill, 1988. A history of the sport which contains Billie Jean King's own comments about her career and the players with whom she competed. An essential book for understanding her impact on the game.

Lumpkin, Angela. *Women's Tennis: A Historical Documentary of the Players and Their Game*. Troy, N.Y.: Whitson, 1981. This overview of women's tennis is a good guide to what has been written about the sport, and it has references to many articles concerning Billie Jean King.

Marble, Alice, with Dale Leatherman. *Courting Danger*. New York: St. Martin's Press, 1991. Marble was Billie Jean's coach, and the book has comments about the impression Billie Jean made on her.

Tinling, Ted. *Love and Faults*. New York: Crown, 1979. The memoirs of the noted designer of tennis dresses and court attire contain some insightful observations on his friendship with Billie Jean King and her role in the sport.

Wade, Virginia, with Jean Rafferty. *Ladies of the Court: A Century of Women at Wimbledon*. New York: Atheneum, 1984. One chapter deals with Billie Jean King's outstanding record as a champion at Wimbledon and her important impact on the tournament.

Karen Gould

MAXINE HONG KINGSTON

Born: October 27, 1940; Stockton, California

Area of Achievement: Literature

Contribution: A writer of memoirs, nonfiction, and fiction, Kingston writes powerfully about the lives of Chinese Americans. Stylistically experimental, her books
merge myth and reality, past and present, female and male voices to universalize
her own, her family's, and her characters' experiences.

Early Life

Born in Stockton, California, Maxine Hong was the oldest of six children of
Chinese immigrant parents. Her father, the youngest of four brothers, had been a poet
and teacher in China before coming to the United States with the hopes of making his
fortune in 1925. After working at a variety of jobs in New York, Tom Hong (who
named himself for Thomas Edison) bought a laundry with some partners. He finally
saved enough money so that he could send for his wife. In January, 1940, Chew Ying
Lan arrived from China to join him, but not before she had been graduated from a
two-year medical school. Her husband wanted an educated wife to join him, not a
simple villager.

Her first two children now dead, Maxine's professionally trained mother came to
New York City to begin a new life as the wife of a laundryman. Soon afterward, she
moved again, when her husband's partners cheated him out of his share of their jointly
owned laundry. The couple eventually opened another laundry in Stockton, California, a working-class city housing people of many different backgrounds. With their
growing American-born family, they lived right near Skid Row, in a rough part of the
city.

Maxine's childhood was filled with contradictions. From her Chinese relatives, she
heard girl children denigrated. "Better raise geese than girls," they said, because
Chinese tradition dictated that after marriage a woman belonged to her husband's
family, not her own. Yet Maxine's mother taught her eldest daughter that she should
be strong, a warrior woman like the legendary Fa Mu Lan, an eleventh century female
avenger whose skill in battle destroyed her family's enemies.

Equally confusing was American school, where Maxine felt tongue-tied by the
English language and institutional racism, and timid about expressing herself. Only
in Chinese school, which she attended after the mandatory public school classes, did
she feel free to let loose and express herself. By the time she was in the fourth grade,
she was writing poems and stories, at least partly as an escape from the tensions of her
life.

By taking a series of odd jobs, Maxine put herself through the University of
California at Berkeley, being graduated in 1962 as an English major. The 1960's
matched her growing idealism. Protesting against the Vietnam War, she and other
young people thought they could change the world. By 1967, however, it became clear

that the war was not ending; it was, instead, escalating. After she married Earl Kingston, whom she had met at Berkeley, and became the mother of three-year-old Joseph, Maxine Hong Kingston moved to Hawaii.

In Hawaii, Kingston began working as a teacher. During her years there, she taught various subjects at all levels: grammar school, high school, business school, and college. Besides English and creative writing, Kingston also taught mathematics, journalism, and English as a second language. The teaching financed her own writing, which, by now, had become central in her life.

Life's Work

In her first book, *The Woman Warrior: Memoirs of a Girlhood Among Ghosts* (1976), Maxine Hong Kingston blends history and legend to tell her own story of growing up as a Chinese American woman. By re-creating and interpreting the stories she grew up hearing, Kingston tries to understand their relationship to her own life. She begins with the story of "No Name Woman," her father's sister, who commits suicide after being ostracized by her family and village for becoming pregnant when her husband was away in America. Next, she considers the story of the legendary Chinese swordswoman Fa Mu Lan, raised as a woman warrior, who donned men's clothing to save her village and rescue the honor of her family. With the story that follows, Kingston demonstrates that her mother, in her own way, was just as brave: After the death of her two children in China, Brave Orchid (as her name translates into English) studied medicine and served as a village doctor before joining her husband in the United States. In her maternal aunt's life, Kingston finds an example of female subservience: Lacking the self-confidence of her sister, Moon Orchid feels lost living outside China and eventually loses her sanity. Appropriately, Kingston ends the memoir with the story of Ts'ai Yen, a second century poet who was captured by a barbarian tribe but whose beautiful songs have survived.

Although these stories may seem to be disconnected, they are not. There are parts of all these women in the young Kingston, struggling to extricate herself from a Chinese culture that tells her that girls are less valuable than boys, that children (especially girls) should be seen but not heard. Like Fa Mu Lan and her mother, Kingston rejects traditional definitions of womanhood: She wants to be a writer. Like her rebel aunt, Kingston refuses to accept society's definition of the role she should play: She refuses to marry a nice Chinese American man and become a homemaker. Although at times she is fearful and silent, like her aunt, Kingston finds strength in her writing, as the captive T'sai Yen did. She refused to become a stereotype for the white culture or the subservient wife valued by the Chinese community.

The Woman Warrior was a huge success, receiving rave reviews and the prestigious National Book Critics Circle Award for nonfiction, but Kingston believed that she had told only half of the story. Her next book, *China Men* (1980), traces the lives of the men in her family, particularly her father, in an effort to understand them. Again, Kingston merges myth and reality to tell their stories, minimizing neither their weaknesses—most were sexist—nor their struggles, particularly against discrimination in their new land. Kingston sees these settlers, poets, teachers, sugar plantation workers, transcontinental railroad builders, laundrymen, and soldiers as American heroes.

As in *The Woman Warrior*, Kingston uses legends to reveal essential truths. In this case, she uses the ancient story of Tang Ao, who was captured when he ventured into the Land of Women. Transformed into a woman—ears pierced, feet bound, perfumed, and painted—the warrior finally sees how restrictive women's lives are. The story suggests both the various transformations her male relatives underwent in coming from China to the United States and the damaging effects of sexism. Although it tells a revenge story, like that of her aunt in Kingston's first book, the book as a whole is about forgiveness and understanding. Recognizing her accomplishment, a Honolulu Buddhist sect honored Kingston as a Living Treasure of Hawaii.

When *China Men* received the American Book Award, Kingston's popularity increased. Other honors followed, including the Hawaii Award for Literature in 1983. In 1987, a collection of essays she had written for *The New York Times* in 1978 appeared, accompanied by woodcuts by the artist Deng Ming-Dao. Called *Hawaii One Summer*, the book includes essays on subjects as varied as her first high school reunion, dishwashing, the Hawaiian landscape, and war.

By the time *China Men* appeared, Kingston had returned to California with her husband and son. She was working on a new book—a novel this time—about San Francisco in the 1960's, a place and time she knew from her own experience. Even more than her memoirs, *Tripmaster Monkey: His Fake Book* (1989) is epic in scope and execution. Wittman Ah Sing, a young Chinese American one year out of Berkeley, is the protagonist. A nonstop talker and aspiring playwright, Wittman is a rebel whose one ambition is to write and stage a play to end all plays: a show that would interweave Chinese novels and legends and include everything from pitched battles to flying horses. In the course of the novel, Wittman gets married, quits his job, falls in love with another woman, gets high on drugs, meets up with his family members, especially his outspoken aunts and his mother, former vaudeville performer Ruby Long Legs, and eventually stages his play.

Kingston alternates perspective in the novel: The reader sees the world not only through Wittman's eyes but also through the eyes of an older, wiser narrator, who is female. This device enables Kingston to experiment with different styles and levels of language: Wittman uses a hip, slangy style, while the narrator is more restrained. Clearly, Kingston intended this book to follow in the tradition of American celebrations such as American poet Walt Whitman's famous "Song of Myself" (1891). Just as Whitman enthusiastically celebrated life in powerful, seemingly unrestrained language, so too Kingston celebrates life in this contemporary comedy. Her hero is as American as the nineteenth century Whitman was; his struggles and triumphs are equally universal.

Summary

As one of the first Asian American woman writers to receive widespread critical attention, Maxine Hong Kingston paved the way for others to follow. Novelist Amy Tan, for example, claims that Kingston's success was a major influence on her own decision to write fiction. By 1989, mainstream presses published Amy Tan's *The Joy Luck Club* and Japanese American novelist Cynthia Kadohata's *The Floating World* to rave reviews, and works by other Asian American women have followed. A few women writers had preceded Kingston: She talks about being influenced by Jade Snow Wong's autobiography, *Fifth Chinese Daughter* (1950). For the most part, however, Kingston grew up never seeing works by people like herself in print. It was Kingston, and writers like her, whose powerful stories and exquisite writing styles convinced mainstream critics that American literature is not limited to recounting the white, middle-class male experience.

By reworking traditional stories, merging fact and fiction, and experimenting with point of view, Kingston has become an important literary innovator. Genre categories such as autobiography, biography, nonfiction, and fiction fail to describe her work: She stretches the limits of the forms and transforms them.

Throughout her career, Kingston has spoken out against sexism, racism, and violence of all kinds. A pacifist and feminist, Kingston sees her life and her work as one: Her goal is to help create a more peaceful world. Explaining what she wants to do in her writing, she said in an interview, "An artist changes the world by changing consciousness and changing the atmosphere by means of language."

Bibliography

Kingston, Maxine Hong. *China Men.* New York: Alfred A. Knopf, 1980. Part two of Kingston's search for her own identity through the lives of her ancestors, this multigenerational study examines her father's life and those of her male relatives.

—————. *The Woman Warrior: Memoirs of a Girlhood Among Ghosts.* New York: Alfred A. Knopf, 1976. A memoir describing Kingston's childhood, interspersing her own life and her mother's life with stories from the family past and Chinese legends.

Lim, Shirley Geok-lin, ed. *Approaches to Teaching Kingston's "The Woman Warrior."* New York: Modern Language Association of America, 1991. This collection of essays by high school and college teachers discusses how they have used Kingston's memoir in their classes. Individual essays examine topics as diverse as the Asian literary background of the book, its place as a postmodern autobiography, and student responses.

Lim, Shirley Geok-lin, and Amy Ling, eds. *Reading the Literatures of Asian America.* Philadelphia: Temple University Press, 1992. These twenty essays provide a comprehensive introduction to Asian American literature. Four of the essays deal directly with Kingston: "Don't Tell: Imposed Silences in *The Color Purple* and *The Woman Warrior*," "Tang Ao in America: Male Subject Positions in *China Men*," "The Production of Chinese American Tradition: Displacing American Orientalist Discourse," and "Clashing Constructs of Reality: Reading Maxine Hong Kingston's *Tripmaster Monkey: His Fake Book* as Indigenous Ethnography."

Perry, Donna, ed. "Maxine Hong Kingston." In *Backtalk: Women Writers Speak Out*. New Brunswick, N.J.: Rutgers University Press, 1993. An in-depth interview with Kingston, who talks about her books, her life, Asian American literature, the politics of publishing, and future writing projects, including a sequel to *Tripmaster Monkey*.

Smith, Sidonie. "Maxine Hong Kingston's *Woman Warrior*: Filiality and Women's Autobiographical Storytelling." In *A Poetics of Women's Autobiography: Marginality and the Fictions of Self-Representation*. Bloomington: Indiana University Press, 1987. In this study of five historically important autobiographies by women writing in English, Smith sees Kingston's memoir as a challenge to the ideology of individualism and gender. Includes excellent descriptive notes on the memoir and related issues.

Donna Perry

JEANE KIRKPATRICK

Born: November 19, 1926; Duncan, Oklahoma

Areas of Achievement: Diplomacy, government and politics, and women's rights
Contributions: The first woman to serve as American Ambassador to the United Nations (1981-1985), Kirkpatrick also wrote one of the first books on women and American politics, giving that new field of scholarship legitimacy.

Early Life

Jeane Duane Jordan was born in Duncan, Oklahoma, a small town forty miles from Texas where her father was an oil business contractor and her mother kept books for the family business. She was born November 19, 1926; her brother Jerry was born eight years later. Like most Oklahomans, the Jordans were Democrats and avid supporters of Franklin D. Roosevelt. Jeane's grandfather Jordan, a Texas justice of the peace, had a collection of law books that Jeane found fascinating. Jeane's mother loved to read and inspired her daughter's lifelong love for reading and writing.

When Jeane was twelve, the family moved to Illinois. By the time she entered high school, Jeane had become an accomplished pianist and had developed a love for literature. She was a straight "A" student at Vandalia High School, edited the school newspaper, and acted in plays. In her senior year, she wrote an essay about George Eliot, the British nineteenth century woman writer who used a male name in order to publish her work. Although Jeane's mother encouraged her daughter to pursue whatever goals she chose, her father wanted her to get married. She chose college.

Jeane embarked on her college years with enthusiasm, focusing on the liberal arts courses at Stephens College in Columbia, Missouri, then moving on to be graduated in 1948 from Barnard College in New York with a degree in political science. She told friends that her goal in life was to be a spinster teacher at a women's college. Her favorite author was Virginia Woolf. Then, daring to do what was quite untraditional at the time, she completed a master's degree from Columbia University and would have continued with doctoral studies had her father not decided it was time for her to support herself. She went to the nation's capital, political science degrees and references in hand, seeking a job. The doctorate would come later.

Jeane was successful in finding jobs in Washington, D.C., including one at the State Department, where she met Evron Kirkpatrick. She also won a fellowship that enabled her to spend a year studying communism in France, and a research position at George Washington University gave her an opportunity to explore Chinese communism while developing research techniques she would use later in life. At the Economic Cooperation Administration, she helped to write a book about the Marshall Plan. Her satisfaction in the work was marred by the author's failure to acknowledge her contributions.

By 1955, Jeane and Evron Kirkpatrick had been dating for about five years. The two intellectuals married, spending their honeymoon at a political science convention near Chicago. Jeane continued working at George Washington University until the first of her three sons was born in 1956. At that point, based on her motto "refuse to choose," she combined motherhood with her career.

During the early 1960's, Kirkpatrick combined her at-home academic work with Democratic Party politics. She and her husband actively supported John F. Kennedy's candidacy in 1960. In 1962, their youngest son entered nursery school and Kirkpatrick took a part-time teaching position at Trinity College, a small women's college near Washington, D.C. While teaching there, she completed her first book, *The Strategy of Deception: A Study in World-wide Communist Tactics*, a collection of essays that analyzed the rise of communist governments outside the Soviet Union.

In 1968, Kirkpatrick completed her Ph.D. at Columbia University. Her dissertation about Perónist politics in Argentina was later published by the MIT Press. Deciding that her children were old enough for her to return to full-time teaching, she applied for and won a position in Georgetown University's political science department. She was to become only the second woman in the university's history to win tenure. It was the beginning of an illustrious career that spanned the academic, political, and journalism professions.

Life's Work

Jeane Kirkpatrick's disillusionment with the Democratic Party began during the late 1960's. During that period, riots took place following the assassinations of Martin Luther King, Jr., and Robert F. Kennedy, a 1968 presidential candidate. It was a time of extreme frustration, violence, and urgent demands for change in cities and on campuses around the nation. Some of the worst violence took place at the August, 1968, Democratic Party Convention in Chicago. Students demonstrated at Columbia University, too, making it difficult for Kirkpatrick to deliver her dissertation to Columbia's library.

Kirkpatrick supported Hubert Humphrey's Democratic Party candidacy in 1968, which he lost to Richard Nixon. In 1972, however, she voted against Democratic challenger George McGovern. In the first of many articles she would write for the journal *Commentary*, she argued that McGovern represented a set of counterculture values that most Americans, herself included, rejected. Nixon, however, established himself as a supporter of traditional American values and as a fervent opponent of communism. The strategy won him Kirkpatrick's vote and a landslide victory over McGovern.

Kirkpatrick's studies of totalitarian governments led her to advocate an anticommunist foreign policy that came to be known as the Kirkpatrick doctrine. It advocated support for right-wing authoritarian leaders if that support would weaken left-wing totalitarianism. It was a policy that the Reagan Administration was to apply to its relations with Central and Latin American governments in the 1980's.

Following the 1972 election, Kirkpatrick became associated with neoconservative thought, which combined opposition to communism and belief in a strong military with liberal views on social issues. Kirkpatrick was very concerned, for example, about the obvious absence of women in government. Her research about that concern led to the publication in 1974 of America's first major book about women in government. *Political Woman* gave Kirkpatrick new recognition outside of academia and gave legitimacy to the emerging study of women in politics. Acclaimed as an expert on the topic, she was asked to represent the United States at a 1975 International Women's Year conference held in West Africa.

In 1976, Kirkpatrick wrote *The New Presidential Elite: Men and Women in National Politics*. Whereas *Political Woman* had focused on state government, the new book studied women at the national level of government. In addition to being well received, the second book also won Kirkpatrick an invitation to join the staff of the American Enterprise Institute (AEI), one of Washington's oldest think tanks. She spent 1977 working full-time at the institute, then returned to Georgetown University while continuing part-time work at the AEI. At the Institute, Kirkpatrick became the first woman to serve as a senior scholar.

During the Jimmy Carter Administration, Kirkpatrick wrote one of her most influential articles for *Commentary* magazine. In "Dictatorships and Double Standards," she argued that Carter failed to appreciate communism's threat and reiterated her belief that the United States sometimes needed to fight totalitarianism by supporting authoritarian regimes. At issue was Carter's support for leftist Sandinistas in Nicaragua. Carter thought that the Sandinistas were more likely to evolve toward democracy than the corrupt Somoza government was. Kirkpatrick pointed out that no communist system in the past had ever become democratic.

Kirkpatrick's article won her the admiration of 1980 presidential candidate Ronald Reagan, who made her foreign policy adviser during his campaign and in 1981 appointed her Ambassador to the United Nations; she was the first woman to hold the latter position. The president won considerable acclaim for his Reagan doctrine, which was an adaptation of the proposal Kirkpatrick presented in "Dictatorships and Double Standards."

As head of her country's U.N. delegation, Kirkpatrick earned a reputation as a capable, if not always popular, negotiator. Her first victory was a difficult compromise she negotiated in response to Israel's 1981 bombing of Iraq's nuclear reactor. President Reagan called her handling of the incident heroic, and Iraq's foreign minister was so impressed that he commented, "One Kirkpatrick was equal to more than two men. Maybe three." That kind of positive response was unusual, however, in the male-dominated United Nations. Ambassador Kirkpatrick often had to cope with sexism among her colleagues.

In addition to sexism, Kirkpatrick had to deal with anti-American attitudes at the United Nations. She developed a theory about why the United States had had difficulty influencing General Assembly decisions since the 1970's. In her view, the United States failed to adapt to a system of coalitions that emerged when dozens of newly independent developing nations became United Nations members starting in the 1960's. Because it refused to participate in any of the new coalitions, the United States lost its ability to influence decisions. During her four years at the United Nations, Kirkpatrick worked to strengthen America's position there while also focusing on the dangers of communism in Central and Latin America.

Early in 1985, Kirkpatrick resigned her U.N. position to return to family and scholarly responsibilities. She continued her association with Georgetown University and the American Enterprise Institute, resuming a heavy schedule of writing that included books, articles, and a syndicated *Los Angeles Times* column on post-Cold War developments. She assumed positions on various foreign-policy related associations, including the Defense Policy Review Board and the Council on Foreign Relations.

Only after her U.N. resignation did Kirkpatrick officially change her voting registration to Republican, prompting discussion of her potential as a 1988 presidential candidate. Although she decided not to run, she had the support of an unusual coalition of conservatives, who appreciated her foreign policy positions, and feminists, who appreciated her stand on women's issues. She had always supported passage of the Equal Rights Amendment, and she generally advocated gender equity.

Summary

Commenting on her years at the United Nations, Kirkpatrick once pointed out that she had been the only woman in history who sat in regularly at top-level foreign policy-making meetings. Those kinds of meetings, she said, had historically been closed to women in most countries. In her view, it matters very much that women have been so excluded. "It's terribly important," she said, "maybe even to the future of the world, for women to take part in making the decisions that shape our destiny."

As a mother of three sons who grew up during the Vietnam War years, Kirkpatrick came to believe that force should be used to resolve conflict only in the most extraordinary circumstances. She believed fervently in using diplomatic negotiation as the primary method for resolving international disputes, and she will be remembered primarily as the first woman to serve as America's principal negotiator at the United Nations. Her scholarly work will also stand as a testament to her commitment to the intellectual analysis of international relations.

Kirkpatrick's advice to women was to "refuse to choose" between motherhood and career. Although many women will not have that luxury, Kirkpatrick is nevertheless an inspiration to those women who want to take control of their own lives so that they can at least expand their range of opportunities. She is especially important as a model for young women who hope to lead productive, satisfying lives.

Bibliography
Crapol, Edward P., ed. *Women and American Foreign Policy: Lobbyists, Critics, and Insiders.* New York: Greenwood Press, 1987. This scholarly volume analyzes women's roles in the historical development of U.S. foreign policy. Judith Ewell's chapter seeks explanations for Kirkpatrick's limited impact on U.S. foreign policy.

Harrison, Pat. *Jeane Kirkpatrick.* New York: Chelsea House, 1991. Part of the American Women of Achievement youth series, this short, illustrated biography describes Kirkpatrick's personal and political life in positive, anecdotal terms.

Kirkpatrick, Jeane. *Political Woman*. New York: Basic Books, 1974. A project of Rutgers University's Center for the American Woman and Politics, this study of women serving in state governments was the first major scholarly examination of women in politics.

——————— . *The Withering Away of the Totalitarian State—and Other Surprises*. Washington, D.C.: American Enterprise Institute Press, 1990. In this collection of columns written between 1985 and 1990, Kirkpatrick analyzes post-Cold War events in the Soviet Union.

LeVeness, Frank P., and Jane P. Sweeney, eds. *Women Leaders in Contemporary U.S. Politics*. Boulder, Colo.: Lynne Rienner, 1987. Naomi B. Lynn's chapter on Kirkpatrick's rise from political science professor to participant in international politics is based on analysis of Kirkpatrick's written work, on interviews with Kirkpatrick, and on interviews with people who have known her.

Susan MacFarland

BLANCHE WOLF KNOPF

Born: July 30, 1894; New York, New York
Died: June 4, 1966; New York, New York
Area of Achievement: Publishing
Contribution: A leading American publisher, Knopf played a key role in shaping the intellectual and cultural climate of the nation. Among other things, she brought Simone de Beauvoir's classic feminist treatise *The Second Sex* to the American public.

Early Life

Blanche Wolf was born on July 30, 1894, in New York City to a relatively wealthy Jewish family. Although she attended New York's Gardner School, her parents saw to it that her education was rounded out by the addition of French and German governesses. Her early exposure to continental literature, language, and thought would later serve her well as she sought out and promoted new talent on the international market.

Blanche met Alfred A. Knopf in 1911 when her family was residing at Long Island for the summer; they were married on April 4, 1916, and two years later they had their first and only child, Alfred A. Knopf, Jr. With Blanche's encouragement, Alfred A. Knopf launched a book publishing company the year before their marriage. After their first child was born, Blanche Knopf hired a full-time nurse so that she would be able to pursue her growing interest in, and talent for, the publishing house she had helped to found.

Knopf's first trip to Europe in 1920 put her in contact with many of the most prestigious publishing firms of England and the Continent—in fact, it was during this trip that her skills at negotiation became apparent. By 1921, she had become a director and vice president of the corporation that bore as its official title her husband's name, Alfred A. Knopf.

In spite of the discrepancies between Blanche's and Alfred's titles within the corporation, the firm's formation had been a joint enterprise, and Blanche's negotiations in Europe firmly established her leadership role within the international book publishing community. This reputation grew when, only a decade later, she began a series of trips that resulted in contractual agreements with writers such as André Gide, Ilya Ehrenburg, Mikhail Sholokhov, and Thomas Mann. Moreover, in 1938, she managed a major publishing coup by convincing Sigmund Freud to publish his last work, *Moses and Monotheism*, with Knopf.

Life's Work

Blanche Knopf was unusually well suited for her chosen field. She had a flair for social intercourse, a love of negotiation and strategic bargaining, a keen sense of cultural and literary trends, an eye for talent, and a talent for gaining political advantage; these qualities combined to make her one of the most formidable publishers of her day.

The period during World War II was especially fruitful for Blanche Knopf. Because travel to Europe was dangerous and often restricted, she turned her attention to a literary source that had been largely ignored by U.S. and European publishing houses: Latin America. Seeking to discover new talent, she traveled extensively throughout Central and South America. She made several successful agreements with authors, such as the Brazilian sociologist Gilberto Freyre, and established an interest in publishing translations, which would become a hallmark of her firm.

As a result of her sponsorship of the great writers of the Southern Hemisphere, she was lauded internationally and frequently given special recognition by foreign dignitaries. In 1950, for example, she was made a Cavaleiro of the Brazilian National Order of the Southern Cross. In 1964, she was again decorated, this time receiving the title of Oficial.

After the end of the war, Knopf was able to return to her interests in promoting the publication and sales of European authors in the American market. Her social and political acumen resulted in contracts with authors such as Jean-Paul Sartre, Albert Camus, and Simone de Beauvoir. These and other authors published by Knopf have had a lasting influence on the development of intellectual trends in the United States.

Blanche Knopf's determination to publish Simone de Beauvoir's famous feminist treatise *The Second Sex* (1953; *Le Deuxième sexe*, 1949) has proved to be one of her most lasting contributions to the study of women's lives. McCarthyism held sway at the time, making Knopf's decision to translate and publish de Beauvoir's work all the more remarkable. *The Second Sex* dealt with important social and political issues such as sexual initiation, prostitution, lesbianism, and role restrictions. Although Knopf was careful to package the book in such a way that the radical nature of its theme was not emphasized, she did take full advantage of its provocative title as part of the larger marketing campaign.

Although Knopf was originally uncertain about the value of the French treatise, she eventually concluded that it was a work that deserved the attention of the American reading public. She spoke enthusiastically of de Beauvoir's book, lauding it as emancipatory and enlightening for both women and men, a work not condemning but convincing. Knopf's commitment to the book's publication became apparent when many peculiar difficulties began to mount.

The publication of *The Second Sex* was no easy matter. Not only was McCarthyism rampant, but de Beauvoir proved to be a difficult author with whom to work. On several occasions the writer refused to meet with Blanche Knopf, and at other times she refused to respond to queries about even the most practical of matters bearing on the book's publication and distribution. Knopf was determined to bring the book to the public, however, and eventually she managed to overcome obstacles posed by both the political climate of the time and the author's stubborn resistance to translation and U.S. publication.

Knopf believed that *The Second Sex* was one of the finest translations her company had produced—it was certainly not the last. For her continued promotion of French literature, and for her graceful recognition of its intellectual and aesthetic value, she was named a Chevalier of the French Legion of Honor by the French Ambassador in 1949. She was later made an Officer.

Blanche Knopf was also responsible for the firm's interest and investment in African American writers. She is especially known for having had a profound impact on the highly talented Langston Hughes. As illustrated by the personal letters exchanged between Knopf and Hughes, the two established a level of closeness and confidence that is rare in publishing circles. Hughes frequently sought her advice on personal matters as well as information on book sales and distribution, and Knopf freely gave her counsel.

Knopf also went out of her way to promote Hughes's best interests, sometimes even acting as his agent in order to negotiate royalties for his work which were normally difficult to obtain. She frequently wrangled extra fees from anthologists when Hughes was too bashful or proud to broach the matter with cutthroat editors. Although the relationship between Knopf and Hughes was later overshadowed with uncomfortable political tension, especially after Hughes's poetry collection *Fine Clothes to the Jew* (1927) came out, they nevertheless managed to remain friends.

Although Knopf was known for having an explosive temper, she was generous in her support and encouragement of budding writers such as Hughes. In a period when publishers often took advantage of the desperate financial straits in which many authors found themselves, Knopf was a notable exception. She wrote numerous personal letters of encouragement or consolation to writers who were struggling not only with their art but also with the gritty exigencies of the need to market their work. Moreover, she frequently added financial aid to moral support, a habit that did much to foster the growth of such writers.

In spite of Knopf's many contributions, however, her chosen profession continued to be openly discriminatory against women. Social organizations such as the Publisher's Lunch Club and the Book Table refused to admit her to their number, a difficult snub to bear when her husband was openly a member of both. In spite of these continued slights, Knopf persevered in her career to become one of the most influential editors to introduce American readers to a larger world of literary culture—a fact that her husband would respectfully acknowledge later in his memoirs.

Knopf's greatest challenge was the erosion of her sight as she aged. As time passed, she was frequently forced to rely on others for opinions about the quality of manuscripts being considered for publication. Rather than relinquish her influence, however, she frequently had passages of manuscripts read aloud to her: The final decision, though influenced by those whose judgment she trusted, was nevertheless always her own. Her influence in the firm did not abate with age, and her prominence as a sculptor of literary inclination lasted until her death in 1966.

Summary

Blanche Wolf Knopf played a key role in founding one of the most influential publishing companies in the United States. In fact, she was the single key figure at Knopf who promoted the works of Latin American, African American, and European writers. An extremely intelligent woman who could recognize talent, promote the good of the author, and still act in the interests of her firm, Knopf played a major role in establishing a receptivity to new literary currents. In a field dominated by men, she was highly competitive, unquestionably successful, and unusually independent. The words that accompanied her honorary degree of Doctor of Letters from Franklin and Marshall College in 1962 aptly summarize her impact: "Her successful career as a publisher, her enlightened understanding of the mutual respect required between author and publisher, her encouragement of promising literary talents have made her one of the most influential women of our time."

Bibliography

Englund, Sheryl A. "Publicity to Overawe the Public: Marketing *The Second Sex.*" *Library Chronicle of the University of Texas* 22, no. 4 (1992): 102-121. Based on information from the Alfred A. Knopf Archive at the University of Texas at Austin, this article delineates the skill required to bring *The Second Sex* successfully to the U.S. market. It also provides a very detailed portrait of Blanche Knopf working against intimidating odds.

Fadiman, Clifton, ed. *Fifty Years: Being a Retrospective Collection . . . Drawn from Volumes Issued During the Last Half-Century by Alfred and Blanche Knopf.* New York: Alfred A. Knopf, 1965. The introduction to this book pays considerable attention to Blanche Knopf's influence on the firm and on the shaping of literary taste more generally.

Flora, Peter. "Carl Van Vechten, Blanche Knopf, and the Harlem Renaissance." *Library Chronicle of the University of Texas* 22, no. 4 (1992): 64-83. Although it focuses mainly on Carl Van Vechten, this article does attest the influence of Blanche Knopf as the key figure behind the contractual agreements set up with African American writers.

Kauffman, Stanley. "Album of the Knopfs." *The American Scholar* 56 (Summer, 1987): 371-381. A semi-autobiographical account of the author's experience as an employee of Knopf. Kauffman is blunt in his depictions but generous in detail.

Lewis, Randolph. "Langston Hughes and Alfred A. Knopf, Inc., 1925-1935." *Library Chronicle of the University of Texas* 22, no. 4 (1992): 52-63. A scholarly, well-researched article that paints an enlightening picture of the relationship between Knopf and Hughes. This article also illustrates the work that remains to be done on the life of Blanche Knopf. Much information about her is available in the archives at the University of Texas, but little serious scholarly attention has been paid to Blanche Knopf's life and influence.

Postgate, John. "Glimpses of the Blitz." *History Today* 43 (1993): 21-28. Provides excerpts from Postgate's wartime correspondence with Blanche and Alfred Knopf. A useful tool for understanding Blanche Knopf's incredible skill at negotiation.

B. R. Siegfried

LEE KRASNER

Born: October 27, 1908; New York, New York
Died: June 19, 1984; New York, New York
Area of Achievement: Art
Contribution: Lee Krasner was a leader in the abstract expressionist movement in the United States. She spoke out for women's rights and became an example of a woman who took her work seriously within a movement that was dominated by males.

Early Life

Lenore "Lena" Krassner was born in Brooklyn, New York, on October 27, 1908. She was the fourth of five children born to Russian parents who had immigrated to the United States. Lenore's parents were Orthodox Jews who owned and ran a produce store in Brooklyn.

As a girl, Lenore was drawn to the visual arts. From 1922 to 1925, she attended Washington Irving High School in Manhattan, the only secondary school that allowed females to study art. From 1926 to 1929, Lenore attended the Woman's Art School of the Cooper Union for the Advancement of Science and Art in New York. In 1929, Lenore enrolled at The National Academy of Design in New York, a traditional art school, where she studied life drawing, painting, and techniques of the Old Masters. It was also during this year that Lenore was first introduced to the more radical, experimental art of modern European artists such as Henri Matisse and Pablo Picasso. The work of both of these artists was to be highly influential in the development of Lenore's own art.

Because of the ensuing Depression economy, Lenore dropped out of art school in 1932 and began working as a waitress. She also attended City College of New York, working toward a high school teaching credential, but she soon realized that she had no interest in teaching. By this time, Lenore Krassner had become dedicated to living her life as an artist; although she had taken many years of traditional art training, she was becoming increasingly interested in more modern, experimental art.

Life's Work

Lee Krasner's career as a professional artist began in 1935, when she was hired by the WPA (Works Progress Administration) Federal Art Project. Krasner was hired as part of the mural division of this government-subsidized project, which had as its goal the decoration of public spaces with large-scale realistic, socially conscious painting. Krasner worked for the WPA until 1943, making murals, posters, and displays for department store windows. During this period, Krasner began calling herself Lee and dropped an "s" from her last name.

Although Krasner's work for the WPA was primarily realistic, her personal style was becoming more abstract. In 1937, Krasner entered the Hans Hofmann School of Fine Arts in New York. Hans Hofmann was a German artist who immigrated to New

York in 1932 and became an influential exponent of modern European art in the United States. He served as a link with major artists such as Picasso and Matisse, and he taught their ideas and techniques at his school. He emphasized the tenets of cubism, spatial tension, and all-over composition. Hofmann believed in painting subjects from nature but emphasizing energy, tension, form, and color rather than detail and scientific accuracy.

Lee Krasner had already become interested in Hoffman's ideas. At Hofmann's school, Krasner studied the cubist style and began creating in a more abstract style that emphasized form, color, line, and rhythm. She retained subject matter but presented it in a simplified, abstract, and geometric manner. Her focus became self-expression rather than the duplication of particular subjects.

By 1937, Krasner had read *System and Dialectics of Art* by the writer and artist John Graham, who was to become a major inspiration to the abstract expressionists. Graham promoted the idea that pure feeling could be represented on canvas through automatic, spontaneous movement of the brush. He emphasized psychological content, emotionality, and drama in painting. Graham's concepts appealed to Krasner, since she was already moving away from the more intellectual, analytical thought of Hans Hofmann. She was searching for a means of painting that would be more directly emotional, spiritual, and psychological in nature.

In 1940, Lee Krasner began to exhibit with the American Abstract Artists (AAA). She participated in the "First Annual Exhibition of the American Modern Artists," held at Riverside Museum in New York (1940), and the "Fifth Annual Exhibition of the American Abstract Artists," which was organized by the WPA and traveled throughout the United States in 1941. At that time, Krasner was showing abstract paintings with thick black outlines, bright colors, and heavily impasted oil paint. Many of her paintings from this period were based on subjects from nature or still lifes, others were nonrepresentational (without recognizable subject matter).

John Graham invited Krasner to show her work in an important exhibition he organized in 1942, entitled "French and American Painting," in which the work of young modern American artists would be shown alongside that of famous modern French artists, including Matisse and the cubist painter Georges Braque. Jackson Pollock, who was to become one of the most famous modern American painters, was also invited to participate in the exhibition. It was at this time that Krasner and Pollock met. They were married in 1945 and purchased an old farmhouse in Springs, East Hampton, Long Island, where they both had studios.

Both Krasner and Pollock are identified as leaders in the first wave of the abstract expressionist movement, which was the first major modern art style to originate in the United States. Abstract expressionism is a nonrepresentational style in which line, form, and color are spontaneously arranged on a canvas or painting surface. Paint is brushed, swirled, dripped, or poured onto the surface in an automatic, gestural manner. The goal is to express one's inner spirit. Many of the abstract expressionists, including Krasner and Pollock, were influenced by the writings of Carl Jung, Eastern religions, and mystical religious traditions in general. The movement stressed the spontaneous expression of the self, emotion, and the spiritual, through color, line, form, and gesture.

Although Lee Krasner's career was less public than Pollock's, she has been recognized as one of the pioneers of the American abstract expressionist movement and as an artist who continually expanded and created innovative forms. While she was married to Pollock, Krasner was inspired by him, dedicated to him, and overshadowed by him. The public most often viewed her simply as Jackson Pollock's wife. The Krasner-Pollock relationship was, however, based on mutual support and encouragement. Krasner was influenced by Pollock, but he was also influenced by her, and much of Krasner's work presents ideas and techniques that are very different from Pollock's.

In 1946, Krasner made two mosaic tables that may have been the inspiration for a series of paintings she executed between 1946 and 1950, called the "Little Image" paintings. On a series of small- to medium-sized canvases, she brushed, scraped, and dripped oil paint into dense arrangements of small rhythmic images encompassing the entire canvas surface and resembling hieroglyphics or intricate webbings.

Cyclical change is one of the hallmarks of Krasner's career: She changed her subject matter, format, and technique every few years, but would often return to ideas that had interested her in the past. In the early 1950's, Krasner made large-scale paintings based on mysterious figural and floral forms. Her technique was automatic drawing done directly on canvas with oil paint. Large, graceful forms moved rhythmically across the canvas, as in her *Blue and Black* (1951-1953). Krasner worked regularly throughout the 1950's, but because the abstract expressionist movement was becoming increasingly male-dominated and because of her association with Pollock, she was not receiving much recognition from the galleries or the press.

Few paintings from Krasner's earlier periods survive. Some were destroyed by fire; others she destroyed herself or cut up to use in collages. During the 1950's, she began including bits of paper and parts of her old canvases in her new paintings. Continuing her interest in expressive, nonrepresentational paintings and nonillusionistic (without perspective) space, Krasner incorporated and overlapped abstract painted forms with frayed, torn, and cut areas of paper and old canvases. These collage paintings, which are among Krasner's most innovative works, were exhibited at Eleanor Ward's Stable Gallery in New York in 1955.

In July of 1956, Krasner took her first trip to Europe. It was there, in August, that she was informed that Pollock had been killed in a car accident. She returned to New York immediately. After Pollock's death, Krasner painted large canvases with brightly colored, intensely energetic abstract compositions based loosely on natural forms such as flowers, fruit, and the human body.

Krasner returned to the medium of mosaic again in 1959, when she executed two large mosaic murals for the exterior of the Uris Brothers office building in New York. In 1959, she also began her series of huge, powerful umber and off-white paintings, which she worked on until 1962. These paintings were shown in solo exhibitions at the Howard Wise Gallery in New York between 1960 and 1962.

After 1962, Krasner returned to a more vibrant color scheme that included brilliant greens, raspberry, yellows, and oranges. Her forms were essentially nonrepresentational, but their organic and flowing quality suggests birds, flowers, and plants boldly surging across the canvases in joyous, lyrical moods. In 1965, Krasner was given a retrospective exhibition at the Whitechapel Art Gallery in London, England, which included these works. In 1966, she joined the Marlborough Gallery in New York.

During the early 1970's, Krasner created several huge canvases in a more hardedged style, composing crisp, spare geometric designs that seem to explode from the canvas, as in *Rising Green* (1972). Throughout the later 1970's, she made another series of collage paintings, this time incorporating cut-up sections of her old charcoal drawings and combining fragments of figural forms with forceful abstract painted forms. In these works, she deconstructed past ideas, reworked them, and brought them into a new realm and into new paintings with titles that play on the idea of time, such as *Past Conditional* (1976) and *Imperfect Indicative* (1976).

Although Krasner was still not taken as seriously as the male artists of the abstract expressionist movement, she began to receive much more attention by the 1970's. In 1974, she was awarded the Augustus St. Gaudens Medal by the Cooper Union Alumni Association and the Lowe Fellowship for Distinction from Barnard College. In 1976, she joined the prestigious Pace Gallery in New York, and in 1978 she was the only woman included in the major exhibition "Abstract Expressionism: The Formative Years," which was shown at the Herbert F. Johnson Museum of Art at Cornell University, the Whitney Museum of American Art in New York, and the Seibu Museum in Tokyo, Japan.

During the early 1980's, Lee Krasner continued to paint and exhibit. She joined the Robert Miller Gallery, New York, in 1981. In 1982, she was awarded the Chevalier de l'Ordre des Arts et des Lettres by the French Minister of Culture. She traveled to Houston, Texas, in 1983 for a major retrospective exhibition of her work which was given at the Museum of Fine Arts. Lee Krasner died in New York on June 19, 1984. She left funds and paintings to create a foundation for needy artists, and she asked that the house in Springs be given to a charitable institution. It was opened as the Pollock-Krasner House and Study Center in 1988.

Summary

Although Lee Krasner is recognized as one of the pioneers of the American abstract expressionist movement and is identified as a member of the first wave, or first generation, of that movement, she has never received as much attention or serious study as the male members of that movement have. Although women were involved in it, the abstract expressionist movement has most often been viewed as a maleoriented phenomenon. For this reason and because of her close association with Jackson Pollock, Krasner has been overshadowed by the male artists of the movement.

Krasner herself was aware of this situation and often spoke out for women's rights. She believed in equality for women and in women's right to express themselves. She took her own work extremely seriously. Although she was married to Pollock and admired his work, her art was experimental and innovative, and her artistic explorations were most often very different from those of Pollock. In 1972, she picketed the Museum of Modern Art in New York because it was not showing enough work by women artists. She received an honorary award from the Long Island Women Achievers in Business and the Professions in 1977, and in 1980 she was presented with the Outstanding Achievement in the Visual Arts Award by the Women's Caucus for Art.

Lee Krasner was a leader in the development of abstract, nonrepresentational, experimental art styles in the United States. She was one of the first artists in the country to explore the use of color, form, line, and gesture to express inner psychological, spiritual, and emotional realities. She was also one of the first artists in the United States to explore widely diverse painting techniques such as automatism, dripping, and collage. For these reasons, Krasner's importance in the history of modern American art cannot be overestimated. The ideas that Krasner brought forth in her art became some of the hallmarks of many modern artists in America in the twentieth century. In particular, her art, as well as the art of the other first wave abstract expressionists, was a direct and profound influence on the second wave of abstract expressionists, including Joan Mitchell and Helen Frankenthaler.

Bibliography
Hobbs, Robert. *Lee Krasner*. New York: Abbeville Press, 1993. This well-written book chronicles Krasner's life and career from childhood to death, with a focus on the development of her art. Includes ninety-three black-and-white and color illustrations as well as a chronology, a bibliography, list of exhibitions, and "Artist's Statements."
Landau, Ellen G. "Lee Krasner's Early Career." Parts 1-2. *Arts Magazine* 56 (October/November, 1981). This two-part article is extremely important. It thoroughly documents Krasner's early career, from her childhood to the 1950's. The focus is on her education, influences, and the "Little Images" paintings. Includes twenty-three illustrations—among them some of the rarely shown early works—and footnotes.
Munro, Eleanor. *Originals: American Women Artists*. New York: Simon & Schuster, 1979. Twenty pages of this book are dedicated to a discussion of Krasner's life and career. The book also addresses the situation of twentieth century women artists in the United States and views Krasner in the context of "Women of the First Wave: Elders of the Century." Includes a bibliography and five illustrations.
Rose, Barbara. *Lee Krasner: A Retrospective*. New York: Museum of Modern Art, 1983. An extremely detailed, important work written in conjunction with Krasner's 1983 retrospective in Houston. Documents Krasner's life and career from childhood to 1983, focusing on her education, work for the WPA, influences, marriage, and philosophy. Includes more than 155 black-and-white and color illustrations, a chronology, and a bibliography.
Tucker, Marcia. *Lee Krasner: Large Paintings*. New York: Whitney Museum of American Art, 1973. A brief but very informative discussion of the development of Krasner's painting and collage styles and techniques, focusing on her work from

the 1930's through the 1960's. Addresses the issues of Krasner's philosophy, influences, and education. Includes eighteen color and black-and-white illustrations of paintings, a chronology, and a bibliography.

Nannette Fabré Kelly

JUANITA KREPS

Born: January 11, 1921; Lynch, Kentucky

Areas of Achievement: Economics, education, and government and politics
Contribution: An economist, higher educational administrator, and secretary of commerce under the Carter Administration, Kreps was dedicated to improving the well-being of people and facilitating the smooth operation of the economy.

Early Life

Juanita Morris, the sixth child of Elmer M. Morris and Larcenia Blair Morris, was of Scots-Irish ancestry. She was born in Harlan County, Kentucky, a very poor region plagued by labor strife. Her father operated a coal mine for United States Steel. When Juanita was four, her parents divorced, and she lived with her mother for the next eight years. At age twelve, Juanita went to a Presbyterian boarding school.

She attended grade school during the Depression and said that, at that time, everyone was poor. Her family was not in any worse financial shape than anyone else's.

In 1938, Juanita enrolled at Berea College. Many students there participated in a work-study program designed to make college affordable for students from this poor region of Appalachia. At Berea, Juanita majored in economics because she thought an understanding of that subject would help foster greater insight into world events. During college, Juanita also was elected to Phi Beta Kappa, a prestigious academic honor society. She said that the spirit of Berea, with its emphasis on integrity, self-reliance, independence, and academic excellence influenced her more than childhood events.

Juanita earned a master's degree and a Ph.D. in economics from Duke University in North Carolina in 1944 and 1948, respectively. While doing graduate work, Morris taught part-time at Duke from 1942 to 1944. She served as junior economist at the National War Labor Board in the summer of 1943 in Atlanta and in the summer of 1944 in Washington, D.C.

On August 11, 1944, Juanita Morris married Clifton Kreps, Jr., who became a professor of banking at the University of North Carolina. The couple had three children, Sarah, Laura, and Clifton.

Life's Work

Juanita Kreps began teaching economics at Denison University as an instructor in 1945. She was promoted to assistant professor in 1947 and held that rank until 1950. She was a lecturer at Hofstra University from 1952 to 1954 and taught at Queens College from 1954 to 1955. In 1955, she returned to Duke as a part-time visiting economics instructor. She has described her progress to the rank of professor as extremely slow.

Kreps was appointed dean of the Women's College and assistant provost at Duke in 1969. Three years later, she was named James B. Duke Professor of Economics, and in 1973, she was the first woman appointed vice president at Duke University.

Writing complemented Juanita Kreps's teaching career. Her earliest books, published in 1955, were *Aid, Trade and Tariffs*, which she coedited with her husband, and *Our National Resources: Their Development and Use*. These were followed by *Automation and Employment* and *Taxing, Spending, and the National Debt*, both published in 1964.

Kreps's next two books, *Sex in the Marketplace: American Women at Work* (1971) and *Sex, Age and Work: The Changing Composition of the Labor Force* (1975), reflected her academic specialty, which was labor demographics. In the former book, she suggested that women move from the few occupations in which they were concentrated into other fields. In the latter, she proposed changing company policies to allow workers to take leaves of absence during their careers without jeopardizing their Social Security status.

A book that Kreps contributed to and edited in 1976 reflected her concern for women's issues. It was titled *Women and the American Economy: A Look to the 1980s*.

Kreps was active in several professional organizations in the 1970's. She served as vice president of the Gerontological Society from 1971 to 1972 and president of the Southern Economics Association from 1975 to 1976. Six colleges and universities awarded her honorary degrees, and she received the North Carolina Public Service Award in 1976.

Issues involving women's employment were important to Kreps, although she once advised women to abandon feminist rhetoric and increase labor union activity to improve their workplace status. She believed that women wanted more education and meaningful work. Kreps believed that women who were serious about careers would find time for them regardless of other responsibilities. In 1964, she urged women to think about possible careers while they were still in college.

Kreps believed that the gender-based pay gap resulted from a combination of sex discrimination and women's concentration in a few occupations. Her proposed solution was to encourage women to gain education to prepare themselves for a wider range of vocational choices.

Kreps favored work force flexibility. She envisioned a labor force composed of more women and fewer men by the year 2000. To accommodate this change, she urged firms to offer flexible scheduling and to give employees more options to enter and leave full-time employment. In the 1970's, she supported flexible daily work schedules and parental leave.

A 1975 conference on Women in the Economy that Kreps organized in Harriman, New York, made several recommendations beneficial to women. Among those were a commitment to strengthen affirmative action plans at universities and an endorsement of the Equal Rights Amendment.

Kreps served on the boards of directors of eleven major U.S. firms, including the New York Stock Exchange, J. C. Penney, Eastman Kodak, and Western Electric. She was serious about her board memberships and tried to get board members to discuss issues they otherwise might ignore. Although she was invariably the lone woman on the boards, Kreps viewed such tokenism as a stage through which women had to pass on their way to equality.

Kreps first met Jimmy Carter in 1976, when she and other economists were invited to Plains, Georgia, to brief him on economic issues. On December 20, 1976, Carter nominated Kreps to be commerce secretary. She was his second choice; Jane Cahill Pfeiffer, a former International Business Machines (IBM) executive, had refused the job.

Before her appointment, Juanita Kreps had gained government experience by serving on various federal and state councils and committees. She was a North Carolina delegate to a White House Conference on Aging, and she served on the Manpower Advisory Committee, as it was then called, and the Labor Department's Small Grants Panel.

Confirmed unanimously, Kreps was sworn in on January 23, 1977, the fourth woman to hold a Cabinet post and the first economist to serve as secretary of commerce. She supervised 38,000 employees and a $2.3 billion budget. With an income of more than $100,000 from her position at Duke, board memberships, and writing, Kreps took a substantial pay cut to accept the job of secretary of commerce at $66,000 per year.

Under Kreps's leadership, government's dialogue with business increased. Besides helping business, Kreps believed that the Commerce Department should be concerned with employee and consumer issues.

Kreps found a unified purpose in the diverse subagencies within the Commerce Department. The Commerce Department included offices as diverse as the Census Bureau and the National Oceanic and Atmospheric Administration; its purpose, according to Kreps, was to facilitate the smooth operation of the economy.

Kreps belonged to an Economic Policy Board that advised President Carter daily. This link to Carter helped offset a perception that the Commerce Department was relatively powerless because other Cabinet departments, such as State and Treasury, strongly influenced Commerce regarding economic issues.

While she was secretary of commerce, Kreps oversaw the growth of the Economic Development Administration (EDA), a subagency established to stimulate long-range economic growth in areas of low income and high unemployment. When Kreps became a Cabinet member, $2 billion had been allocated to the EDA to spend on public works projects.

Kreps was involved with many other activities while she was secretary of commerce. She tried to convince businesses to adopt social responsibility indexes to permit comparisons based on firms' commitment to preserve the environment and promote women and minorities as well as on profit. Kreps favored economic impact studies to identify costs of government programs and budgets to analyze the costs of regulatory activities. Another one of her duties was to encourage the use of ocean resources while minimizing environmental damage. Kreps also helped the domestic shoe industry and expanded U.S. exports, particularly to China.

Kreps thought that more women should hold top federal government positions. When Carter mentioned the difficulty he experienced finding qualified women for high-level posts, she urged the Administration to do a better job of looking for them.

One of Kreps's most controversial suggestions was to raise the age at which people would be eligible for full Social Security benefits. At the time, that idea was very unpopular.

Juanita Kreps resigned as secretary of commerce for personal reasons in October of 1979 and returned to Duke University. In 1981, she received an achievement award from the American Association of University Women.

Summary

Juanita Kreps is a good role model for women who wish to succeed in higher education and government. She was persistent when striving to achieve goals but was never arrogant. As an educator, administrator, and Cabinet executive, she listened to others' ideas. She tried to build consensus rather than resort to divisive conflict.

Despite excellent credentials, her progress through the academic ranks at Duke was painstakingly slow because of her gender. In the 1970's, Kreps believed, it was acceptable for women to be viewed as patient teachers at universities, but they were not supposed to think about their fields seriously or write books. Juanita Kreps did both.

Many of Kreps's ideas and actions were ahead of their time. She believed that business should be socially responsible not only for ethical reasons but also in order to enhance long-run profitability and avoid additional government regulation. She believed that women should plan for careers, expanding their choices beyond the narrow range of occupations into which they had been channeled previously. In return, business should adapt to the changing work force by allowing flexible work schedules and granting parental leaves.

Kreps was part of a dual-career couple and a commuter marriage before those terms were commonly used. She and her husband seemed to have balanced career and family successfully.

When asked how she wanted to be remembered, Kreps said that she hoped people would recall her efforts to deal with prices, unemployment, family income, and human rights. She also supported greater roles for women in the economy and anticipated a time when a woman's nomination to a Cabinet position would no longer be unusual.

Bibliography
Jones, Peter M. "Juanita Kreps: Captain of Commerce." *Senior Scholastic* 110 (January 26, 1978): 4-6. Kreps's childhood, education, Commerce Department appointment, and commuter marriage are discussed. In an interview format, Kreps explains her views on government bureaucracy, a social responsibility index, and job creation programs. She says she would like to be remembered for dealing with unemployment, prices, human rights, and family income.
"Juanita Kreps: More Active Role for Commerce." *Nation's Business* 65 (Septem-

ber, 1977): 30-34. Kreps's views on costs of government programs, inflation, social audits and economic development are presented. The article describes the prevailing business climate in the late 1970's. Kreps's experience in higher education is mentioned, as is the pay cut she took to accept the Cabinet post.

Langway, Lynn, and Thomas Rich. "The Cabinet: First Lady of Commerce." *Newsweek* 89 (February 7, 1977): 61. This article presents an overview of the new responsibilities Kreps assumed at the Commerce Department. It mentions Kreps's role as the first woman in several positions she held and discusses her career change from higher education administration to Cabinet executive.

"Secretary Kreps Defines Department's Goals." *Commerce America* 2, no. 4 (February 14, 1977): 11. Kreps discusses her overriding goal for the Commerce Department, which is to facilitate balanced economic growth. She explains her plans to reduce unneeded paperwork and to seek input from business, consumers, and employees. Her corporate board memberships and academic achievements are listed, as are the government committees on which she served and books she wrote.

Margaret Foegen Karsten

ELISABETH KÜBLER-ROSS

Born: July 8, 1926; Zurich, Switzerland

Area of Achievement: Psychiatry

Contribution: A leading researcher in the field of thanatology (the study of death), Kübler-Ross is most widely recognized for having identified five stages in the process of dying that have provided a framework for further work by professionals in the area of counseling the terminally ill and their families. Her work has helped remove former taboos from the subject of death and brought a compassionate and humane approach to the care of the dying.

Early Life

Elisabeth Kübler, daughter of Ernst and Emmy (Villiger) Kübler, was the first-born of triplet girls. Although Elisabeth and one of her sisters weighed barely two pounds, the triplets survived as a result of their mother's diligent care. The close-knit Kübler family was dominated by a father who was a firm disciplinarian yet who also sang songs with his children around the parlor piano and led them on summer nature hikes at the family's Swiss mountain retreat in Furlegi. These trips instilled in young Elisabeth a lasting love and respect for nature. Never a religious person in the traditional sense, Elisabeth favored a sort of pantheism and exhibited compassion for all living creatures. As a child attempting to escape from the constant company of her sisters, she chose a secret place atop a flat rock in the woods near her home to which she returned even as an adult when in need of solace.

Elisabeth struggled for personal identity since her childhood was spent with very few belongings or activities that were different from those of her sisters. This situation was further complicated by the fact that she was physically identical to Erika, for whom she was often mistaken. Elisabeth developed a fascination for African history that became the source of the first personal possession she later recalled was not shared by her sisters. As a reward for recovering from a near fatal case of pneumonia, Elisabeth's father bought her an African rag doll for which she had been yearning. This fascination with a culture that differed radically from her own resulted in the creation of a sort of tribal nonsense language used by the imaginative triplets that only they understood.

Although their older brother, Ernst, was educated to enter the business world, the girls were sent to local schools with the objective that they be properly prepared for marriage. The basics bored Elisabeth, who longed for more challenge and saw education as her doorway to important work. She soon discovered a passion for science. Because Elisabeth received no parental support for her goals, her educational pursuits beyond secondary school were entirely self-motivated.

Several events in Elisabeth's youth were key factors in determining the direction of her life and her profession. The peaceful death of her hospital roommate when Elisabeth was five, the release from the suffering of meningitis of a young girl in her hometown, and memories of a neighboring farmer with a broken neck calmly preparing his family for his death were never forgotten. These early experiences with death intensified the belief that later became the crux of her professional credo—that death is only a stage of life and people should be able to face death with dignity and the support of those they trust.

September 1, 1939, marked in some ways the most crucial day in her life. When Elisabeth heard on the radio that the Germans had invaded Poland, she made a vow to go help the Polish people as soon as she was able. First, she was involved with refugees sent to the Swiss hospitals where she worked as a laboratory assistant during the war. She joined the International Volunteers for Peace in 1945 hoping to have found the right avenue to reach the Polish people. In intervals between her laboratory work, she worked on the French-Swiss border and in Sweden before her dream of being sent to Poland was finally realized in 1948. She worked at numerous jobs, including those of camp cook, gardener, carpenter, and nurse, as she assisted war victims in rebuilding.

These postwar experiences, combined with poignant memories of butterfly signs of hope left on barrack walls at Maidanek concentration camp, made it clear to Elisabeth that her purpose in life was to channel her energy and compassion into the healing of human minds as well as bodies. She worked tirelessly to complete her preliminary medical school exams in two years instead of the usual three while meagerly financing her studies working as a lab assistant in an eye clinic. In 1951, she was admitted to the University of Zurich Medical School and she embarked upon the winding trail that led her to the field of psychiatry. Having come to believe without question that people's bodies often achieve healing only after their minds and souls are healthy and free, Elisabeth was convinced that psychiatry offered the perfect venue for the combination of her special instincts and intellect.

Life's Work

Elisabeth Kübler was graduated from the University of Zurich in 1957 and practiced for a few months as a Swiss country doctor. On February 7, 1958, she married Emanuel Robert Ross, a fellow medical student to whom she was wed for eleven years. Elisabeth Kübler-Ross came to the United States with her new husband, a native New Yorker, and they were able to secure internships at Community Hospital in Glen Cove, Long Island. This experience was followed by a three-year residency in psychiatry at Manhattan State Hospital in Ward's Island and a concurrent year at Montefiore Hospital in the Bronx. Even patients with the most severe psychoses seemed to respond to Kübler-Ross's compassionate yet persistent and simple way of communicating with them. The lack of humane concern in psychiatric hospitals was appalling to the young doctor, and the more freedom she was given to work in her own way, the more successful were her treatments.

The couple felt a need to leave the city environment after the arrival of their new child, Kenneth. In 1962, they accepted positions at the University of Colorado School of Medicine in Denver. Kübler-Ross was given a fellowship in psychiatry and the next year became an instructor at Colorado General Hospital. In 1965, the family, with the addition of a daughter Barbara, moved to Chicago, where Kübler-Ross became an assistant professor of psychiatry and assistant director of psychiatric consultation and liaison services at the University of Chicago Medical School. All through her working years, she had been disturbed by the attitude of avoidance that existed in dealing with the anxiety of terminally ill patients. She found the situation the same almost universally and began to quietly develop her own methods for recognizing the anxiety of the dying and also guiding them in expressing their feelings. It was in Chicago that fame for her work in thanatology began. Against administrative pressures to bring as little attention to her work as possible, she networked with nurses, willing doctors, priests, and seminarians to further her studies of the counseling of the dying. She held weekly seminars that attracted overflow crowds. These seminars were eventually canceled by administrators who were concerned about public reaction to discussions about death rather than recovery of patients.

In these seminars, dying patients were interviewed by Kübler-Ross behind a one-way glass through which those who attended could observe. Kübler-Ross viewed death as the final stage of life and began to identify five stages in the process of dying that she found all patients to experience, though not necessarily in the same order. The five stages were denial, anger, bargaining, depression, and acceptance. These stages and other conclusions were the subject of many guest lectures and of her best-selling work *On Death and Dying* (1969). The book became a standard resource for counselors, physicians, and laymen as they helped patients, friends, and relatives deal with the issue of death. *Life* magazine published an article on November 21, 1969, that related to the public for the first time the boldness with which Kübler-Ross approached the issue of death with patients and their open dialogue with her. The public response was overwhelming, and Kübler-Ross saw this as a turning point in her career. Her work turned solely to assisting dying patients and their families.

In 1977, she established "Shanti Nilaya" ("Home of Peace"), a healing center for dying persons and relatives in the hills north of Escondido near San Diego, California. She moved her residence there from Chicago, and profits from her lectures and books supported the center. In 1990, she moved the Elisabeth Kübler-Ross Center to her own 200-acre farm in Headwater, Virginia, where she had retired in 1984. Kübler-Ross continued to keep abreast of current issues and attempted in 1986 to establish a hospice for babies with acquired immune deficiency syndrome (AIDS); because of heated community dissent, however, she abandoned the idea. Nevertheless, the center was enormously successful in its efforts to offer assistance to professionals and laypersons in dealing with terminally ill patients. The center is supported by proceeds from Kübler-Ross's workshops and lectures and by volunteer help.

Since the advent of *On Death and Dying*, Kübler-Ross has published a number of other books based on her studies, including *Questions and Answers on Death and Dying* (1974), *Death: The Final Stage of Growth* (1975), *To Live Until We Say Good-bye* (1978), *Living with Death and Dying* (1981), *Working It Through* (1982), *On Children and Death* (1983), *AIDS: The Ultimate Challenge* (1987), and *On Life After Death* (1991).

Over the years, Kübler-Ross has been recognized for her selfless devotion and tireless efforts by numerous organizations, including the Teilhard Foundation (1981) and the American Academy of Achievement (1980). She was named a "Woman of the Decade" by *Ladies' Home Journal* in 1979. She was one of the founders of the American Holistic Medical Association and is a member of other major medical and psychological associations. Honorary degrees have been bestowed upon her by Smith College, University of Notre Dame, the Medical College of Pennsylvania, Albany Medical College, Hamline University, and Amherst College.

Summary

Elisabeth Kübler-Ross is almost solely responsible for the humanitarian focus on the care of the dying patient which currently exists. Her workshops and lectures continue and she assists where she is needed. She responds also to individual pleas and has flown to the bedside of patients in their final stages of life to listen and give comfort to them and their families. Elisabeth Kübler-Ross's name has become synonymous with the idea of respect for the dying. Over the years, her work has literally revolutionized for doctors and patients the world over the area of psychology dealing with death and dying.

Bibliography

Bartlett, Kay. "No Stranger to Death, Kübler-Ross Turns Her Attention to AIDS." *Los Angeles Times*, May 10, 1987, sec. 1, p. 25. Kübler-Ross discusses her feelings about the after-life of the human spirit and the application of her thanatological research to the counseling of children and adults suffering with AIDS.

Gill, Derek. *Quest: The Life of Elisabeth Kübler-Ross*. New York: Harper & Row, 1980. The first full-length biography of Kübler-Ross. An intimate volume that contains an epilogue by Kübler-Ross and covers her life through 1969, the year that *On Death and Dying* was published and her attentions turned solely to work with the terminally ill.

Goleman, Daniel. "We Are Breaking the Silence About Death." *Psychology Today* 10 (September, 1976): 44-47. Kübler-Ross discusses her work and traces the path of her career. The article includes an interview about dealing with the death of children, the difficult subject of much of her recent writing.

Kübler-Ross, Elisabeth. *On Death and Dying*. New York: Macmillan, 1969. Kübler-Ross's first work and the one in which she defines her famous "five stages" in the process of death. The best-known treatise in the field, this work set the standard for later research.

Wainwright, Loudon. "Profound Lesson for the Living." *Life* 67 (November 21, 1969): 36-43. This was the first article addressed to a general audience that publicized Kübler-Ross's controversial Chicago seminars on dying. Her unorthodox method of working is revealed in his observation of an emotional interview between the doctor and a twenty-two-year-old leukemia patient.

Sandra C. McClain

K. D. LANG

Born: November 2, 1961; Edmonton, Alberta, Canada

Area of Achievement: Music

Contribution: A songwriter and Grammy-winning singer, Lang has achieved success in the genres of country-western and alternative pop music while challenging stereotypes of female popular entertainers.

Early Life

Kathryn Dawn "K. D." Lang was born on November 2, 1961, in Edmonton, and was reared with her three older siblings in Consort, a town of almost seven hundred people in the eastern central plains of Alberta, Canada. Her father, Fred, purchased and operated the town pharmacy, and her mother, Audrey, taught elementary school.

Supported by her parents, especially her mother, Lang began to sing at local music festivals when she was five years old, and she continued to perform at school shows and weddings until she finished high school. At the age of seven, she started weekly piano lessons in the town of Castor (about an hour's drive from Consort), but after three years she switched to playing the guitar. Throughout her childhood, she listened to a wide variety of musical genres, ranging from classical music to Broadway tunes to rock and roll.

Lang's parents also taught her to challenge gender stereotypes. She actively participated in sports as a javelin thrower and volleyball player. Although her father left the family when Lang was twelve, she had a close relationship with him prior to his departure, and from her father she learned how to ride motorcycles and target shoot. She also exhibited a nonconformist sense of fashion, wearing leather pants and favoring "hippie" headbands and sunglasses.

Life's Work

When she was eighteen, K. D. Lang left Consort to study music and voice at Red Deer College, ninety miles south of Edmonton, but the combination of her frustration with academic requirements and job opportunities in Edmonton led her to quit college and pursue a career as an entertainer. Her early work was eclectic and included performance art, but increasingly she defined herself as a country-and-western singer.

This identity was strengthened in 1981, when Lang appeared in Edmonton in a musical, *Country Chorale*, playing a part loosely modeled on American country singer Patsy Cline, who died in a plane crash in 1963. Lang felt strongly drawn to Cline as an artistic role model and especially appreciated the pain-filled songs of lost love for which Cline had been famous.

Lang also continued to defy traditional gender stereotypes and to develop her own distinctive style. She began to use her first and middle initials instead of Kathy Dawn, and to spell her name entirely in lower-case letters. She also drew attention with her unusual stage costumes, which might combine heavy socks and boots with long square-dance skirts or false sideburns with a cowboy hat.

In 1982, Lang auditioned for and received a job as vocalist for an Edmonton country swing group, but when the band folded after one public performance, she decided to form her own group. With the help of Larry Wanagas, an Edmonton recording studio owner who became her manager, Lang created "The Reclines" and began to appear with this band at Edmonton nightclubs.

In 1984, K. D. Lang and the Reclines released *A Truly Western Experience* on the independent Bunstead label and toured Canada to promote the album. Initially, Lang and the Reclines appeared in smaller Canadian cities. Her act combined an exotic blend of country crooning and rockabilly with vigorous dancing and light-hearted clowning. These elements, plus her gender-bending appearance (enhanced by a new, close-cropped hairstyle), seemed to puzzle audiences. Some wondered if Lang's performances were serious efforts at country music or humorous spoofs of the genre. In Toronto, however, she and her band found enthusiastic audiences and received good reviews. Based on this success in a major urban center, Lang and the Reclines were booked in 1985 at The Bottom Line, a well-known New York City nightclub. After watching Lang perform, Seymour Stein of Sire Records, famous for his interest in offbeat musical performers, signed her to a recording contract.

Angel with a Lariat (1986), Lang's first album with Sire, sold more than 460,000 copies and brought her a Juno Award as Canada's best Country Female Vocalist. On that album and her next for Sire, *Shadowland* (1988), Lang offered mixtures of country music standards (rearranged to feature her energetic "cowpunk" style) and tunes cowritten by Lang and Ben Mink, a member of the Reclines. She also paid homage to Patsy Cline with deeply emotional torch songs and through her choice of Owen Bradley, Cline's longtime producer, as the producer of *Shadowland*. The torch songs enabled Lang to use her rich voice to full advantage and to develop a romantic quality in her performances.

Lang began to win both a large audience and praise from much of the music industry. *Shadowland* sold more than a million copies and won praise from numerous critics, as did her next Sire album, *Absolute Torch and Twang* (1989). Lang also won the Grammy award for Best Country Vocal Collaboration in 1988, for her duet with Roy Orbison on a remake of his hit song "Crying," and the 1989 Grammy for Best Country Female Vocal Performance for *Absolute Torch and Twang*.

Yet such success did not translate into full acceptance in the ranks of country-and-western music. Centered in Nashville, Tennessee, the country music industry did not respond with uniform enthusiasm to Lang's willingness to combine country tunes with blues, rock, and punk music. Her unwillingness to conform to industry standards of feminine appearance also drew criticism, as did her growing reputation as a model of female independence and strength. Although individual country performers (including Minnie Pearl, Brenda Lee, and Loretta Lynn) did embrace Lang and work with her, few country radio stations would play her songs. Despite this lackluster response from mainstream country-and-western supporters, Lang continued to expand her base of fans, especially among enthusiasts of alternative pop music and from critics writing for publications such as *Rolling Stone* and *The New York Times*. She toured widely in North America and Europe to promote her albums, and developed a strong reputation as a live performer. Her appearances with Sting and Bruce Springsteen on the Amnesty International Tour of 1988 helped to cement her position as a favorite with rock-and-roll audiences.

The year 1990 brought new levels of acclaim and new criticisms for Lang. Although the Country Music Awards continued to ignore her, Lang won a 1990 Grammy for Best Female Country Vocalist. She also recorded a television commercial at the request of People for the Ethical Treatment of Animals (PETA). In the commercial, Lang spoke strongly against the beef industry and meat-eating. A longtime vegetarian, Lang referred to her own upbringing in the cattle country of Alberta and bluntly stated, "Meat stinks." Furor over the advertisement developed before its planned release, and although it aired only on news programs, Lang became notorious for her statements.

Although her animal rights activism did not seem to damage Lang's reputation with most of her fans and won strong approval from some, it did give country music another reason to reject Lang. Many country radio stations in Canada and the United States announced that they would no longer play her music (even though most never had).

Rather than run from such condemnation, Lang took new paths in her career and life. In 1991, she released *Harvest of Seven Years (Cropped and Chronicled)*, a compilation of her videos and taped performances since 1984. She tried dramatic acting in *Salmonberries* (1992), a film directed by Percy Adlon and set in Alaska and Berlin. Lang played an Inuit woman in love with a German widow, and while the film was only released in theaters in Europe and then appeared once on Canadian television in 1993, Lang's performance won praise. In her fifth album, *Ingenue* (1992), Lang abandoned most of her country sound and instead featured her voice in ten yearning and introspective love songs, all cowritten by Lang and Ben Mink.

Both *Salmonberries* and *Ingenue* increased rumors about Lang's sexual orientation, since she portrayed a lesbian in the former and sang of unrequited passion in the latter. Although Lang had never denied her sexual orientation, in an interview in the summer of 1992 she eliminated the rumors by clearly stating that she was a lesbian. She explained that her earlier reticence reflected her concern that her mother, who had been targeted by hate mail following Lang's PETA advertisement, would suffer an additional round of attacks.

Lang's openness about her sexual orientation did not have a negative effect on her popularity as a singer and songwriter. In 1993, she won a Grammy for Best Female Pop Vocal on "Constant Craving," a single from *Ingenue*. The album achieved platinum status in sales, and "Constant Craving" reached the Top Ten on *Billboard*'s Adult Contemporary chart and Top 100 Singles chart. Lang and Ben Mink also wrote the soundtrack for *Even Cowgirls Get the Blues* (1994).

Summary

K. D. Lang is renowned for her commitment to musical innovation and her ability to fuse a wide variety of musical styles in her songwriting and performances. Her work drew new listeners to country-and-western music, and alongside artists such as Lyle Lovett, Lang successfully broadened the image of country performers. With her song "Constant Craving," Lang also established herself as a popular alternative pop artist and ballad singer. Her performance in *Salmonberries* also indicated her ability as a dramatic actor, and Lang expressed interest in developing a film career as a complement to her musical work.

Beyond her contributions to popular music, Lang has challenged gender stereotypes and proved that female performers can draw fans and praise without conforming to a particular model of appearance or behavior. From the onset of her career, she playfully tested and teased the established, rather demure style of many female country singers, even as she clearly demonstrated her respect for her colleagues' choices of style and appearance. Although Lang considers herself to be a musician first and a social activist second, her advocacy of animal rights and openness about her sexual orientation remain significant aspects of her public image. In the latter decades of the twentieth century, as a number of women challenged the limits placed on female entertainers, K. D. Lang became one of the most prominent examples of a female artist committed to honesty and independence in both her work and her public life.

Bibliography
Bufwack, Mary A., and Robert K. Oermann. *Finding Her Voice: The Saga of Women in Country Music*. New York: Crown, 1993. This comprehensive history and analysis of women in the country music industry includes a thorough assessment of Lang's impact in the 1980's and since. References to Lang's work with other female country performers and to her performances of classic country songs are also offered. This work, the best source available, analyzes Lang's place in the history of female country artists.
Gillmor, Don. "The Reincarnation of Kathryn Dawn." *Saturday Night* 105 (June, 1990): 27-35. A detailed examination of Lang's life and career, with discussions of her childhood, her early studies in music, and the various stages of her career development. Brief interviews with Lang, her family, and her fellow musicians are included.
Gore, Lesley. "Lesley Gore on k.d. lang." *Ms.* 1 (July-August 1990): 30-33. This transcript of a lengthy conversation between Lang and pop singer Gore provides information about the musical influences in Lang's career, the reception given to women in popular music in the late twentieth century, and Lang's methods as a songwriter.
Robertson, William. *k.d. lang: Carrying the Torch*. Toronto: ECW Press, 1992. This biography of Lang is the first book devoted entirely to her life and career. It is an honest, detailed account, and is written for a general audience.
Udovitch, Mim. "k.d. lang." *Rolling Stone*, no. 662 (August 5, 1993): 54-57. This article briefly summarizes Lang's musical career and more extensively discusses

her public image and iconoclastic style. It includes an interview with Lang and comments on reactions to her open status as a lesbian.

Beth Kraig

DOROTHEA LANGE

Born: May 26, 1895; Hoboken, New Jersey
Died: October 11, 1965; San Francisco, California
Areas of Achievement: Photography and social reform
Contribution: Considered by many to be the country's most distinguished documentary photographer, Dorothea Lange brought her photographic vision to bear most memorably on the living conditions of Depression America's rural poor and Japanese Americans detained in World War II internment camps.

Early Life

Dorothea Lange was born Dorothea Margaretta Nutzhorn on May 26, 1895, in Hoboken, New Jersey. She was named for her father's mother, Dorothea Fischer. Later in her life, she would drop her middle name and the surname Nutzhorn, using instead her mother's maiden name, Lange. Her father was Heinrich (Henry) Martin Nutzhorn, a lawyer and the son of German immigrant parents. Her mother, Joanna (Joan) Caroline Lange, also of German heritage, enjoyed music and worked as a clerk or librarian until the birth of Dorothea, her first child.

In 1902, Dorothea Lange suffered poliomyelitis, an ailment for which there was not yet a vaccine. As a result, Dorothea had limited mobility in her right leg, particularly from the knee down. This condition caused her to walk with a limp, and she was teased throughout childhood. In her own accounts, Lange described the experience of illness and subsequent paralysis as being formative in her life. She found people's reactions to be both humiliating and instructive, and Lange claimed never to have gotten over this experience. Later in life, though, she did report that her physical disability inspired photographic subjects to be open with her.

When Dorothea was twelve years of age, her father left his wife and children. Details remain uncertain, but it is widely speculated that his departure represented flight from some criminal offense. Throughout her life, however, Dorothea Lange spoke little of her father. In 1907, Joan Nutzhorn took her children to live with her mother in Hoboken. Joan Nutzhorn began work at the New York Public Library on the Lower East Side.

By traveling to New York with her mother and posing as a New York resident, Dorothea was able to attend Public School No. 62, also on New York's Lower East Side. On February 5, 1909, Dorothea Lange enrolled at Wadleigh High School in Harlem; later, she attended the nearby New York Training School for Teachers. When Wadleigh failed to hold Dorothea's interest, which proved to be often, she would explore the city—attending concerts, viewing museum exhibits, and the like. Before launching her career as a photographer, Dorothea also accompanied her mother on home visits in her new capacity as investigator for a juvenile court judge. Dorothea Lange's sensitivity to the plight of others likely had its roots in her exposure to New York's poverty and its immigrant ghettos. As a result of her experiences in the New York area, Lange knew well the adverse conditions in which many people were forced to live, and her mind filled with these vivid images.

Life's Work

At about the time of her high school graduation, Dorothea Lange informed her mother of her plans to become a professional photographer. At that point in her life, however, Lange had never taken a photograph. She began work in the studios of several New York City photographers, though, and one of her first positions was with studio photographer Arnold Genthe. Genthe taught Lange the basic techniques of photography, and Lange continued her photographic apprenticeship in 1917 and 1918 by studying at Columbia University under photographer Clarence H. White. She also worked with a variety of other portrait photographers in the vicinity. Lange abandoned her teacher-training school at this point, finding her experiences in teaching displeasing, and devoted herself to a life in photography.

At age twenty, Dorothea Lange started to travel, selling photographs along the way to help finance her journey. When her money ran out, Lange found herself in San Francisco, California, where she settled and opened her own portrait studio in 1916. On March 21, 1920, she and the painter Maynard Dixon were married. She spent the 1920's in San Francisco, working as a society photographer. She and Dixon became known within San Francisco's bohemian circles. On May 15, 1925, Dorothea gave birth to her first child: Daniel Rhodes Dixon. The couple's second child, John Eaglefeather Dixon, arrived on June 12, 1928. After the stock market crash of 1929, Lange and her family ventured to a Taos art colony presided over by writer Mabel Dodge Luhan. On their return trip, Lange and her family observed America's homeless, unemployed, and migrant workers.

Upon returning to California, Lange could not reconcile studio work for those who could afford professional portraits with the poverty she saw around her. In 1932, she left the comfort of her portrait studio and began to make photographs of the social conditions she observed, including soup kitchens and breadlines. A 1933 image of this kind, "White Angel Bread Line," went a long way toward establishing Lange's reputation as a documentary photographer. With her images, Lane also made an extensive and change-making chronicle of the plight of California's migrant workers. Similar images of migrant labor and poverty would later be rendered in fiction by John Steinbeck in the novel *The Grapes of Wrath* (1939).

When one of Lange's photographs of an "agitator" was chosen to accompany a *Survey Graphic* article by economist Paul Schuster Taylor, Lange and Taylor began a close association. In 1935, Taylor was asked by the Division of Rural Rehabilitation to design a program to assist migrant workers. His first decision was to secure Lange's services as project photographer, although for official purposes, she was listed on the payroll as a typist. Lange and Taylor were married a short time later, two months after Lange and Dixon divorced. In that same year, Taylor and Lange presented a monograph of their findings in Southern California, entitled *Notes from the Field* (1935). After a copy of this report arrived in Washington, D.C., it was forwarded by Columbia University economist Rexford Guy Tugwell to Roy Stryker, head of the photographic section of the Resettlement Administration, later renamed the Farm Security Administration (FSA). Upon seeing Lange's potential, Stryker hired her to produce government photographs of Depression America.

Lange worked chiefly in the southern and southwestern United States. She began government photography in 1935, and her images for the FSA featured California, New Mexico, and Arizona. At times, she photographed as many as five states a month, sometimes traveling from Mississippi to California in a month's time. Lange used a Berkeley darkroom to hasten the availability of her images, although it was general policy for exposed film to be returned to Washington, D.C., for filing and processing at national headquarters. Lange's insistence on retaining this California darkroom allowed her to direct immediate aid through the Emergency Relief Administration to Nipoma Valley pea pickers, such as the woman who became the subject of one of her signature photographs, "Migrant Mother." Lange remained on the staff of the FSA until budgetary concerns led to her firing in October of 1936. By January of 1937, Lange was rehired, released, and rehired again in October of 1938. Her last photographs in the government photographic files date from 1939. In that same year, Lange and Taylor published a collaborative volume entitled *An American Exodus: A Record of Human Erosion* (1939).

Lange's release from the FSA did not curtail her productivity. On February 1, 1940, not long after the end of Lange's association with the FSA, she was hired as head photographer for the Bureau of Agricultural Economics, another division of the U.S. Department of Agriculture. In 1941, she was offered a Guggenheim Fellowship to make photographic studies of rural communities in the United States. Her proposed work concentrated on the Mormons of Utah, the Hutterites in South Dakota, and the Amana society in Iowa. Before Lange reached the Mormon community, war conditions changed her plans. In the wake of the Japanese attack on Pearl Harbor, Lange opted to photograph the relocation camps where Japanese Americans were being detained. For a time, she photographed internees for the government's War Relocation Authority. She then did photographic work for the Office of War Information. After World War II, she completed numerous photo-essays for *Life* magazine, including "Mormon Villages" and "The Irish Countrymen." Her work focused on cooperative religious communities, such as the Shakers, and other dimensions of agrarian America. She also photographed delegates to United Nations conferences.

Illness kept Lange from photography for a few years during the 1940's. In 1951, she returned to active work as a photographer. She spent the 1950's creating photo-essays, including some collaborative work with Ansel Adams, and consulting on exhibition designs. She also began teaching seminars in photography. In the late 1950's, she took photographic trips to Egypt and the Far East. Dorothea Lange died of cancer on October 11, 1965, a short time before a one-woman show of her work was to open at New York's Museum of Modern Art.

Summary

The Women's Book of World Records and Achievements lists Dorothea Lange as "The United States' Greatest Documentary Photographer." She was the first woman to earn distinction within the field of documentary photography, the first woman to receive a photography grant, and the first woman to be honored with a photographic retrospective at the Museum of Modern Art. Perhaps her best-known image, and arguably the most widely recognized of the 270,000 photographs presented by the FSA's photographic team, "Migrant Mother," was published throughout the world. In addition to raising awareness of the plight of the poor, this particular photograph proved to be instrumental in raising funds for medical supplies. Whether working in conjunction with the Farm Security Administration, California's Emergency Relief Administration, or the War Relocation Authority, Dorothea Lange produced striking and memorable images that bore poignant testimony to the historical events she witnessed. With these images, she reached a wide audience of viewers who otherwise would have been unfamiliar with the arduous lives of other Americans. Lange's photographs became evidence for needed reforms as well as valuable historical documents. Her career in documentary photography has inspired women photographers in their efforts not only to chronicle conditions but also to change them.

Those wishing to find out more about the career of Dorothea Lange may explore a variety of archival sources. The Dorothea Lange Collection, including both photographs and writings by Lange, is housed by the Oakland Museum's Prints and Photographs Division in Oakland, California. Other photographs and notebooks may be found in the Library of Congress and the National Archives.

Bibliography
Becker, Karin E. *Dorothea Lange and the Documentary Tradition.* Baton Rouge: Louisiana State University Press, 1980. Although Becker does not engage in very much close analysis of specific Lange photographs, she has much to say about Lange's role within the emerging genre of documentary photography.
Curtis, James. *Mind's Eye, Mind's Truth: FSA Photography Reconsidered.* Philadelphia: Temple University Press, 1989. The third chapter of this historical treatment of FSA images is devoted to Lange's most recognized photograph: "Migrant Mother." Curtis includes a thorough account and critique of the photograph's origin and reception.
Dorothea Lange. New York: The Museum of Modern Art, 1966. This exhibition catalog urges viewers to read Lange's images closely and to return to them for successive viewings. It comments in some detail on specific photographs, comparing Lange's portrait work favorably to the streetscapes and architectural photographs of fellow photographer Walker Evans.
Fisher, Andrea. *Let Us Now Praise Famous Women: Women Photographers for the U.S. Government, 1935-1944.* New York: Pandora Press, 1987. Fisher argues that Lange is as important to the documentary tradition as her male FSA colleague Walker Evans, and she explores the implications of Lange's reputation as the mother of documentary photography.
Guimond, James. *American Photography and the American Dream.* Chapel Hill: University of North Carolina Press, 1991. This volume is especially helpful in its discussion of Lange's later life, particularly her photographs in internment camps,

her blacklisting as a member of the Photo League in the late 1940's, and her impact on the design of photographer Edward Steichen's landmark 1955 exhibition "The Family of Man."

Meltzer, Milton. *Dorothea Lange: A Photographer's Life*. New York: Farrar, Straus & Giroux, 1978. Meltzer supplies a thorough and well-researched biography, including a bibliography of archival sources, writings by Lange, and writings concerning Lange. Of particular interest is the incorporation of Lange's reflections about her experiences and images, culled from interviews and oral histories.

O'Neal, Hank. *A Vision Shared: A Classic Portrait of America and Its People, 1935-1943*. New York: St. Martin's Press, 1976. This volume features thirty-one well-reproduced Lange photographs from the FSA years and includes a brief but solid biographical sketch of the photographer. A helpful introductory section discusses the Farm Security Administration's Photographic Division.

Linda S. Watts

SUSANNE K. LANGER

Born: December 20, 1895; New York, New York
Died: July 17, 1985; Old Lyme, Connecticut
Areas of Achievement: Philosophy and education
Contribution: A leading American philosopher in an historically male-dominated
field, Langer was one of the major influences on twentieth century thought in the
fields of philosophy and aesthetics. Her work in the realm of "symbolic transformation" helped to establish logical philosophical framework for art and social
science, areas not formerly thought to adhere to any ordered system of ideas.

Early Life

Susanne Katherina Knauth was born to Antonio and Else M. (Uhlich) Knauth on
the Upper West Side of New York City just before the turn of the century. Along with
her two brothers and two sisters, Susanne was surrounded by a rich German heritage
of academic and artistic influences. Her father, a lawyer from Leipzig, was an
accomplished pianist and cellist. One of his fondest diversions was to invite friends
to his home to play chamber music in the evenings. The children all played musical
instruments. Susanne was a pianist, but later, as an adult, she became a proficient
cellist.

Else Knauth instilled a love of poetry in her children, and as a young child, Susanne
often created and recited her own verses. Later, her creative flair extended to drama,
and she wrote pageants drawn from classical subjects that she and her siblings
presented to family and friends. A wealthy family, the Knauths had a vacation retreat
at Lake George in upstate New York, where they spent many happy summers. A love
of nature and of the natural sciences was born here that was evident in all aspects of
Susanne's later life and writings.

Else Knauth never became easily fluent in English, so German became the preferred language at home. This had its disadvantages when Susanne attended school,
and as a result, much of her learning was self-motivated, with reading constituting a
large portion of her activity. Her childhood thirst for knowledge of all subjects was
prodigious: In a 1960 *New Yorker* interview with Winthrop Sargeant, she spoke of
having read Louisa May Alcott's *Little Women* and Immanuel Kant's *Critique of Pure
Reason* simultaneously as a teenager. In spite of the respect for knowledge in the
home, Susanne's father hated what he interpreted as masculine qualities in females
and would not agree to send any of his daughters to college. After his death, however,
Susanne enrolled at Radcliffe College with the encouragement of her mother. Out of
her broad early education arose an interest in philosophy, and she received her
bachelor's degree in the field in 1920. In 1921, Susanne was married to William
Leonard Langer, a Harvard graduate student of history, and the couple spent a year
studying in Vienna, Austria. Upon their return to Massachusetts, Susanne began
graduate studies in philosophy and earned a master's degree in 1924 and her Ph.D.
from Harvard in 1926. For the next fifteen years, she served on the Radcliffe faculty

and taught occasionally at Smith and Wellesley Colleges as well, while her husband was a respected professor of history at Harvard from 1936 to 1964.

Life's Work

Susanne Langer's ventures as a published writer began not with philosophical works but with a volume entitled *The Cruise of the Little Dipper, and Other Fairy Tales* (1924). The book was illustrated by Helen Sewell, an artist who was a lifelong friend and upon whom Langer depended later for critique of her writing about aesthetics. Since childhood, Langer had been fascinated by the world of myth and fantasy. The subject carried over into her later work as myth became a central focus in her study of the human formulation of symbols. At Radcliffe, Langer was in contact with the major philosophical minds of the age, and their influence can be traced throughout her work. Her professors—Alfred North Whitehead, the English mathematician and philosopher, and Henry Sheffer—were largely the catalysts for her writing.

The Practice of Philosophy (1930), Langer's first philosophical treatise, contained a preface by Alfred North Whitehead. The book discusses the purposes and methods of philosophy and the importance of symbolic logic in contemporary thought. The book's premise was that training in logic frees the mind. Henry Sheffer's influence on Langer is most obvious in her second book on philosophy, *An Introduction to Symbolic Logic* (1937). She employed his methods of symbolic logic to create a textbook on the subject and an essay on logic.

Langer defined philosophy as the clarification and articulation of concepts. She saw the purpose of philosophy as making explicit what is implicit in people's beliefs and actions. An awareness that modern society seemed to function without a defined philosophical base was always of major concern to Langer. In 1942, she published *Philosophy in a New Key: A Study in the Symbolism of Reason, Rite, and Art*. The book, which was dedicated to Whitehead, established Langer as a leading figure in the field of aesthetics.

The most direct influence on her thinking at this time was the German philosopher Ernst Cassirer, whose 1925 book *Sprache und Mythos* was translated into English as *Language and Myth* by Langer in 1946. His work in the philosophy of symbolism served as a framework for Langer's formulation of "new key" concepts. This book had varied reception among scholars in the field, but was nevertheless a landmark. Langer expounded upon the idea that there are things inaccessible to language that have their own forms of conception. She refused to accept the common premise that language represented the limits of rational experience. It was in this book that she delved into what she considered the human need for "symbolic transformation"—that man is constantly creating new symbols for different areas of life and thought. Langer intended to create a frame of mind that would lead people to treat with the same seriousness as is given to the sciences, areas such as art and social sciences that had previously not been thought to lend themselves to philosophical logic. The book laid the groundwork for Langer's work on the larger problem of the structure and the nature of art, a subject that became the focus of her continued writing.

In what Langer termed a sequel to *Philosophy in a New Key*, she wrote *Feeling and Form: A Theory of Art* (1953), in which she further developed her theories of symbolism and logic. Dedicated to the memory of Ernst Cassirer, *Feeling and Form* is the application of her theories to each of the arts separately. She defined such words as expression, creation, symbol, and intuition in such a way that art might be better understood in those particular terms. The book was not intended to further the cause of such things as criticism of artistic masterpieces nor was it to help in the creation of art. The expressed purpose was to define simply the logical and philosophical basis on which art rests and the relationship of art to feeling. Langer's *Problems of Art* followed in 1957 and remained true to the concepts set forth in her previous book. She maintained that art is not an expression of the artist's own feeling, but is rather an expression of his knowledge of feeling in nondiscursive terms (symbols). It is an expression not possible to the same extent by verbal means and for which art provides humans with a set of symbols whose meanings may vary as necessary. Langer believed strongly that the importance of this concept was that once an artist is supplied with a secure framework in logic and symbolism, it is possible for his knowledge to exceed even the limits of his own experience.

Langer had left Radcliffe in 1942 and spent a year teaching at the University of Delaware in Newark before teaching from 1945 to 1950 at Columbia University. With the support of the university and a Rockefeller Foundation Grant, she wrote *Feeling and Form*. She continued to work as a guest lecturer and to contribute articles and chapters to books in the area of art and aesthetics. In 1954, she was made chair of the Department of Philosophy at Connecticut College in New London, Connecticut. She remained there until her retirement in 1962, when she was named a professor emeritus and a research scholar in philosophy. In 1956, with a grant from the Edgar J. Kaufmann Charitable Trust of Pittsburgh, Langer began the project that was to be the pinnacle of her career. The depth of the work was such that she committed herself totally to the writing and in 1967, the first volume of *Mind: An Essay on Human Feeling* was published. Two more volumes were to follow; the second in the series was published in 1972 and the final installment appeared in 1982. These products of Langer's latest years assumed a certain familiarity with the earlier suppositions she advanced in *Philosophy in a New Key* and *Feeling and Form*. Langer examined in great detail the course of development of human feeling as it departed from the level of the animal who possesses feeling without intellect. The work was the culmination of her understanding of philosophical symbolic logic as applied to abstract areas of human existence.

Langer was recognized by a number of disciplines for her work through the years. Equally comfortable lecturing to educators, philosophers, artists, or scientists, she was a frequent guest at conventions and conferences. In 1950, she was the recipient of the Radcliffe Alumnae Achievement Award and in 1960, she was elected to the American Academy of Arts and Sciences. Honorary doctorate degrees were bestowed upon her by Wilson College, Wheaton College, and Western College for Women.

Upon her retirement from Connecticut College, she remained in her colonial home in Old Lyme, retreating when necessary to the solitude of an old farmhouse in Ulster County, New York, where she avoided all modern conveniences including electric lights and especially the telephone. Fiercely independent, she organized her life to suit her needs. Communing with nature, quiet time spent writing and thinking, and occasionally playing chamber music with friends filled her days with favorite activities. After her husband died in 1977, her children and grandchildren provided companionship during their welcome visits as did her lifelong friends from her professorial days. Langer died in 1985 at her Connecticut home at the age of eighty-nine.

Summary

Susanne Langer entered a field in which few women had ever achieved serious recognition and her work had a profound effect on philosophical thought of the twentieth century. Her hunger for knowledge and experience in almost every realm of human existence from the most scientific fields to simple, as well as sophisticated, artistic forms of expression provided a rich backdrop for her ideas. From her thinking emerged some of the most scholarly work which exists in the fields of philosophy and aesthetics. Her contributions to education in these fields and her influence on the approach to philosophy and education brought about a distinct change in the framework of the logic upon which human feeling and art are interpreted.

Bibliography

Danto, Arthur C. "Mind as Feeling, Form as Presence; Langer as Philosopher." *The Journal of Philosophy* 81 (November, 1984): 641-646. Danto follows the progression and development in philosophical thought that occurred in Langer's literary career. The article is one of three in this special issue that formed the basis of a symposium entitled "The Philosophy of Susanne K. Langer" for the American Philosophical Society in December, 1984.

de Sousa, Ronald B. "Teleology and the Great Shift." *The Journal of Philosophy* 81 (November, 1984): 647-653. The "great shift" from animal to human behavior and its philosophical implications are explored by de Sousa based on Langer's *Mind: An Essay on Human Feeling.*

Hagberg, Garry. "Art and the Unsayable: Langer's Tractarian Aesthetics." *British Journal of Aesthetics* 24 (1984): 325+. Hagberg reconsiders Langer's theory that art is a creation of forms that symbolize human feeling, picking up where language ends.

Langer, Susanne. *Philosophy in a New Key.* Cambridge, Mass.: Harvard University Press, 1942. This book, with a preface by the author, is the treatise upon which all Langer's later writing in the area of philosophy and aesthetics is based. Her basic tenets about the importance of symbolic logic as applied to human expression are detailed.

_____ . "Why Philosophy?" *The Saturday Evening Post* 234 (May 13, 1961): 34-35. Langer discusses her personal life and career and major factors which influenced the direction of her philosophical thought. Her views about the lack of apparent philosophical framework in modern society are also presented.

Morawski, Stefan. "Art as Semblance." *The Journal of Philosophy* 81 (November, 1984): 654-662. Morawski grapples with Langer's theories of symbolic logic in aesthetics and Langer's role as a pivotal philosophical figure in the 1950's.

Sargeant, Winthrop. "Philosopher in a New Key." *The New Yorker* 36 (December 3, 1960): 67-68. In a lengthy and intimate interview, Sargeant questions Langer about her life and career, revealing information about her method of working and lifestyle not available in a formal biography.

Sandra C. McClain

ANGELA LANSBURY

Born: October 16, 1925; London, England

Areas of Achievement: Theater and drama and film
Contribution: Lansbury has been an award-winning actress on stage, screen, and television.

Early Life

Angela Brigid Lansbury was born on October 16, 1925, in London, England. Edgar Isaac Lansbury, her lumber merchant father, married Moyna Macgill, a London actress. Her mother's example, however, did not automatically interest the young Angela in a theatrical career: When she was six, George Lansbury, her grandfather, became leader of the British Labour Party, and her earliest career interests were in politics.

When Angela was high-school age, however, World War II had begun and the Nazis were bombing London. Her mother gave her a choice: Either study acting with a tutor at home or evacuate to a boarding school in the country (a scenario that Lansbury would later re-create in the Walt Disney film *Bedknobs and Broomsticks*). Angela chose acting as the lesser of two evils, but wound up enjoying it so much that she enrolled in the Webber-Douglas School of Singing and Dancing in London in 1940. As the bombing intensified, however, Angela and her mother moved to New York, where Angela received a scholarship at the Feagin School of Drama and Radio.

A fellow student at the Feagin School, Arthur Bourbon, helped Angela develop a variety act, and in 1942 she was signed as a nightclub singer at the prestigious Samovar Club in Montreal, Canada. When her six-week run was over, Angela joined her mother in Los Angeles in 1942, where they worked during the Christmas season at Bullock's department store as sales clerks. After the Christmas rush, Angela was retained in cosmetic sales.

Late in 1943, Angela received a tip from an actor friend that Metro-Goldwyn-Mayer (MGM) was looking for an English actress for *The Picture of Dorian Gray*. When she applied, however, the studio had her test for a cockney role in *Gaslight*. The test so impressed Louis B. Mayer that he offered her a seven-year contract with options. Her performance in *Gaslight* (1944) was nominated for a Best Supporting Actress Oscar, as was her performance in *The Picture of Dorian Gray* (1945), which won a Golden Globe award. Critics praised her; it was clear that Angela Lansbury had arrived as a film actress. In 1945, she married actor Richard Cromwell; they were divorced after nine months.

Life's Work

For the next twenty years, Angela Lansbury would be typecast in some of the least likable female roles Hollywood could produce. Two roles in 1946 set the tone: In *Hoodlum Saint* she was the less-than-virtuous love interest who supplied a foil to the ideal woman Esther Williams, and after filming *The Harvey Girls*, she found herself hissed in public for her meanness to Judy Garland. After her role as a teenager in *National Velvet* (1945), Lansbury was invariably cast older than she was. In two films released in 1948, the twenty-two-year-old actress grew progressively older: In *If Winter Comes* she played a thirty-five-year-old jealous wife, and in *State of the Union* she played a thirty-eight-year-old millionaire who tries to lure a presidential candidate away from his wife. In the same year, she played the naughty Queen Anne in *The Three Musketeers*.

On August 12, 1949, Lansbury was married to Peter Shaw, who later became a Hollywood agent and then an MGM executive. Angela became an "instant mom," rearing Peter's son from a previous marriage, David. Two years later, she became a U.S. citizen, and the following year, 1952, she gave birth to a son, Anthony Peter. In 1953, her daughter Dierdre Angela was born.

When her MGM contract expired in 1950, Lansbury found work in other studios. The 1950's also marked the beginning of the television era, however, and Lansbury was in demand as a character actress in such early television drama venues as *Revlon Mirror Theater* (1953), *Star Time* (1955), in which she was the only female to receive star billing, *Ford Television Theater* (1956), and *Playhouse 90* (1956-1961). She was also a regular panelist on the television game show *Pantomime Quiz* in the late 1950's.

Because most television drama in the 1950's originated from New York, Lansbury's work in the medium brought her close to Broadway. On April 11, 1957, she made her Broadway debut at the Henry Miller Theatre in *Hotel Paradiso*. The show had a modest run of 108 performances, though the critics praised her performance. Nevertheless, Lansbury did not believe that the stage was her medium, and she returned to film, where she continued to be typecast as a painted lady or an adulteress in *The Long Hot Summer* (1958), *The Dark at the Top of the Stairs* (1960), and *A Breath of Scandal* (1960). She played the same type of character in her return to Broadway in *A Taste of Honey*, which opened at the Lyceum on October 4, 1960. Critics praised both her and the play, which ran for 376 performances.

Her film roles in the early 1960's continued to make her older than she was: In 1962, at age thirty-six, she played the mother of twenty-seven-year-old Elvis Presley in *Blue Hawaii* and twenty-four-year-old Warren Beatty in *All Fall Down*, and the following year, at thirty-seven, she played the mother of thirty-four-year-old Laurence Harvey in *The Manchurian Candidate*—a role that brought her third Oscar nomination. Lansbury was also nominated for an Emmy that year (1963) for a guest-star role in the psychological-medical television series *Eleventh Hour*.

In April of 1964, Angela Lansbury returned to Broadway in another hard-boiled matron role, as the corrupt mayor of a dying town, in Stephen Sondheim's avant-garde musical *Anyone Can Whistle*. Unfortunately, the musical was too avant-garde: It closed after nine performances. Nevertheless, Lansbury did not give up on Broadway, and in 1965, for the first time in her career, she actively pursued a stage role instead of having to be cajoled into it.

The role of Mame Dennis made theatergoers realize what film director Frank Capra had said two decades earlier: Angela Lansbury was a consummate character actress who could play virtually any part. The role also won Lansbury her first major award: the Antoinette Perry (Tony) award for Best Actress in a Musical. *Mame* ran for 1,508 performances.

Lansbury's new success was darkened by family difficulties: Like many parents of teens in the late 1960's, her life was shaken by her children's addiction to drugs. At the same time, her mother developed throat cancer and had her vocal cords removed— a crushing blow to her actress mother.

Keeping busy on stage helped Lansbury to cope with such turmoil. In 1969, she returned to Broadway in the lead role of a Jerry Herman musical, *Dear World*, which enjoyed only a modest run. The critics, however, were not disappointed, and Lansbury won her second Tony.

In 1970, another personal tragedy became the last straw that made Lansbury pull back from the Hollywood-Broadway lifestyle. Her Malibu home was destroyed in a brushfire. Remembering the therapeutic effect of her visits to Ireland with her mother when she was a teenager, Angela settled there with her husband and children, living in rural simplicity for nine years. Although she spent more time in a less hectic pace with her family, she did not avoid acting. In 1971, she filmed the Walt Disney musical *Bedknobs and Broomsticks*, and in the summer of 1972, she reprised her role in *Mame* for the Westbury Music Fair in Long Island. She played the lead (Mama Rose) in a 1973 London production of *Gypsy*, which was brought to Los Angeles in 1974, and then to Broadway as a revival in 1975, winning Lansbury her third Tony for Best Actress in a Musical. Later that year, while rehearsing the role of Gertrude in *Hamlet*, which her mother had taught her as an audition piece thirty-five years earlier, she received the news of her mother's death.

Angela Lansbury once more captured Broadway in the character role of the scheming Mrs. Lovett in Stephen Sondheim's dark musical *Sweeney Todd* (1979). She captured her fourth Tony and a Drama Desk award, and took the show on tour and filmed it for the PBS television series *Great Performances*. Her film roles at this time seem, in hindsight, almost like preludes to her best-known television role as mystery writer and amateur sleuth Jessica Fletcher in the CBS series *Murder, She Wrote*. She appeared in *Death on the Nile* (1978), which was based on an Agatha Christie novel, and *The Lady Vanishes* (1979), playing a character much like Christie's Miss Marple, whom she did play in *The Mirror Crack'd* (1980).

The Miss Marple character quite obviously contributed to the Jessica Fletcher character in the script Lansbury received in 1983 for a proposed television series. In fact, a Miss Marple story, "Murder, She Said," suggested the title for the series, *Murder, She Wrote*. Lansbury had been approached regularly with television offers since her success in 1979 with *Sweeney Todd*, but the long-range commitment to a series did not appeal to her. Yet there was something in this character, part Miss Marple, part Agatha Christie, that touched a chord in Lansbury. She accepted the role and was an immediate success. The series was rated eighth in its first season and third in its second. For her work in the series, Lansbury won two Golden Globe Awards

(1984 and 1987) for Best Actress in television drama.

In 1988, Lansbury produced a successful exercise video for older men and women, *Positive Moves*, which also sold well in book form. Another new venture was lending her voice to the cartoon character Mrs. Potts in the Walt Disney animated feature *Beauty and the Beast* (1991), for which she also sang the title song. Her previous voice-overs for cartoons included the made-for-television *First Christmas Snow* (1975) and *The Last Unicorn* (1982).

Summary

Angela Lansbury's contributions to American drama—film, stage, and television—go beyond her awards and high ratings. Her professionalism in turning some of the least desirable Hollywood roles into moving portraits of real people provided an example to a film industry too often accused of shallow characterization. Lansbury's portrayals of endless Hollywood harridans show that she understands what Shakespeare understood so well and what Stanislavsky taught: A villain is never a villain in her own eyes. By finding the person within the "bad girl" roles she was given, Lansbury pointed the way to characterizations subtler than those film audiences were led to expect.

In the same roles, and in her later career, Lansbury also became an example of grace triumphing over one of Hollywood's deepest prejudices: the bias against age. In her twenties and thirties, she did so almost against her will, taking roles as characters ten and twenty years older than she was. This sent an unspoken message to actresses who would refuse such casting: The enemy is not age itself, but the prejudice against it. In her later career, Lansbury helped to erode this prejudice simply by being herself: a graceful attractive woman who achieved beauty on camera not by trying to look younger, but by embracing the beauty of maturity. In 1988, she hosted the Tony awards show on television in a daring Bob Mackie gown that another era would have thought "too young for her."

Yet Lansbury fought ageism in more direct ways, too. Exercise was a part of her preparation for roles long before it was popular: In 1966, she spent three hours a day in the gym preparing for her role in *Mame* (once the show opened, she got all the exercise she needed on stage). Twenty years later, she continued her exercise regimen and showed others how to stay fit in her 1990 exercise book and video *Positive Moves*.

Bibliography

Blum, Richard A., and Richard D. Lindheim. *Primetime: Network Television Programming*. Boston: Focal Press, 1987. Though this is a general book about television programming, the second chapter uses Lansbury's series *Murder, She Wrote* as an example of how a series is developed, including script changes to reflect Lansbury's personality.

Culhane, John. "Angela Lansbury Takes the Lead." *Reader's Digest* 130 (June, 1987): 20-26. Employing interviews with Lansbury after the success of her television series, this article contains a balanced account of Lansbury's triumph over personal difficulties in the 1970's. The account is direct without being sensational.

Lansbury, Angela. "Angela Lansbury." In *The Player: A Profile of an Art*, by Lillian Ross and Helen Ross. New York: Simon & Schuster, 1962. This very revealing 3,500-word autobiography is the ultimate source of most of the biographical information published elsewhere on Lansbury. It provides insight into Lansbury's attitudes and feelings, gives factual information, and is very readable.

Lansbury, Angela, with Mimi Avins. *Positive Moves*. New York: Delacorte Press, 1990. Though primarily an exercise and self-help book based on her successful exercise video, this brief volume is also sprinkled with biographical information and personal insights, especially in the opening chapter.

Nolan, Patricia. "I Had to Save My Family." *50 Plus* 28 (October, 1988): 20-21. A frank interview with Angela Lansbury regarding her family's health difficulties and the steps she took to improve them: namely, moving to Ireland, away from the Hollywood lifestyle and influences.

John R. Holmes

JULIA C. LATHROP

Born: June 29, 1858; Rockford, Illinois
Died: April 15, 1932; Rockford, Illinois
Areas of Achievement: Government and politics and social reform
Contribution: As the first woman to head a federal agency, the U.S. Children's Bureau (1912-1921), Lathrop identified and shaped significantly twentieth century public policy for children.

Early Life

Julia Clifford Lathrop was born on June 29, 1858, in Rockford, Illinois. She was the first of five children, two girls and three boys, born to Sarah Adeline Potter Lathrop and William Lathrop. Her mother was graduated as valedictorian from the first Rockford Seminary (later renamed Rockford College) class in 1854. An enthusiastic woman suffrage advocate, Sarah Lathrop also urged the creation and maintenance of art and cultural organizations in her community. William Lathrop was a prominent attorney and one of the founders of the Illinois Republican Party. Elected to the state general assembly and Congress, William Lathrop was a reform-minded politician who supported civil service legislation, woman suffrage, and various social welfare issues.

Julia Lathrop attended her mother's alma mater for one year before transferring to Vassar College, where she earned a degree in 1880. During the next ten years, Lathrop worked in her father's law office and as a secretary for two local manufacturing companies. In 1890, she moved to Chicago, where she joined Rockford College graduates Jane Addams and Ellen Gates Starr at their recently established Hull House settlement. Lathrop remained at Hull House for twenty years.

Life's Work

Julia Lathrop's association with Hull House placed her in contact with one of the most significant social reform networks of the Progressive Era. In addition, beginning in 1893, she began volunteer work as a Cook County agent visitor. Assigned to investigate relief applicants living within a ten-block radius of Hull House, Lathrop had the opportunity to observe the desperate circumstances of many ordinary people in an increasingly industrial and urban America. Many of her findings were published two years later in *Hull-House Maps and Papers* (1895). Her work came to the attention of reform governor John P. Altgeld, who appointed Lathrop to the Illinois State Board of Charities in 1893. In this capacity, she visited each of the state's 102 county poorfarms and almshouses. Particularly appalled by the grouping of children, the elderly, the mentally handicapped, and the sick in the same institutions, Lathrop spent the next twelve years lobbying for the creation of separate facilities for these constituencies. As a result of her efforts and those of other prominent activists, Illinois built new state hospitals for the insane and, in 1899, established the nation's first juvenile court system in Cook County. In 1901, Lathrop resigned her state appointment in protest when Altgeld's successor circumvented the board's authority by giving jobs to political supporters rather than adhering to the state's civil service laws.

Lathrop believed that the political spoils system resulted in the appointment of poorly qualified staff. From 1903 to 1904, she and another member of the settlement house network, Graham Taylor, devised and implemented courses designed to produce trained individuals for careers in social work. Educators Edith Abbott, Sophonisba Breckinridge, and others later joined Taylor and Lathrop in this effort. Their "college" was incorporated in 1908 as the Chicago School of Civics and Philanthropy (made part of the University of Chicago in 1920). In the meantime, newly elected Governor Charles Deneen had reappointed Lathrop to the State Board of Charities, where she served from 1905 to 1909. She also became one of the founders of the Illinois Immigrants' Protective League (1908) and continued to work as a trustee for that organization until her death.

These years also brought Lathrop deeper into child welfare work. In 1909, she attended the first White House Conference on the Care of Dependent Children. At that meeting, participants heartily endorsed a proposal to establish a federal children's bureau. New York's Henry Street Settlement founder Lillian D. Wald and the National Consumers' League's Florence Kelley had first suggested the idea for a federal bureau mandated to investigate and report on American children as early as 1903. In 1905, the National Child Labor Committee (NCLC) made the creation of such an agency its highest legislative priority. The measure received little attention, however, until the 1909 White House meeting. Over the next three years, supporters lobbied Congress on the proposal's behalf.

On April 9, 1912, President William Howard Taft signed legislation establishing the U.S. Children's Bureau in the Department of Commerce and Labor. The next step was to find a Children's Bureau chief who would be acceptable to all concerned. Taft asked the NCLC for advice. In response, members of the NCLC board met with President Taft on April 15 and named Julia Lathrop as their first choice. Although she was well known to most social welfare reformers in Illinois, Lathrop was not a nationally recognized children's rights advocate. NCLC board member Jane Addams lobbied strongly on her behalf. A year earlier, Lathrop had published a report on public schools in the Philippines after completing a trip around the world with her sister Anna Case. This study, combined with the NCLC's recommendation, Lathrop's experience in Illinois, and assurances from Attorney General George Wickersham that there was no legal restriction to appointing a woman, led Taft to name her as Children's Bureau chief on April 17, 1912. Although national woman suffrage was not made a part of the constitution for another seven years, many Americans believed that child welfare work was a proper domain for women. Therefore, Lathrop became the first woman to head a federal bureau.

Under Lathrop's direction, the Children's Bureau hired a staff, selected fields of work, and designed and implemented a program for the "whole child." The U.S. Children's Bureau was the first national government agency in the world created solely to consider the problems of children. Limited by a paltry appropriation of $25,640 and a staff of only fifteen, Lathrop was determined that financial obstacles should not hinder the bureau's beginnings. She built on statistical work already completed by other government agencies and supplemented her staff with volunteers from the General Federation of Women's Clubs and other private organizations. This tactic proved to be a valuable source of public support for the agency.

The chief also made an astute choice of infant mortality as the bureau's first subject of original investigation. Although its institution was generally a popular idea, some individuals believed that the Children's Bureau might violate parental and states' rights as well as serve as a wasteful duplication of federal activities. The American Medical Association complained that the Public Health Service should deal with child health issues. Other critics questioned the suitability of a childless "spinster" for such a job. Sensitive to such criticism, Lathrop realized that the study of infant mortality was probably the least debatable topic under the Children's Bureau's mandate. The United States lagged far behind many other countries in the collection and analysis of such data. Furthermore, no branch of the federal government, including the Public Health Service, had investigated why so many babies died before their first birthday.

The Children's Bureau found that the United States' 1913 rate of 132 deaths per 1,000 live births ranked behind seven comparable nations. The effort to save babies' lives became the flagship issue for the Children's Bureau. The popularity of this work enabled Lathrop and her staff later to address more controversial issues, such as child labor regulation, juvenile delinquency, and mothers' pensions. Although her political prowess is often overlooked, Lathrop was an astute politician as well as a competent administrator.

During her tenure as chief, the Children's Bureau's budget increased tenfold and the effort to reduce the nation's high infant mortality rate resulted in passage of the pioneering 1921 Sheppard-Towner Maternity and Infancy Act. In addition, the agency was given the responsibility for enforcing the first federal child labor law, the 1916 Keating-Owen Act. Lathrop brought former Hull House resident Grace Abbott to Washington to head the bureau's Child Labor Division. Although the Supreme Court declared the Keating-Owen law unconstitutional in 1918, this legislation and the Sheppard-Towner Act served as blueprints for the children's programs included in the 1935 Social Security Act and the 1938 Fair Labor Standards Act. Thousands of mothers wrote the bureau for advice, and the chief and her staff carefully answered every letter. Overall, Lathrop's strategy firmly established the Children's Bureau as the major source of information and advocate for America's children. By 1921, Julia Lathrop was one of the most popular and well-known federal bureaucrats. Her election to presidency of the National Council of Social Work in 1918 also shows her status as a political insider who had contacts with a vast reform network. Confident that the Children's Bureau was a permanent part of the federal bureaucracy, Lathrop resigned as Children's Bureau chief in August, 1921. Ill with a hyperthyroid condition but not wanting to jeopardize the pattern of work she had established, Lathrop convinced President Warren G. Harding to appoint Grace Abbott as her successor.

For the remainder of her life, Lathrop lived in Rockford with her sister. During these years, she remained active and served as president of the Illinois League of Women

Voters (1922-1924), as an assessor for the League of Nations' Child Welfare Committee (1925-1931), and as an adviser to a presidential committee examining conditions at Ellis Island (1925), and she continued to work for the rights of minors. Two months before her death, Lathrop orchestrated a campaign to keep Russell Robert McWilliams, a seventeen-year-old Rockford boy convicted of killing a motorman, from execution under Illinois' death penalty. McWilliams was granted a reprieve after Lathrop's death. Lathrop died in Rockford on April 15, 1932, at the age of seventy-three.

Summary

Although Julia Lathrop never married or had children of her own, her legacy is most important in the field of child welfare. In its first decade of work, the U.S. Children's Bureau identified major issues and designed the blueprint according to which federal child welfare policy has developed. Furthermore, even though she did not seek the appointment of chief and actually had little to do with the effort to establish the bureau, Lathrop's acceptance of the job and the strategy she implemented secured a role for women in child welfare policy development and implementation. Her appointment also set a precedent that was not broken until President Richard M. Nixon appointed the Children's Bureau's first male chief in 1973. Although Lathrop's "whole child" philosophy did not survive federal restructuring in 1946, which reduced the agency's influence, the Children's Bureau's first decades of work highlighted the vulnerability of children and opened public debate on how best to preserve "a right to childhood." Julia Lathrop's ability to act as "statesman" as well as politician made her a successful bureaucrat who helped to legitimize the notion that the federal government's responsibilities include the welfare of its youngest citizens.

Bibliography

Addams, Jane. *My Friend, Julia Lathrop*. New York: Macmillan, 1935. To date, the only biography of Lathrop's life. This work focuses on her life to 1912.
Ladd-Taylor, Molly. *Mother-Work: Women, Child Welfare, and the State, 1890-1930*. Urbana: University of Illinois Press, 1994. This work underscores the role of women in the development of the American social welfare system and includes a discussion of Lathrop's part in this process.
_____ , ed. *Raising a Baby the Government Way: Mothers' Letters to the Children's Bureau, 1915-1932*. New Brunswick, N.J.: Rutgers University Press, 1986. An edited collection of letters sent to the U.S. Children's Bureau asking for advice or other assistance. Includes some of Lathrop's responses and an overview of the bureau's early work.
Lathrop, Julia, et al. *The Child, the Clinic and the Court: A Group of Papers by Jane Addams, C. Judson Herrick, A. L. Jacoby, and Others*. New York: New Republic, 1927. An excellent source of Lathrop's opinions concerning the role of the state in child welfare.
Meckel, Richard A. *"Save the Babies": American Public Health Reform and the*

Prevention of Infant Mortality, 1850-1929. Baltimore: The Johns Hopkins University Press, 1990. While focusing on the national effort to reduce infant mortality, this work includes an examination of the Children's Bureau's role in the effort to save babies' lives.

Muncy, Robyn. *Creating a Female Dominion in American Reform, 1890-1935*. New York: Oxford University Press, 1991. An important work examining how Julia Lathrop and Grace Abbott worked to keep child welfare policy as a proper domain for women.

Parker, Jacqueline K., and Edward M. Carpenter. "Julia Lathrop and the Children's Bureau: The Emergence of an Institution." *Social Service Review* 55 (March, 1981): 60-77. An excellent brief overview of the Children's Bureau and its work under Lathrop's tenure.

Kriste Lindenmeyer

EMMA LAZARUS

Born: July 22, 1849; New York, New York
Died: November 19, 1887; New York, New York
Areas of Achievement: Literature and social reform
Contribution: Lazarus began writing poems as a girl and published volumes of poetry,
  plays, translations, a novel, and many influential essays in *Century* magazine and
  in the American Jewish press. She is best remembered for her sonnet "The New
  Colossus," which is engraved on the base of the Statue of Liberty.

Early Life

On July 22, 1849, Emma Lazarus was born into an American Jewish family that
had lived in New York for generations. One of her ancestors was a Sephardic Jew from
Portugal who had fled the Spanish Inquisition and emigrated to the West Indies.
Emma's father, Moses Lazarus, was a successful sugar merchant and one of New
York's wealthiest men. He was a founder of the Knickerbocker Club and belonged to
the influential Spanish-Portuguese Synagogue. Emma's mother, Esther Nathan Lazarus, belonged to a prominent New York family whose members were distinguished
in the legal profession.

Emma, the fourth daughter born to the family, was named for one of the novelist
Jane Austen's heroines. A boy and two more girls followed. The family enjoyed
summers in fashionable Newport, Rhode Island. Emma and her older sisters were
educated at home by private tutors; Emma in particular was considered too frail for
schooling outside the house. She had a gift for languages and learned French, Italian,
and German. She also immersed herself in children's stories and then in the volumes
of her father's library. She was particularly taken with Walter Scott, the Scottish
novelist and poet, and with Greek and Roman mythology.

When the Civil War broke out, Emma was only eleven, but she was aware of the
uncles and male cousins, dressed in Union blue, who arrived at her home at all hours
to say tearful goodbyes to her parents. She wrote poems on war and on nature themes,
and translated French and German poets. Her father retired in 1865 at the age of
fifty-two and devoted himself to his children. When he saw Emma's notebooks, he
was taken with her thirty original poems as well as with her translations of Heinrich
Heine and Victor Hugo. He decided to have the manuscript printed for private
circulation. *Poems and Translations by Emma Lazarus. Written Between the Ages of
Fourteen and Sixteen* appeared in 1866. The book was received enthusiastically and,
with the addition of ten new poems, was reprinted the following year for general
circulation. To crown the events of her eighteenth year, Moses Lazarus introduced
Emma to Ralph Waldo Emerson, who was then in his sixties. Emerson, one of the most
influential poets and writers of his time, asked the young poet to send a copy of her
book to him in Concord, Massachusetts. He praised the book and offered constructive
criticism, which led to a long and fruitful correspondence. He was to be an important
influence on her work.

Life's Work

In the next few years, Emma Lazarus pursued nature, classical, and Jewish themes in her poetry. She wrote one of her best-known poems, "In the Jewish Synagogue at Newport," drawing on the historical resonance of the oldest synagogue in the United States and patterning it after Henry Wadsworth Longfellow's "The Jewish Cemetery at Newport." "Admetus," a long, romantic poem with scenes from Greek mythology, was accepted by *Lippincott's*, the leading literary magazine of the day, and became the title poem of her second collection. Emerson praised *Admetus and Other Poems*, and Lazarus dedicated it to him over his objections. Published in 1871, the book was well received in the United States and earned rave reviews in England, where one critic compared Lazarus favorably to Robert Browning, one of the most erudite living English poets.

Lazarus' next project was a romantic novel titled *Alide*, based on a love incident in the life of Johann Wolfgang von Goethe, the great German writer whose work she had translated. When *Alide* was published in 1874, Lazarus sent a copy to Ivan Turgenev, a world-famous Russian novelist whom she revered. His response was reserved but positive; he praised her grasp of the German spirit and admired her depiction of character. Lazarus treasured his letter, and it may have offered her some comfort when *Parnassus*, a poetry anthology edited by her friend Emerson, appeared shortly afterward. It was an important anthology in which English and American poets were published together for the first time. When she found that she was omitted from *Parnassus* despite Emerson's years of praise for her work, Lazarus was deeply wounded. She wrote him a proud letter questioning his sincerity, but he did not answer.

Lazarus' mother died early in 1876, breaking up an unusually close-knit family circle and prompting new poems on the theme of mother love. The following summer, after a year and a half of silence, Emerson and his wife invited Lazarus to visit them in Concord. It was a great adventure for the twenty-seven-year-old poet. She was immediately taken with Mrs. Emerson and developed a friendship with Emerson's daughter Ellen, who was ten years her senior. Among the people she met there was the poet and biographer William Ellery Channing, who took Lazarus to Henry David Thoreau's cottage at Walden Pond and presented her with the pocket compass that his old friend Thoreau had carried on his walks.

Lazarus returned to her literary life in New York, interspersed with summers in elegant Newport. Her poems continued to appear, and her name became widely known as her activities branched out into critical essays, book reviews, and profiles of prominent artists. Lazarus now began to recognize the limitations of her knowledge of the world and started to question the importance of her work. At about that time, Gustave Gottheil, a New York rabbi, asked her to translate some medieval Jewish hymns from German. These were the first of many that she was to translate from German, Spanish, and Hebrew sources and that were to appear over the years in the *Jewish Messenger*. She next wrote a long, ambitious work titled *The Dance to Death*. This powerful verse-drama in five acts chronicles the martyrdom of the Jews of

Nordhausen in 1349, when they were accused of causing the Black Plague and were sentenced to be burned to death. At the time, Lazarus neither showed it to anyone nor submitted it for publication. Her interest in her Jewish heritage found a new outlet in the life and work of the German Jewish poet Heinrich Heine. She translated many of his poems and wrote others based on Heine's notes that were found after his early death in 1856. A book grew from these endeavors, *Poems and Ballads of Heinrich Heine*, which included Lazarus' biographical study of the German poet.

The early years of the 1880's were marked by historical events that were to have a profound effect on Lazarus' work. A series of bloody riots against the Jewish population in Russia had caused hundreds of thousands of destitute Jews to flee to the United States. Lazarus visited the refugees at Ward's Island in the East River, where they were temporarily housed. The first task was to resettle the refugees, and she immediately started to raise funds for that purpose from her wide circle of acquaintances. In April of 1882, *Century* magazine carried an article by a Russian historian that justified the pogroms by vilifying Jews. Incensed, Lazarus wrote an answering essay that appeared in the May issue. She had found her cause, and with it, a new voice.

She wrote many new poems on Jewish themes and sent them to Philip Cowen, editor of the *American Hebrew*. She also sent him *The Dance to Death*, which he published in installments. In September of 1882, the verse-drama was published together with new poems in *Songs of a Semite*. Lazarus continued to visit the refugees on Ward's Island, occasions that stimulated new perspectives. In a burst of energy, Lazarus wrote "An Epistle to the Hebrews," which grew into fifteen articles that appeared in the *American Hebrew* between November, 1882, and February, 1883. The work was an appeal to American Jews to reflect upon their history and try to retain their special identities. "An Epistle" provoked great controversy, particularly in its support for the establishment of a Jewish state in Palestine.

Her reputation preceded her when Lazarus sailed to England in the spring of 1883 with her younger sister Annie. She was showered with invitations from the artistic elite of British society. She returned home in the autumn, and shortly after, she received an appeal from a fund-raising committee for the gigantic new Statue of Liberty to be erected on Bedlow Island in New York Harbor. The committee requested an original manuscript to sell at an auction along with manuscripts by Henry Wadsworth Longfellow, Walt Whitman, and Mark Twain. In reply, Lazarus wrote the sonnet "The New Colossus," a poem that was to ensure her immortality in a world of changing tastes and fashions.

The following year Lazarus fell ill, but she persevered in her work, writing a long poem that was intended to sum up her beliefs about the Jews. Influenced by Walt Whitman, she chose a new form: a cycle of lyrics made up of long, sprawling lines, which became "By the Waters of Babylon." Lazarus had apparently recovered from her illness when her father died in May of 1885. It was a numbing shock, and eight weeks later she departed for a tour of Europe with her sister Josephine. Lazarus spent two years abroad, although she was an invalid for much of that time. She finally returned to New York in 1887, where she died of cancer at the age of thirty-eight.

Summary

Emma Lazarus' popular fame rests on her sonnet on the Statue of Liberty. Ironically, the author never assigned any particular importance to the poem. Only through the efforts of a friend, Georgiana Schuyler, was "The New Colossus" inscribed on a plaque on the base of the Statue of Liberty in 1903, sixteen years after the author's death. During her lifetime, hers was a strong and eloquent voice advancing provocative ideas on the history and future of the Jews. At a time when anti-Semitism was widespread, she wrote convincingly of the proud Jewish spirit. An ardently patriotic American, she had no difficulty reconciling this patriotism with her ethnic loyalty. She was one of the first Americans to take up the cause of a Jewish homeland, an idea that was not welcomed by the American Jews of her time.

Quiet, almost withdrawn, Emma Lazarus became an influential writer and intellectual who was admired by major contemporary figures. It cannot be known what Emma Lazarus might have accomplished if she had lived, but in her thirty-eight years she became a widely known artist and important public advocate for causes whose time had not yet arrived.

Bibliography

Gordh, George. "Emma Lazarus: A Poet of Exile and Freedom." *The Christian Century* 103 (November 19, 1986): 1033-1036. In a careful reading of Lazarus' poetry, Gordh compared her early, romantic verse with the later work, which he finds imbued with a religious sensibility. "The New Colossus" is discussed at length.

Jacob, Heinrich E. *The World of Emma Lazarus*. New York: Schocken Books, 1949. Jacob uses a Freudian model to understand Lazarus, concluding that the major influence on her life was her father. This study is fanciful but interesting.

Lichtenstein, Diane. "Words and Worlds: Emma Lazarus's Conflicting Citizenships." *Tulsa Studies in Women's Literature* 6, no. 2 (Fall, 1987): 247-263. Lichtenstein demonstrates that Lazarus used her writing to achieve a resolution between her American and Jewish identities in the last decade of her life. The article also raises the issue of the poet's gender, another form of marginality that Lazarus forged into her unique identity.

Merriam, Eve. *Emma Lazarus: Woman with a Torch*. New York: Citadel Press, 1956. This biography studies Lazarus' life as it was reflected in her work. Merriam traces the poetry from the early focus on history and myth to its later engagement with events of her own time.

Vogel, Dan. *Emma Lazarus*. Boston: Twayne, 1980. This work, one of a standardized series of monographs, offers the general reader a well-organized, concrete overview of the poet's life and work.

Sheila Golburgh Johnson

ANN LEE

Born: February 29, 1736; Manchester, England
Died: September 8, 1784; Niskeyuna, New York
Area of Achievement: Religion
Contribution: Ann Lee was the founder of the United Society of Believers in Christ's
  Second Coming, a religious sect commonly known as the Shakers. Members of the
  sect believed Mother Ann to be the female embodiment of Christ and the maternal
  component of the Father/Mother God.

Early Life

Information about Ann Lee's childhood is scarce. According to Shaker tradition, she was born on February 29, 1736, in the slums of Manchester, a manufacturing town in northwest England. Cathedral records indicate that she was baptized in the Anglican church on June 1, 1742. Apparently, she was the second of eight children, five boys and three girls, in the John Lee household. Her father was a blacksmith. Little is known about her mother, whose name is unknown, except that she was a pious woman in the Anglican church.

Like most eighteenth century girls born into English working-class families, Ann received no formal education and remained illiterate throughout her life, but was industrious from her youth. As a teenager, she worked in the textile mills; at age twenty, she became a cook in a public infirmary. A turning point in Ann's life occurred in 1758, when she joined a society of religious dissenters led by Jane and James Wardley.

The Wardley group, called the Shaking Quakers by their critics, called people to repent and to be prepared for the imminent reappearance of Christ, who would sweep away all anti-Christian denominations and establish a millennial kingdom on earth. Worship at the Wardleys was informal and spirited. Believers gathered, sat briefly in silent meditation, and then responded to the impulses of the spirit. The services included ecstatic utterances, prophecies concerning the end of the world, physical manifestations such as falling and jerking, and personal testimonies of supernatural assistance.

In 1762, Ann was persuaded by her parents to marry Abraham Standerin, an illiterate blacksmith who may have worked for Ann's father. Historians have speculated that this marriage was arranged in order to wean Ann from her association with the Wardley sect. The marriage, which Ann apparently never desired, resulted in the birth of four children, all of whom died in infancy. The delivery of her last child was especially difficult. Forceps were used; Ann lost much blood and almost her life. When the infant died in October of 1766, the physically weak and emotionally dispirited mother sought divine consolation. In the midst of her anguish, Ann became convinced that sexual cohabitation was the source of not only her trevails but also of all evil. For Ann and for her future religious followers, salvation from sin demanded public confession and holy, celibate living after the pattern of Jesus.

Life's Work

After the death of her fourth child, Ann Lee assumed a more vocal and prominent role in the Wardley society. By the early 1770's, this religious sect was engaging in confrontational tactics designed to attract attention to its teachings. On several occasions, for example, the Shakers invaded the sanctuaries of congregations gathered for worship in order to disrupt the church services and proclaim their message of apocalyptic judgment. For these actions, they were prosecuted for assault, the destruction of property, and the breaching of the Sabbath. Among those fined and imprisoned was Ann Lee Standerin. While in prison, Ann received a "grand vision." In this vision, Christ appeared to Ann and told her she was to be his special instrument. As the "Mother of the New Creation" she would teach confession as the door to regeneration and celibacy as its "rule and cross."

Like many other groups of religious dissenters throughout history, the Shakers thrived on opposition, which united them against the "wicked world." Persecution, however, also brought much unpleasantness. Neighbors, disliking the noise, speaking in tongues, and dark prophecies of the Shaker meetings, verbally abused the members of the sect, charged them with heresy and witchcraft, and even threatened mob violence. Local authorities permitted the sect to worship together in private, but no street preaching or disruptive intrusions into other public services of worship were allowed. Although the sect won a few converts, such as John Lee, Ann's father, and William Lee, her brother, under these difficult circumstances, the prospects for evangelical success in England were limited.

In the spring of 1774, Ann received another vision informing her that a harvest of souls awaited her ministry in the United States. Shortly thereafter, eight members of the sect, plus Abraham Standerin, who never joined the group, left England for New York. The immigrants did not include the Wardleys, who by now disagreed with some of the teachings of Mother Ann. After a three-month voyage across the Atlantic Ocean aboard the ship *Mariah*, the group arrived in New York City on August 6. Financial problems forced the scattering of the small Shaker band. Several members sought work in upper New York state, near Albany. Ann herself remained in Manhattan, finding employment as a domestic servant. At this time, Ann still lived in a platonic relationship with her husband. Within a few years, however, the couple formally separated. Unlike Ann, Abraham Standerin refused to accept the Shaker commitment to celibacy.

In 1779, the Shakers purchased an isolated piece of land in Niskeyuna, near Albany. The dozen disciples of Mother Ann constructed a small building that served as both their communal quarters and meetinghouse. In April of 1780, two travelers stumbled upon the Shaker site. After receiving Shaker food, shelter, and religious instruction, the men promised to tell others in the New Light Baptist Church, where they were members, about the witness of Mother Ann. On May 19, 1780, the Shakers held their first worship service that was open to the general public. According to Shaker tradition, on this "Dark Day in New England" the sun did not shine, a phenomenon that may have been caused by smoke from burning farmland. In the excitement of the meeting, several visitors experienced religious conversion. News about the spiritual quickenings at Niskeyuna spread throughout the towns of New Lebanon and Albany, and soon the Shaker site was deluged with curious and spiritually hungry guests.

Upstate New York, like other areas in the former British colonies at this time, was bitterly divided between the American patriots who supported and the Loyalists (or Tories) who opposed independence from England. When a born-again Shaker convert was found by American patriots bringing some sheep to the commune at Niskeyuna, the anti-Tory forces became suspicious. Believing the Shaker sect to be a front organization for the British Crown, the American authorities issued a warrant for Ann Lee's arrest. To secure her release, William Lee, Ann's brother, asked General James Clinton of Albany to write a letter about the situation to the New York governor. The American general agreed, and with his assistance, Mother Ann was freed on December 4.

Publicity surrounding the arrest and release of Mother Ann aroused public sympathy from many New Yorkers who questioned why the authorities, who were allegedly fighting for freedom and personal liberty, would harass and imprison a religious pacifist who caused no harm to anyone. Buoyed by this positive response from the public, Mother Ann, William Lee, and James Whittaker, another Shaker elder who had come with the group from England, decided to begin a missionary tour into the neighboring states. Between May of 1781 and September of 1783, the three itinerant English evangelists traveled throughout Massachusetts and Connecticut spreading the tenets of the Shaker faith.

In New England, as in England, Shaker success and opposition went hand in hand. In community after community, Mother Ann's simple message, regeneration through confession and perfection through celibacy, provoked a great response. On several occasions, opponents stormed the meetings and quarters of the itinerant preachers, insulting, threatening, and even stoning and beating them nearly to death. In Harvard, Massachusetts, for example, when rumors circulated that the Shakers refused to support the American revolutionary cause, local officials called the militia to drive the Shaker leaders out of town. After a three-week stay in Stonington, Connecticut, the Shaker ambassadors were warned by members of the local Baptist society to leave town within twenty-four hours or face brutal beatings. In Petersham, Massachusetts, an angry mob attacked Mother Ann, dragged her down a flight of stairs feet first, and ripped off her garments. Despite, or perhaps in some cases because of, the fierce opposition, the saintly female pacifist won committed new converts to the Shaker faith in nearly every town she entered. Her evangelistic successes during this twenty-eight-month missionary tour laid the foundation for the establishment of future Shaker communities in Harvard, Shirley, and Hancock, Massachusetts, and in Enfield, Connecticut.

In September of 1783, the weary itinerants returned to their home in New York. Shortly after their arrival, the elders at Niskeyuna began the economic experiment in joint ownership for which later Shaker communities would become well known. The resulting form of Shaker communism, established so "that the poor might have an equal privilege of the gospel with the rich," rested on the common understanding that whatever was gained by individual industry would be used for the benefit and good of the whole society. The Shaker edict "Give all members of the Church an equal privilege, according to their abilities, to do good, as well as an equal privilege to receive according to their needs" became a central tenet of Shaker culture for the next two centuries.

Despite the tenacious spirit of the English immigrants, the years of toil, travel, persecution, and poverty took their toll on the Lee family. On July 21, 1784, William Lee died. According to Shaker tradition, he did not "appear to die by any natural infirmity; but he seemed to give up his life in sufferings." The death of Ann's brother and spiritual comrade saddened the founder of the faith. The ailing leader, harassed in both body and spirit from her youth, yearned to be freed from her earthly travails. Less than two months after William's death, early in the morning of September 8, 1784, Mother Ann exclaimed her final words, "I see Brother William coming, in a golden chariot, to take me home."

News of the passing of the "Mother of Zion" shocked many of Ann Lee's followers, who believed, in spite of her rejection of the doctrine, that her earthly ministry would last a thousand years. Although many followers lost faith and fell away from the church, the United Society of Believers under the leadership of James Whittaker—the sole remaining member of the Shaker triumvirate—survived this time of crisis. Notwithstanding its twentieth century demise, the Shaker movement exhibited an inner vitality and strength that enabled it to outlive all subsequent nineteenth century utopian experiments in New World socialism.

Summary

The daughter of an illiterate blacksmith from Manchester, England, Ann Lee lived most of her life in dire poverty. She never attended school and never read a book. None of her children survived infancy. She suffered through a difficult marriage and divorce. Yet Ann Lee was revered as the female embodiment of God by thousands of American men and women who called her "Mother," who pledged all their belongings to her cause, and who, in time, attempted to recall and publish for future generations every word she uttered.

As the charismatic leader of a millennialist movement. Mother Ann possessed an extraordinary power over people. For her followers, her saintly life was proof enough of the truth of her teachings. Although she never attempted to develop a systematic theology, her thoughts on the importance of public confession, celibate living, and the need to share one's worldly possessions inspired many people to strive for human perfection. Moreover, her understanding of God as a feminine as well as a masculine deity provided future generations of Shakers with a theological basis for promoting equal rights for women.

Bibliography

Andrews, Edward Deming. *The People Called Shakers: A Search for the Perfect*

Society. New York: Oxford University Press, 1953. Until the publication of Stephen Stein's 1992 text, this was the definitive work on the Shaker movement. Although dated, this sympathetic treatment remains an excellent introduction to the study of Shaker origins.

Brewer, Priscilla J. *Shaker Communities, Shaker Lives*. Hanover, N.H.: University Press of New England, 1986. A scholarly yet sympathetic treatment of the origins of and developments within Shakerism to 1904.

Campion, Nardi Reeder. *Mother Ann Lee: Morning Star of the Shakers*. Hanover, N.H.: University Press of New England, 1990. Perhaps the best biography of Ann Lee, this volume is a revised edition of Campion's 1976 book *Ann the Word*. Includes bibliographic references.

Humez, Jean M., ed. *Mother's First-Born Daughters: Early Shaker Writings on Women and Religion*. Bloomington: Indiana University Press, 1993. Although Mother Ann never wrote a book, reminiscences of her life and many of her sayings were later compiled and published by her followers. Chapter 1 of this interesting volume includes a number of these testimonies about the beloved Shaker founder.

Joy, Arthur F. *The Queen of the Shakers*. Minneapolis: Denison, 1960. An unscholarly but very readable biography of Ann Lee drawn largely from uncritical Shaker sources.

Stein, Stephen J. *The Shaker Experience in America: A History of the United Society of Believers*. New Haven, Conn.: Yale University Press, 1992. The best single-volume textbook to survey the history of the Shaker church from its origins to its recent demise.

Terry D. Bilhartz

GYPSY ROSE LEE
Rose Louise Hovick

Born: January 9, 1914; probably Seattle, Washington
Died: April 26, 1970; Los Angeles, California
Areas of Achievement: Dance and film
Contribution: Although she began her career in vaudeville and burlesque, Lee's charisma and intelligence brought her success on the stage, in films and television, and as an author.

Early Life

Rose Louise Hovick was born somewhere on the West Coast on January 9, 1914, to John Hovick, a newspaperman, and Rose Thompson Hovick. After a second girl (Ellen, later called June) was born, the couple divorced, and Rose Thompson Hovick took her daughters to live with her father in Seattle. When Rose Louise was four and June was two and a half, they made their singing and dancing debut at the Knights of Pythias lodge. From the beginning, the cute and talented June was the star, and Louise, who was tall and chubby, was the supporting player. Their act was so successful that they appeared at various lodges around Seattle.

After making an unsuccessful assault on Hollywood, Rose Thompson Hovick and the girls returned to Seattle and played lodges again. Rose Hovick, who was described by both of her daughters as an overbearing and ruthless stage mother, added a boy and a dog and booked the act as Dainty June, the Hollywood Baby, and Her Newsboys.

By 1922, the act traveled the Pantages vaudeville circuit; soon it graduated to the Keith-Orpheum circuit, which paid as much as $1,500 per week. Dainty June and her Newsboy Songsters now included the girls, six boys, and more animals. Rose Louise sang "Hard-boiled Rose" in boys' clothes. (Her sister claims that Louise never really sang, but talked to music.) Although the girl's education was spotty, Rose Louise read such authors as Giovanni Boccaccio, François Rabelais, Honoré de Balzac, and William Shakespeare.

Life's Work

Rose Louise Hovick's life changed as she matured into a tall, beautiful teenager. After her sister eloped with a "newsboy," the act became all female: Rose Louise and Her Hollywood Blondes. The Depression and talking pictures doomed vaudeville, however, and the act was forced into seedy clubs and burlesque houses.

It was probably at the Gaiety Theater in Toledo, Ohio, that Rose Louise's lifetime career began in earnest. When the show's star landed in jail, the sixteen-year-old Louise went on in her place to perform her first striptease. Lee says she insisted that her new name, Gypsy Rose Lee (she may not have used that name regularly for several years), appear on the marquee. Legend has it that, embarrassed by her awkwardness, she wrapped the stage curtain around her at the end of her act and tossed a rose to the orchestra leader. Her debut was a stunning success, and she was signed for the rest of the season. Tossing a rose and using the curtains became her trademarks; she regularly closed her act by standing between the curtains and slowly drawing them together, as if sharing a secret with the audience.

Her career skyrocketed. In 1931, she starred at Minsky's Republic Theater on Forty-second Street at Broadway in New York; by 1935, she made $1,000 per week. In addition to making regular burlesque appearances, she appeared on Broadway in *Hot-Cha!* (1932) with Bert Lahr and in the *Ziegfeld Follies* (1936) with Fanny Brice. Although she spent two years in Hollywood, she returned to her burlesque role at the World's Fair in *The Streets of Paris* (1940) and on Broadway in Mike Todd's *Star and Garter* (1942). Her act was, compared to those of other strippers, refined and even literate; she was witty and frank as well as sexy. She compared her act to holding a toy just out of a baby's reach in order to make it laugh.

Lee's verve, her intelligence, and her reading made her a hit offstage. She first charmed Broadway denizens such as Walter Winchell and Damon Runyon. Magazines ran stories about her. Intellectuals were delighted that a stripper could discuss ideas. Among her early friends were Deems Taylor, Mark Van Doren, Carson McCullers, and Janet Flanner. H. L. Mencken coined the word "ecdysiast" to give some dignity to Lee's profession, combining the Greek words for "getting out" and "moulting." Her fame was assured when Richard Rodgers and Florenz Hart satirized her intellectual side with the song "Zip" in their Broadway musical *Pal Joey* (1940).

Rodgers and Hart may have been inspired by rumors of Lee's first book, *The G-String Murders* (1941), a mystery novel set in a burlesque house. Although the book may have been partly ghostwritten, Lee clearly provided the backstage detail about managers, stagehands, strippers, and the strippers' boyfriends. The book's sales encouraged Lee to issue a second mystery, *Mother Finds a Body* (1942), which was not a success. Her career as an author continued; over the next twenty years she wrote many articles for *The New Yorker* and other magazines.

Lee's film career began in Hollywood in 1937. In that and the next year, she made five films under her real name, since film executives feared that the name "Gypsy Rose Lee" would draw protests. She played supporting roles, often women who briefly distracted the hero. In *You Can't Have Everything* (1937), according to critics, Lee played a nasty character with gusto. Next came *Ali Baba Goes to Town* (1937), a conflation of Mark Twain's *A Connecticut Yankee* with the story of the 1,001 Arabian Nights; Eddie Cantor was Ali, and Lee played The Sultana. In the next year, Lee appeared in *Battle of Broadway* (1938) and in *Sally, Irene, and Mary* (1938). Her last film as Louise Hovick was *My Lucky Star* (1938), a vehicle for the skating champion Sonja Henie.

During her stay in Hollywood, Lee was married to Arnold R. Mizzy, a manufacturer of dental supplies. They were wed in a water taxi in 1937 and divorced in 1941. Lee was married twice more: to an actor, Alexander Kirkland (1942; divorced 1944), and to a painter, Julio De Diego (1948; divorced 1955). In 1944, she gave birth to a son, Erik. Many years later, Otto Preminger, the film director, acknowledged that he was Erik's father; Lee herself said that she chose Preminger to father her child.

Lee's success as a writer took her again to Hollywood. She helped write *Lady of Burlesque* (1943), which was based on *The G-String Murders*. The film, which critics say is better than the book, starred Barbara Stanwyck. In the star-studded wartime extravaganza *Stage Door Canteen* (1943), Lee did a mock striptease. She then starred with Randolph Scott in the dance-hall drama *Belle of the Yukon* (1944).

In New York, Lee attempted to conquer the stage. She wrote a comedy, *Ghost in the Woodpile*, in which a burlesque queen has a book ghostwritten. After being revised by George S. Kaufman and receiving a new title, *The Naked Genius* (1943) opened in New York. It starred Joan Blondell and ran profitably for a month, despite critical condemnation. The film version, *Doll Face* (1945), was probably written with Lee's assistance.

Lee continued to perform her burlesque act well into the 1950's and made three films in that decade. *Babes in Bagdad* (1952), starring Paulette Goddard, depicted a harem on strike; critics praised Lee's humor but not much else. Lee also appeared in *Screaming Mimi* (1958), an odd psycho-thriller starring Anita Ekberg. In *Wind Across the Everglades* (1958), she was praised for her humor as the owner of a brothel frequented by Christopher Plummer. The film also featured Burl Ives, the boxer Tony Galento, and the famous clown Emmett Kelly.

Lee's first television appearance was in "Sauce for the Goose" on *The U.S. Steel Hour* in 1956. She later appeared on many variety and talk shows, and she had her own syndicated talk show in 1966. That year she was a regular cast member on the short-lived television series *The Pruitts of Southampton*. She played in summer theaters, most notably starring in *Auntie Mame*.

Although she continued to write magazine pieces, her greatest literary success was *Gypsy: A Memoir* (1957), an autobiography that provided the basis for the musical *Gypsy*. On Broadway in 1959, Ethel Merman played Mama Rose and Sandra Church played Gypsy herself; in Hollywood in 1962, those roles were played by Rosalind Russell and Natalie Wood.

Lee's last major show was *A Curious Evening with Gypsy Rose Lee*. Lee combined reels of her home movies, bits from her films, and old newsreel clips to create a documentary of her life; she provided a running commentary. It was presented first in Palm Beach, Florida, in 1958, had showings both on and off Broadway in 1961, and was produced in a few other cities, including Los Angeles, during that year. Although it received polite reviews, the show was a flop, as was a revival of Bertolt Brecht's *Threepenny Opera*, starring Lee as Jenny. Lee continued to appear on television and also toured Vietnam for the USO.

Lee was a star and demanded that she be treated as one. She could be astonishingly overbearing. In spite of her early profession, friends noted that she had a Victorian primness. Since her vaudeville days, Lee had been an expert seamstress, and from childhood she had been surrounded by pets—usually, dogs.

Even though she had lived in magnificence on New York's upper East Side for many years, she moved permanently to Beverly Hills, California, in 1962. She cooked, gardened, traveled, and collected art and antiques. After undergoing surgery in 1966, she was in ill health, and she died of lung cancer in 1970. She was survived by her father, her son Erik, and a grandson.

Summary

Although Rose Louise Hovick moved from vaudeville to burlesque in a conventional way, what happened next could not have happened to any other striptease artist. She admitted, and critics agreed, that she did not dance well and sang even worse, but, as Gypsy Rose Lee, she became famous. All those who knew her or saw her agreed that the secret of her success was her charisma. From the moment she appeared on stage as a star, audiences loved her and clapped for more. Critics and friends spoke of her magical glowing presence, her intelligence, her wit, and her self-confident force. This force shows in her early photographs; other girls in the pictures seem to be inert, but Lee is alive.

As a result of her star qualities, some said, Lee made the profession of stripteaser almost respectable; if that was ever true, the respectability did not last. By gaining respect for partial stage nudity, however, Lee probably did help to teach audiences of her era to appreciate the beauty of the human body and to acknowledge that sexuality was healthy. Even though she decried complete nudity on stage, she must be given some thanks or blame for the abundance of nudity on stage and in films in the years after her death.

Her real impact has probably been general. By means of her achievements on the legitimate stage, in films, on television, and as an author, she showed how an intelligent, witty, and forceful woman can shape her life and enjoy it.

Bibliography

Allen, Robert C. *Horrible Prettiness: Burlesque and American Culture*. Chapel Hill: University of North Carolina Press, 1991. The last chapter of this academic book describes Lee's era; burlesque houses turned to strippers as a last resort to attract customers. Good on burlesque's backgrounds and cultural context.

Havoc, June. *Early Havoc*. New York: Simon & Schuster, 1959. Lee's sister tells what their life as child vaudevillians was like. Havoc discusses her mother and describes in detail what she and Louise did on stage. Some illustrations show the young Rose Louise Hovick.

Lee, Gypsy Rose. *The G-String Murders*. New York: Simon & Schuster, 1941. Also published as *Lady of Burlesque* in the United States and as *The Strip-Tease Murders* in England. This mystery made a splash when it was published, since it was the first novel written by a striptease artist. It is a weak, mildly risqué story in which the central character, named Gypsy Rose Lee, is implicated in a series of backstage crimes. Its dialogue and descriptions give a vivid picture of backstage life as it was—or as Lee wishes the reader to think it was. Some experts think that it and Lee's other mystery novel were ghostwritten by Georgiana Ann Randolph.

_____ . *Gypsy: A Memoir*. New York: Harper & Brothers, 1957. Illustrated. An invaluable, detailed, and probably slightly fictionalized account of Lee's career up to about 1937. The anecdotes of backstage life are convincing, and Lee's picture of her domineering, loving, conniving mother is irresistible.

Preminger, Erik Lee. *Gypsy and Me: At Home and on the Road with Gypsy Rose Lee.* Boston: Little, Brown, 1984. Lee's son tells of his often unhappy relations with his mother from about 1956, when she finished her own autobiography, until her death. These were not happy years for Lee. Many of the anecdotes about her are sad; those about Erik are dull.

Sobel, Bernard. *A Pictorial History of Vaudeville.* New York: Citadel Press, 1961. Lee came in at the end of a long tradition of popular entertainment, which this book briefly chronicles and profusely illustrates. Provides good background for Lee's childhood. Two pictures of the pre-burlesque Lee are included.

George Soule

PEGGY LEE

Born: May 26, 1920; Jamestown, North Dakota

Area of Achievement: Music

Contribution: After rising to fame as a big band vocalist, Lee achieved lasting success in many other areas of American entertainment.

Early Life

Norma Deloris Egstrom was born to Scandinavian parents on May 26, 1920, in Jamestown, a small city in central North Dakota. She grew up there and in nearby towns: Nortonville and Wimbledon.

Norma had a hard childhood. After her mother died, Norma was badly beaten by her sadistic stepmother. Her beloved father, a railroad station agent, was an alcoholic. Even when he was home, Norma ran the Wimbledon depot for him. She also worked on farms and washed blackboards at school. Norma loved music, however, and from the time she was ten, she knew she wanted to be a singer.

Before graduating from Wimbledon high school in 1938, she sang in the glee club and came in second in a statewide vocal contest. Her career in show business started when she was fourteen. Legend has it that she impulsively entered an amateur contest in nearby Valley City and won; the prize was a singing job in a local restaurant. What is certain is that at age fourteen she joined a college band there and sang on radio station KOVC. Even then, success was not easy to achieve. One Wimbledon neighbor later recalled that when Norma's stepmother disparaged her singing and forbade her to travel to Valley City, he gave Norma a ride and helped start her career.

Life's Work

After she was graduated from high school, Norma Egstrom got her breaks in radio. She moved back to Jamestown and sang on station KRMC. A friend insisted that she audition at Radio Station WDAY in Fargo, where Program Director Ken Kennedy (Kenneth Sydness) hired her in the morning, put her on the air in the afternoon, and suggested a new name: "Peggy Lee." In Fargo, she supported herself, not only by singing but also by slicing and wrapping bread for Regan's bakery. Kennedy teamed her with four male vocalists and billed the act as Four Jacks and a Queen; she wore a gingham dress and a straw hat. The quintet appeared weekly on the Hayloft Jamboree program and toured the region.

When Lee was seventeen, she headed for Los Angeles to become a star. She worked as a waitress and as a carnival barker until she landed a singing job at the Jade Room, a Chinese restaurant on Hollywood Boulevard. Her throat gave her trouble, however, and she returned to North Dakota for a tonsillectomy. She had turned eighteen, and when she recovered she sang at the Belmont Cafe in Grand Forks, in Fargo over WDAY again, and for a collegiate crowd at the Powers Hotel and Coffee Shop.

Peggy Lee hit the big time when she left her native state. Kennedy got her an audition in Minneapolis, Minnesota, and she became the vocalist with Sev Olson and his orchestra at the Radisson Hotel and at the Marigold Ballroom. In November, 1940, she joined the Will Osborne band, but it folded a few months later. Trying her luck in California, Lee next sang at the Doll House in Palm Springs. She was spotted there and hired by the Ambassador West Hotel in Chicago.

Then came the break that would lead her to fame. On August 1, 1941, Benny Goodman, the great clarinetist and big band leader, heard her at the Ambassador; he hired her the next day. "Pretty Peggy Lee" replaced Helen Forrest with the Goodman band, which was then at the height of its popularity. Despite Lee's initial nervousness, and despite having to sing arrangements written for Forrest, she won over the critics. Although Goodman's was a "swing" band, to compete with bands such as Glenn Miller's, Goodman began to feature Lee's vocals on hits such as "I Got It Bad and That Ain't Good," "Somebody Else Is Taking My Place," "Don't Get Around Much Anymore," "The Way You Look Tonight," and "Where or When." During a memorable engagement at the New Yorker Hotel, Lee first met a number of jazz greats, including Fats Waller, Count Basie, and Louis Armstrong.

Lee toured with Goodman for two years, playing hotels, theaters, and college dances, and making radio broadcasts. She sang with the band in two motion pictures: *The Powers Girl* (1942) and *Stage Door Canteen* (1943). The cast list for this wartime extravaganza reads like a Who's Who of popular music, stage, and screen. Lee sang her greatest early hit, "Why Don't You Do Right? (Like Some Other Men Do)." This song, which she had suggested to Goodman, established her as a woman who could belt out songs that were anything but cute and sweet. "Why Don't You Do Right?" had a jazz beat, and its lyrics were frank and colloquial.

In 1943, Lee married her first husband, Goodman's guitarist Dave Barbour, the love of her life. The Barbours quit the band and settled in Los Angeles. Their daughter, Nicki, was born in 1944. While she was pregnant, Lee began to write songs whose harmonies Barbour completed. She began to record again, eventually signing a contract in 1944 with Capitol records. Barbour's alcoholism strained their marriage (although, in the euphoria of his recovery from bleeding ulcers, they wrote "Mañana" together). When his condition deteriorated, Barbour realized that their marriage had to end; they were divorced in 1951. Lee's subsequent marriages have been to actor Brad Dexter (1955; they were divorced the same year); actor Dewey Martin (1956; they were divorced in 1959); and Jack Del Rio (1964; they were divorced the same year). In 1965, she and a sober Barbour decided to remarry, but he died four days later.

With Capitol, Lee recorded such hits as "Golden Earrings," "I'll Dance at Your Wedding," "I'm a Woman," and several of her own songs, such as "It's a Good Day!" "I Don't Know Enough About You," and "Don't Smoke in Bed." "Mañana," in which Lee was accompanied by Carmen Miranda's Brazilians, was the Barbours' biggest and most profitable hit of that era; it may have been the first recording to end in a fade out, created by having the band samba out of the studio. When someone else claimed to have written the song, performer Jimmy Durante's testimony in court gave the Barbours a victory.

Lee was named Best Female Vocalist by both *Metronome* and *Down Beat* magazines in 1946 and Most Popular Vocalist in 1950. Her later best-selling records include an upbeat Latin version of Richard Rodgers' waltz "Lover" (with Decca) and the steamy "Fever" (with Capitol again), for which she wrote additional lyrics. In 1969, Lee won a Grammy for Best Contemporary Vocal Performance by a Female Artist. In 1990, she became only the ninth recipient of the Pied Piper Award, the highest honor given by ASCAP (the American Society of Composers, Authors, and Publishers).

Beginning in the 1940's, Lee appeared regularly on radio and television shows starring such performers as Jimmy Durante, Frank Sinatra, Johnny Mercer, Perry Como, Steve Allen, Jackie Gleason, Bing Crosby, Lena Horne, Julie Andrews, and Ed Sullivan. She also continued to appear in clubs such as the Copacabana in New York City and Ciro's in Hollywood. In 1960, she had a dramatic role in *So Deadly, So Evil*, a General Electric Theater presentation aired on CBS-TV.

Not counting her appearances with the Goodman band, Lee's film career began in 1950 with *Mr. Music*, starring Bing Crosby. In this forgettable film, Lee sang a duet with Crosby, "Life Is So Peculiar." Her next film (in 1953) was a remake of *The Jazz Singer* starring Danny Thomas; in it, Lee sang "This Is a Very Special Day."

Her last appearance on film was her most memorable. In 1955, she played a down-and-out club singer in *Pete Kelly's Blues*, directed by and starring Jack Webb. The cast also included Janet Leigh, Edmund O'Brien, Lee Marvin, and Ella Fitzgerald. Although the melodramatic plot was panned by some critics, Lee's singing and acting were praised. She recalls that it was hard playing an alcoholic vocalist, because she had to sing off-key. She was nominated for a Best Supporting Actress Oscar in 1955, the same year film patrons voted her an "Audie" award.

She not only acted in films but also wrote for them. She provided theme music for *Johnny Guitar* (1954) and *About Mrs. Leslie* (1954) as well as songs for the animated cartoon features *tom thumb* (1958) and *The Time Machine* (1960). She collaborated with Duke Ellington in writing "I'm Gonna Go Fishing" for *Anatomy of a Murder* (1959).

The film for which she is best known is Walt Disney's animated feature *Lady and the Tramp* (1955). She and Sonny Burke wrote the score, and she provided voices for four of the film's characters (two cats, a dog, and a human); in the Siamese cats' duet, the lyrics, sound effects, and voices are hers. In 1987, when Disney released the film as a videocassette, Lee (who had been paid $3,500 for her work) sued for a share of the profits. A California court awarded her some $3 million, and this award was confirmed on two appeals.

In later years, despite several life-threatening medical conditions, Lee has regularly performed in clubs in New York (Basin Street East, the Ballroom), New Orleans, Toronto, Atlantic City, and Las Vegas. She has appeared in London, Amsterdam, Monaco, and Japan; in Britain, she was the Sugar Plum Fairy in a jazz version of Peter Ilich Tchaikovsky's *Nutcracker*. She has sold paintings and designed fabrics. In 1962, she followed Marilyn Monroe on stage at President John F. Kennedy's famous birthday party in New York. She did research for, wrote, and performed in *The Jazz*

Tree (1963), which told the story of the beginnings and development of jazz in America. In 1983, she and Paul Horner created the musical presentation *Peg* for Broadway; drama critics panned it, and it closed after four performances. Her songs have been issued on many records and compact discs.

All the while, Lee has lived in and around Los Angeles; she gardens enthusiastically (a rose is named for her), and her autobiography is jammed with the names of her friends, many of them famous. Her daughter Nicki is married, and Lee is a grandmother. Her autobiography, *Miss Peggy Lee*, was published in 1989.

Summary

Peggy Lee has been one of the great female popular vocalists of her era. She began as a big band singer, but her style shows many jazz influences. Jazz critic Whitney Balliett describes her singing as follows: "She avoids long notes and glissandos," he writes, "and if she uses a Billie Holiday bent note she lets it die almost immediately. . . . She does not carry a tune; she elegantly follows it." Her style has always been distinctive, and the songs she has recorded have often gone well beyond the conventional, in both their words and their melodies.

She has been much more than a singer. She wrote popular songs when there were few other female songwriters, and she has branched out into another male-dominated field: film scoring. Although she has appeared on radio, on television, and in films, unlike many popular artists, she has continued to perform in public. In short, she has worked in many areas of the entertainment business with great success.

The most remarkable aspects of Lee's career have been her energy and daring. She herself sees her life as a series of triumphs over adverse situations. Unlike most popular singers, she has not faded into obscurity. She has not been afraid to put her hand to new projects, and she has succeeded in almost everything she has attempted. She has showed that, with courage and talent, a female artist can rise quickly from great obscurity. She has also diversified her goals so as to remain a loved and respected force in American popular music and popular culture for more than four decades.

Bibliography

Balliett, Whitney. "Still There." *The New Yorker* 68 (August 5, 1985): 64-67. An engaging interview that includes thoughtful descriptions of Lee's singing style by Balliett, perhaps the best writer to be a jazz critic, and by three musicians.

Dahl, Linda. *Stormy Weather: The Music and Lives of a Century of Jazzwomen.* New York: Proscenium, 1984. Dahl makes appreciative references to Lee while discussing big band "canaries," jazzwomen, solo singers, and instrumentalists from 1890 to the mid 1980's. She treats these artists' working conditions and their problems in general.

Firestone, Ross. *Swing, Swing, Swing: The Life and Times of Benny Goodman.* New York: W. W. Norton, 1993. Contains a brief, unflattering account of Lee's joining of the Goodman band and her early months with it. Some interesting photographs are included.

Lee, Peggy. *Miss Peggy Lee*. New York: Donald I. Fine, 1989. Lee's autobiography provides details of her career, her unhappy childhood, her loves, and her successes. She describes her religious life and her throat, lung, and heart problems. A discography is included.

Mellers, Wilfrid. *Angels of the Night: Popular Female Singers of Our Time*. New York: Basil Blackwell, 1986. A readable and evocative survey of several generations of female singers. Lee is treated in the "Jazz Singer as Little Girl Lost" category, along with Anita O'Day and Blossom Dearie.

George Soule

EVA LE GALLIENNE

Born: January 11, 1899; London, England
Died: June 3, 1991; Weston, Connecticut
Area of Achievement: Theater and drama
Contribution: A leading actress of classical plays, Le Gallienne also founded a repertory company with which she introduced dramas by Anton Chekhov and Henrik Ibsen to American audiences. Hoping to build an audience, she drastically reduced the price of theater tickets, which was an innovation in its day.

Early Life

Eva Le Gallienne was born on January 11, 1899, to an English father of French extraction and a Danish mother. Her father, Richard Le Gallienne, was a successful poet and novelist, the friend of such writers as Irish playwright George Bernard Shaw and Irish poet William Butler Yeats. Her mother, Julie Norregaard, was a correspondent for a well-known Danish newspaper, *Politiken*, and a friend of such distinguished English actors as Constance Collier and William Faversham.

When Eva was about seven, her parents separated and her mother took her to live in Paris, where she studied at the Collège Sévigné. They attended theater and ballet performances, and Eva was privileged to see the fabled French actress Sarah Bernhardt in some of her most popular roles. The experience made a deep impression on her, and she was determined to make the stage her career.

Life was difficult for mother and daughter, since Richard Le Gallienne contributed almost nothing to their support. (The couple's divorce became final in 1911). When her newspaper efforts did not bring in enough money, Julie Le Gallienne opened a dress shop in Paris, which became moderately successful thanks to her good taste and to the patronage of her eminent acquaintances. Every summer, mother and daughter returned to England to stay with friends. One of them, actress Constance Collier, noticed Eva's interest in theater and volunteered to give her acting lessons. In 1914, Collier invited Eva to take the role of a page in Belgian dramatist Maurice Maeterlinck's *Monna Vanna* (1902), and Eva's career was officially launched at the age of fifteen.

Feeling the need for more formal training, Eva enrolled in Herbert Beerbohm Tree's Academy for actors. Tree was one of the best-known actor-managers in England, and at his school Eva took classes in dancing, fencing, voice production, and elocution. In 1915, she had a role in playwright George Du Maurier's *Peter Ibbetson* (1891), and soon the young actress was besieged with offers to do other plays. Some came from overseas. Eva, worried that the war, which had just broken out, might cause the curtailment of theater in England, decided to accept an offer from Broadway.

When Eva Le Gallienne, accompanied by her mother, arrived in New York, she found that the so-called little theaters—groups committed to producing plays for their artistic merit rather than for their financial rewards—were in full swing. The Neighborhood Playhouse, the Provincetown Players, and the Washington Square Players were offering dramas by such new writers as Eugene O'Neill, as well as the work of Germany's Georg Kaiser, Hungary's Ferenc Molnár, and Russia's Leonid Andreyev. This discovery gave Eva Le Gallienne a taste for the kind of theater she would prefer and would come to champion in later years. From 1915 to 1920, however, she appeared in a number of negligible plays, most of them opening in New York and touring the country as far as San Francisco. Her employment was steady but her roles were unsatisfactory until she was cast as Julie in Ferenc Molnár's *Liliom* (1921), when play and player came together to make Le Gallienne a name in the theater.

Life's Work

The producers of *Liliom*, whose group had developed from the Washington Square Players into the Theatre Guild, were uneasy about the play, which had failed at its Budapest opening in 1909. (Many years later, it found another life as the successful Broadway musical *Carousel*.) The script possessed such charm and the acting, notably Eva Le Gallienne's, was so powerful that both critics and audiences were captivated by it. Eva Le Gallienne's performance was judged perfect: One critic noted that she was not poetic but was sheer poetry. Her early training at the Academy and her experience had prepared Le Gallienne for this moment; she enriched the role of a waiflike character whose love transcends tragedy with her attention to realistic detail, her imagination, and her perfectionism. Above all, her admiration of French actress Sarah Bernhardt had given way to her worship of Italian actress Eleonora Duse, because Bernhardt projected her own personality on to the part she was playing, while Duse submerged her personality in the role. These are two entirely different approaches to interpretation: One proclaims the star; the other, the actor. As she grew in her understanding, Le Gallienne chose the second, truer way.

After *Liliom* concluded its successful run, it was sent on tour with the company; again, when she was free to perform, Le Gallienne appeared in a few more mediocre plays, good scripts always being difficult to find. In 1923, however, another Molnár play, *The Swan* (1914), was offered to her, and she took the leading role of a princess who for a moment falls in love with her brother's tutor but knows that she may not marry him because she is destined to be a queen. Although it is a slight comedy, the play is full of rueful charm. At the end of the play, the audience gave Le Gallienne a standing ovation (much rarer then than it is now), and the critics all agreed that she had surpassed her performance in *Liliom*. Le Gallienne gave full credit to the art of Eleonora Duse, saying that it would have been easy to stress the play's winsome quality, but by bringing a sturdy reality to the part she was able to make the princess not only believable but also sympathetic. *The Swan* ran for more than a year in New York and then toured for the entire 1924-1925 season.

The next year, Le Gallienne decided to take a new play by Mercedes de Acosta, *Jeanne d'Arc*, to Paris, her background in French making the occasion a major event. American designer Norman Bel Geddes directed the play, but he so overwhelmed it with spectacle and the play itself was so lacking in power (George Bernard Shaw's 1923 *Saint Joan* made every other portrait of the Maid of Orléans seem faded), that the result was a resounding failure. Le Gallienne returned to New York to appear in a play by Viennese dramatist Arthur Schnitzler, *Call of Life* (1925); this time, the critics believed that the role of a young woman who poisons her father and runs away with her lover was an unsuitable vehicle for Le Gallienne. She was beginning to experience the difficulty that every prominent actor (and every playwright) undergoes: excessive praise followed by damnation that is not always justified but is dependent on the mood of an audience and the atmosphere of the times. Le Gallienne began to think about starting her own theater, where she could pick the scripts she preferred, rehearse them in the time she required, and present them to an audience at an affordable price. Before she could realize her dream, however, she had to find the financial backing necessary for such a project.

To her great good fortune, she was offered the role of Hilda Wangel in Henrik Ibsen's *The Master Builder* (1892) in 1925, which was a busy year for her. It opened at the Maxine Elliott Theatre in New York for an announced run of four matinees, but it was such a resounding success that the engagement was extended. The critics once more sang her praises, because the role seemed tailor-made for her. It is probably true that Le Gallienne achieved her best effects playing women of strong character; she was never at home in the lighter pieces that were so popular in the commercial theater. The success that Le Gallienne enjoyed in playing Hilda Wangel, who defies convention, challenges authority, and would even storm the ramparts of Heaven, made her realize that she had to make her own place in the theater.

Because she was again the darling of the critics, Le Gallienne was able to raise money for her project, and such patrons of the arts as banker Otto Kahn, who almost single-handedly rescued the Metropolitan Opera in its early days, gave her his enthusiastic support, both verbal and financial. Le Gallienne took a lease on a building in the lower part of Manhattan, on 14th Street, and she called it the Civic Repertory Theatre. She knew that there were many good young actors who would be willing to work with her in classical plays because there were so few opportunities to do so on Broadway; she also knew that there were dedicated people who cared more for art than for money. If they could make a living from their work, they had no need for riches. Fired with such idealism, she was able to attract a good company and to present plays unfamiliar to the public which would later prove to be theatrical landmarks: The dramas of Ibsen and, especially, Russia's Anton Chekhov would form the basis of her repertory.

On October 25, 1926, the newly refurbished theater, which seated eleven hundred and which offered tickets for a top price of $1.50 (comparable Broadway tickets at that time cost at least five times as much), opened with Jacinto Benavente y Martínez's *Saturday Night* (*La noche del sábado*, 1903), chosen because it needed a large cast that Le Gallienne wished to introduce to her audience. It was received with hostility: England's favorite actor-playwright, Noël Coward, announced that "Eva was terrible, the production awful, and the play lousy." Fortunately for Le Gallienne, however, the repertory system which made it possible to produce several plays in one season and alternate them in the course of a week, saved her. The next evening, Chekhov's *The

Three Sisters expunged the previous night's disaster: Le Gallienne was praised for her acting, for her directing, and for her determination to create an ensemble company instead of a collection of stars. Soon, William Shakespeare's *Twelfth Night* and Carlo Goldoni's *La locandiera* (*The Mistress of the Inn*, 1753) were added to the list. Although all the productions were artistic and critical successes, they did not find favor with audiences; the playhouse was operating only at 60 percent of its capacity. Gregorio Martinez Sierra's *The Cradle Song* (1921), however, turned the tide: It was a genuine triumph, and all fifty-six performances sold out. Le Gallienne was urged to take the play uptown to Broadway, where she could make more money, but she refused, noting that by raising the price of the tickets she would be defeating the purpose of her "mission." She would not compromise.

By the end of her first season, Le Gallienne had won enough acclaim to be convinced that she could make a success of the enterprise, even though she had barely broken even at the box office. The *Nation* magazine chose her for its Roll of Honor, along with Eugene O'Neill and novelist Ernest Hemingway, among others. She received an honorary degree, the first of many, from Tufts University in Massachusetts and was awarded a gold medal by the Society of Arts and Sciences for her contributions to the theater. The second season at the Civic was less impressive: Only Henrik Ibsen's *Hedda Gabler*, with Le Gallienne in the title role, was well received. The next two seasons, however, were profitable as well as artistically satisfying, with such plays as Chekhov's *The Cherry Orchard* and *The Sea Gull*, Molière's *The Would-Be Gentleman*, James Barrie's *Peter Pan*, and Alexandre Dumas' *Camille*, with Le Gallienne in the lead. *Camille* was the greatest box-office success in the Civic's short history. In 1931, Le Gallienne decided to close her theater for one year, to rest and map out plans for the future, which looked grim because the stock market had crashed, play attendance was falling everywhere, and even bankers with seemingly limitless funds could no longer subsidize the arts.

In June of 1931, while she was in the basement of her home in Connecticut trying to light the hot-water heater, the heater exploded, engulfing Le Gallienne in fire. Her entire body was burned, and for a week it was believed that she would not live. Part of her face and both of her hands were severely burned. Yet within a year, despite great pain and innumerable operations, Le Gallienne was back. She reopened the Civic in 1932, repeating some of the productions she had presented before and adding an adaptation that she and actress Florida Friebus had made of Lewis Carroll's *Alice's Adventures in Wonderland* (1865). The play, which was extremely successful, was moved uptown to Broadway.

Growing financial pressures forced Le Gallienne to lease out her theater and take her company on the road with some of the plays that had done well. By 1936, it was clear that the Civic could not survive. Le Gallienne disbanded the company, allowing its members to go their separate ways and find work wherever they could. In the ensuing years, she appeared on Broadway sporadically but spent most of her time in the hinterlands playing in the classics. Gradually, she fell out of favor with the public, which was becoming more interested in American playwrights such as Arthur Miller and Tennessee Williams. For a brief time in 1946, Le Gallienne, director Margaret Webster, and producer Cheryl Crawford banded together to form the American Repertory Theatre, presenting plays by Shaw, Ibsen, Chekhov, and Shakespeare, playing in New York and on the road. Financial problems doomed their efforts. Yet Le Gallienne kept touring, convinced of the rightness of her cause. In 1975, a new company headed by Ellis Rabb and Rosemary Harris invited Le Gallienne to appear in a revival of a 1927 comedy, *The Royal Family*, by Edna Ferber and George Kaufman. Both Le Gallienne and the production were successful. A new generation discovered Le Gallienne and listened to what she said about the theater. In 1986, she was awarded the National Medal of the Arts by President Ronald Reagan in recognition of her service to the drama. Gradually, her strength began to ebb, and she died in her ninety-second year.

Summary

When Eva Le Gallienne first made her mark on the American stage, audiences were not prepared for her concept of theater. She believed in producing plays that had stood the test of time and in holding down ticket prices so that nonaffluent audiences would not be driven away. To her, the theater was a necessity; no one should be kept from it because of cost. She believed in a repertory system that would keep actors fresh in their roles because they would not be performing the same piece night after night. She believed that actors should have a permanent place in which to work, a theater that belonged to them, such as existed in Paris, Berlin, and Moscow. She believed that a theater should be supported by the government, just as public schools and libraries were supported. Above all, she believed in improving the taste of the audience, not because of snobbery, but because people deserved the best.

Although her Civic Theatre failed, Le Gallienne's dream did not. In subsequent years, professional groups have formed throughout the United States. Actors are engaged on a more permanent basis, the classics as well as new plays are produced, local audiences are loyal in their attendance, and the best companies are now supported not only by ticket sales but also by local, state, and even federal monies.

Bibliography

Brown, John Mason. *Upstage*. New York: W. W. Norton, 1930. The drama critic of the *New York Post* discusses the structure and contributions of the Civic Repertory Theatre and analyzes the character of its founder. He mentions Le Gallienne's strength in the face of adversity and her enjoyment in doing battle for her principles.

Le Gallienne, Eva. *At Thirty-three*. New York: Longmans, Green, 1934. This is Le Gallienne's own account of her early years and the beginning of her work to establish the Civic Repertory Theatre. The photographs are particularly valuable.

—————. *With a Quiet Heart*. New York: Viking Press, 1953. This book continues the story of the Civic, detailing Le Gallienne's attempts to keep it open. It also deals with her later venture, the American Repertory Theatre, and its problems. Excellent photographs.

Middleton, George. *These Things Are Mine*. New York: Macmillan, 1947. An account of the Civic by a playwright who studied acting with Le Gallienne. He also discusses her detailed study of Eleanora Duse's acting technique.

Schanke, Robert A. *Eva Le Gallienne: A Bio-Bibliography*. New York: Greenwood Press, 1989. This comprehensive annotated bibliography of the actress covers her articles, reviews by critics, and records of her performances. A photograph of Le Gallienne as Hedda Gabler is included. An invaluable reference work.

_____ . *Shattered Applause: The Lives of Eva Le Gallienne*. Carbondale: Southern Illinois University Press, 1992. This exhaustive biography of the actress discusses both her career and her troubled personal life. The author based his book on many interviews he had with Le Gallienne. Many excellent photographs, a complete record of the actress' performances, and a short bibliography are included.

Mildred C. Kuner

ANNIE LEIBOVITZ

Born: October 2, 1949; Westbury, Connecticut

Area of Achievement: Photography

Contribution: A leading photographer since the early 1970's, Leibovitz has become
known for her bold portraits of celebrities.

Early Life

Anna-Lou Leibovitz was born on October 2, 1949, in Westbury, Connecticut, to
Sam Leibovitz, a United States Air Force lieutenant colonel, and Marilyn Leibovitz,
a modern-dance instructor. The third of six children, Annie (as she became known)
was close to her brothers and sisters. Because her father was in the Air Force, the
family frequently had to move from one military base to another. She attended
Northwood High School in Silver Spring, Maryland. As a teenager, Annie channeled
her creative energies into painting and playing the guitar. In 1967, she decided to
enroll at the San Francisco Art Institute. Through her studies, Annie hoped to become
a painter and possibly become a painting instructor. During this time, her father was
stationed in the Philippines. After her freshman year at the institute, Annie visited her
family in the Philippines. During her visit, she got the chance to travel with her mother
to Japan, where Annie bought a camera and began taking photographs. Upon returning
to San Francisco for her sophomore year, Annie decided to take a night class in
photography.

In 1969, she joined an archaeological team that was excavating the site of King
Solomon's temple in Israel. Annie was able to travel to Israel because she had
convinced the art institute to allow her to have a year of independent study in order to
become a better photographer. While in Israel, she lived and worked in Kibbutz Amir.
After completing her independent study program, she returned to San Francisco in
1970 to continue her formal education. With the encouragement of her boyfriend,
Christopher Springmann, a photographer for the *San Francisco Chronicle*, Annie
submitted a photograph she had taken of the poet Allen Ginsberg smoking marijuana
at a peace demonstration to *Rolling Stone* magazine. Within a half hour of her arrival,
Annie had met the art director of the magazine, Robert Kingsbury, and he had bought
her photograph of Ginsberg. With this transaction, Annie Leibovitz launched her
career as a professional photographer.

Life's Work

Annie Leibovitz was only twenty years old when she sold her first photograph to
Rolling Stone in 1970. When she was in the *Rolling Stone* office, Leibovitz noticed
that everyone who walked by her was under thirty years old and was casually dressed.
Although she knew that the publication was staffed and controlled primarily by men,
she was convinced that she could find employment with the magazine. Leibovitz was
a young, talented, and ambitious photographer who was not about to allow her gender

to prevent her from finding work in the male-dominated world of photojournalism. She continued her formal education at the San Francisco Art Institute, but increasingly sought out opportunities to become a working photographer. *Rolling Stone* eventually offered her an assignment to photograph Grace Slick, the lead singer of the rock group *Jefferson Airplane*. As a result of this successful assignment, Leibovitz was able to promote herself as someone who could do a top-notch job.

Leibovitz did her job well and avoided becoming overwhelmed by the hectic pace of her work. As a dedicated photojournalist, she willingly placed the demands of her art before those of her personal life. After she returned from her first assignment, *Rolling Stone* put Leibovitz on a $47 a week retainer. Although Leibovitz was new to the magazine, she spoke up and convinced the editors to send her to New York City to photograph legendary rock star John Lennon. She came back with some remarkable photographs, one of which was chosen to appear on the cover of *Rolling Stone* in 1970. Leibovitz had a way of capturing the essence of her subject in a way that spoke directly to the generation that read *Rolling Stone*. In the process of becoming an important photographer to the counterculture, she did more than merely take pictures of famous people. Leibovitz would do research on her subject before she picked up a camera. She also attempted to understand the celebrities she photographed by observing them closely in their own environments. Standing six feet tall, Leibovitz often used her physical presence to establish an aura of authority, but she also worked to establish a personal rapport with her subjects. To her, the assignment came first, and she wanted her subjects to relate to her on a professional level.

In 1973, *Rolling Stone* magazine decided to make Leibovitz its chief photographer, and she remained with the magazine until 1983. During her tenure with the magazine, Leibovitz took some of the most amazing photographs of rock stars and other celebrities. In 1975, she was hired to be tour photographer for the British rock group the Rolling Stones. It was an enormous and challenging assignment, since Leibovitz understood that anything involving the Stones would combine the heady excitement and danger surrounding the world-famous rock band. It was her instinct as a photographer that made it possible for Leibovitz to capture the tension, the exhaustion, and the magnetism of the group's performances and private moments on the tour with her camera. The experience was enervating for her, though, and after the six-week American tour had ended, Leibovitz took her first break from work.

After her experience with the Rolling Stones, Leibovitz decided that she no longer wanted to be involved in photographic assignments that lasted more than two days. She began to restructure her portrait style by maintaining a certain distance from her subject. The background study that she conducted before any photographs were taken became the key element in Leibovitz's creative pursuit of the exaggerated pose that would make for a stunning portrait. Leibovitz's ingenuity and her ability to persuade the celebrity to collaborate with what she was trying to do made for a winning combination. One of the subjects with whom this collaboration was most successfully realized was John Lennon. On December 8, 1980, Leibovitz took her last photograph of him only two hours before his tragic murder. The portrait of a naked Lennon curled up in a fetal position and wrapped around his fully clothed wife, Yoko Ono, would become one of Leibovitz's most famous photographs. In addition to her work with noted male rock musicians, Leibovitz's assignments during the 1970's and early 1980's for *Rolling Stone* included photographs of such public figures as Daniel Ellsberg, Roman Polanski, Ron Kovic, Dan Rather, Arnold Schwarzenegger, Linda Ronstadt, Patti Smith, Lauren Hutton, to name a select few.

In 1983, Leibovitz took some time off to organize her first major exhibit, which opened in the fall of 1983 at the Sidney Janis Gallery in New York City. During the year, Leibovitz also decided to leave *Rolling Stone*. She continued her work with celebrities after accepting a post as a contributing photographer for *Vanity Fair* magazine. Her sixty-print exhibit toured the United States and Europe from 1983 to 1985, and the exhibit's companion book, entitled *Photographs*, came out in 1983. One of the primary reasons that Leibovitz chose to leave her post at *Rolling Stone* was that she wanted to have more control of her time. For thirteen years, she had been moving from assignment to assignment at a furious pace, and her discontentment had led to serious friction between Leibovitz and the magazine's founder, Jann Wenner. Leibovitz finally realized that she was losing touch with how to construct a portrait before she would shoot it.

Tina Brown, the editor of *Vanity Fair*, was more than happy to welcome such an accomplished and imaginative photographer as Leibovitz. Whereas *Rolling Stone* represented rock-and-roll and counterculture, *Vanity Fair* focused on sophistication and high society. In her new job, Leibovitz was given the chance to photograph poet Robert Penn Warren and the business tycoon Donald Trump. She still tried to remain innovative, though, in her approach to celebrity portraits. Leibovitz had Warren pose without a shirt, snapped a portrait of comedian Roseanne Arnold and her husband mud-wrestling, and created a cover shot of a coyly nude and extremely pregnant Demi Moore. As always, Leibovitz's portraits were eye-catching images. They occasionally were also quite controversial, but Leibovitz refused to be confined by convention or public criticism. She had mastered her irreverent style with *Rolling Stone*, and she was not about to abandon it. In addition to contributing photographs to *Vanity Fair*, Leibovitz took on a variety of outside projects, including advertising campaigns for Rose's Lime Juice, Honda, American Express, and others.

In 1991, a retrospective of Leibovitz's work opened at the National Portrait Gallery in Washington, D.C. The exhibit then moved to other major cities of the United States, Europe, and the Far East. HarperCollins published *Photographs: Annie Leibovitz, 1970-1990*, a companion book to the exhibit, in 1991. In the course of her career, Leibovitz has won numerous awards, including the American Society of Magazine Photographers' Photographer of the Year in 1984, their Innovation in Photography Award in 1987, Clio Enterprises' Clio Award in 1987, and the International Center of Photography's Infinity Award for applied photography in 1990. Although she had received criticism over the years for neglecting socially relevant topics because she took photographs of celebrities, there can be no doubt that Leibovitz was a major innovator in photojournalism. She also expanded her subject matter beyond the realm of celebrities by taking poignant shots of war-torn Sarajevo in 1993. Leibovitz was determined to create photographs that would endure the test of time.

Summary

Since she first started with *Rolling Stone* magazine in 1970, Annie Leibovitz was a vibrant and innovative photographer. Inspired by the gains made by the women's movement during the 1970's, she was persistent and fought for creative control of the work she had done. The work—the finished product—was always her primary concern, and her instinct and talent allowed her to produce extraordinary results. Her photographs of rock stars during her tenure at *Rolling Stone* helped to define how the stars were viewed by the public. Leibovitz was able to capture the energy and the destructiveness of rock music and the counterculture which grew up around it. During the 1970's, Leibovitz was the master photographer who influenced the visual tastes of the younger generation that read *Rolling Stone*, listened to rock music, questioned authority, and experimented with alternative lifestyles. Through her work, she stretched the boundaries of what constituted a proper portrait. In the 1980's, she turned her attention to shaking up popular culture through her work with *Vanity Fair* magazine. The one constant in Leibovitz's varied career has been her wonderful eye for creating something quite unique. Unwilling to rest on her laurels, she began striking out into new areas in the 1990's. Her willingness to work hard and her fearlessness in adopting new approaches and techniques have made Annie Leibovitz one of the eminent American photographers of the second half of the twentieth century.

Bibliography
Biema, David Van. "The Eye of Annie Leibovitz." *Life* 17 (April, 1994): 46-54. Besides providing a solid overview of her career and the celebrities whom she has photographed, this interview includes Leibovitz's own comments about her time in Sarajevo and the tragedy of its destruction in the region's bitter civil war. She believes that she does her best work when she is willing to take risks. Realizing that her vast experience has made her more wise, Leibovitz admits that she has no desire to be twenty again, but places full confidence in her current artistic ability and in what she can do in the future. Illustrated with photographs by John Loengard.
Brantley, Ben. "Annie's Eye." *Vanity Fair* 54 (September, 1991): 204-213. Brantley makes the point that Leibovitz has been driven to photograph celebrities in the context of what personality traits they may possess. A successful portrait for Leibovitz is one that conveys some knowledge or a truth about her subject. The article includes photographs from Leibovitz's book *Photographs: Annie Leibovitz, 1970-1990.*
Groer, Anne. "Shooting Star." *Washingtonian* 26 (April, 1991): 74-79. In 1991, Leibovitz became only the second living American photographer to have a one-person show at the National Portrait Gallery in Washington, D.C. The profile speaks to how Leibovitz has helped to define what it means to be a celebrity in American culture.

Hagen, Charles. "Annie Leibovitz Reveals Herself." *ARTnews* 91 (March, 1992): 90-95. Leibovitz discusses her career, her life, and the famous people she has photographed. Hagen is a well-respected journalist on the subject of art and photography who has written frequently for *The New York Times*. Except for a few factual errors, this is a detailed and insightful profile of a hardworking and imaginative photographer whose possibilities for even greater triumphs in the future seem guaranteed.

Lacayo, Richard. "Shadows and Eye Candy." *Time* 138 (September 30, 1991): 72-74. Lacayo compares the careers of *Vogue* photographer Irving Penn and Leibovitz. He surmises that the world must have drastically changed between 1943, when Penn joined *Vogue*, and 1983, when Leibovitz left *Rolling Stone* and moved to *Vanity Fair*. The similarities and differences between the two eminent photographers are analyzed.

Leibovitz, Annie. *Photographs: Annie Leibovitz, 1970-1990*. New York: Harper-Collins, 1991. The definitive collection of Leibovitz photographs. The book opens with Ingrid Sischy having a conversation with Leibovitz, in which Leibovitz talks about her career and her approach to photography. The photographs span twenty years and speak volumes about American popular culture.

Marcus, Adrianne. "Annie Leibovitz: One Frame at a Time." In *The Photojournalist: Mary Ellen Mark and Annie Leibovitz*. Los Angeles: Alskog/Thomas Y. Crowell, 1974. Although this book was published four years after Leibovitz had started as a professional photographer for *Rolling Stone*, it serves as a solid introduction to her career and the motivation behind her photographic style. In addition to "One Frame at a Time," Marcus also includes other chapters concerning Leibovitz, "Photographing Folk Heroes as Folk Heroes," "Documenting the Counterculture," and "Interpreting Personality Through Portraits." At the end of the book is a "Technical Section: Tools of the Photojournalist," which details the cameras and the photographic tricks of the trade used by Leibovitz and Mark. This book is part of the Masters of Contemporary Photography series.

Schonauer, David, Russell Hart, Carol Squiers, et al. "Photography's Top 100." *American Photo* 5 (Jan.-Feb., 1994): 61-101. Leibovitz is profiled as one of the top 100 most influential individuals working in photography. In addition to photographers, there are curators, dealers, models, gallery owners, agents, museum directors, and critics also profiled. In the section devoted to Leibovitz, she expresses how profoundly affected she was by her trip to Sarajevo. Leibovitz's concluding statement relates her love for what she does: "I'm doing photographs for their own sake again. . . . The most important thing I've rediscovered in the last few years is that photography is greater than magazines."

Jeffry Jensen

EDMONIA LEWIS

Born: 1845(?); probably near Albany, New York
Died: after 1909; probably Rome, Italy
Area of Achievement: Art
Contribution: A talented sculptor, Lewis drew on her African American and Native
   American heritage to expand the range of American neoclassic sculpture.

Early Life

Little is known about the early or late life of Mary Edmonia Lewis. She was born
in poverty and obscurity and, after an exciting forty or so years of adulthood,
disappeared from public view. She was born about 1845, probably near Albany, New
York (although she herself sometimes gave Greenhigh, Ohio, as her birthplace). Her
father was an African American who apparently worked as a gentleman's servant, and
her mother was a Chippewa Indian. Her father never played much of a part in
Edmonia's life. Both of her parents died when she was a child, and she was reared by
her mother's tribe in upstate New York. In later life, Lewis enjoyed telling stories
about her youth when she was known by the name Wildfire and was busy selling
baskets and moccasins and traveling with her mother's tribe.

Although Lewis began her formal schooling during her teens, it is unclear how she
secured the necessary funds to do so. Somehow—perhaps with the aid of a brother
who mined gold in California—Lewis was able to enter Oberlin College in 1859.
Since its founding in 1835, Oberlin had permitted women of all races to enroll. With
some thirty other black women, Lewis attended Oberlin from 1859 to 1863. It was
during her years at Oberlin that she changed her name from Wildfire to Mary Edmonia
Lewis. She studied music, French, zoology, and a host of other liberal arts subjects, but eventually left Oberlin under something of a cloud. In her senior year, she
was accused of poisoning two of her classmates. She was beaten by vigilantes and
then brought to trial. A prominent black lawyer, James Mercer Langston, secured
Lewis' acquittal. In early 1863, Lewis was accused of stealing art supplies and was
denied permission to graduate. She traveled to Boston, intending to pursue a musical
career.

She carried with her to Boston a letter of introduction to the abolitionist William
Lloyd Garrison. A public statue of Benjamin Franklin impressed Lewis greatly, and
she began to think for the first time of studying art. Garrison introduced her to the
sculptor Edmund Brackett, who took her on as a pupil. The first task he gave her was
to sculpt a replica of a human foot; he smashed copy after copy until she got it right.
His tutoring was to be her only real training in sculpture.

She achieved popular success with her first works: a bust of Colonel Robert Gould
Shaw (1865), leader of a black Civil War regiment, and a medallion with the likeness
of John Brown. At her first public exhibition, a benefit for the Soldiers' Aid Fund,
Lewis sold nearly one hundred plaster copies of the Shaw bust. She used the proceeds
to travel to Rome, Italy, in 1865.

Life's Work

From her initial artistic successes, Edmonia Lewis both benefited and suffered from the attentions paid her by liberal Bostonians. Although they were well meaning, Lewis' patrons saw in her a representative of oppressed, downtrodden people—and they could not refrain from commenting on her background at every turn. The observation was made many times that, because of her African heritage, she ought to have excelled in painting. It must be because of her Indian heritage, it was reasoned, that she was able to sculpt.

Lewis was generally amused by such remarks and, as her benefactors (including reformer Lydia Maria Child) were truly kind and generous, she accepted what help she could find. But although she begged that her work be judged on its own merits, not as examples of what a "colored girl" could do, she was more often than not held up as the proverbial credit to her race.

Like many artists of her time—most notably, like many women artists—she moved to Italy. She was barely twenty at the time. For sculptors of the nineteenth century, Italy provided cheap labor as well as countless examples of fine classical sculpture to study and a plentiful supply of pure white Carrara and Serravezza marble with which to work. For women, Italy offered the further advantage of acceptance. At home, there was too much criticism of women who wore pants, or climbed ladders, or wielded heavy tools, or knew enough about anatomy to sculpt the human figure.

In Rome, Lewis fell in with a company of American expatriate artists, including actress and patron of the arts Charlotte Cushman and sculptors Harriet Hosmer and Emma Stebbins. With their help, Lewis set up a studio and began carving.

The common practice for American neoclassic sculptors—those sculptors attempting to copy the style, and often the subjects, of classical Roman sculpture—was to fashion a small model from plaster or clay and to hire local craftsmen to do the actual carving in stone. Edmonia Lewis and Harriet Hosmer created something of a stir by doing some of their carving themselves. For Lewis, it meant the chance to learn more about technique and also to declare her independence. Also, because of the public's condescending attitudes toward her gender and racial origins, she wanted to be sure that her work was recognized as her own.

Lewis' first subjects in marble drew their subject matter from slavery and abolition. She received favorable criticism for *Freedwoman* (1866), a full figure of a freed slave and her son. Like most of Lewis' work, the statue has been unfortunately lost. *Freedwoman* was said to be very like Lewis' next big success, a piece called *Forever Free* (1867; earlier called *The Morning of Liberty*). This piece, nearly life-size, depicts a standing black man comforting a kneeling black woman. They have broken chains at their feet. The figures are sculpted along classical lines, showing strength of body and spirit.

Lewis turned again and again to slavery and abolition for her themes. In 1870, she made busts of Abraham Lincoln and the abolitionists Wendell Phillips and Charles Sumner. In 1871, she carved the biblical figure *Hagar*. For nineteenth century Americans, Hagar represented Egypt, and Egypt represented Africa. For blacks,

Hagar symbolized alienation. Lewis said she carved the piece as a tribute to all women who have suffered.

Other works reflected Lewis' Indian heritage. Always proud of her mother's people, she worked to show their strength and dignity, reacting against the stereotypes of the uncivilized savage. Her Indian figures, for the most part, have traditional dress and accessories, but idealized Roman features.

She was drawn to Henry Wadsworth Longfellow's poem "The Song of Hiawatha" (1855), and made small groups of figures from the story, *The Wooing of Hiawatha* (1867) and *The Marriage of Hiawatha* (1867). She also created small busts of Hiawatha and Minnehaha, and in 1871 a life-sized bust of Longfellow, who sat for it and appreciated Lewis' work enormously.

One of her most famous works also features Indian subjects. Called *The Old Arrow Maker and His Daughter* (1872), it depicts a seated man working with arrows while his daughter, making moccasins, kneels beside him. The statue was very popular, and Lewis made at least three identical versions of it.

Besides Longfellow, Lewis met other important writers of her day. It was common for British and American travelers on the Grand Tour of Europe to visit to artists' studios, and Lewis' studio was a popular stop, in part because her race and gender made her exotic. She wore a red cap, rakishly tilted, and was outspoken, witty, and charming. She became friendly with the British poets Robert Browning and Elizabeth Barrett Browning as well as American novelists such as Nathaniel Hawthorne and Henry James. In 1886, she met the great black abolitionist and writer Frederick Douglass in Rome.

Throughout her career, Lewis carved copies of classical works as a way to improve her skills. She copied a bust of "Young Octavian" (1873) and a Michelangelo work, "Moses" (1875), and several other pieces. These copies sold well to tourists, and funded Lewis' larger works. She also made a sculpture entitled *Madonna and Child* in 1867 (a common enough subject, but rare for American sculptors), and small fanciful pieces such as her *Poor Cupid* (1876), which also sold well in the United States.

Once she moved to Rome, Lewis rarely returned to the United States. In 1873, she had an exhibition of five pieces at the San Francisco Art Association. In 1876, her *Death of Cleopatra* in marble won a medal at the Centennial Exposition in Philadelphia. The sculpture, which was later lost, attempted to show the ravaging effects death has on beauty. The figure was at once beautiful and horrifying; it received powerful, but not uniformly positive, reviews. Lewis herself was welcomed and celebrated.

By the late 1880's, she had faded from celebrity. The demand for neoclassical sculpture had waned, and she had no more major commissions. Although one report claims that she was seen in Rome in 1911, the date and place of her death are unknown.

Summary

Edmonia Lewis is often referred to as the first female African American sculptor, or the first major African American/Native American artist, or something of the kind, but her importance is not only in her being early and exotic. She did overcome racial and gender bias and condescension to create a body of work. She did realize her dream to set up a studio in Rome, and funded it largely through the sales of her own work. In doing so, she became an example of what even "uncivilized" people could accomplish. Her example played a small but real part in educating nineteenth century Americans about the potential of its black, Indian, and female citizens and citizens-to-be.

Lewis' primary importance lies in her contributions to art. She was one of many neoclassic American sculptors working in the nineteenth century, all of them using traditional technique and style, Italian marble, and classical themes. Lewis was unusual—although not unique—in using the classical forms to express modern themes. Her pieces dealing with issues of human rights, instead of with subjects from classical history and literature, brought fresh energy to the tradition. She was unusual among black artists of her time in freely expressing racial themes in her work.

Unfortunately, of forty-six documented pieces she created during her career, fewer than fifteen could be located by the end of the twentieth century. Of these, several remained in the Boston area, where they continued to inspire and delight.

Bibliography
Gerdts, William H. *American Neo-Classic Sculpture: The Marble Resurrection*. New York: Viking, 1973. A thorough and clear examination of the important influences, techniques, and products of American Neoclassic sculptors, showing the context for appreciating Edmonia Lewis' work. Includes high-quality photographs of seven of her sculptures.

Hartigan, Lynda Roscoe. *Sharing Traditions: Five Black Artists in Nineteenth-Century America*. Washington, D.C.: Smithsonian Institution Press, 1985. The chapter on Lewis is the fullest and most sympathetic treatment available of Lewis' life and art. The author emphasizes Lewis' contributions to art and her reception (and treatment as a curiosity) by writers and other celebrities of the day. Includes several photographs of the sculptures, and two likenesses of Lewis herself.

Leach, Joseph. *Bright Particular Star: The Life and Times of Charlotte Cushman*. New Haven, Conn.: Yale University Press, 1970. A fascinating account of the circle of expatriate women in Rome with whom Lewis lived, worked, and socialized. An actress and patron of the arts, Cushman took young Edmonia Lewis under her wing and helped Lewis establish friendships and a studio in Rome.

Lynes, Russell. *The Art-Makers of Nineteenth-Century America*. New York: Atheneum, 1970. An attempt to examine all the important American artists of the nineteenth century to arrive at what makes their work "American." The short analysis of Lewis' work is sensitive to the special difficulties posed by her race and gender and is appreciative of her accomplishments.

Murray, Henry Morris. *Emancipation and the Freed in American Sculpture: A Study in Interpretation*. 1916. Reprint. Freeport, N.Y.: Books for Libraries Press, 1972.

The first volume in the author's "Black Folk in Art" series, this work is an appreciation rather than a technical criticism. A short chapter on Lewis' *Freedwoman* is included.

Porter, James A. *Ten Afro-American Artists of the Nineteenth Century*. Washington, D.C.: Gallery of Art, Howard University, 1967. The interesting introduction to this exhibition catalog establishes a contrast between the high achievement levels of black craftsmen in nineteenth century America with the rather lower levels of achievements in the so-called higher arts. A short chapter on Lewis proposes her as a surprising exception. Includes photographs of two of her works.

Cynthia A. Bily

LILIUOKALANI

Born: September 2, 1838; Honolulu, Hawaii
Died: November 11, 1917; Honolulu, Hawaii
Area of Achievement: Government and politics
Contribution: The last monarch of Hawaii, Liliuokalani witnessed the end of the
 Hawaiian kingdom and the beginning of the islands' annexation as a territory of the
 United States.

Early Life

Liliuokalani was born into Hawaii's royal family. She was the daughter of a chief named Kapaakea and his wife Keohokalole, who was one of the fifteen counselors of the king, Kamehameha III. Immediately after her birth, she was adopted into another family. A woman named Konia was her foster-mother, and her foster-father was a chief named Paki. This practice of adoption was the custom among the leading families of Hawaii; it was a way to cement alliances among the chiefs, who were the nobility of Hawaii. All of Liliuokalani's ten brothers and sisters were also adopted into and reared by other families.

When she was four years old, the little princess was enrolled in the Royal School, a boarding school run by American missionaries. The students of this school were all members of the royal extended family, which was made up of the families of the king and chiefs. In this school, Liliuokalani learned English and was taken to church every Sunday, but she said that she never got enough to eat.

The school closed in 1848, when she was ten years old, and after that she attended a day school also run by American missionaries. Learning was very important to Liliuokalani throughout her life.

After Paki's death in 1855, Liliuokalani continued to live in his home, along with her sister Bernice and Bernice's husband, Charles R. Bishop. The Bishops were to be a major influence on Liliuokalani's life.

Although at one time she was engaged to be married to Lunalilo (also known as Prince William), who would become king in 1873, she ultimately was married to the son of an Italian-born sea captain and a New England woman. The man was named John O. Dominis, and the marriage took place on September 16, 1862. The couple began their married life at Washington Place, the estate built by the groom's father for his family. This was to remain Liliuokalani's private residence throughout her life.

Much of Liliuokalani's adulthood before her accession as queen was spent on benevolent work for native Hawaiians. She was also a composer of music, and she wrote several Christian hymns as well as the famous Hawaiian song "Aloha Oe." In 1887, she attended Queen Victoria of England's Jubilee celebration as an honored guest. She never had any children.

Life's Work

A year after Liliuokalani's marriage, King Kamehameha IV died, on November 30,

1863. Since the young king had recently lost his only son to illness, there was no direct heir to the throne. According to the Hawaiian Constitution of 1852, the king's brother was elected as the new monarch by the cabinet, the privy council, and the *kuhina nui* (the queen, who served as coruler with the Hawaiian king). He became known as Kamehameha V. When he died in 1872, a new constitution had been passed (in 1864) that gave the king the right to choose his own successor. The successor he had named, however, his sister Princess Victoria, had died in 1866, and he had named no one else.

Now it was up to the Hawaiian legislature to elect a new king from among the nobility. This was when Liliuokalani's former fiancé, Lunalilo, ascended the throne. He lived only a year longer, however, and also died without naming an heir. This time, Liliuokalani's brother Kalakaua was elected, and in 1877 she was chosen as heiress to the throne. She served as regent from January to October of 1881 while the king was making a trip around the world, which gave her a taste of what it would later be like to be queen. She took this role again in 1890 and 1891 while the king was in California on a trip meant to restore his failing health. He died in January of 1891, however, leaving his sister Liliuokalani as queen.

Liliuokalani was proclaimed queen on January 29, 1891, at the age of fifty-two. She inherited a government that had been, throughout the nineteenth century, a mixture of Hawaiian tradition, British constitutional ideals, Victorian influence, and American interference brought by missionaries, adventurers, and politicians. Symbolic of this mixture were the combinations of names held by the Hawaiian nobility. (Liliuokalani was also known as Lydia Kamekaeha Paki and Mrs. John O. Dominis.) This mixture was strengthened by the frequency of intermarriage between Hawaiians and people of European-American extraction, of which Liliuokalani's own marriage was an example.

Liliuokalani's brother, influenced by American businessmen, had led Hawaii on a course toward ruin by trying to return to a more despotic form of government. This led to revolution in 1887 and to increased American influence, since in the new constitution of that year members of the nobility were to be elected by voters of large income and property, which in practice meant large numbers of Americans and others of foreign birth or ancestry. Hawaii was also under the grip of an economic depression as a result of the McKinley Tariff Act, which removed tariffs on other importers of sugar to the United States. Since sugar had become the center of Hawaii's economy, this act devastated the island nation.

This was the situation the new queen faced: political turmoil and economic difficulty. Her solution was to strengthen the monarchy. Liliuokalani was firmly opposed to the Constitution of 1887, which was far more democratic than previous constitutions had been. At the same time, the political strife and economic difficulties in the islands made the idea of annexation by the United States look rather appealing to some Hawaiians, and by 1892 there were secret organizations working toward that end.

After an attempt by the queen to promulgate a new constitution giving the monarchy more power, in January, 1892, a revolutionary committee took over the government and ended the monarchy, setting up a provisional government until a union with the United States could be worked out. The queen assented against her will, in order to avoid bloodshed, and retired to Washington Place. A treaty of annexation by the United States was drawn up and signed by the provisional government on February 14, 1893. It had not been acted upon, however, by the Senate of the United States by the time Grover Cleveland became president a few days later. Cleveland, a friend of Liliuokalani, had received a letter from her about the coup d'état. After his inauguration, he withdrew the treaty from the Senate's consideration and launched a lengthy investigation into the matter. Meanwhile, the provisional government remained in power.

When it became clear that annexation was not imminent, a constitutional convention in 1894 set up what was to be the Republic of Hawaii. Liliuokalani protested to both the United States and Great Britain, but to no avail. An attempt to restore the monarchy was quickly squelched, leading to Liliuokalani's arrest and conviction on charges of treason. She was imprisoned in the Iolani Palace and forced to sign abdication papers. Hawaii was officially annexed to the United States on August 12, 1898, but the Republic continued to govern the islands under the authority of the president of the United States.

Liliuokalani was pardoned in 1896, and in that year she traveled to the United States to visit her late husband's relatives, trying to forget her sorrows over recent events. She returned in August of 1898, her enthusiastic welcome home showing how much support she still retained among both native-born and foreign-born Hawaiians.

While in the United States, she wrote her autobiography, *Hawaii's Story by Hawaii's Queen* (1898), as well as translating an ancient Hawaiian poem. Liliuokalani died on November 11, 1917, in Honolulu, Hawaii.

Summary

Although her reign was Hawaii's last as an independent nation, Liliuokalani's impact on Hawaii's history cannot be denied. Because she was part of a tradition in which women played important roles, she never questioned her right to rule. Although she believed in a strong monarchy, Liliuokalani organized institutions for the improvement of the health, welfare, and education of her native Hawaiian compatriots. She was an educated woman who valued learning, and she was both an author and a composer. A native Hawaiian, she was also an enthusiastic participant in the Victorian-inspired society of her times. Her downfall was her accession to the throne at a time when her tiny kingdom, influenced as it was by both European and American values and politics, could no longer remain independent. Although she resigned herself to Hawaii's annexation to the United States, she never agreed with the idea, always remaining convinced of the value of national autonomy for her islands.

Liliuokalani is something of a tragic figure. Trained and educated as a potential ruler, passionate about her country and her people, a woman of cosmopolitan learning and taste, she nevertheless came to power at a time when her method of rule came into conflict with the movement of history.

Bibliography

Kuykendall, Ralph S., and A. Grove Day. *Hawaii: A History, from Polynesian Kingdom to American State.* Englewood Cliffs, N.J.: Prentice-Hall, 1948. The parts of this book labeled books 3 and 4 (chapters 11 through 12) give a very helpful chronicle of the events of the latter years of the Hawaiian kingdom. They help the reader understand the background to the situation that Liliuokalani inherited, as well as the outcome of her own reign.

Liliuokalani. *Hawaii's Story by Hawaii's Queen.* Rutland, Vt.: Tuttle, 1964. The queen's autobiography is the best source for learning about her early life. Although it is somewhat rambling, it is invaluable in that it gives Liliuokalani's perspective on events in her own words. It ends with her return from the United States in 1898.

Loomis, Albertine. *For Whom Are the Stars?* Honolulu: University Press of Hawaii, 1976. A highly readable and sympathetic account of the end of the Hawaiian monarchy, discussing the revolution and events leading up to it, the first failure to annex Hawaii to the United States, the founding of the Republic, the rebellion of 1895, and the queen's arrest and trial.

Russ, William Adam, Jr. *The Hawaiian Republic, 1894-98, and Its Struggle to Win Annexation.* Selinsgrove, Pa.: Susquehanna University Press, 1961. This book follows up on Russ's earlier book (below). This volume analyzes the years of the Hawaiian Republic, between the time of Liliuokalani's abdication and Hawaii's annexation by the United States.

_____ . *The Hawaiian Revolution, 1893-94.* Selinsgrove, Pa.: Susquehanna University Press, 1959. Analyzes in readable detail the events of the revolution that deposed Queen Liliuokalani. It also examines the involvement of the United States and American interests in the overthrow of Hawaiian autonomy.

Tate, Merze. *The United States and the Hawaiian Kingdom: A Political History.* New Haven, Conn.: Yale University Press, 1965. This book focuses on the period of Hawaiian history that included Liliuokalani's life and work: 1864 to 1898. Chapters 4 through 7 deal specifically with various events of her reign: her attempt to change the constitution, the Revolution of 1893, and annexation by the United States.

Young, Lucien. *The Real Hawaii: Its History and Present Condition.* New York: Doubleday & McClure, 1899. An eyewitness account of the Revolution of 1893 and the events that followed. The author was on a ship stationed at Honolulu at the time. Written to discount the reports of James H. Blount, the envoy of Liliuokalani to President Cleveland, the book gives an account of Hawaiian culture, history, and economy as well as of the revolution and its aftermath.

Eleanor B. Amico

MAYA YING LIN

Born: October 5, 1959; Athens, Ohio

Area of Achievement: Architecture
Contribution: Lin designed the Vietnam Veterans Memorial in Washington, D.C., and the Civil Rights Memorial in Montgomery, Alabama.

Early Life

Architect Maya Ying Lin was born on October 5, 1959, in Athens, a small midwestern town in southern Ohio. Her father, Henry Huan Lin, was a highly respected ceramicist and dean of fine arts at Ohio University. Her mother, Julia C. Lin, was a poet and professor of Asian and English literature. Both of her parents were born to culturally prominent families in China. Maya Lin's grandfather, Lin Changmin, along with Liang Qichao, whom the author Orville Schell calls "China's First Democrat," and Xu Zhimo, the greatest Chinese lyric poet of his generation, worked to establish democratic rule in China in the early 1900's. Her grandfather was also the director of the Chinese League of Nations Association and was stationed in London, England. While in England, the Lin family socialized with many of the brightest intellectuals of the day, a group that included H. G. Wells, Thomas Hardy, Bertrand Russell, and Katherine Mansfield. Lin Changmin's daughter, Lin Huiyin (Maya Lin's aunt), married the son of Liang Qichao, Liang Xucheng. Liang later became China's greatest architectural historian. After marrying, they moved to the United States, where both received degrees in architecture from the University of Pennsylvania. Lin Huiyin then went to Yale University to study architecture and stage design. The Lins eventually returned to China. Following World War II, however, when the communist forces overtook the Nationalists in a bitter civil war, Maya Lin's parents, like many other Chinese, fled the country. Henry Lin left to escape possible death or imprisonment and Julia left to attend Smith College on scholarship. They met for the first time in the United States and later settled in Athens, Ohio.

Maya Lin grew up in a typical middle-class home in a small midwestern university town. Her home environment included art and literature, and she was surrounded by books. An avid reader, she especially liked works by existentialists Jean-Paul Sartre and Albert Camus as well as fantasies such as J. R. R. Tolkien's *The Hobbit* and *Lord of the Rings*. She learned silversmithing, ceramics, and jewelry design, and she worked at McDonald's.

Although she was a loner at school, Maya Lin was an outstanding student. During her senior year in high school, she was covaledictorian of her graduating class. When she enrolled at Yale University in 1977, she had not selected a major. Eventually, she chose to enroll in a program in architecture. During her junior year she studied in Europe. While traveling in Europe, she became interested in cemetery architecture. She was particularly moved by Sir Edwin Lutyens' memorial to those who died in 1916 during the Somme offensive in World War I, called the Great Arch. This structure is considered one of the world's most outstanding war memorials. She received her bachelor's degree in architecture from Yale in 1981 and her master's degree in architecture from Yale in 1985.

Life's Work

After Maya Lin returned from Europe for her senior year at Yale, she enrolled in a class in funerary architecture. As a part of her coursework, she and her classmates were encouraged to enter the nationwide competition for designing a Vietnam Veterans Memorial in Washington, D.C. This competition attracted 1,420 entries, many of them submitted by noted architects and sculptors. It was the largest design competition in U.S. history. The entries were to be judged by a panel of experts, much as the designs for the U.S. Capitol and the Washington Memorial had been. Maya Lin traveled to Washington with two classmates to view the site of the planned memorial in Constitution Gardens near the Lincoln Memorial. Within a half-hour, she chose her design. She saw people gathered in the park and children playing and decided to make a structure that would not destroy the harmony of the park. When she finally completed her sketch for the entry, she was one of the last people to turn her entry in, only five minutes before the deadline. One month later, she received a telephone call informing her that she had won the competition.

The design, like the Vietnam War itself, was very controversial. The design featured a wall consisting of two segments, each 246.75 feet long, that came together to form a "V"-like structure. One segment points to the Washington Memorial; the other, to the Lincoln Memorial. Each segment consists of seventy polished black granite panels. The names of the 58,156 soldiers who died in the war, including those missing in action, are inscribed on the panels in the order in which they fell, along with a brief inscription. At the intersection, the highest point, the panels are 10.1 feet high; they taper to a width of eight inches at each end. On the back side, the entire structure is below ground. The front is open so that people can walk by and touch the wall if they choose to. Because of the reflective quality of the black granite, the wall gives back to those who visit images of themselves and the surrounding landscape.

The structure was praised by architects, the judges, and Jan Scruggs, the founder of the Vietnam Veterans Memorial Fund. Several veterans and other prominent figures, however, opposed it. Some of them called it "a black ditch," "an outrage," and the "black gash of shame." Its supporters called the design "moving" and praised its "extraordinary sense of dignity." As the controversy became more heated and opposition and support for the memorial increased, a compromise was reached, and James Watt, secretary of the interior, issued final approval. The memorial was dedicated on November 13, 1982. A bronze statue of three servicemen, sculpted by Frederick Hart, was placed near the wall and dedicated on November 11, 1984.

Maya Lin's second major design, the Civil Rights Memorial in Montgomery, Alabama, was dedicated in the fall of 1989. The inspiration for the project came from a paraphrase of a verse in the biblical Book of Amos that was spoken by the Reverend Martin Luther King, Jr., "We will not be satisfied until justice rolls down like waters and righteousness like a mighty stream." The main idea of the memorial is that water flows over those words and over the names, each carved into the black granite, of forty men, women, and children who were killed during the course of the Civil Rights movement. Like the Vietnam Veterans Memorial, the work invites visitors to touch the names, this time through the water, and therefore bring some part of themselves to the act of honoring the dead.

In the case of the Civil Rights Memorial, Edward Ashworth, a board member of the Southern Poverty Law Center contacted Lin to see if she would be interested in designing it. The center sent her books about the Civil Rights movement and about various hate groups, including the Ku Klux Klan. Maya Lin was deeply moved by the stories of various people who gave their lives for civil rights. She was especially moved by the story of Michael Donald, a black teenager who was lynched by the Klan in 1981, and the successful prosecution by the center of the person guilty of the murder. Like many people in America, Lin had never learned about these people in school and was shocked to discover that many of them had been killed during her lifetime. She readily agreed to design a memorial that would occupy the plaza in front of the center in Montgomery, Alabama.

The Civil Rights Memorial consists of two parts, both of which are made of Canadian black granite. One part is a large nine-foot-tall panel with the carved inscription ". . . until justice rolls down like waters and righteousness like a mighty stream—Martin Luther King Jr." Water cascades down the panel, covering the inscription but allowing it to be read. The second part is a circular tabletop, almost twelve feet in diameter, resting on a pedestal. On the top of the structure are fifty-three brief entries carved into the stone in chronological order. Forty of the entries describe individual deaths; thirteen describe landmark events in the Civil Rights movement. Water comes out of the middle of the tabletop and gently flows over the inscriptions. As envisioned by Morris Dees, the director of the Southern Poverty Law Center, the Civil Rights Memorial has become a teaching tool for those who come and read the inscriptions. It is also a place of quiet reflection where visitors can come to understand that these individuals' deaths influenced history and helped to make things better.

Maya Lin has also excelled in sculpture and various kinds of architectural work during her professional career. Her public artwork includes "TOPO," an environmental sculpture for Charlotte, North Carolina; "Groundswell," the first sculpture commissioned for the Wexner Center for the Arts in Columbus, Ohio; and the "Women's Table," an outdoor sculpture dedicated to women at Yale University, in New Haven, Connecticut. Her architectural work has included the Museum for African Art in the SoHo district of New York City; the Rosa Esman Gallery, also in New York City; and private homes in Santa Monica, California, and in Williamstown, Massachusetts.

She has also pursued her interest in her own studio sculpture, creating human-scaled works made from beeswax, lead, steel, and broken glass. These works have been exhibited in New York, Los Angeles, San Francisco, and Columbus, Ohio.

Like both of her parents, Maya Lin has also taught at the university level. She has taught at Yale University and as a visiting artist at the Yale School of Art. She has also lectured at many museums and educational institutions, including the University of Washington, the Wexner Center for the Arts, the Metropolitan Museum of Art, the San Francisco Museum of Art, Wellesley College, and Qinghua University of Beijing, China.

In addition to doing her professional work, Maya Lin also serves on several community boards. Her interest in environmental issues has led her to serve on the board of the Energy Foundation and on the national advisory board to the Presidio Council in San Francisco. She also serves on the board of the Ohio University Museum of Art and on the advisory board of the Southern Poverty Law Center.

Summary

Maya Lin has made two significant contributions to architecture, a field dominated by males. Lin, a Chinese American, was selected to create two public memorials in the United States that celebrate two of the most important social issues of the past half-century. The Vietnam Veterans Memorial has become the most visited memorial in Washington, D.C., and has been described as "perhaps the most moving war memorial ever built." On November 20, 1984, the U.S. postal service issued a twenty-cent stamp commemorating the Vietnam Veterans Memorial. The Civil Rights Memorial has also received great praise.

She has received the Presidential Design Award, the American Institute of Architects' Honor Award, and the Henry Bacon Memorial Award. She is a recipient of a National Endowment for the Arts visual artists' grant and has received honorary doctoral degrees of fine arts from Yale University, Smith College, and Williams College.

Maya Lin owns a studio in New York City's Bowery district. Early in her career, Maya Lin has already become one of the most celebrated and accomplished architects in the United States. She has proved that women can succeed in architecture and in sculpture and has opened the doors for others to follow.

Bibliography

Ashabranner, Brent. *Always to Remember: The Story of the Vietnam Veterans Memorial*. New York: Dodd, Mead, 1988. This book, which is appropriate for middle and high school students, gives a very good background of the controversy surrounding the Vietnam War as well as the memorial itself.

Ezell, Edward Clinton. *Reflections on the Wall: The Vietnam Veterans Memorial*. Harrisburg: Stackpole Books, 1987. A very good account of various positions toward and impressions of the memorial.

Lopes, Sal. *The Wall: Images and Offerings from the Vietnam Veterans Memorial*. New York: Collins, 1987. An excellent pictorial that captures the beauty and emotions of the memorial.

Scruggs, Jan C., and Joel L. Swerdlow. *To Heal a Nation: The Vietnam Veterans Memorial*. New York: Harper & Row, 1985. An excellent overview of the history of the Vietnam Veterans Memorial, including the controversy surrounding the selection of Maya Lin's design for the memorial and the harsh politics of getting a memorial approved.

Spence, Jonathan D. *The Gate of Heavenly Peace: The Chinese and Their Revolution, 1895-1980.* New York: Viking Press, 1981. Provides an excellent account of Maya Lin's family in China as well as one of the best histories of modern China.

Zinsser, William. "Deeds and Deaths That Made Things Better." *Smithsonian* 22 (September, 1991): 32. An excellent article detailing the background and the impact of the Civil Rights Memorial in Montgomery, Alabama.

Gregory A. Levitt

BELVA A. LOCKWOOD

Born: October 24, 1830; Royalton, New York
Died: May 19, 1917; Washington, D.C.
Areas of Achievement: Law, women's rights, and peace advocacy
Contribution: Lockwood obtained passage of federal legislation giving women equal pay for equal work in government service, became the first woman to be granted the right to plead cases before the U.S. Supreme Court, and was a committed activist for women's rights.

Early Life

Belva Ann Bennett, the second of the five children of Lewis Bennett and Hannah Green Bennett, was born on October 24, 1830, in Niagara County, New York. She attended country schools and completed her education by the age of fifteen. Her father's opposition to her educational ambitions, as well as a lack of funds, led her to begin a career in teaching. She taught school for four years before marrying Uriah McNall, a local farmer. The young couple moved to the country near Gasport, where Belva gave birth to a daughter, Lura. When her husband died in a sawmill accident in 1853, Belva returned to school to further her education in order to support herself and her child.

Belva McNall sold the farm and entered Gasport Academy. She also continued to teach school. As a teacher, she experienced at first hand inequities toward women when she was offered half the salary paid to male teachers. Angry and upset, she left her daughter with her parents and entered Genessee College, where she studied law, political economy, and the U.S. Constitution. On June 27, 1857, she received a bachelor of science degree from the college that was to become Syracuse University.

In 1857, Belva McNall became headmistress of Lockport Union School, where her daughter studied. For the next four years, she supervised the staff, taught courses, and, despite conservative disapproval, encouraged gymnastics, public speaking, nature walks, and skating for young women. She also taught at the Gainesville Female Seminary and later became proprietor of the Female Seminary in Oswego, New York. In 1866, while in her middle thirties, Belva McNall, with her daughter Lura, left for Washington, D.C. Her profession was still teaching, but she had political ambitions that would eventually take her far beyond the classroom.

In 1867, Belva McNall opened a school of her own. On March 11, 1868, she married Ezekiel Lockwood, a dentist and former Baptist minister. Their only child, Jessie, died in infancy. Ezekiel Lockwood assumed the administrative duties of his wife's school so that she could pursue a law degree. Denied admission to Columbia, Georgetown, and Harvard because she was not only a woman but a married one, Lockwood was finally accepted at the National University Law School. She completed her studies in 1873 but was awarded her diploma only after she petitioned President Ulysses S. Grant, the school's ex officio president, to intervene on her behalf. Her husband, who had continued to supervise her school in Washington, was finally forced to close it because of his ill health. He died in 1877.

Life's Work

After judicial rules were changed and women were allowed to practice law in the District of Columbia, Belva Lockwood was admitted to the bar on September 24, 1873. At the age of forty, she embarked on a distinguished career in law. When one of her cases came before the Federal Court of Claims that winter, Lockwood was refused, because she was a woman, the right to plead a case. Her petition for admission to the Supreme Court of the United States (1876) was denied on the basis of custom, but Lockwood would not admit defeat. She petitioned Congress to pass a Declaratory Act or Joint Resolution "that no woman otherwise qualified, shall be debarred from practice before any United States Court on account of sex." Reasoning that if women had the right to practice law they were entitled to pursue legal matters through the highest courts in the country, Lockwood pushed enabling legislation through Congress. By means of energetic lobbying, and with the support of such pro-suffrage senators as Aaron A. Sargent of California and George F. Hoar of Massachusetts, Lockwood secured the passage of the Lockwood Bill, which permitted women to practice before the Supreme Court. On March 3, 1879, she became the first woman to be admitted to the Bar of the United States Supreme Court. Three days later, she was admitted to the U.S. Court of Claims.

A year later, on February 2, 1880, in a striking demonstration of her commitment to racial equality, Belva Lockwood appeared before the Supreme Court of the United States and made a motion that Samuel R. Lowery, an African American, be allowed to practice before the Supreme Court. Lowery, who was the principal of the Huntsville Industrial University in Alabama, became the first southern African American to practice law before the Supreme Court of the United States.

Belva Lockwood became a familiar sight in Washington as she pedaled throughout the city on "Challenge No. 2," an English tricycle that she introduced to the nation's capital. She rode the vehicle to the Capitol, the courts—wherever her work led her. By 1890, Belva was well established in her law career, specializing in pension and claims cases against the U.S. government. It was this specialty that led her to one of the greatest legal triumphs of her career. The Cherokee Indian Nation secured Lockwood to represent it in claims against the U.S. government related to an 1891 treaty involving the sale and purchase of more than eight million acres of land known as the Cherokee Outlet. Lockwood was entrusted with defending nearly fifteen thousand Cherokee clients. After reviewing the numerous treaties and statutes that governed the history of the Cherokees, she filed a petition to uphold the claim of her Indian clients.

On March 20, 1905, the case of the Eastern and Emigrant Cherokees against the United States was decided before the Court of Claims. Following an impassioned argument by Lockwood, the Chief Justice agreed that the United States had broken and evaded the letter and spirit of its agreement with the Cherokees. Nevertheless, although he decreed that the Cherokees recover certain amounts due in the account rendered by the government, he could not bring himself to allow the full interest on those amounts. The case was appealed to the Supreme Court, where, on April 30,

1906, Lockwood again argued for the Indians and their rights. The court agreed and awarded the Cherokees five million dollars.

As a feminist, Lockwood did much to further women's rights. In 1867, she was one of the founders of Washington's first suffrage group, the Universal Franchise Association. During the 1870's and early 1880's, she was active in the Washington conventions of the National Woman Suffrage Association (NWSA). In January, 1871, Belva Lockwood presented a memorial to the United States Senate on "The Right of Women to Vote."

She addressed congressional committees and drew up innumerable resolutions and bills that would help bring equality to women in the United States. She circulated a petition at the meetings of the National and American Woman Suffrage Associations in New York that hastened the passage, in 1872, of legislation giving women government employees equal pay for equal work. In 1873, she represented a woman in a divorce case, charging the defendant with drunkenness, cruel treatment, desertion, and refusal to support. She won the case for her client, obtaining the decree of divorce and alimony with costs. Later, in 1896, as a member of a committee of the District Federation of Women's Clubs, she helped Ellen Spencer Mussey and others secure passage of a law liberalizing the property rights of married women and equal guardianship of their children in the District of Columbia. In 1903, she proposed the inclusion of woman suffrage clauses in the statehood bills for Oklahoma, Arizona, and New Mexico, which were then under consideration.

In 1872, Belva Lockwood spoke at Cooper Union in New York on behalf of Victoria Woodhull's candidacy for president of the United States. Lockwood herself was nominated for president in 1884 by women representing the National Equal Rights Party. Her platform reflected her commitment to civil rights, temperance, and feminism. She encompassed equal rights for all, including African Americans, Indians, and immigrants. She advocated curtailment of the liquor traffic, reform in marriage and divorce laws, and universal peace. She flourished a banner inscribed on one side with the words "Women's Rights" and on the other with the word "Peace." Although her campaign alienated many members of the organized suffrage movement, including Susan B. Anthony, it generated much public interest. Astonishingly, she won the electoral vote of Indiana, half that of Oregon, nearly captured New Hampshire, and made a respectable showing in New York. A second campaign four years later was less successful. Her political aptitude was recognized by President Grover Cleveland, who sent her as the U.S. delegate to the Congress of Charities and Correction in Geneva, Switzerland.

Increasingly committed to the cause of world peace, Lockwood put much of her energy into peace organizations after the 1880's. One of the earliest members of the Universal Peace Union, Lockwood served at various times in the 1880's and 1890's on the union's executive committee and the editorial board of its paper, the *Peace-maker*, as a corresponding secretary and vice president, and as one of the union's chief lobbyists. She was the union's delegate to the International Peace Congress of 1889 and its successors; served as the American secretary of the International Bureau of

Peace, founded in Berne in 1891; and served on the nominating committee for the Nobel Peace Prize. In all these organizations, she agitated for the arbitration principle as a means of settling world problems.

Belva Lockwood remained politically active into her later years. She continued lecturing well into her eighties, and at the age of eighty-seven she campaigned for Woodrow Wilson. In 1909, she was awarded an honorary LL.D. degree by Syracuse University, and in 1913, she was presented with an oil portrait of herself by the women of Washington, D.C. The portrait now hangs in the Art Gallery of the National Museum.

Following the death of her daughter Lura in 1894, Lockwood's financial fortunes collapsed, and her last years were spent in ill health and relative poverty. She died at George Washington University Hospital in 1917 and was buried in the Congressional Cemetery in Washington. The funeral service held in the Wesley Chapel of the Methodist Episcopalian Church recalled the triumphs of her life, and the newspapers recorded her history. A scholarship was established in Lockwood's name, and a bust of Lockwood was unveiled by the Women's Bar Association of the District of Columbia to commemorate the seventy-fifth anniversary of her admission to the Supreme Court.

Summary

Legally and socially, Belva A. Lockwood scored important victories for women. Marriage, she concluded, should be a civil contract in which property rights were equal. She rebelled against the law in the District of Columbia that could compel a man to support his illegitimate child but could not compel him to support his wife and his legitimate children. She worked for the reform of probate law and recognition of the rights of widows and orphans. Single-handedly, Lockwood moved the U.S. Congress to open the highest court to women lawyers. She fought for civil rights for all Americans. Up to the day she died, she worked for world peace.

Over the years of her practice, Lockwood gave aid, advice, and encouragement to women from all parts of the country who were attempting to become attorneys-at-law. Belva Lockwood's hard-won battles, confidence, and fortitude are an inspiration to women throughout the world.

Bibliography

Curti, Merle. *Peace or War*. New York: Garland, 1972. Curti discusses Lockwood's pacifism and her efforts to advance peace on the national and international scenes.

Fox, Mary Virginia. *Lady for the Defense: A Biography of Belva Lockwood*. New York: Harcourt Brace Jovanovich, 1975. A useful, relatively recent treatment of Lockwood's life and work.

Stanton, Elizabeth Cady, et al. eds. *History of Woman Suffrage*. New York: Arno Press, 1969. Contains informative accounts of the NWSA's Washington conventions, 1870 to 1874, in volumes 2 through 4 (1882-1902) and useful chapters on the District of Columbia in volumes 3 and 4.

Stern, Madeleine. *We the Women*. New York: Schulte, 1963. This work contains the most complete account available of Belva Lockwood's life. Stern discusses, at length, Lockwood's most celebrated court cases, including her own quest to practice before the Supreme Court. This is the best source to consult regarding Lockwood's commitment to women's rights, civil rights, and pacifism.

Whitman, Alden, ed. *American Reformers*. New York: H. W. Wilson, 1985. A brief but fairly thorough account of Lockwood's life, highlighting her women's rights and peace activism.

Diane C. Vecchio

ALICE ROOSEVELT LONGWORTH

Born: February 12, 1884; New York, New York
Died: February 20, 1980; Washington, D.C.
Area of Achievement: Government and politics
Contribution: Often referred to as "Washington's other monument," Alice Roosevelt
   Longworth reigned for more than eight decades as one of the most controversial
   and influential individuals within the political and social arenas of America's
   capital city.

Early Life

Alice Lee Roosevelt was born at the Manhattan home of her paternal grandmother, socialite Martha "Mittie" Roosevelt, on February 12, 1884. Her twenty-four-year-old father, Theodore Roosevelt, received the happy news in Albany where, as the New York state assembly's youngest member, he was busily wrapping up business before a planned leave of absence. Having been advised that his beautiful young wife, the well-pedigreed Alice Hathaway Lee, was recovering without difficulty, Roosevelt was stunned to receive an urgent telegram a few hours later urging him to come home immediately. A grim situation awaited his arrival at midnight on the fourteenth of February. Mittie lay dying of typhoid fever in her bedroom on the first floor of the house; two floors above, Roosevelt's eighteen-year-old wife also lay gravely ill. Mittie died within hours of her son's arrival, only to be followed at two in the afternoon by Alice Lee, who succumbed to a severe kidney infection, later diagnosed as Bright's disease. Roosevelt would later mark that tragic day with a cross in his 1884 diary, and the words "The light has gone out of my life." Stunned by the dual loss, he managed to remain composed throughout the funeral. He then left abruptly for his ranch in North Dakota. Baby Alice was put in the care of Roosevelt's older, unmarried sister, Anna—an arrangement that Roosevelt was perfectly willing to consider as permanent.

Young Alice lived with Anna, whom she called Auntie Bye, for the first three years of her life. She would later praise her aunt as the most important and positive influence in her life. A homely, gregarious, and cultured woman, Auntie Bye had a gift with people that endeared her to many. She loved Alice deeply and was the only one to provide the little girl with information about her mother as she was growing up. Theodore never once spoke of Alice Hathaway Lee to his daughter.

In 1887, Theodore Roosevelt married a former sweetheart, Edith Kermit Carow. Although he was content to leave young Alice in the custody of Auntie Bye, Edith insisted that she wanted the child. Alice left the cherished security of Auntie Bye's house and entered a household where she was ignored by her father and treated as a necessary responsibility by her stepmother. During this time, Alice contracted polio, a disease that left her nearly crippled. Edith, who distrusted the nurse, stretched the young girl's legs each evening. Alice would later attribute her impeccable posture to this experience and would credit her stepmother for her unflagging commitment to this task.

Over the next several years, Roosevelt's political career began to soar. During this time, Edith gave birth to five children: Theodore, Jr. (1887), Kermit (1889), Ethel (1891), Archie (1894), and Quentin (1897). While adored by her siblings, Alice often felt like an outsider in the family. Starved for attention at home, the shy little girl eventually matured into a beautiful and rebellious young woman who craved that attention from an adoring American public.

On November 6, 1900, Republican William McKinley was elected to the office of president of the United States, with Theodore Roosevelt as his vice president. After McKinley's assassination in September of 1901 (an event that Alice admitted feeling "rapturous" about), the Roosevelt family moved into the Executive Manor, which Theodore renamed the "White House." In the fall of 1901, seventeen-year-old "Princess Alice" (as she was dubbed, to her disgust, by the press) became the first presidential daughter to debut in the White House. The magnificent celebration captured America's attention and officially launched Alice's lifelong affair with the nation's capital. It was also an event that Alice would later note as a disappointing and dowdy affair arranged by her stepmother, Edith.

Life's Work

President Theodore Roosevelt once remarked to Owen Wister, author of *The Virginian* (1902), that he could run the country or he could manage Alice, but that he could not possibly do both. The American public, just emerging from the repressed Victorian era, was simply fascinated with the headstrong and spoiled Princess Alice. Her looks were much admired—the translucent eyes, beautiful face, and perfect posture (cultivated by Alice's determination not to appear a "cripple" after her childhood bout with polio). Alice Lee Roosevelt was also blunt, opinionated, scandalous, and highly unpredictable. Her antics—the smoking, drinking, racing around in cars, betting on horses—were intoxicatingly naughty. Women fashioned dresses in "Alice blue," a shade favored by the president's daughter because it enhanced her natural coloring. "Alice, Where Art Thou," and "Alice Blue Gown," were popular songs of the day. Her image, so closely linked to the pen-and-ink Gibson girl illustrations created by Charles Dana Gibson, was admired and imitated both at home and abroad.

Alice was featured regularly in *Town Topics*, a weekly gossip sheet published in Washington, D.C. The fervid publicizing of his precocious, society-struck daughter's indiscretions proved a constant worry for the image-conscious Roosevelt and his rather reclusive wife. In time, however, the president would come to find Alice a political asset, as his own popularity received a boost from the country's love affair with his free-spirited daughter. Alice's trip to the Far East in 1905, with an American delegation that happened to include her future husband, Nicholas Longworth III, swelled national pride and only whetted the public's appetite for more tales of the dazzling Alice.

On February 17, 1906, American newspapers headlined the marriage of Princess Alice to Longworth, a plain-looking but promising politician from a prominent family. Alice was twenty-two years of age, he was thirty-six. Within two years, the marriage was in trouble. Although well loved by his peers, Longworth had a reputation for drinking and womanizing. Alice Roosevelt Longworth, thriving on her father's newfound appreciation for her political savvy and contacts, focused on Roosevelt's career over that of her husband. Her father's death on January 6, 1919, devastated Alice; she blamed Woodrow Wilson for his demise and vowed political revenge. Alice embarked on a career in politicking that would make her one of the most influential personalities in Washington, D.C.

In 1920, Alice supported woman suffrage—not because she believed in it, but because it was controversial. A few years later, she shocked Washington society by announcing her pregnancy only months before her forty-first birthday. It was rumored that the father was not Longworth, but Senator William Borah of Idaho, a powerful (and married) politician with whom Alice had become quite friendly. On February 14, 1925, her daughter, Paulina, was born. Alice was an indifferent mother, but her husband accepted and cherished the little girl. Nicholas Longworth, who had been elected Speaker of the House in 1925 and who had earned political respect and admiration among his colleagues, died in 1931. His six-year-old daughter was crushed by the loss. Bereft of any real love and subjected constantly to her mother's sharp tongue and controlling ways, Paulina Longworth developed into a strange, emotionally stunted young woman who made a bad marriage, had an only daughter of her own, and died—a probable suicide—from an overdose of barbiturates and alcohol at the age of thirty-two. Those close to Alice said that she was greatly saddened by the loss of her daughter. Like her father, however, she denied any emotion and carried on as though Paulina had never existed. Alice's relationship with her orphaned ten-year-old granddaughter, Joanna, provided her with a second chance. After a rocky start, the two, more than sixty years apart in age, remained devoted to each other until Alice's death.

When her husband died, voters urged Alice to run for Longworth's seat in the House of Representatives. Later, they invited her to run for the Senate. In both cases, Alice politely declined the offer, stating family obligations; the real reason was her terrible fear of public speaking. In 1933, *Crowded Hours* was published—a book of reminiscences that Alice agreed to write out of financial need. She hated writing and always preferred the art of intimate conversation.

The 1930's and 1940's were a busy time for Alice as she vigorously opposed the politics of her cousins, Franklin and Eleanor Roosevelt, and preached isolationism in the face of Adolf Hitler's atrocities. After the war years, she began to mellow, and as time passed no longer concerned herself with voting a particular party. She concentrated on the qualities and qualifications of the individual.

Alice remained an important fixture in Washington politics. She was noted for her quick wit and sharp tongue, tempered by her own self-mocking nature. Alice was also a self-taught intellectual with broad interests. Gatherings at her home often included writers and poets, such as Ezra Pound. The main requirement of a guest was that they not be boring.

In time, Alice established relationships with many important political people: the Kennedys (Bobby was a special favorite), the Johnsons (she considered Lyndon to be a masterful politician), and the Nixon family. Richard Nixon was the last American president to pay homage to Alice, even braving critics to attend her ninetieth birthday party, held during the height of the Watergate controversy.

Always "February's child," Alice died of pneumonia on February 20, 1980, and was buried beside her daughter, Paulina. The occasion of her passing recalled a 1935 quote from British author, Dame Rebecca West: "Intellectually, spiritually, the city [Washington, D.C.] is dominated by the last good thing said by Alice Roosevelt Longworth."

Summary

As Washington's most important and controversial hostess, for years Alice Roosevelt Longworth signified American style and glamour. Known as "Mrs. L" to her friends, her concise, opinionated observations, sharp wit, and stinging one-liners were well-respected in the political and social circles of America's capital city. A voracious reader, Alice often attributed her success to her "monkeylike quality to catch on"—she prized cleverness in others as well. She was unself-pitying in the face of tragedy, and intolerant of weakness in others. Her energy and blunt honesty were addictive to those who were allowed into her inner circle. Alice had a gift for mingling and conversing with people, and it was this ability that enabled her to become one of the most significant and memorable individuals in Washington.

As the daughter of a U.S. president, wife of the Speaker of the House, belle of the Washington social scene, and as a woman who had watched America move from the horse and buggy to the SST, Alice Roosevelt Longworth truly enjoyed her particular vantage point in history. She saw eighteen administrations come and go, shared many secrets, and knew an enormous number of people. Her gatherings were considered to be exclusive, important events with snob appeal. Those who sought her favor, as well as those who did not, recognized the persuasive power she held in her role as a shrewd and valued confidante to the leading figures of her day.

Bibliography

Brough, James. *Princess Alice: A Biography of Alice Roosevelt Longworth*. Boston: Little, Brown, 1975. A detailed biography of Alice Roosevelt Longworth up to her ninety-first year. The text is entertaining and accented with photos throughout.

Felsenthal, Carol. *Alice Roosevelt Longworth*. New York: G. P. Putnam's Sons, 1988. A highly readable and thorough study of Longworth's remarkable life. More current than the biographies of Brough and Teichmann, Felsenthal carries the story forward until Longworth's death in 1980. Includes a good collection of photographs.

Hagedorn, Hermann. *The Roosevelt Family of Sagamore Hill*. New York: Macmillan, 1954. The classic biography of Theodore and Edith Roosevelt, their children, and life at the family estate at Sagamore Hill. Offers a rather romanticized version of

Alice's early years, told in glowing tones.

Longworth, Alice Roosevelt. *Crowded Hours: Reminiscences of Alice Roosevelt Longworth*. New York: Charles Scribner's Sons, 1933. Longworth's autobiography, a labor of necessity rather than love. Presents a somewhat dry and highly selective set of memoirs.

McCullough, David. *Mornings on Horseback*. New York: Simon & Schuster, 1981. An excellent biography of the Roosevelt family. Covers Theodore Roosevelt's frail boyhood to the years just prior to his presidency. McCullough, a noted historian, provides excellent background material on Alice's mother, the tragic circumstances surrounding young Alice's birth, and her early years with Auntie Bye.

Teague, Michael. *Mrs. L: Conversations with Alice Roosevelt Longworth*. New York: Doubleday, 1981. The culmination of six years of taped conversations with friend Alice at teatime, Teague's book offers an excellent balance to the biographical material published by other authors. Longworth tells her own version of stories and events. Important reading for a complete picture of Longworth; a sensitive and interesting treatment complete with photographs.

Teichmann, Howard. *Alice: The Life and Time of Alice Roosevelt Longworth*. Englewood Cliffs, N.J.: Prentice-Hall, 1979. A chatty biography covering Longworth's life in detail. Biographer and playwright Teichmann uses lots of dialogue to propel the story along. Photographs scattered throughout the text.

Cynthia Breslin Beres

ANITA LOOS

Born: April 26, 1888; Sissons, California
Died: August 18, 1981; New York, New York
Areas of Achievement: Literature and film
Contribution: A pioneering scriptwriter who developed the use of intertitles during the silent film era, Anita Loos also wrote the famous jazz-age novel *Gentlemen Prefer Blondes.*

Early Life

Corinne Anita Loos was born on April 26, 1888, in Sissons (later Mount Shasta), California, to Minerva and R. Beers Loos. "Minnie" Loos was a proper, patient wife who socially abided the flamboyant, philandering ways of her husband, an itinerant journalist whose wanderlust led him to one small-town California newspaper after another. The wayward father also loved everything theatrical. A self-proclaimed "Edwin Booth of amateur theatre," he opened (and closed) as many drama societies as he did newspapers.

When a San Francisco weekly, *Music and Drama*, went on the market, Anita's father bought it and moved the family once again. San Francisco's frontier spirit and Barbary Coast pleasures fascinated him as he prowled the city's bustling waterfront, often with the diminutive Anita. He introduced Anita and her younger sister Gladys to theater when the youngsters made their dramatic debut in the Alcazar Stock Company's production of *Quo Vadis?* (1894).

The close bond between Anita and her father survived a family tragedy when eight-year-old Gladys Loos died after an emergency appendectomy performed on the family's kitchen table while R. Beers Loos was out on the town. The family's fortunes dipped again when Anita's father's paper failed because of lax supervision. R. Beers Loos next managed the Cineograph in San Francisco's Mexican district, where short one-reel films alternated with vaudeville acts. When that venture failed, the family moved to San Diego, where R. Beers managed the Lyceum, a theater featuring pirated Broadway plays that often starred Anita, who by now was a versatile teenage actress and an increasingly important source of the family's income.

In spite of the promise of a successful theatrical career, Anita Loos concluded that acting was a profession for numbskulls and narcissists and turned her attention to writing. In 1912, after penning gossip items for the local paper, Loos tried the "galloping tintypes." Her target was New York's Biograph Company, the nation's top studio thanks to innovative director D. W. Griffith. Biograph responded to Loos's unsolicited script for *The Road to Plaindale* with a check for twenty-five dollars and a release form. Within months, at age twenty-four, Anita Loos had sold three scripts to Biograph and a fourth to the Lubin Company. One of these, *The New York Hat* (1912), was directed by Griffith as a swan song for Mary Pickford, who was making her final appearance for Biograph. The film was a barometer prefiguring Loos's penchant for satirizing provincialism and busybody moralists.

Life's Work

During the first phase of Anita Loos's career with D. W. Griffith at Biograph and then at Triangle, the attractive four-foot, eleven-inch comedic dynamo churned out more than one hundred scenarios. In the process, she revolutionized the "art" of writing intertitles, the printed snippets of dialogue and expositional narrative that helped audiences follow the melodramatic unfolding of a film's plot and the development of its characters. Typical of her approach was an early film for Lubin in which she identified the antagonist, Proteus Prindle, as "a self-made man who adored his maker." The wittily turned intertitle soon would become her stock-in-trade.

Although Loos had met Griffith briefly in 1914 on one of the director's winter sojourns to shoot under Southern California's sunny skies, their professional relationship did not move from correspondence to direct collaboration until 1915. Griffith, who along with Mack Sennett and Thomas Ince headed one of Triangle's three production units, hired Loos to help the ambitious tripartite studio keep pace with an urgent need for fresh material. At the time, with Europe consumed by World War I, the American film industry was growing at a rapid rate in order to meet growing domestic and international demands for new films. Loos could not have been at a better place (Hollywood) at a better time (1915).

Griffith, keenly aware of his need for smart writing talent, tendered Loos a contract for seventy-five dollars a week plus a bonus whenever one of her scripts was produced. Fresh from his triumph with *The Birth of a Nation* (1915) and preoccupied with his independent production of Intolerance, Griffith turned Loos over to Frank Woods, head of Triangle's script department. The paternal Woods, affectionately known on the Triangle lot as "Daddy," at first kept Loos busy with wise-cracking titles for Sennett's Keystone Kops and rewrites for the progressively longer melodramas, which by 1920 would become standardized at a feature length of one to two hours. Her first major assignment was an adaptation of *Macbeth* (1915) for renowned English actor Sir Beerbohm Tree. It was a "prestige production" for which, thanks to Daddy Woods, she received her first screen credit: "*Macbeth* by William Shakespeare and Anita Loos." She later wrote, "if I had asked, Daddy Woods would have given me top billing."

Loos was soon assigned to one of Triangle's secondary directors, John Emerson, who had been charged with trying to find some way of using former Broadway leading man Douglas Fairbanks. Loos penned *His Picture in the Papers* (1916) for Fairbanks, a project that poked fun at America's love of publicity and instant celebrity. Loos had a field day with the titles, which horrified Griffith, who ordered the picture shelved on the assumption that if audiences wanted to read, they would stay home with a book. A shortage of product prompted the film's release. To Griffith's surprise, *His Picture in the Papers* was a huge hit that made Fairbanks a film star and the intertitle a basic part of film technique. For his part, the savvy Griffith, recognizing Loos's unique talents, hired her to work, uncredited, on the titles for his mammoth production of *Intolerance* (1916).

Meanwhile, Loos and Fairbanks collaborated on nine more pictures for Triangle, most of which were directed by Emerson. Almost all of these films deflated current fads and fashions. In *The Mystery of the Leaping Fish* (1916), Fairbanks' hyped-up Coke Ennyday, "the scientific detective," parodies applied empiricism and cocaine. In *Reaching for the Moon* (1917), Coueism, a then-popular self-help regimen based on an autosuggestive mantra, "Every day in every way I am getting better and better," was cheerfully sent up and shot down. In *Wild and Woolly* (1917), Hollywood itself is mocked. In the process, the Loos-Emerson-Fairbanks team capitalized on Fairbanks' athletic ability, boundless cheer, good humor, and winning smile to fashion one of Hollywood's greatest icons and embodiments of American optimism.

In 1920, Loos married director John Emerson, a relationship that perplexed her friends, who resented the director for putting his name as coauthor on Loos's scripts. Loos seemed to have an affection for domineering, unfaithful men. In her autobiography, *A Girl Like I* (1966), Loos explains that she could not fall in love with an especially ardent suitor because "he gave me full devotion and required nothing in return, while John treated me in an offhand manner, appropriated my earnings, and demanded from me all the services of a hired maid. How could a girl like I resist him?"

In 1925, on sabbatical from Hollywood, Loos wrote the novel *Gentlemen Prefer Blondes* (1925). Loos was praised by literary lions such as H. L. Mencken for "making fun of sex, which has never before been done in this grand and glorious nation of ours." The novel's durable Lorelei Lee, the ditzy gold-digging blonde from Little Rock, first appeared on the silver screen in a silent version directed by Mal St. Clair in 1928. (Howard Hawks's 1953 remake featured the incandescent Marilyn Monroe as Lorelei Lee.)

Loos returned to Hollywood in the late 1920's to work with Irving Thalberg at Metro-Goldwyn-Mayer (MGM). Like her friend and fellow scenarist Francis Marion, Loos negotiated the switch to "talking" pictures smoothly. In *Red-Headed Woman* (1932), for example, the combination of Loos's wise-cracking dialogue and Jean Harlow's gold-digging glamour and genius for comic timing clicked with precision and panache. Among Loos's own favorites was the melodramatic *San Francisco* (1936), set around the earthquake of 1906, starring Clark Gable, Jeannette MacDonald, and Spencer Tracy; Gable's role was based on the great yet unrequited love of Loos's life, Wilson Mizner, the bon vivant she later traced in her book *Kiss Hollywood Goodbye* (1974). Loos also coscripted with veteran MGM writer Jane Murfin a sharp-edged adaptation of Clare Boothe Luce's venomous comedy The Women (1939), which was directed by George Cukor and featured Norma Shearer, Rosalind Russell, Paulette Goddard, and Joan Crawford.

After John Emerson's attempt on her life in 1937 and his subsequent confinement in a sanitarium as an uncurable schizophrenic for the final twenty years of his life, Loos became one of the few Hollywood scriptwriters to move successfully to the writing of plays, novels, and memoirs. She continued to produce various kinds of work for many years. Anita Loos died in New York in 1981 at the age of ninety-three.

Summary

The name Anita Loos promises to live long as the author of *Gentlemen Prefer*

Blondes, whether its form be novelistic, cinematic, or theatrical. Indeed, the golden-haired Lorelei Lee—whose sexual politics are summed up in Leo Robin's and Jule Styne's aphoristic "Diamonds Are a Girl's Best Friend," from the 1949 Broadway musical adaptation of Loos's novel—remains an entertaining though increasingly problematic representation of American womanhood, since it trades heavily on the stereotype of the dumb, submissive blonde bombshell.

In the history of the American film, especially during the silent era, Loos will continue to occupy a prominent place on the strength of her crisp satirizations of American foibles, her innovative exploitation of intertitles, her shaping of Douglas Fairbanks' exuberant screen persona, and her collaboration with D. W. Griffith on the intertitles for the director's masterwork, *Intolerance*.

Critic Marjorie Rosen suggests that although Loos's tender age may have limited the scope of her early scripts, it may also have accounted for their success. "For it is unlikely," Rosen concludes, "that in any other era the thoughts of a teen-aged girl—granted an exceptional one—could have so directly corresponded to the dreams of millions of women who were just beginning to take their moviegoing seriously."

Bibliography
Acker, Ally. *Reel Women: Pioneers of the Cinema, 1896 to the Present.* New York: Continuum, 1991. Acker's invaluable set of profiles places Anita Loos under the category "From the Silents to the Sound Era" in the chapter "Reel Women Writers."
Bartoni, Doreen. "Anita Loos." In *International Dictionary of Films and Filmmakers,* edited by Nicolas Thomas, et al. 2d ed. Vol. 4, *Writers and Production Artists.* Detroit: St. James Press, 1993. A concise biographical profile supplemented with a useful filmography and bibliography.
Carey, Gary. *Anita Loos: A Biography.* New York: Alfred A. Knopf, 1988. Based on extensive interviews with Loos and a cadre of her associates, Cary's lively and meticulous account is the definitive biography of the writer. Illustrated with fascinating photos from the Loos family collection.
Loos, Anita. *Cast of Thousands.* New York: Grosset & Dunlap. 1977. This handsomely produced scrapbook of Loos memorabilia is crammed with revealing photos, posters, newspaper items, and magazine covers that bring the reader face-to-face with Fairbanks, Emerson, and the other members of the incredible cast that swirled around the diminutive dynamo Anita Loos.
——————. *A Girl Like I.* New York: Viking Press, 1966. Loos's autobiography paints a rich picture of Hollywood's golden age and her exotic associates, who paraded through "a life that was never boring."
Rosen, Marjorie. *Popcorn Venus: Women, Movies, and the American Dream.* New York: Coward, McCann & Geoghegan, 1973. Rosen's groundbreaking survey of women's contributions to the classical Hollywood film includes a concise, penetrating account of Loos's unique talents.

Charles Merrell Berg

NANCY LOPEZ

Born: January 6, 1957; Torrance, California

Area of Achievement: Sports

Contribution: Success as an amateur and professional golfer established Nancy Lopez as a predominant figure in the world of golf, and her presence stimulated the growth of women's professional golf in the United States and internationally.

Early Life

Nancy Lopez was born on January 6, 1957, in Torrance, California. Shortly after her birth, she and her older sister, Delma, moved with their parents, Domingo and Marina, to Roswell, New Mexico, where her father opened an auto repair shop. As a youth, Nancy was a Girl Scout and participated in basketball, flag football, gymnastics, swimming, and track. Although her heritage was Mexican American, her upbringing was generally anglicized, and she spoke very little Spanish.

Lopez's involvement in golf was the result of her father's interest in golf as a form of exercise for himself and his wife. At the age of seven, Lopez began following her parents when they played golf at the Roswell public course. Her father cut off a four wood for her to swing when she was eight, and in less than a year she was playing golf on the course with him. She won her first "pee wee" tournament at age nine, and her father began coaching her more seriously, emphasizing that a happy, relaxed mental attitude would allow her to enjoy golf as a game.

Lopez's development as a golfer was fostered by her parents' encouragement, support, and sacrifice. Her father helped her develop the skills and attitudes of a champion, and her mother nurtured her warm and outgoing personality. The parents skimped financially, forgoing a new house to provide braces for her teeth and to pay for her traveling to tournaments as a youth. Their daughter's amateur success rewarded them.

At age twelve, Lopez won the New Mexico Women's Amateur. She ranked number one on the otherwise all-male golf team at Godard High School in Roswell and led the team to a state championship. During her teens, she won two United States Junior Girls Championships (1972, 1974), three Western Juniors (1972, 1973, 1974), and the 1975 Mexican Amateur. In 1975, she finished second in the United States Women's Open Championship to Sandra Palmer, a renowned professional on the women's tour.

While attending Tulsa University on an athletic scholarship, Lopez won the 1976 Trans-National, Western Amateur, AIAW National Collegiate Championship, and four other collegiate titles. She was a member of the 1976 Curtis Cup and World Amateur teams that competed internationally. She left Tulsa University at the end of her sophomore year, concluding her amateur career. Lopez decided to turn to professional golf as the next challenge to her talents.

Life's Work

Nancy Lopez had developed an unusual golf swing—characterized by a deliberate

Nancy Lopez

takeaway of the club from the ball, a pause at the top of the backswing, adjustment in the downswing with a smooth and powerful generation of speed through the striking of the ball, with a graceful, balanced follow-through. Her unique style resulted in a consistency that enabled her to maintain a high level of skill in ball-striking distance and accuracy. That talent, combined with a delicate, accurate putting stroke, enabled her to become a player of professional caliber.

Lopez began her career as a professional at the 1977 U.S. Women's Open, finishing in second place. She then participated in the Ladies Professional Golf Association (LPGA) Qualifying School in July of 1977 in order to earn the right to play on the LPGA tour. She finished third in the qualifying tournament and earned playing privileges as a tour member. Two second-place finishes on the tour in 1977, at the Colgate European Open in Sunningdale, England, and at the Long Island Charity Classic in the United States, highlighted her start as a professional.

In the early days of her professional career, Lopez wondered how she would respond if she took the lead toward the end of a tournament. Lopez admitted to playing in the safe, prevailing style of the LPGA at that time, trying to avoid bogeys (one over par for a hole) rather than going for birdies (one under par for a hole). Her attitude changed, however, after the death of her mother following an appendectomy, in September, 1977. Coping with her mother's death made Lopez feel mentally stronger, and in memorial tribute to her mother, Lopez won her first professional tournament, the Bent Tree classic in Sarasota, Florida, by one stroke over Jo Ann Washam. Lopez's father, Domingo, believed that the motivation for her victory was ironic, because previously his daughter had been trying too hard to win for her mother. He commented that as long as a competitor tries too hard in any sport, he or she will not be able to win.

The beginning of Nancy Lopez's professional career was impressive, but 1978 held even greater success for her. In the Sunstar Tournament at the Rancho Park Course in Los Angeles, California, on March 12, Lopez shot one under par to pass Debbie Austin and win her second straight LPGA victory. She narrowly missed a third straight victory in losing a playoff to Sally Little in San Diego in April. What followed raised Lopez to stardom.

On May 14, Lopez won the Greater Baltimore Classic by three strokes over Donna Caponi. She came from behind to win a playoff against JoAnn Carner at Jamestown, New Jersey, a week later. On May 29, she won again at New Rochelle, New York, in the Golden Knights Tournament. On June 11, she set a new tournament record in winning the LPGA Championship at the Kings Island Course in Ohio. The following week, she won the Bankers Trust Classic in Rochester, New York, thereby setting a new record with her five consecutive victories on the LPGA Tour.

During 1978, Nancy Lopez won nine tour events—seven in the United States, one in Japan, and one in England. She was the LPGA tour's leading money winner with a record $189,813. Lopez earned the Vare Trophy, awarded for the lowest scoring average for the year, with her 71.76 stroke average per eighteen-hole round. Her accomplishments led to her selection as Rookie of the Year and Player of the Year on the LPGA tour.

I

Her personal preferences in many areas are detailed, as is her life with her husband, Ray Knight, and their daughters Ashley and Erinn. Includes photographs.

Raymond J. Sobczak

s

ca
tor
the
tive
She

H
incre
prize
adver
indivi
the tor
players

JULIETTE GORDON LOW

Born: October 31, 1860; Savannah, Georgia
Died: January 18, 1927; Savannah, Georgia
Area of Achievement: Social reform
Contribution: The principal founder of the Girl Scouts of the United States of America, Low spent the last fifteen years of her life working for an organization which would be similar to, but independent of, the Boy Scouts of America.

Early Life

In the midst of the secession crisis of 1860, Juliette Magill Kinzie Gordon was born in Savannah, Georgia, on October 31, 1860. She was the second of six children and the second of four daughters. Juliette's mother, Eleanor Lytle Kinzie Gordon, a Chicago native, had learned about the frontier experience from her father, who was a government agent to the Indians. Juliette's father, William Washington Gordon II, was a cotton broker who served during the Civil War as an officer in the Confederate army and later served as a general and peace negotiator for the United States in the Spanish-American War.

Full of energy, quick of wit, and blessed with an artistic nature, Juliette Gordon displayed much of the wit and charm attributed to her mother. She early exhibited the strong will and organizational abilities of her father, often taking charge of the childhood activities that she, her sisters, and more than a dozen cousins engaged in every summer at The Cliffs, the home of her aunt in northern Georgia. The Gordon girls and their cousins swam, camped, and sometimes hunted, and they often acted in and wrote several plays. Daisy, as Juliette was called by her family, usually acted several parts in each play.

Juliette attended private schools in Georgia, Virginia, and New York. The private school in New York City, nicknamed "The Charbs" by its students, was a finishing school run by the Charbonnier sisters, two extremely circumspect Frenchwomen who had emigrated to the United States following the Franco-Prussian War. While in New York City, Juliette wrote additional plays, acted in amateur productions, and studied painting. Once her formal education was finished, Juliette Gordon began dividing her time between living in the United States and visiting Britain and Europe, a pattern she would continue until her death.

While on one of her visits to Britain, Juliette Gordon fell in love with William Mackay Low, the son of a wealthy Englishman with Savannah connections. After a four-year courtship, which she attempted to conceal from a doting and protective father who viewed William Low as a social playboy, Juliette Gordon and William Mackay Low were married in Savannah, Georgia, in December of 1886. Juliette Gordon Low became part of the social elite in Britain, where her multimillionaire husband owned substantial property and was a close friend of the Prince of Wales and his entourage. The Lows hunted at their own estate in Scotland and entertained extensively in England and the United States. In addition, Juliette Gordon Low was presented at Court to Queen Victoria.

Beneath the surface, however, all was not well. Increasingly Low was left alone as her husband went throughout the world on game-hunting expeditions and engaged in other gentlemanly pursuits. Kept even from her favorite pursuit of horseback riding by an injury, Low took up sculpting and oil painting to fill the lonely hours. She also carved a mantlepiece for the smoking room at her Warwickshire estate, forged a pair of iron gates for the entrance to the Wellesbourne property, and often traveled without her husband (but always properly with a female companion). When the Spanish-American War began in 1898, Juliette Low helped her mother operate a hospital for soldiers in Miami, Florida.

Meanwhile, Low's marriage continued to disintegrate. In 1902, she consented to a separation and, after her husband's affair with an attractive widow became common knowledge to English society, agreed to begin proceedings for a divorce. William Low died before the divorce was concluded, leaving his estate to his lover. After several months of tense negotiations with estate lawyers, Juliette Gordon Low was granted a settlement of approximately $500,000, making her financially secure for the remainder of her life. Low resumed her active social life, alternating her time between London and Scotland while wintering in Savannah, Georgia, and other parts of the United States.

Life's Work

A turning point in Juliette Gordon Low's life came in 1911, when she met Sir Robert Baden-Powell, the hero of the defense of Mafeking in the Boer War and the founder of the Boy Scouts. She admitted later that she had disliked Baden-Powell before she met him, believing that he had received public acclaim at the expense of some of her friends who had participated in the rescue of Mafeking during the Boer War, but she and Baden-Powell soon became close friends and quickly discovered they had much in common. She shared with him a book that her mother had written about the frontier experiences of Juliette's maternal grandfather; he introduced her to his sister, who had founded the Girl Guides in England.

Low had found the rewarding service she had been seeking throughout her life. She organized a troop of Girl Guides in Scotland and two troops of Girl Guides in London before deciding to expand the movement to include girls in her native country. Upon her return to the United States, Low established a Girl Guide unit on March 12, 1912, consisting of sixteen young girls in two troops that met in the carriage house in the rear of the garden of her house in Savannah, Georgia. The first Girl Guide was her niece, Margaret Eleanor ("Daisy") Gordon. The young girls, dressed in middy blouses, dark blue skirts, light blue ties, and dark cotton stockings, wearing large black ribbons in their hair, engaged in camping and other sports and were soon the envy of the young girls of Savannah. Juliette Low rapidly moved to make the Girl Guides a national organization.

William Gordon's death, although a serious blow to his worshipful daughter, caused only a slight delay in Low's plans. After a year abroad in England with her mother,

Low returned to the United States and resumed her efforts to make the Girl Guides a national organization. At first, she hoped to merge the existing Campfire Girls organization, founded in 1910, with her Girl Guides organization and call the new organization the Girl Scouts, but the merger fell through. Undaunted, Low continued her dream of a national organization. She began organizational efforts in various states, created a national headquarters, and enlisted prominent Americans to serve on the national board. In 1915, the Girl Scouts of the United States of America was incorporated, with Low serving as its first president. By early 1916, more than 7,000 young women in the United States had registered as Girl Scouts.

Although World War I did not appear to affect Low's travels between the United States and Britain, it did take its toll upon her finances. She had been the major financial supporter of the Girl Scouts before the outbreak of the war; with the increasing success of the organization, however, she discovered that even her substantial finances were insufficient to keep pace with the growth of the organization. She adopted little economies to save money for her Girl Scouts. Her famous teas began to feature cakes that were recycled until either they were eaten or ingeniously disposed of by her guests. She refused to permit the electric lights to be turned on in her home until half past five, regardless of how dark the day might be. Her friends and relatives claimed that she was saving pennies while spending hundreds of dollars on the Girl Scouts. Others suspected that her "economies" were a ruse to encourage donors to give more generously to the cause of Girl Scouting.

With the advent of their nation's entry into World War I, the Girl Scouts performed valuable services for their country, donations increased, and the organization soon grew too large to be staffed by volunteers alone. Juliette Low, recognizing that her responsibilities could be handled by a new generation of leaders, resigned as the president of the Girl Scouts in 1920, but remained active in her support and was granted the title "The Founder."

Diagnosed with cancer in 1923, Juliette Low continued to demonstrate the energy and will she had exhibited throughout her life. She attended the World Camp of the Girl Scouts in England the following year and soon became involved in plans to hold the World Camp of 1926 in New York state. When told by a friend to wait until 1928 to bring the World Camp to the United States, Juliette Low responded that she would not be around in 1928.

Although she found it difficult to conceal the increasing pain of her illness, Juliette Low summoned the energy to engage in the week-long meeting of the World Camp in New York state in 1926. Following the World Camp's closing, she sailed for England, bidding her farewells to friends who were unaware of her condition, and returned to her beloved Savannah, where she died on January 18, 1927.

Summary

Juliette Gordon Low would not be surprised by the size and importance of the Girl Scout movement today. She had faith in her abilities and the abilities of the young women she attracted to the Girl Scouts. Her indomitable will, boundless energy, and belief that physical challenges, such as her own increasing deafness, only slowed advances, never stopped them, proved to be an inspiration both to the young girls fortunate enough to know her personally and the young women who would follow in their footsteps. The last message that she received from the national headquarters of the Girl Scouts shortly before her death adequately sums up her life: She was, the telegram read, "not only the first Girl Scout," she was "the best Scout of them all."

Bibliography
Choate, Anne Hyde, and Helen Ferris, eds. *Juliette Low and the Girl Scouts: The Story of an American Woman, 1860-1927.* Garden City, N.Y.: Doubleday, 1928. Rev. ed. New York: Girl Scouts of America, 1960. First published for the Girl Scout organization shortly after Juliette Low's death, this collection of reminiscences by friends and family members is filled with anecdotal information about the eccentricities of the Girl Scout founder. The revised edition, prepared by Ely List, who was the assistant to the director of the public relations department of the Girl Scouts, is an updated and shortened version of the Choate collection.
Kludinski, Kathleen. *Juliette Gordon Low: America's First Girl Scout.* New York: Viking Children's Books, 1988. Designed for juveniles, this brief book provides a useful introduction to the life of Juliette Low.
Saxton, Martha. "The Best Girl Scout of Them All." *American Heritage* 33 (June/July, 1982): 38-47. Although brief, this article could be used as an introduction to an examination of Juliette Low's life.
Schultz, Gladys D., and Daisy Gordon Lawrence. *Lady from Savannah: The Life of Juliette Low.* New York: J. B. Lippincott, 1958. Although it does not have either a bibliography or an index and nearly half of it concentrates on the Kinzie and Gordon family histories, this book continues to be useful as the most thorough treatment of the life of Juliette Gordon Low.
Strickland, Charles E. "Juliette Low, The Girl Scouts, and the Role of American Women." In *Women's Being, Women's Place: Female Identity and Vocation in American History*, edited by Mary Kelley. Boston: G. K. Hall, 1979. Strickland uses Erik Erikson's life-cycle model to analyze the reasons why Juliette Low became the founder of the Girl Scouts of the United States. Although designed for specialists in gender and child development studies, this essay can be read with benefit by the nonspecialist. Contains useful bibliographical references.

Robert L. Patterson

AMY LOWELL

Born: February 9, 1874; Brookline, Massachusetts
Died: May 12, 1925; Brookline, Massachusetts
Area of Achievement: Literature
Contribution: A leading poet of her day and leader of the Imagist movement, Amy
  Lowell also worked enthusiastically to popularize poetry and the other arts. She
  supported the work of other writers by editing collections of their works and by
  giving popular lectures on literature.

Early Life

Amy Lowell was a member of the Lowell family which arrived in America in 1639,
twenty years after the arrival of the *Mayflower*, and rose to become one of the leading
New England families. (It was the Cabots who spoke only to the Lowells, and the
Lowells who spoke only to God.) Amy's older brother Lawrence was president of
Harvard University from 1909 to 1933. Amy was the last of seven children, five of
whom survived infancy. Amy's mother remained a semi-invalid for all of Amy's life
(she suffered from Bright's disease), and Amy was raised mainly by her nurse-
governess at Sevenels, the Lowells' home in Brookline, Massachusetts.

Amy did not have the companionship of other children and was often lonely, and
as a result she took up the interests that her father and older brothers had. She preferred
outdoor games and activities and was considered a tomboy by the age of eight.

Stimulated by the distinguished adults in her family and those who visited the
Lowells, Amy was precocious. She became a good conversationalist and could amuse
her parents' guests with puns. She liked to write, and at age ten she started a
mimeographed magazine called *The Monthly Story-Teller*. Her mother encouraged
her to put together a book for sale at a charity bazaar: *Dream Drops*.

She was sent to private schools, but after attending some lectures at Radcliffe
College, which she found boring, she left school at the age of seventeen. She educated
herself by reading, both at home and at the Boston Athenaeum, a private library
founded in 1807. She developed a special fondness for the English poet John Keats
and later began a collection devoted to him. Her two older brothers had both published
books (Percy on the Orient and astronomy and Lawrence on government), and Amy
decided that she too would pursue a writing career. She experimented for several years
with various literary forms, including plays, novels, and short stories.

After her mother died in 1895 and her father died in 1899, Amy bought the ten-acre
family Brookline estate from her siblings. She created a large library and designed a
music room. She had the house electrified, and she bought a summer home in New
Hampshire. She joined various civic boards and shocked the local gentry by speaking
up in meetings (which was unusual for women in those days).

Amy was plump and had always felt self-conscious about her weight, and in 1897
she may have been jilted by a suitor. She gave up thoughts of marriage and contented
herself with friends. In 1912, she met the actress Ada Dwyer, and their friendship grew

to such an extent that Ada quit the stage in 1914 to become Amy's full-time secretary-companion until Amy's death.

Amy had made many contacts in the social and political world by meeting and becoming friends with the many guests her family had entertained at Sevenels as she grew up. After the death of her parents, Amy was helped in her endeavors not only by Ada but also by her many friends; for example, Carl Engel, a composer and music publisher. With his encouragement, she put on and acted in plays at Sevenels and organized monthly concerts. At her salons, she introduced her audiences to new music, including that of Béla Bartok, Claude Debussy, and Erik Satie.

Amy's position in a wealthy and influential family (whose wealth came mainly from the cotton mills that its members owned), combined with the support of her parents and older siblings, allowed her to have a larger role in determining the course of her life than many young women of her day had. The death of her parents by the time she was twenty-five relieved her of any need to secure their approval for her plans, and the wealth she inherited permitted her to live as she wished, writing, being a patron of the arts and salon hostess, or traveling wherever she wished. Thus, she was in a position to be much more independent than most other women of her era.

Life's Work

In 1902, when she was twenty-eight, Amy Lowell was inspired by a performance of the European actress Eleonora Duse to write a poem, and she decided to focus on poetry. Amy's first published poem appeared in *Atlantic Monthly* in August of 1910. She organized her first book of poems and persuaded Houghton Mifflin to publish it. *A Dome of Many-Colored Glass* came out in October of 1912 to tepid reviews. The poems were not seen as very exciting. Amy came across an article by Ezra Pound on a group of poets to which he belonged: the Imagists. She traveled to London to meet the poets in the group and began both to write in the Imagist style and to campaign for the recognition of the group in the United States.

Amy worked hard at selling her work and that of other poets whom she admired. She read her poetry whenever she was asked, and she soon began to be in demand as a lecturer on both poetry and music. Her lectures were well prepared and were usually published, first as magazine articles and then as books (for example, *Tendencies in Modern American Poetry*, 1917). She visited editors of magazines and her publishers, selling them on her poems and ideas for books. She worked at first with local magazines and publishers, such as Houghton Mifflin, but soon extended her forays to New York, where she worked with Macmillan. She edited several volumes of poems by Imagists (the first, *Some Imagist Poets*, appeared in 1915) and a volume on six French poets (*Six French Poets*, 1915), followed by several other similar volumes, the royalties from which Amy delighted in dividing into portions and sending to the authors, some of whom desperately needed money.

Soon Amy began to be noticed by the media. She had begun to smoke cigars, and her behavior made headlines in the *New York Tribune*. Amy saw that this kind of publicity would help her establish a public image and contribute to the success of her poetry, so she cultivated the image, even though it was natural for her to behave in the way she did. She smoked, she bullied, and she stayed in bed till past noon, even receiving visitors there. Such behavior was most unusual for a woman of that era, but Amy's financial independence and social position led others to see her actions as interesting rather than shocking.

Her second volume of poems, *Sword Blades and Poppy Seeds,* made a splash in 1914. The poems had varied rhythms and versification, and the reviews came in angry, favorable, or puzzled. No one viewed her work as bland anymore. The criticism, rather than depressing her, made her ready to do battle to convert people to the "new poetry." She hired two full-time secretaries. She wrote letters, ran dinner parties, worked on anthologies, lectured, and continued to write poems and give readings. Eventually, she was speaking to audiences of more than a thousand people at a time throughout the United States.

Although Lowell had suffered from occasional depressions and somatic disorders such as jaundice and gastritis (developed during a trip to Egypt to lose weight), she was not seriously ill until she developed a hernia while attempting to extricate her carriage from mud in 1916. From this time on, her health deteriorated rapidly. The injury and its complications required several operations, none of which satisfactorily resolved the problem (the practice of medicine at the time was severely limited in its treatment of internal problems), and she developed several symptoms of stress, perhaps as a result of the deaths of close relatives and fears of political action by the workers at the Lowell family cotton mills.

In the midst of the series of operations for her hernia, Amy worked on a translation of Chinese poems into English (*Fir-Flower Tablets,* 1920) and on a book of poems about North American Indians (*Legends,* 1921). Critics liked *Legends* but disapproved of *Fir-Flower Tablets.*

She suffered a mild heart attack and retinal hemorrhages, and the hernia broke through again, but she kept working frenetically. In 1922, she determined to finish a biography of Keats she had begun to write, but first she wrote an anonymous spoof of modern poets (including herself), a hoax to which she did not admit for over a year (*A Critical Fable,* 1922). She was upset in 1922 when Edna St. Vincent Millay became the first woman to win a Pulitzer Prize for poetry. (Amy's came posthumously, in 1926.) A final lecture tour was completed in January of 1923. The eleven-hundred-page manuscript on Keats (*John Keats*) finally reached the publisher in November of that year, and the biography was released in February, 1925, to good reviews in America but poor reviews in England, where they seemed to be jealous that an American could write a good biography on Keats.

By March, Amy's weight was down to 160 pounds from a high of 250. (She was only slightly more than five feet tall.) An operation to correct her hernia was scheduled for May, but the day before the operation, on May 12, 1925, Amy had a stroke and died.

Summary

Although only a few of Amy Lowell's poems are considered good enough to merit inclusion in modern anthologies, she was an accomplished poet of her day, if not the leading poet. She received a Pulitzer Prize for poetry in 1926, shortly after her death. In the 1920's, Lowell was one of the most striking figures in American literature. She replaced Ezra Pound as the leader of the Imagist group, and she experimented with form and technique in poetry, becoming especially good at free verse. She is remembered particularly for her enthusiasm for the enterprise of poetry and for her efforts to promote it. She edited collections of works by authors whom she admired and gave lectures to large audiences across the country, attempting to arouse their enthusiasm for the arts. Her published essays established her as a literary critic, and her scholarly biography of Keats was received favorably. Her comfortable financial and social position permitted her a great deal of freedom to act, and she took advantage of that freedom to promote literary causes, including her own poetry.

Bibliography

Benvenuto, Richard. *Amy Lowell*. Boston: Twayne, 1985. This work contains a brief biography of Amy Lowell but consists mostly of a critical appraisal of her work, focusing on her prose, early poetry, narrative poetry, and lyrical works.

Coffman, Stanley K. *Imagism: A Chapter for the History of Modern Poetry*. New York: Octagon Books, 1972. Coffman reviews the history and development of the poets who became known as the Imagists, who were led first by Ezra Pound and then by Amy Lowell.

Damon, S. Foster. *Amy Lowell: A Chronicle with Extracts from Her Correspondence*. Boston: Houghton Mifflin, 1935. This is an early biography of Amy Lowell and a review of her work. Unlike later biographies, it contains long extracts from her letters.

Gould, Jean. *Amy: The World of Amy Lowell and the Imagist Movement*. New York: Dodd, Mead, 1975. This biography focuses on Lowell's life, providing much information about her personal habits and day-to-day activities. It does not attempt a literary analysis or critical appraisal of her poetry or essays.

Heymann, C. David. *American Aristocracy: The Lives and Times of James Russell, Amy, and Robert Lowell*. New York: Dodd, Mead, 1980. This book traces the history of the Lowells in America from their arrival in 1639 but concentrates on the lives of three members of the family, each of whom wrote poetry: James Russell Lowell (1819-1891), Amy Lowell (1874-1925), and Robert Lowell (1917-1977).

Ruihley, Glenn, R. *The Thorn of a Rose: Amy Lowell Reconsidered*. Hamden, Conn.: Archon Books, 1975. This work is both a biography and a critical appraisal of Amy Lowell's writing.

David Lester

CLARE BOOTHE LUCE

Born: April 10, 1903; New York, New York
Died: October 9, 1987; Washington, D.C.
Areas of Achievement: Journalism and government and politics
Contribution: As a journalist, playwright, and political appointee, Luce became an eminent example of how women could overcome gender stereotypes that limit their goals.

Early Life

Ann Clare Boothe was born on April 10, 1903, in New York City. Her mother, Ann Clare Snyder Boothe, was the daughter of Bavarian Catholic immigrants and was a former chorus girl. Her father, William F. Boothe, was a Baptist minister's son who played the violin and worked as an executive for the Boothe Piano Company. Young Clare was related to the theatrical Booth family, Edwin and John Wilkes Booth. After the Lincoln assassination, however, some family members changed the spelling of their name to camouflage the relationship.

When Clare was eight, her father abandoned his family and business to become a musician. Clare's mother worked to provide her only child with the kind of education normally given to children of much wealthier families. She lived with friends, put Clare to work as a child actress, and invested in the stock market. Unwilling to let Clare attend public schools, Ann Boothe sent her daughter to private schools when she could afford it. She supplemented her daughter's intermittent formal education with home schooling and with trips abroad, and instilled in her a lifelong love for books. Clare graduated from Castle School in Tarrytown in 1919.

After her graduation, Clare ran off to Manhattan, where she stayed in a boarding house and worked in a candy factory. Having taken the pseudonym Joyce Fair as a child actress, Clare took the name Jacqueline Tanner as a factory worker. An attack of appendicitis forced her to return to her mother's home for surgery. After Mrs. Boothe married a wealthy physician, Albert E. Austin, Clare lived with her mother and stepfather in Sound Beach, Connecticut. In 1919, she left the United States to visit Europe with her parents. On the return voyage, Clare met Mrs. O. H. P. Belmont, a wealthy Manhattan socialite, who introduced her to millionaire George Brokaw. In 1923, Clare Boothe and George Brokaw were married; she was twenty, and he was forty-three.

Life's Work

Clare Boothe's high-fashion Manhattan marriage ended in 1929 when she sued George Brokaw for divorce, claiming mental cruelty. The generous divorce settlement enabled her to move into a fashionable Beekman Place penthouse with three servants and a governess for her daughter. It also enabled her to begin a new life that was to include remarkable success in publishing, playwrighting, politics and diplomacy.

Following her divorce, Boothe went to work in New York's publishing industry. By

1933, she was managing editor of *Vanity Fair*. She also began writing on her own, and after only a year as a *Vanity Fair* editor, resigned to devote her full attention to writing plays. A rapid and prolific writer, Boothe had her first major success with *The Women*, which opened on Broadway on December 26, 1936. Although it was much more successful than her first play, *Abide with Me*, it was not considered great theater by critics. The author herself assessed it modestly, but audiences enjoyed the satire, which features a cast of thirty-eight women. Two motion picture versions and a television special were made of the play, which has been produced throughout the world. Described as a satire about men without a single man in the cast, it also satirizes the pretensions of bored, wealthy women.

Clare Boothe had become a highly successful independent woman by 1935, the year she married Henry Luce, cofounder of *Time* magazine. Together, the couple collaborated in developing *Life* magazine, soon to become one of the world's most popular magazines. Her work in the publishing business prompted Clare Boothe Luce to stay well informed about political developments throughout World War II. Although she had been a supporter of Franklin Roosevelt and the New Deal Democrats, by 1940 she was ready for new leadership in the White House. She decided to support the Republican Party's candidate, Wendell Willkie, making some forty speeches and appearances on his behalf. Although her candidate lost, Luce had gained important experience as a political activist.

In 1941 and 1942, Luce traveled as a *Life* magazine correspondent to China, the Philippines, Egypt and the Far East. Her description and analysis of the war in Europe, *Europe in Spring*, appealed to Republican party leaders, who convinced her to run for Congress in 1942 from Connecticut's Second District, a seat held previously by her late stepfather, Albert Austin. She won the nomination easily, but had to work hard to oust the Democratic incumbent, using criticism of Roosevelt's handling of the war as her campaign theme.

Although Clare Boothe Luce entered Congress with a reputation for being rich, beautiful, and clever, she relied on intelligence and hard work to get things done. Like all new lawmakers, she learned about the importance of compromise. She wanted a seat on the House Foreign Affairs Committee but settled for the Committee on Military Affairs.

In a celebrated 1943 speech, "American and the Postwar Air World," Luce criticized the Roosevelt Administration's foreign policies, referring to them as "globaloney." The press focused on her cleverly coined word, but failed to discuss her analysis of America's ongoing air policy. It was a pattern that concerned Luce. Journalists tended to emphasize her minor comments, but ignored her major themes. Media coverage of her views was further complicated by her failure to comply consistently with Republican Party platforms. She was independent and unpredictable—characteristics not always appreciated by politicians or journalists.

Luce's policy interests included both foreign and domestic issues. She proposed gender equality in the armed services, affordable housing for veterans, independence for India, and an end to restrictions on immigration from China. She voted against the

1943 anti-labor Smith-Connally Act and was instrumental in developing Senator J. William Fulbright's Resolution of 1943 calling for creation of "international machinery" to establish and maintain a just and lasting peace. That line of reasoning contributed to creation of international agencies such as the United Nations and the North Atlantic Treaty Organization (NATO).

Although Luce opposed isolationism and favored American participation in international organizations, she criticized politicians who expressed sentimental principles instead of developing specific foreign policy goals and objectives. She was particularly critical of the Atlantic Charter, a joint declaration that had been issued by President Roosevelt and British Prime Minister Churchill in 1941. The two leaders proclaimed their commitment to "Four Freedoms": freedom from fear and want, and freedom of speech and religion. Luce called the proclamation wartime propaganda, not real foreign policy.

After winning a close election race in 1944, Luce toured Europe with a congressional delegation. The devastation she saw there bolstered her opposition to America's wartime foreign policy, which she considered incoherent and inconsistent. As the war ended, Luce continued her criticism of the Democratic administration, warning against Soviet aggression in Eastern Europe and condemning Roosevelt for his participation in the Yalta conference. America's foreign policy, in her opinion, was to "drift and improvise."

By 1944, Luce had given Republican leaders ample evidence that she could develop and present ideas forcefully, both in writing and in speeches. They selected her to deliver the keynote address at the Republican National Convention, the first woman of either party to be so honored.

Luce's extensive legislative output during her second term included proposals to rewrite immigration quotas, to help veterans get civil service jobs, to study profit sharing for workers in order to reduce strikes, to permit physicians tax breaks for charity work, to ban racial discrimination in the workplace, to promote scientific research, and to require popular election of U.S. representatives to the United Nations.

In 1945 Luce wrote to Congressman Everett Dirksen describing a plan for helping Europe recover from the war. She did not believe her staff had the expertise to write sufficiently comprehensive legislation, and so she called on Dirksen to do so. Dirksen did, but no immediate action was taken. In 1947, Secretary of State George C. Marshall proposed an almost identical approach to the problem. Although historians have traced the origins of the Marshall Plan to several men, they have generally overlooked Luce's early insight into that foreign policy situation.

In spite of her accomplishments and her interest in a wide range of political issues, Luce did not particularly enjoy the legislative process. In 1946, she decided not to pursue reelection. She continued working for the Republican Party, however, and was particularly forceful in expressing her concern that America's former ally, the Soviet Union, had become a threat to world peace.

In 1952, Luce campaigned for Dwight Eisenhower and was offered a position as secretary of labor in his presidential cabinet. She declined that offer but accepted an appointment as ambassador to Italy, becoming the first woman to represent the United States in a major foreign embassy. She handled the difficult job successfully until 1957. In 1959, Eisenhower asked her to take a position as ambassador to Brazil. She accepted, but when the confirmation process turned into a heated attack on her anti-Roosevelt stance during World War II, she withdrew her name.

Because of her friendship with the Kennedy family, Luce kept a low profile during the 1960 campaign, but in 1964 she worked for Republican Barry Goldwater's candidacy. She moved to Hawaii during the 1970's, then returned to the East Coast to serve on the President's Foreign Intelligence Advisory Board under the Nixon, Ford, and Reagan administrations. She died in 1987, the holder of numerous awards and honors for her contributions to political and cultural life in America.

Summary

Clare Boothe Luce was an intelligent, talented, hard working woman who succeeded in an unusually wide range of endeavors. The term "multivalent" probably describes her best as a person with unusually diverse abilities and ambitions. For American women who want a role model who inspires them to set high goals and to pursue them vigorously, Luce is a good choice. *The Women* will endure as part of America's cultural history. The very different story of Clare Boothe Luce herself as writer, politician and diplomat will also endure as a reflection of America's cultural and political development during the twentieth century.

Bibliography

Harriman, Margaret Case. *Take Them up Tenderly: A Collection of Profiles.* New York: Alfred A. Knopf, 1944. A cleverly written sketch of Luce as congresswoman and playwright. It is a witty, subjective profile rather than an objective analysis of Luce's life and accomplishments.

Luce, Clare Boothe. *Europe in the Spring.* New York: Alfred A. Knopf, 1940. In this analysis of pre-war conditions in Europe, Luce describes the factors that made war virtually inevitable. A popular book, this work was reprinted eight times.

──────── . *The Women.* New York: Random House, 1937. Popular among audiences, this play depicts upper-class women at their worst. It satirizes relationships between women and those between women and men.

Lyons, Joseph. *Clare Boothe Luce.* New York: Chelsea House, 1988. Written as part of the American Women of Achievement series, this biography is written for juvenile readers. Provides a good introduction to Luce's accomplishments as ambassador, legislator, dramatist and journalist.

Shadegg, Stephen. *Clare Boothe Luce: A Biography.* New York: Simon & Schuster, 1970. Based on his friendship with Luce, his correspondence with her and on documents from her files, Shadegg presents a sympathetic yet well-written account of her personal and political life.

Sheed, Wilfrid. *Clare Boothe Luce.* New York: E. P. Dutton, 1982. Sheed's biography, written with the cooperation of Luce, is notable for its informality and popular appeal. As Sheed himself notes in his preface to the book, many people have deified or demonized Luce, and his own portrait strives for a somewhat objective tone in dealing with the various facets of Luce's personality.

Susan MacFarland

IDA LUPINO

Born: February 4, 1918; London, England

Area of Achievement: Film

Contribution: After achieving stardom, Ida Lupino became dissatisfied with the limited roles available to Hollywood actresses and went on to pioneer as a director specializing in films about problems of women in a patriarchal society.

Early Life

Ida Lupino was born in London on February 4, 1918, while World War I was still in progress. Although she was born in England, her father, Stanley Lupino, was of Italian descent. He came from a long line of Italian entertainers, some of whom had been banished from Italy during the seventeenth century for political reasons. Her mother, Constance O'Shay Lupino, was a musical-comedy actress who had been on the stage since childhood and also came from a long line of entertainers.

Acting was in Ida's blood, and she was immersed in a theatrical environment from infancy. Her parents built a small theater where she produced, directed and starred in amateur plays while only a child. This experience was invaluable to her in later years, giving her the incentive and background to pursue a multifaceted career. She also had a good musical education. In later years, Ida told friends she had often felt tempted to give up acting in favor of a career as a musician and composer. One of her compositions, *Aladdin Suite*, was performed by the Los Angeles Philharmonic after she had become a Hollywood star.

Lupino became a professional actress at the tender age of thirteen. She stated in later years that she never had a real childhood. Her initial film appearance was in *Her First Affair* (1933), in which she was cast in the ingenue lead with bleached platinum blond hair and plucked eyebrows to make her resemble the American superstar Jean Harlow. By age fourteen Lupino was regularly playing ingenue roles in British films, attracting critical praise because of her talent and beauty.

Lupino was soon discovered by American producers and brought to Hollywood under contract to Paramount Studios. A majority of the Hollywood films produced in the 1930's featured male stars in stories about men's adventures and achievements. For years Lupino played ingenue roles which did little to challenge her dramatic talents. She attracted enough critical praise to win roles opposite some of the biggest male stars of the period, including Gary Cooper and Bing Crosby.

Lupino was married three times. She blamed her demanding career and lifelong dedication to the dramatic arts for her domestic problems. Her third marriage, to fellow actor Howard Duff, gave her some of the domestic security she had always been seeking.

Life's Work

As Ida Lupino grew older, her face developed more character; her voice became an instrument with which she could express a rich variety of emotions. It was recognized that she was not a beauty queen, but was more suited to roles exposing the darker side of human character. She began playing aggressive, manipulative, conniving, immoral, tormented, even wicked women; these are the types of roles for which she is remembered.

One of her greatest successes came when she played a London Cockney prostitute in *The Light That Failed* (1939) opposite Ronald Colman, another imported British actor who achieved Hollywood stardom. In 1940, she scored another success as a mentally unstable murderess in *They Drive by Night*, playing opposite George Raft and Humphrey Bogart, two of the leading hardboiled actors of the period. Warner Bros. was so pleased that they signed her to a seven-year contract. Most of her best work as an actress was in films made with Warner Bros. during the 1940's.

The two films for which Lupino is best remembered are *High Sierra* (1941), in which she plays the moll of "Mad Dog" Earle (Humphrey Bogart), and *The Sea Wolf* (1941), in which she plays a fugitive from the police in an adaptation of Jack London's story about shanghaied sailors, sadistic officers, and mutineers. In both roles she proved that the public would respond favorably to films in which women were portrayed as something other than passive sex objects. Her performance as "a female Svengali" in *The Hard Way* (1942) won her the coveted New York Film Critics Award.

Lupino's outstanding characteristic was professionalism. One critic wrote: "She works with an economy of effort, a sense of just exactly the right gesture and intonation, so right you hardly realize the affair must have had careful planning behind it." She said of herself: "I study and work hard. I take a script and mull over it and underline the bits I want to emphasize. When I go on the set I know exactly what I want to do and how I want to do it."

All her life, Lupino demonstrated remarkable enterprise, independence, courage, and intelligence. When her acting career was stagnating, she became an independent producer-writer-director. Her first venture was a low-budget filmed television drama which she wrote and produced. The success of this project encouraged her to set up an independent production company with a wealthy partner. Lupino collaborated on the script for their first venture, *Not Wanted* (1949), a story about the psychological torments of an unwed mother.

Between 1949 and 1953, Lupino directed six feature films for her independent companies. The other features were *Young Lovers* (1950), about the effects of polio on a young woman's life; *Outrage* (1950), about the psychological effects of rape; *Hard, Fast and Beautiful* (1951), about a domineering mother driving her daughter to become a champion athlete; *The Hitch-Hiker* (1953), about a serial killer; and *The Bigamist* (1953), about two women who discover they are married to the same man. In addition to her directing credits, Lupino received sole or joint credit for screenplay authorship on *Not Wanted, Young Lovers, Outrage*, and *The Hitch-Hiker*.

Operating on low budgets, Lupino gained experience she could apply to directing for television, a medium which was mushrooming in popularity during the 1940's and 1950's in a way that threatened the very existence of motion picture theaters. She directed for such series as *Have Gun Will Travel*, *General Electric Theater*, *The Untouchables*, *Breaking Point*, and *Gilligan's Island*. Altogether she directed more than 100 films for television, making her one of the most successful directors in that field.

During her career she acquired more varied experience in filmmaking than almost any other man or woman in cinema history: she was a star, a supporting actress, a screenwriter, a director of major productions, a director of television features and television series, and an independent producer.

Lupino costarred with husband Howard Duff in a popular television comedy series titled *Mr. Adams and Eve*, which ran for sixty-eight episodes between 1957 and 1958 before going into syndication. Lupino was one of the few actors who could play both comedy and tragedy with credibility. The only major motion picture she directed after going into television work was *The Trouble with Angels* (1966), starring Rosalind Russell. Lupino continued to appear as an actress in feature films and television films until 1976. Like many another aging actor, she was forced to accept roles in low-budget films that have been described as "shlock movies," including *Food of the Gods* (1976), a film adaptation of an H. G. Wells novel in which she plays a woman being pursued by giant rats and caterpillars; however, she understood the practicalities of the business, was always a trouper, and always gave her best.

Although Ida Lupino never became a superstar, was never regarded as a "glamour queen," and never won an Academy Award, she was internationally famous and enjoyed a longer film career than almost any other man or woman. Many actresses' careers faded when they lost their youthful beauty, but Lupino survived because of her multiple talents. Colleagues respected her as a skilled, hard-working, nontemperamental professional. She usually received appreciative reviews from critics, and her name on the marquee always attracted customers to the box office.

Summary

As an actress, Ida Lupino influenced the filmgoing public to demand more realistic roles for women and to develop a distaste for the traditional film heroines who were sweet, helpless, housebound, unworldly, and totally dependent upon males. Since filmed drama has such an influence on styles, taste, and behavior, Lupino's career had a powerful impact upon American and European women.

As a motion picture director, Lupino pioneered in introducing important feminist issues to mass audiences. Her career proved that women could direct as effectively as men and helped to break down the chauvinistic barriers that traditionally prevented women from holding important positions in film production. She also demonstrated entrepreneurial skill by starting her own independent film production company in one of the world's most competitive industries.

As a television director, Lupino proved that a woman could be just as capable as any man of working on a tight schedule, often with inexperienced actors and on a limited budget, while still turning out a good product. She broke the barriers against women working behind the camera and opened the way for such important directors as Elaine May, Barbra Streisand, Goldie Hawn, Claudia Weill, Jodi Foster, Joan Micklin Silver, Susan Seidelman, Martha Coolidge, Donna Deitch, and Joyce Chopra.

Lupino was never a militant feminist. She liked men and got along well with them. She was married three times and stated that she enjoyed marriage and only regretted that her work made such demands on her home life. Her intelligent diplomacy in dealing with male colleagues in a male-dominated industry set an example that other women followed when breaking into the production end of the Hollywood film business. Although Lupino is best known as a film star, it was as a filmmaker that she set an original example for creative women to follow.

Bibliography

Dozoretz, Wendy. "The Mother's Lost Voice in *Hard, Fast and Beautiful.*" *Wide Angle* 6, no. 3 (1984): 50-57. A pro-feminist, psychoanalytic examination of one of the films written and directed by Ida Lupino. This edition of the influential cinema journal *Wide Angle* is devoted to "Feminism and Film." Contains a variety of interesting articles.

Johnston, Claire. "Women's Cinema as Counter-Cinema." In *Movies and Methods: An Anthology.* Vol. 1, edited by Bill Nichols. Berkeley: University of California Press, 1976. Johnston takes an unsympathetic view of Lupino's approach to film-making because her female protagonists have "the mark of disablement"—they are helpless and dependent.

"Mother Lupino." *Time* 81 (February 8, 1963): 42. A brief and amusing article about Lupino as a television director. Describes her "motherly" approach to handling actors and film crews. Contains a photo of Lupino at work on the set.

Quart, Barbara Koenig. *Women Directors: The Emergence of a New Cinema.* New York: Praeger, 1988. Quart discusses the phenomenon of women emerging as important film directors since the late 1970's. Chapter titled "Antecedents" considers Lupino's contribution as a pioneer filmmaker and the psychological strain of battling the patriarchal motion picture industry endeavoring to present credible female characters and significant women's issues.

Scheib, Ronnie. "Ida Lupino." In *American Directors,* edited by Jean-Pierre Courso-don with Pierre Sauvage. Vol. 2. New York: McGraw-Hill, 1983. Scheib discusses Lupino as an innovator of early "problem" films that were shot on location working on tight time schedules with small budgets. Some discussion of Lupino's work from 1950 to 1966 when Lupino directed many segments of such popular television series as *Have Gun Will Travel* and *The Untouchables.*

Stewart, Lucy Ann Liggett. *Ida Lupino as Film Director, 1949-1953: An Auteur Approach.* New York: Arno Press, 1980. The best available discussion of Lupino's work as a film director. Exhaustively researched. Contains an excellent bibliography of books, articles and film reviews as well as extensive footnoting.

Vermilye, Jerry. *Ida Lupino.* New York: Pyramid Publications, 1977. This short, heavily illustrated book gives a good account of Lupino's life and work as an actress and director. Contains a valuable bibliography and list of the productions in which Lupino was cast as an actress or employed as director.

Weiner, Debra. "Interview with Ida Lupino." In *Women and the Cinema: A Critical Anthology*, edited by Karyn Kay and Gerald Perry. New York: E. P. Dutton, 1977. Lupino tells about her experiences as a director and screenwriter. She explains the problems of being a woman in a male-dominated profession and recalls male directors who influenced her work.

Bill Delaney

GREAT LIVES
FROM
HISTORY

AREAS OF ACHIEVEMENT